D0534520

Life on the Russian Country Estate

With photographs by WILLIAM BRUMFIELD

YALE UNIVERSITY PRESS   New Haven and London

Life on the Russian Country Estate

A SOCIAL AND CULTURAL HISTORY

Priscilla Roosevelt

**Published with the assistance of the
Getty Grant Program.**
Published with assistance from the
Kingsley Trust Association Publication Fund
established by the Scroll and Key Society
of Yale College.

Copyright © 1995 by Yale University.
All photographs not otherwise credited in this book are
© William C. Brumfield.

All rights reserved.
This book may not be reproduced, in whole or in part, including
illustrations, in any form (beyond that copying permitted by Sections 107
and 108 of the U.S. Copyright Law and except by reviewers for the public
press), without written permission from the publishers.

Designed by Sonia L. Scanlon.
Set in Trump type by The Composing Room of Michigan, Inc.
Printed in Singapore by C. S. Graphics.

Library of Congress Cataloging-in-Publication Data

Roosevelt, P. R. (Priscilla R.)
Life on the Russian country estate : a social and cultural history
/ Priscilla Roosevelt ; with photographs by William Brumfield.
p. cm.
Includes bibliographical references and index.
ISBN 0–300–05595–1 (cloth: alk. paper)
ISBN 0–300–07262–7 (pbk.: alk. paper)
1. Russia—Social life and customs—1533–1917. 2. Country life—
Russia. I. Title.
DK142.R66   1995
947—dc20   94–42337
CIP

A catalogue record for this book is available from the British Library.

The paper in this book meets the guidelines for permanence and
durability of the Committee on Production Guidelines for Book
Longevity of the Council on Library Resources.

Frontispiece: N. P. Bogdanov-Belsky. *Among the Flowers*. 1913. (*Stolitsa i usadba*, no. 3)

10 9 8 7 6 5 4 3 2

To my parents, Lloyd and Mary Reynolds

to Marc Raeff, teacher and friend

and to Nicholas Volkov-Muromtsov and Alona Vassiloff,
my personal guides to the world of the estate

Contents

Acknowledgments

Russian estate life is an enormous theme, and the sources for studying it immense and varied. I could never have assembled the pieces of such a puzzle without the active assistance of many institutions, friends, and colleagues here and abroad. My research was generously supported by the National Endowment for the Humanities, the Kennan Institute for Advanced Russian Studies of the Woodrow Wilson Center for Scholars, and IREX. At the Kennan Institute, I was fortunate to have Joanna Levison as my talented and energetic research assistant. For encouragement, information, or comments on the text I am greatly indebted to Willis Brooks, Marina Carney, Kyra Cheremeteff, Patricia Chute, Philip Clendenning, Michael Confino, Anthony Cross, Abbott Gleason, George Grabowicz, Peter Hayden, Alison Hilton, Sherry Houghton, Edward Kasinec, Adele Lindenmeyr, Jakov Luria, Olga Matich, Olga Nosova, Anne Odom, Marc Raeff, Blair Ruble, Serge Schmemann, Niente Smith, John Massey Stewart, Richard Stites, and Richard Wortman. The dedicated librarians at the Slavonic Library in Helsinki, the New York Public Library, the Widener and Fogg Libraries at Harvard, and the Library of Congress helped me in all aspects of my research. For generous assistance while I was in Russia I wish to thank Andrei Anikin, Alexander Dynkin, Viktor Kulakov, Irina Pozdeeva, Galina Razdoburdina, Vladimir Sedov, Alla Sevastianova, Dmitry Shvidkovsky and his wife, Katya Shorban, Elena Stolbova, Elena Varshavskaya, and Vsevolod Vygolev. I am indebted to the staff of the Moscow Institute of Architecture, to the editors of *Nashe Nasledie,* and to the directors and curators of the Abramtsevo, Arkhangelskoe, Bogoroditsk, Karabikha, Khmelita, Kuskovo, Ostafievo, Ostankino, and Spasskoe-Lutovinovo museums for their enthusiastic support. I am grateful to the editors of *Slavic Review* and the *Russian Review* for allowing me to use adapted versions of articles published in their journals in 1990–91 for chapters 3 and 5 of this book; and to the directors of the numerous museums that granted me permission to reproduce images from their collections.

The visual side of this project owes much to William Brumfield's skill and generosity, to assistance from Marina Grigorovich-Barsky, Sylvia Steiner, Elsie Hull, Kyra Cheremeteff, and Philip Frisbee, and to Sonia Scanlon, the designer of my book. I wish to thank Judy Metro and Karen Gangel of Yale University Press for their careful readings and commentary on the manuscript, not to mention their patience and sense of humor during its long gestation. Last, I owe a number of special debts. Nicholas Volkov-Muromtsov (who left Khmelita at age eighteen) has been a major source of information, photographs, and constant encouragement. Alona Davydova Vassiloff (who fled Kamenka at sixteen) has generously shared with me the memoirs and paintings of her mother, Mariamna Lopukhina Davydov, as well as her own photographs, additional information about the Davydov family, and her personal recollections. Mopsy Lovejoy's unerring eye was invaluable while I was selecting the images, and her humor made what seemed at times an endless process positively fun. Finally, no words can adequately convey the thanks I owe my husband, Kermit, for his unstinting support and for his extraordinary efforts in collecting illustrations.

Introduction

"Well to be sure," sais I. "Russia! & good luck to you, you are a comical place! & you'll give me something to talk of many a long day." —**Eleanor Cavanaugh**

All old houses have stories to tell. Of these sagas, few are as rich and dramatic as those embedded within the walls of Russia's country estates. Compelling images first drew me to my subject—towering columns beneath massive porticoes, overgrown gardens with Chinese bridges and Gothic gates, mobcapped countesses and pensive lace makers, bejeweled courtiers and provincial harems, scenes of teatime in the park, bear hunting, and aged family retainers, and, most of all, the voiceless but evocative ruins of rural Russia today. As I matched these varied images to written accounts of estate life, I found my attention captured by three quite different visions that seemingly ordered the world of the Russian landowner. The first, it appeared to me, celebrated the estate as an aristocrat's playground, a luxurious arena of delight and fantasy. The second enshrined the estate as a patriarchal, self-contained world of ritualized tradition and festival. The third transformed the estate into the pastoral arcadia of poets and artists.

Visions are, as a rule, imperfectly enacted. I found that the lines between these concepts of what country life could or should be often blurred. In Russia, some aristocratic estate owners were also major cultural figures. Many ruled their private princedoms in patriarchal fashion, while less wealthy landowners envied and imitated their aristocratic neighbors. Some estates, though small, were of major cultural significance. A few (notably, Leo Tolstoy's Yasnaya Polyana, meaning "clear meadow") united elements from all three visions. Yet because Russians themselves used terms similar to my own to distinguish between what they perceived as distinct variants of estate life, I have chosen to adopt these visions as a framework, for they provide the most illuminating structural guide to the complex social and cultural world of the estate.

The Russian estate's lifespan—slightly over two centuries, from the reign of Peter the Great to the Bolshevik revolution—was short by European standards yet of immense historical significance. Almost all the great houses were built between the mid-eighteenth and mid-nineteenth centuries, and the majority were constructed during the nobility's brief "golden age"—from the reign of Catherine II (1762–96) through that of Alexander I (1801–25). The aristocratic emblem of this era, the large neoclassical house surrounded by a spacious natural garden carefully laid out to lure visitors along its paths and across its bridges to strategically positioned belvederes, pavilions, grottoes, and hermitages, was imitated by lesser nobles on whatever scale they could afford. To outward appearances, therefore, the Russian estate was for the most part Western.

Yet the peculiarities of Russian development made its estate life sui generis as well. Certain elements, particularly the institution of serfdom, were unknown in Western Europe at that time. Serfdom and Russian custom made the estate, like the nation to which it belonged, a study in contrasts, paradoxes, and extremes. Good taste sometimes gave way to ostentatious displays of wealth; refined manners sometimes concealed baser impulses. European habits competed with Russian tradition in estate culture to produce a unique way of life. The three visions of estate life and the reality they engendered are major chapters in the story of the Russian elite's conflicting cultural allegiances and its search for a national identity.

The object of this book is to describe both the world of the estate and the different visions it embodied: to determine which attitudes inspired estate building and how it took shape; to explore how estate life was lived, what emotions this life generated, and how they were conveyed in literature and art; and to examine the relationship of the estate to the larger environment, both geographical and cultural. Russia's country estates began as isolated islands in a rural vastness. As these islands multiplied to form an interconnected archipelago, they acted as powerful cultural agents. Up to the emancipation of the serfs in 1861 estate owners were the main, if not the sole, purveyors of culture in the Russian provinces, bringing new styles, manners, information, and entertainment to the country-side. Moreover, the art, music, and ideas the cultural world of the estate engendered both set the tone of Russian high culture and transformed it throughout the imperial period.

Estate culture was at its pinnacle from the late eighteenth century to 1861; the purest expression of this existence was found in the region around Moscow, in the contiguous provinces, and in the rich "black earth" agricultural areas to the south. My book reflects this: of the fifty provinces of imperial Russia, the central European provinces are best represented. This is not, however, the story of the entire nobility inhabiting the countryside. Russians measured their wealth in the number of *dushi* (literally "souls," referring to adult male serfs) they owned. Five thousand or more souls signified that the landowner was enormously wealthy; from eight hundred to five thousand, extremely well off; from two hundred to eight hundred, prosperous; from eighty to two hundred, average; and below eighty, not self-sufficient. The vast majority of Russian nobles were in the last two categories—that is, too poor to do more than subsist on their estates. I touch upon this group only slightly.

Although the decline of the estate accelerated after 1861, its economic decline was well under way long before, and its cultural significance strong well after that date. Prior to the emancipation, estate life and nobility were virtually synonymous in that only hereditary nobles could own populated estates. Even after this bond was ruptured, the vision of the good life associated with the estate continued. Between emancipation and revolution a veritable flood of memoirs and several new journals devoted to estate life appeared. Wealthy merchants, the new would-be aristocracy, commissioned country mansions designed in the evocative neoclassical style of a century earlier or bought out impoverished nobles—a phenomenon Anton Chekhov immortalized in *The Cherry Orchard*.

A major reason for the resonance of estate culture was that on the estate landowners could replicate, transform, or reject the ruling hierarchical structures of imperial Russia—the autocracy, the bureaucracy, and the family—in any way they found psychologically satisfying. Each of the three forms of estate life portrayed in this book had deep roots in the idiosyncrasies of Russian culture and affected its further development, for each reflected a particular notion of the landowner's personal identity and of his larger social and cultural role. The first, that of the aristocratic playground, inaugurated estate culture and gave it color. From the reign of Catherine to the war of 1812, courtiers and grandees used their palatial estate complexes for cultural fantasy and displays of personal refinement. The regal entertainments ordered by aristocrats reflected a sense of boundless power within a realm where their word alone was law. This approach to estate life rapidly became anachronistic, for such levels of spending could not be sustained and a more refined morality began to condemn excess. Yet the habits of these early aristocrats cast a long shadow on Russia's cultural development.

But in imperial mythology the tsar was not merely an autocrat but also the father of his people: the Russian realm was his *votchina*, or patrimony. Many owners of estates both large and small considered themselves "little fathers" to their peasants. They viewed the estate as a patriarchy; its traditions embodied the best characteristics and the proper role of their social class. Indeed, in the absence of access to real political power, the landed nobility clung to this vision of estate life as a compensatory way of defining its position. The patriarchal approach to the countryside outlived the emancipation of the serfs, persisting as the mainspring of estate life in a Russia poised on the brink of the industrial era.

Russia's educated elite—its writers, artists, visionaries, and prophets—had yet a third vision of estate life. For many of them the estate was a retreat, a refuge from an official world they despised. It offered an idyllic space where ideas could be expressed without fear of censorship, where the true Russia might be found, where artistic talent could be nurtured. On the estate the cultured were free to develop their ideas and gifts. Some also championed the talents of the numerous serfs whose work as craftsmen, artists, musicians, and actors made the splendor of estate life possible and who were laying the foundations for Russian culture at its height. Others seized on the thorough but inefficient exploitation of serf labor as the most glaring example of Russia's inequalities, injustices, and economic and social backwardness. Among a critical minority of nobles, from Alexander Radishchev through the Decembrists to the Westerners of the 1840s, this aroused a call for rebirth in the image of the West. But other thinkers, concerned by the elite's apostasy from the culture of Old Russia, searched for their native roots in the countryside and found them in peasant traditions and values. By the 1830s this search had given birth to Slavophilism, which embraced patriarchal estate life as the natural order for Russia. Even after the emancipation a cultural elite no less obsessed with peasant Russia continued to use estates to experiment with reclaiming its native heritage, a cultural *ricorso* cut short by the Bolshevik revolution.

Few ways of life have caused more controversy, or vanished more completely, than the world I have set out to describe. The backwardness of rural Russia and the plight of its peasants polarized Russian public opinion both before and after 1861, coloring much of what was written about estate life. Revolutions and wars are notoriously hard on historical artifacts and evidence. The revolution of 1905, the outbreak of war in 1914, and a second, greater revolution in 1917, followed by civil war, brought doom to the Russian estate. In the maelstrom, virtually all these properties were physically damaged or totally destroyed, and the records and possessions of generations of owners scattered or obliterated. In contrast to English family seats such as Chatsworth, alive today with centuries-old, meticulously maintained archives, some once-grand Russian estates now survive only in paintings or a chance photograph. Others we know only by name.

These facts have required that my methodology be emphatically eclectic. I have gathered information and drawn inspiration from everything available to me: a mass of written material, physical artifacts (from estate houses to objects used in daily life and the art generated on and by the estate), and the oral reminiscences of some of the last representatives of Russia's landed elite. In its prime, the life of the Russian country estate reflected ideals and a way of life that evolved under particular historical circumstances. In recent times an army of skilled restorers in the former Soviet Union has turned its talents to re-creating the outward appearance of this lost world. Currently the tourist can visit Arkhangelskoe, Kuskovo, or Ostankino near Moscow; private palaces or elegant dachas near St. Petersburg; Alupka and Livadia in the Crimea; estates associated with great Russian writers and composers; and even the agronomist A. T. Bolotov's modest and newly restored Dvoryaninovo. But the elapsed centuries have erected a wall between us and the life on most former Russian manors. Modern historians have attempted in numerous ways to remove some of the bricks obscuring our view. Social historians have acquainted us with the demographics of landownership. Economic historians have sketched aspects of the manorial economy, anthropological historians the social matrix of peasant life on the estate, and cultural historians the architecture of surviving estate houses. Each approach has pierced the wall at a particular vantage point, and I have taken advantage of these apertures to glimpse one or another discrete aspect of estate life.

My goal, however, has been the re-creation of the larger scene behind the wall. In search of it I have reexamined the literary legacy: the memoirs, diaries, travel journals, and contemporaneous literature in which estate life was recorded and portrayed and which offer a more complete and compelling portrait of estate life than do statistics. I hope that my book will give new insight into a world that Russia's greatest writers alternately celebrated and bemoaned. In *Eugene Onegin* Alexander Pushkin was perhaps the first to portray country living as the source of natural Russian virtue, a theme taken up by Ivan Turgenev, Leo Tolstoy, and continued by writers right up to today. In reality, Russian estate owners, like their European counterparts, were divided between transient aristocrats and permanent inhabitants, sensitive, cultivated men and women and semiliterate boors. Pushkin's lyrical portrait of the Larin family on its rural estate was soon challenged by its literary counterimage, evident in the chicanery of Nikolai Gogol's provincial traders in dead souls.

Russia's writers and artists, called upon to be prophetic, to address current social evils and provide solutions, inevitably drew on their own experiences. Turgenev's *A Sportsman's Notebook* describes the area near Orel, where his family estate was located, and Gogol's stories the Ukrainian countryside of his boyhood. Sergei Aksakov's *Family Chronicle* and *Years of Childhood* narrate his family history and his upbringing in the eastern steppes. Leo Tolstoy's passionate attachment to Yasnaya Polyana gave rise to his lyrical portrait of childhood on the estate and permeated his later epics. In *War and Peace* he creates the fictitious young countess Natasha Rostova, whose Russian instincts emerge as she dances; in *Anna Karenina* his alter ego Constantine Levin finds the true meaning of existence as he mows the hay alongside his peasants. Ivan Goncharov's Oblomov, lying on his bed in St. Petersburg in a state of spiritual paralysis, finds solace in a mental retreat to the childhood delights of his small country estate, modeled on Goncharov's memories of his upbringing among the provincial nobility. This sunlit, gentle world stands in sharp contrast to Chekhov's later portraits of estates populated by bewildered nobles unable to deal with their new circumstances, a world no less lyrical but one that evokes an ominous grayness, a mood of uncertainty and pathos, the suggestion of an imminent, menacing storm.

With few exceptions, the literary portraits are brilliant but oversimplified and, even when nostalgic or elegiac, largely negative. We are presented with the hedonistic, cruel, or improvident aristocrat, the ignorant, coarse, or helpless smallholder, or the "superfluous man," as Russian intellectuals dubbed the many eccentric or aimless nobles to be found in the provinces. These were powerful stereotypes that unduly influenced both contemporaries and later historians. Russian memoirs to some extent correct the picture by portraying more prosaic or moral landowners along with these exaggerated types. Yet memoirists are infuriatingly selective, some failing to tell us how many souls they owned, others ignoring the trivia of daily life. Many, consciously writing for a public audience, were affected by literary conventions and ideological quarrels, particularly the debate over serfdom. They were also undoubtedly influenced by literary portraits of estate life, as authors of fiction were by memoirs. Because the extent or direction of the modeling is in most cases unclear, I have confined my task to pointing out the many correspondences but also the divergencies between fictional estate worlds and remembered real worlds where they occur. I have also used foreigners' accounts, particularly the tidbits these outsiders provide on subjects Russian memoirists found too normal to describe. The Wilmot sisters, for instance, wrote lively and lengthy accounts of their daily life and adventures as guests of Princess Dashkova in the early nineteenth century. As the epigraph to this introduction suggests, even their Irish maid was astounded by aspects of life in a country most Europeans viewed as either barbarous or enigmatic.

I have endeavored to combine all these sources of information into a full-scale portrait, as close as possible to the vivid reality, of life on the estate, a topic that has fascinated me since I read my first Turgenev novel. A single volume can do no more than sketch the visions and realities of this life and suggest their greater impact. I hope my work will provoke new avenues of investigation, inspire the detailed family and estate histories the subject deserves, and encourage other scholars to venture beyond Russia's capitals to its provinces. Above all this book is an attempt to re-create, for both those who are familiar with the country estate of Russian literature and those who are not, the real world on which it was based.

A few technical matters. In the text, I have rendered names ending in **ий** or **и** as *y*; throughout, I have omitted soft signs and rendered **я** as *ya*, **ю** as *yu*. I have used English translations of literary works where available. Where my source is in a language other than English, the translation is my own unless otherwise noted.

Last, a word on the two maps. Some of the estates featured in this book have vanished entirely and cannot be precisely located today. Of the estates that have survived to the present, some do not appear in my text because I could find no significant information about the life on them. These considerations governed my selection of estates for the maps. For the Moscow region, whose surviving architectural monuments have been extensively mapped, I have included some estates not mentioned in the text to provide an idea of the density of estate ownership and of family holdings in a single province. For provincial Russia, I used a detailed map of 1851, on which I was often, but not always, able to locate an estate my sources described. I have omitted some extant estates not mentioned in the text. I hope these maps, incomplete as they are, will provide some sense of the vast network of estates that at one time constituted the social and cultural world of rural Russia.

Life on the Russian Country Estate

Estates of Moscow Province

The estates in this key are listed alphabetically, with numbers designating their location on the map. Modern variants of estate names appear in parentheses. Families or individuals who owned estates are listed chronologically following the location number.

Abramtsevo: 15, Golovin, Molchanov, Aksakov, Mamontov

Akhtyrka: 14, Trubetskoy, Matveev

Aleshkovo: 139, Novikov, Kozhin, Shcherbakov

Almazovo: 46, N. A. Demidov

Andreevskoe: 9, E. F. Orlova

Annino: 65, Miloslavsky, Savin, Belavin

Anosino: 43, E. N. Meshcherskaya

Arkhangelskoe: 52, Cherkassky, Golitsyn, Yusupov

Arkhangelskoe: 106, Naryshkin

Bogorodskoe: 96, Guriev

Bogorodskoe: 140, Sheremetev

Bogorodskoe (Kishkino): 115, N. A. Oltseva, N. A. Kavetskaya

Bogoslovo: 33, P. F. Astafieva

Boldino: 1, V. N. Tatishchev

Bolshye Vyazemy: 80, B. A. Golitsyn

Brazhnikovo: 39, P. I. Prozorovsky

Bykovo: 95, M. M. Izmailov, Vorontsov-Dashkov

Cherkisovo: 132, Cherkassky

Danilovskoe: 4, I. F. Golitsyn

Dedevshino: 30, V. M. Golitsyn

Dednevo-Novospasskoe: 12, Golovin

Demyanovo: 3, G. Ya. Naumov, M. I. Rimskaya-Korsakova, A. A. Poltoratskaya, D. B. Mertvago

Denezhnikovo: 107, I. L. Talyzin

Drovnino: 99, Bulygin

Dubrovitsy: 103, Golitsyn, Potemkin, Dmitriev-Mamonov

Dubrovky: 13, I. A. Beloselsky

Dyakovo: 11, Zhukov

Eldigino: 26, Kurakin

Ershovo: 50, Saltykov, Olsufiev

Fedorovskoe: 17, P. A. Shakhovskoy

Fili: 53, Naryshkin

Filimonki: 85, Lachinov, Svyatopolk-Chetverinsky

Fryanovo: 28, I. L. Lazarev

Glinki: 48, Jacob V. Bruce, E. A. Musina-Pushkina

Golovin mansion: 58, Fyodor A. Golovin

Golubino: 71, Gerard

Gorenki: 60, Dolgoruky, Razumovsky, Volkov, Panteleev, Tretyakov

Gorky: 10, Yankov

Gorky: 92, Pisarev, Sushkin, Prokofiev, Gerasimov, Z. G. Morozova-Reinbot

Gorodnya: 129, Sheremetev

Grebnevo: 37, Trubetskoy, G. I. Bibikov, Golitsyn, Pantaleev

Ilinskoe: 70, S. L. Streshnev, A. I. Ostermann-Tolstoy

Islavskoe: 67, Arkharov

Ivanovskoe: 29, Gagarin, Bludov, A. S. Menshikov

Ivanovskoe: 104, Golovin, Zakrevsky, F. A. Tolstoy

Izmalkovo: 83, Samarin, Komarovsky

Khrabrovo: 5, Obolensky

Konstantinovo: 105, Romodanovsky, P. E. Tatishchev

Konstantinovo: 119, A. M. Pushkin

Korenevo: 78, A. V. Nabrekov

Krasnaya Pakhra: 101, D. N. Saltykova

Krivyakino: 120, Lazhechnikov

Kuskovo: 57, P. B. Sheremetev

Kuzminki: 76, Stroganov, Golitsyn

Letovo: 86, P. I. Bibikov

Lobanovo (Troitskoe): 117, Lobanov-Rostovsky, S. F. Volkonsky

Lopasnya-Zachatevskoe: 124, A. S. Vasilchikov

Lyakhovo: 114, Vasilchikov, A. D. Zalivskaya, A. A. Vargin

Lyublino: 75, V. P. Prozorovsky, N. A. Durasov

Marfino: 24, Golitsyn, Saltykov, Orlov, Panin

Marinka: 118, Buturlin

Melikhovo: 126, Anton Chekhov

Meshcherskoe: 112, Sheremetev

Mikhailovskoe: 98, M. N. Krechetnikov, Sheremetev

Mogiltsy: 27, P. M. Shcherbachev

Molodi: 111, F. A. Golovin, Saltykov, Domashnev

Muranovo: 16, Engelhardt, Putyata, F. I. Tyutchev

Nepetsino: 131, Novikov

Neskuchnoe: 54, N. Trubetskoy

Neskuchnoe: 55, P. A. Demidov

Nikitskoe: 108, A. F. Apraksin

Nikolskoe: 77, F. M. Apraksin, A. I. Osterman

Nikolskoe-Arkhangelskoe: 62, A. V. Dolgoruky

Nikolskoe-Gagarino: 40, S. S. Gagarin

Nikolskoe-Obolyanovo (Podyachevo): 6, P. M. Vlasov, Obolyaninov, Olsufiev

Nikolskoe-Prozorovskoe: 25, A. A. Prozorovsky

Nikolskoe-Uryupino: 51, N. I. Odoevsky, N. A. Golitsyn

Novinki: 135, B. N. Dolgov

Olgovo: 8, Chaplin, Soimonov, Apraksin

Ostafievo: 88, A. I. and P. A. Vyazemsky, S. D. Sheremetev

Ostankino: 45, N. P. Sheremetev

Ostashevo: 38, A. V. Urusov, Muraviev, N. P. Shipov, K. K. Romanov

Ostrov: 93, A. D. Menshikov, A. G. Orlov

Otrada-Semenovskoe: 136, V. G. Orlov, Orlov-Davydov

Pekhra-Yakovlevskoe: 47, Golitsyn, I. A. Gagarin, A. D. Naryshkin, Shelashnikov

Perkhushkovo: 81, Yakovlev

Petrovskoe: 94, Miloslavsky, Naryshkin, Demidov, D. P. Shelaputin, L. L. Chernyshev, Bariatinsky

Petrovskoe (Petrovo Dalnee): 69, Prozorovsky, Golitsyn

Petrovskoe Alabino: 97, N. A. Demidov

Podzhigorodovo: 22, Yuriev

Pokrovskoe: 127, Sheremetev

Pokrovskoe-Rubtsovo: 41, Nashchokin

Polevshchina: 34, Polevoy

Polivanovo: 102, Saltykov, Naryshkin, K. G. Razumovsky

Poreche: 63, A. G. Razumovsky, S. S. Uvarov

Rai-Semenovskoe: 133, Nashchokin

Rozhdestveno: 23, D. V. Golitsyn

Rozhdestveno: 42, I. I. Kutaisov

Rozhdestveno-Telyatievo: 134, Arkharov, Sollogub

Sadki: 123, Eropkin, Riumin

Sekerino: 100, Borozdin

Serednikovo: 35, Vsevolozhsky, A. A. Nesterov, G. A. Saltykov, I. Z. Malyshev, Stolypin

Shabolovo: 56, P. A. Prozorovsky

Shchapovo: 128, S. F. Volkonsky

Shkin: 130, G. I. Bibikov

Spasskoe: 121, N. M. Smirnov

Staro-Nikolskoe (Pervomaisky): 82, I. P. Musin-Pushkin, E. A. Bibikova

Subbotino: 109, P. A. Smirnov

Sukhanovo: 91, Volkonsky

Sukovo: 138, E. A. Yaroslavova

Tabolovo: 90, P. M. Apraksin

Tarychevo: 74, E. N. Golovina

Teploe: 20, Soimonov

Teply Stan: 72, D. Saltykova

Tikhvinskoe (Avdotino): 116, N. I. Novikov

Timonino: 49, Valuev

Troitskoe-Kainardzhi (Fenino): 59, P. A. Rumyantsev

Troitskoe-Ratmanovo (Ivashevo): 61, Nebolsin, M. N. Bibikova

Troitskoe-Sheremetevo: 32, Sheremetev

Tsaritsyno: 87, imperial family

Tsesarka: 31, Shchepotin, Martynov

Ubory: 68, P. B. Sheremetev the younger

Valuevo: 84, P. Tolstoy, D. Shepelev, Musin-Pushkin, Chetverinsky

Vasilievskoe: 79, Yakovlev, A. I. Herzen

Vasino: 122, Velyaminov

Vaskino: 125, D. M. Shcherbatov

Verzilovo: 137, Shakhovskoy

Vinogradovo (Dolgoprudnee): 36, Pushkin, Vyazemsky, Glebov, Benckendorff

Volynshchina: 64, Dolgorukov-Krymsky

Vorobievo: 113, E. S. Ershova

Voronino: 2, Blagovo

Voronovo: 110, Volynsky, Vorontsov, Rostopchin, Tolstoy, Sheremetev

Vvedenskoe: 66, Lopukhin, Zaretsky, Golovin, Shtakelberg

Vysokoe: 21, Volkov

Yaropolets: 18, A. P. Doroshenko, Chernyshev

Yaropolets: 19, A. P. Doroshenko, Zagryazhsky, Goncharov

Yartsevo: 7, A. V. Rimsky-Korsakov

Yasenevo: 73, Lopukhin

Znamenskoe-Gubailovo (Krasnoyorsk): 44, Volynsky, V. M. Dolgorukov-Krymsky

Znamenskoe-Sadki (Butovo): 89, Urusov, Trubetskoy, Orlova, M. N. Katkov

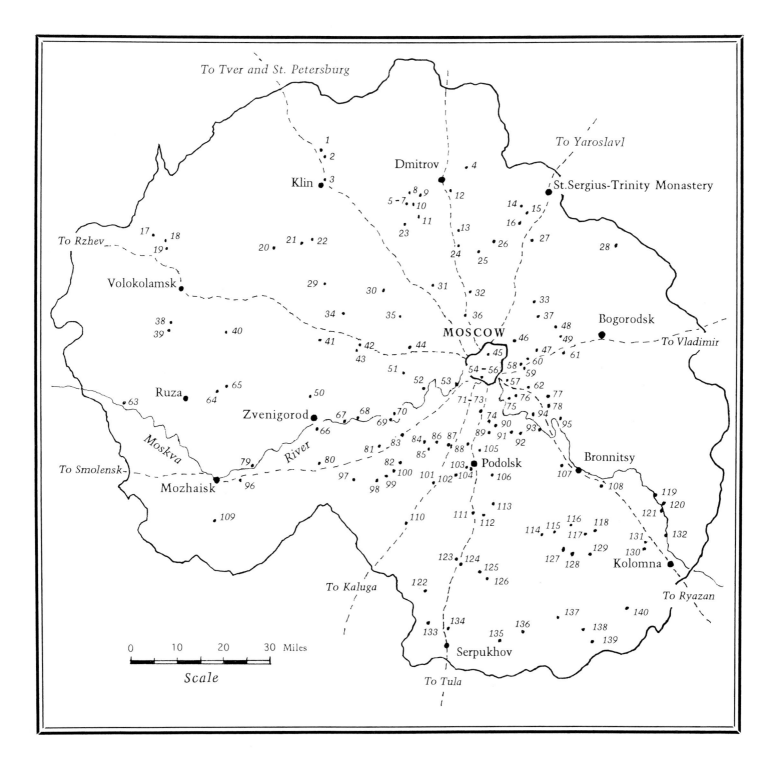

To Tver and St. Petersburg

To Yaroslavl

1
2
3 Klin
Dmitrov *4*
St.Sergius-Trinity Monastery

8 *9*
5 - 7 *10*
12
14 *15*
11
16
23 *13*
27

To Rzhev
17 *18*
19
20 *21* *22*
24 *25* *26*
28

Volokolamsk
29 *30* *31*
32
33
Bogorodsk

38
39 *40*
34 *35*
36
37
48
49
To Vladimir

MOSCOW
41 *42* *44*
46
47
61
43
51
45
58 *60*
59

Ruza
65
50
52 *53*
54 - 56 *57* *62*
63
64
Zvenigorod *67* *68* *70*
71 *73* *76* *77*
75 *78*
66 *69*
74 *94* *95*
90
83 *84* *86* *87* *89* *91* *93*
Moskva River *81* *85* *88* *92*
79 *80* *82* *105*
96 *97* *100* *101* *102* *104* *106*
103 Podolsk
Bronnitsy
107

To Smolensk
Mozhaisk
98 *99*
108
119
120

109
110 *111* *112* *113*
121
114 *115* *116* *118*
117
131 *132*
129
127 *128* *130*
Kolomna

To Kaluga
123 *124* *125*
126
122
137 *140*
134 *136* *138*
133 *135* *139*
Serpukhov
To Ryazan

To Tula

0   10   20   30 Miles

Scale

Estates of Central Russia

The estates in this key are listed alphabetically, with numbers designating their location on the map. Modern variants of estate names appear in parentheses. Families or individuals who owned estates are listed chronologically following the location number.

Aksheno: 83, Ogarev
Aleksandrovka: 144, Somov, Golubev
Aleksino: 46, Baryshnikov
Annino: 100, Yankov
Avchurino: 62, Poltoratsky
Balovnevo: 98, Muromtsov, Volkov-Muromtsov
Bartsovka: 21, A. I. Bibikov, Kozlovsky
Baturin: 126, K. G. Razumovsky
Bekovo: 106, A. M. Ustinov
Belaya Tserkov: 139, Branicki
Beloomut: 79, Ogarev
Bobrovo: 60, E. V. Rimskaya-Korsakova
Bobylevka: 120, Lvov
Bogdanovskoe: 33, Filosofov
Bogoroditsk: 91, Bobrinskoy
Bogorodskoe: 49, Lykoshin
Boldino: 39, Pushkin
Bolshaya Aleshnya: 93, Kikin, A. S. Ermolov
Borisoglebskoe: 15, Musin-Pushkin
Darovoe (Khotyaintsev): 71, Dostoevsky
Dikanka: 136, Kochubey
Dolbino: 88, Kireevsky
Dolzhik: 134, Shcherbinin, Golitsyn
Dugino: 40, Panin, Meshchersky
Durasovka: 110, Durasov
Dvoryaninovo: 69, A. T. Bolotov
Elagin Island: 4, Elagin, imperial family
Elizavetino: 16, D. A. Yankov
Gatchina: 9, Grigory Orlov, imperial family
Glubokoe: 37, Heiden
Golitsyno: 86, Golitsyn, G. A. Rimsky-Korsakov
Golovchino: 129, I. O. Khorvat
Gomel: 111, P. A. Rumyantsev
Gorodnya: 58, N. P. Golitsyna

Gorodok: 48, Ozerov
Gremyach: 113, Ladomirsky, Korsakov, V. D. Golitsyn
Grigorievskoe: 44, Lykoshin
Gruzino: 12, A. Arakcheev
Gruziny: 31, M. Poltoratsky
Ignatovskoe: 64, E. I. Naryshkina
Ilovna: 14, Musin-Pushkin
Isa: 85, M. S. Vorontsov
Kachanovka: 124, Rumyantsev, Tarnovsky
Kamarichi: 114, V. B. Golitsyn
Kamenka: 141, G. A. Potemkin, Davydov
Karabikha: 18, A. P. Golitsyn, N. A. Nekraskov
Karaul: 105, N. V. Chicherin
Kareyan: 118, Goncharov
Kazulino: 42, Lykoshin
Khmelita: 45, Griboedov, Volkov-Muromtsov
Kholm: 41, D. I. Uvarova
Khoten: 128, Kondratiev, Stroganov
Kimora: 32, M. L. Vorontsov
Kotovka: 142, N. D. Urusov
Krasnoe: 130, G. S. Wolkenstein
Kurakino-Preobrazhenskoe: 115, Alexei B. Kurakin
Lopatino: 65, A. I. Naryshkina
Lyalichi: 95, P. V. Zavadovsky, Engelhardt, Atryganev
Lyubichi: 102, Nikolai Krivtsov
Mara: 104, imperial family, Baratynsky
Marino: 127, Bariatinsky
Matussov: 140, Orlov, Lopukhin
Mednoe: 3, Yakovlev
Medvedevo: 10, V. V. Golitsyn
Mikhailovka: 131, Golitsyn, T. Potemkina
Mikhailovskoe: 17, M. M. Shcherbatov

Mikhailovskoe: 34, Pushkin
Mitino-Vasilievo: 30, Lvov
Molodenki: 92, Samarin
Nadezhdino: 107, Alexander B. Kurakin
Nikolskoe: 59, Kropotkin
Nikolskoe-Cherenchitsy: 29, N. A. Lvov
Novospasskoe: 56, M. I. Glinka
Ogarevo: 82, Bakhmetev, E. Golitsyna
Orzhevka: 101, Martynov
Ostrovki: 23, N. P. Miliukov
Ovinovtsina: 47, Engelhardt
Pady: 122, Naryshkin
Panurovka: 112, Miklashevsky
Parshino: 11, Makarov
Pavlovsk: 7, imperial family
Peterhof: 4, imperial family
Petrishchevo: 89, Yushkov
Petrovo: 75, Yankov
Petrovskoe: 35, Gannibal
Petrovskoe: 119, Gagarin
Podmoklovo: 67, N. S. Dolgoruky
Pogorelets: 96, Granovsky
Pokrov: 43, N. P. Panin
Pokrovskoe: 50, Engelhardt
Pokrovskoe: 55, Nikolev
Polenovo: 68, V. D. Polenov
Polotnyany Zavod: 57, Goncharov
Ponezhskoe: 19, Obreskov
Priyutino: 5, A. N. Olenin
Pryamukhino: 28, Bakunin
Pushchino: 78, Strekalov
Rostashi: 121, Raevsky
Ruzaevka: 81, N. E. Struisky
Safonkovo: 22, A. G. Venetsianov
Saltyki: 117, Yu. Golitsyn
Sergievskoe: 99, Bibikov
Sergievskoe (Koltsovo): 61, Ossorgin
Shchelykovo: 20, N. Ostrovsky
Sheremetevo: 123, Sheremetev
Shklov: 87, S. Zorich

Spasskoe-Lutovinovo: 90, Turgenev
Spas-Ugol: 25, M. E. Saltykov
Stolnoe: 125, Musin-Pushkin, Kushelev-Bezborodko
Studenets: 76, Vyazemsky
Svyatye Gory: 143, A. B. Golitsyn, T. Potemkina
Talashkino: 52, M. K. Tenisheva
Teploe: 74, A. A. Yankova
Tikhvinskoe: 16, N. I. Tishinin
Titovo: 66, Miliutin
Trigorskoe: 36, Wulf
Troitskoe: 63, E. R. Dashkova
Trostyanets: 133, Golitsyn
Tsarskoe Selo: 6, imperial family
Uderevka: 132, Stankevich
Ulyanka: 1, D. N. Sheremetev
Umatovo: 26, P. V. Esipov
Umet: 103, B. D. Khvoshchinsky
Uruchya: 97, Ogarev
Urusovo: 108, Gagarin
Ushakovo: 54, P. N. Rimsky-Korsakov
Ustinovo: 24, V. I. Likhachev
Vasilievskoe: 51, Grabbe
Vasilievskoe: 137, Gogol
Verkhnee Ablyazovo: 94, A. N. Radishchev
Veryakushki: 38, P. A. Koshkarov
Vodolagi: 138, Dunin
Vyra: 8, Nabokov
Yagotin: 135, Razumovsky, Repnin
Yakhontovo: 84, A. A. Tuchkov
Yasnaya Polyana: 77, Volkonsky, L. N. Tolstoy
Yuskovo: 73, Engelhardt
Zheleznovka: 80, Yablochkov
Zhernovka: 72, N. S. Mosolov
Zhukovo: 53, Yakushkin
Zlobino: 70, Gorchakov
Znamenskoe-Raek: 27, F. I. Glebov
Zubrilovka: 109, Golitsyn
Zvanka: 13, D. A. Derzhavina

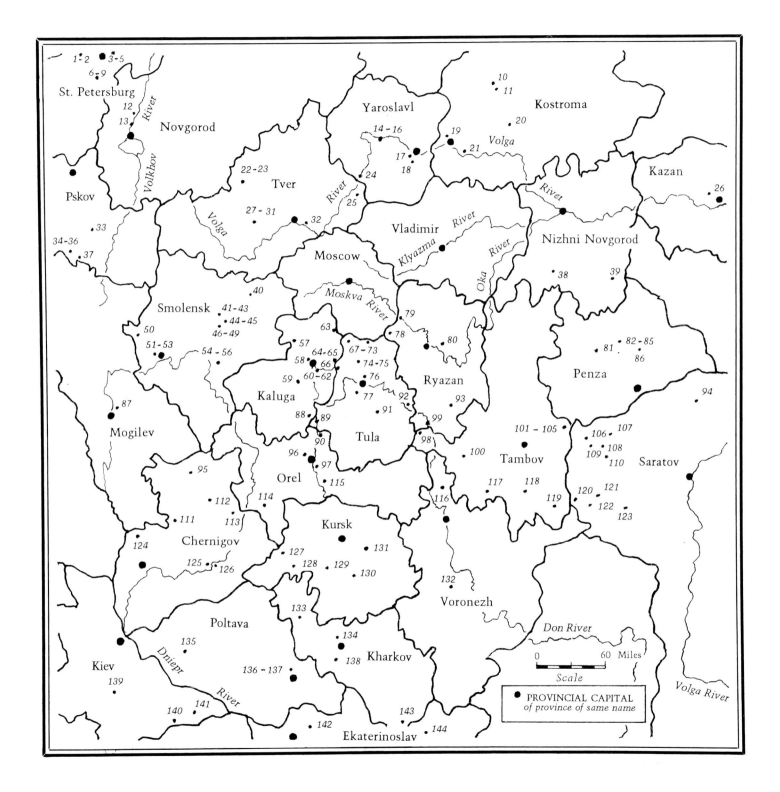

St. Petersburg
Novgorod
Pskov
Volkhov River
Volga River
Tver
Volga
Yaroslavl
Kostroma
Volga
Kazan
Vladimir
Klyazma River
Oka River
River
Nizhni Novgorod
Smolensk
Moscow
Moskva River
Mogilev
Kaluga
Orel
Ryazan
Penza
Tula
Saratov
Tambov
Chernigov
Kursk
Voronezh
Poltava
Kharkov
Don River
Kiev
Dniepr River
Ekaterinoslav
Volga River

0   60 Miles
Scale

● PROVINCIAL CAPITAL
  of province of same name

1. Artist unknown. *On the Estate*. 1780s. Silhouette. (Courtesy of the State Historical Museum, Moscow)

I
The Aristocratic Playground

I have resolved to embark on a new residence that, at

the least, will demonstrate to posterity that, in our century and in our

country, taste was known.—**Prince A. A. Bezborodko**

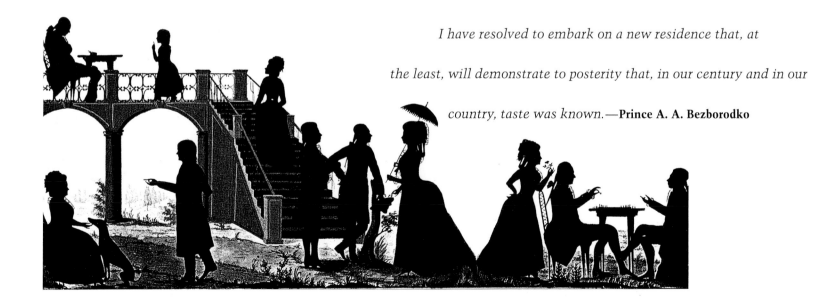

1
The Russian Noble

FROM MUSCOVITE TO EUROPEAN

Russia is but in the 12th century. Have you ever seen a clumsy romping Ignorant

Girl of 12 years old with a fine Parisian Cap upon her head? So seems to

my eye this Imperial Realm.—**Catherine Wilmot**

FROM ANTIQUITY, EUROPEAN COUNTRY RESIDENCES have either embodied intellectual and cultural ideals or symbolized personal power. In England these two stimuli had fused by the early eighteenth century to create a culture of country living that was unique and widely envied. Nowhere else did the country house so clearly express not just national culture, family wealth and status, and self-confident taste but also a clear connection between land-ownership and political power.

The Russian nobility was the last European elite to express its identity in country living. Russians began building elaborate country houses in the mid-eighteenth century in an attempt to replicate, virtually overnight, a way of life that elsewhere had developed over centuries. The Russian mania for building was driven by new cultural appetites and class instincts and fueled by recently acquired wealth. Moreover, estate builders in Russia were operating in a political and social context quite different from that of any other European elite of the time. For all these reasons, a seventeenth-century Muscovite boyar (an official of the highest rank) would have found the appearance, values, and way of life of his eighteenth-century descendants incomprehensible and, most likely, reprehensible. To gauge the remarkable changes that occurred between these generations one need only glance at the travel notes of Adam Olearius, the Duke of Holstein's envoy to Muscovy (as Russia was then known in the West) in the 1630s and 1640s. He describes Muscovite boyars as Oriental in appearance and slavishly dependent: "The magnates even have their heads shaved, imagining this to be an ornament. . . . However, when anyone . . . learns that he has fallen into disgrace, he allows his hair to grow long and in disorder. . . . All subjects, whether of high or low condition, call themselves and must count themselves the Tsar's *kholopi*, that is, slaves and serfs." Muscovites, Olearius reported, had no interest in learning. "Most Russians express crude and senseless opinions about the elevated natural sciences and arts. . . . They re-gard astronomy and astrology as witchcraft." As for the fine arts, Muscovite walls were bare save for religious icons, which he described as "wretchedly colored and ill-proportioned."[1]

Olearius noted that a few magnates had built "costly palaces" in the preceding thirty years and that their wives traveled in carriages or sleighs lined with red satin. Yet most of the tsar's lords lived in nondescript dwellings, with "not more than three or four earthen pots and as many clay and wooden dishes. . . . Very few people have feather beds, in lieu of which they lie on benches covered with cushions, straw, mats, or their clothes; in winter they sleep on flat-topped stoves. . . . Side by side lie men, women, and children, as well as servants, both male and female" (figs. 2, 3). Olearius reported finding "chickens and pigs under the benches and stoves."[2] In travels beyond Moscow, Olearius was surprised to find that one prince's country seat was nothing more than a small wooden farm.

Foreigners as a rule had little chance to see Muscovite houses, for Muscovy was a closed society, and most Muscovites xenophobic. Convinced that the dogma and rituals of Russian Orthodoxy encompassed truth and salvation, Muscovites equated foreign ways with heresy and a fall from grace. In the middle of the century, this fear of things foreign expressed itself in a wave of witch hunts and serious urban rioting directed against the foreign dress and habits of some nobles close to young Tsar Alexei (who reigned between 1645 and 1676). In response to the popular mood, Alexei ordered foreigners restricted to a particular area outside Moscow's walls, known as the German Suburb. In addition, he outlawed foreign dress and ordered that all foreign musical instruments in Moscow be confiscated and destroyed.[3]

Against this backdrop, the cultural reorientation of the Russian elite in the reign of Alexei's son, Peter the Great (1682–1725), seems all the more prodigious a feat. In a single generation the xenophobic Muscovite boyar was transformed into a polyglot cosmopolitan. By the time his

3

2. Sketch of a seventeenth-century Muscovite bridal procession.
(Olearius, *Travels in Muscovy*, 1669)

3. Sketch of seventeenth-century Muscovite costumes.
(Olearius, *Travels in Muscovy*, 1669)

grandsons reached adulthood, the entire way of life of the upper classes had radically changed. This transformation was reflected in their dress and manners, education and reading, work and entertainment, houses and carriages, the art they collected and commissioned, the language they spoke and wrote—in other words, in almost everything that defines a person. Both contemporaries and later generations tended to ascribe the entire process to Peter's iron will alone. Yet the evidence shows that even in the reign of Peter's pious father, Alexei, who for many epitomized the old Muscovite ideals, certain members of the elite close to the throne were flirting with Western ideas, adopting Western habits, and in quiet fashion challenging the foundations of Muscovite culture (fig. 4).

Artamon Matveev, guardian of Natalya Naryshkina (Alexei's second wife and the mother of Peter the Great), is a prime example. Matveev's case shows that although before the reign of Peter, a publicly expressed interest in things Western might bring official condemnation or popular retribution, such inclinations not only existed but were tolerated. A childhood friend of Alexei, Matveev was to outward appearances a traditional Russian. Yet his house contained Western items such as clocks, he employed a small group of musicians and, most significantly, he had almost eighty foreign books "on subjects ranging from landscape gardening to horses, including . . . a treatise on 'the nature of stones.'" Thus he was clearly, albeit privately, breaking the rules. Shortly after Alexei's death Matveev was betrayed by an angry subordinate, tried, and exiled, having been found guilty of sorcery and of summoning spirits "in the company of a foreigner, using a foreign book."[4]

Had Alexei, Matveev's powerful protector, been alive, Matveev would probably have avoided trial. Rank at court and family wealth depended on appointment to state service and the rewards that flowed from service; thus the tsar's favor alone determined the composition of the wealthy Muscovite elite (figs. 5–8). By contemporaneous

4. The Savvin-Storozhevsky Monastery in Zvenigorod. On the right is the red brick palace Tsar Alexei Mikhailovich had built for the visits of his wife, the tsaritsa, to this monastery. Across the courtyard is the tsar's palace. (Author)

Four courtiers costumed as Muscovites for the imperial ball at
the Winter Palace, February 1903.

5. E. F. Lazareva (née Countess Sumarokov-Elston) costumed as a
boyar's wife.
(Author's collection)

6. Count S. D. Sheremetev costumed as Field Marshal Boris
Sheremetev, from a portrait at Kuskovo. (Author's collection)

7. Count D. I. Tolstoy in the boyar dress traditionally worn at home.
(Author's collection)

8. Countess E. V. Musina-Pushkina (née Countess Kapnist) costumed
as a boyar's wife.
(Author's collection)

European standards seventeenth-century Russia did not have a nobility, that is, a titled, privileged elite with inalienable, hereditary rights. The title of prince—which signified descent from Riurik (the mythical first Russian prince), from Prince Gedimin of Lithuania, or from Georgian or Tatar princes—meant little unless accompanied by high court rank. The protocol of Muscovite appointments was governed by two elaborate hierarchies of status: family status (determined by the service rank of the head of the family), and order of birth within the family. Both determined the service positions to which a young man could aspire; neither could be openly circumvented.[5] Ranks were all-important, for if one family member accepted a rank beneath the family's current position in the hierarchy, the status of the entire family was lowered. Rank in service determined one's wealth, measured in land worked by income-producing peasants, which the tsar awarded to trusted servitors either as a *votchina* (hereditary tenure) or a *pomestie* (personal possession in return for service). Muscovite servitors were constantly maneuvering, trying either to convert temporary holdings into hereditary lands or to improve their status—without, however, incurring the tsar's anger. To offend the tsar meant ruin, because what he had granted, he could (and frequently did) take away.

Even before Peter's reign, the deficiencies of this awkward system of rank and precedence were acknowledged. In 1682 it was abolished and Russia's first book of heraldry created, laying the basis for a Western-style nobility. This register included families who claimed descent from the royal house of Riurik, such as the Naryshkins; families descended from appanage princes, such as the Apraksins, Golitsyns, Dolgorukys, Vorontsovs, Tatishchevs, Gagarins, and Sheremetevs; and noble families of foreign origin, such as the Davydovs, Yusupovs, and Karamzins (all descended from Tatars), or the Volkovs, who traced their lineage back to the illegitimate son of a wealthy eleventh-century Polish cardinal. The family history of the Volkovs

illustrates the making of the Russian nobility. In 1505 a Gregory Volk arrived in Moscow as ambassador of the grand duke of Lithuania, bringing with him three sons. Fyodor, the oldest, joined the Muscovite servitor class, made a name for himself as a soldier, and was granted large estates near Yaroslavl. Fyodor's grandson Michael served as head huntsman for Ivan IV, who was notorious for confiscating boyar lands (fig. 9). By this time, marriage into and among the leading Muscovite families had become (and would remain) the most common way of protecting and enlarging family fortunes. In the late seventeenth century Michael Volkov's son Abram solidified the family status by marrying a sister of Natalya Naryshkina. As a result Abram's son Alexei was brought up with Peter the Great and became a captain of Peter's prestigious Semenovsky Guards regiment.[6] Before his death in battle in 1708 Alexei married the oldest daughter of the wealthy Prince Romodanovsky and produced heirs. His sons and grandsons continued to build the Volkov fortune, establishing family ties with the powerful Dolgorukys, Mamontovs, Bibikovs, Dmitriev-Mamonovs, and Muromtsovs. In the course of the eighteenth century all these families adopted a style of life their Muscovite ancestors could not have imagined, a life based on vast wealth and European tastes.

During the long reign of Peter I (fig. 10) the nobility's ground rules for advancement changed dramatically. Peter was an egalitarian who wanted not a *noblesse d'épée* but a *noblesse de robe*, a dynamic elite whose energies would transform Russia into a modern military power. Peter had spent much time as a child in the German Suburb, fascinated by Western inventions like music boxes and by his foreign friends' dress and manners. From this experience Peter may have derived the important assumption that underlay his reforms: that technology and culture are inseparable. A military man all his life, Peter was intensely concerned with acquiring Western technology. But he came to assume that to think like a European—that is, to understand Western technology, warfare, and statecraft—

9. The sixteenth-century tent-style Church of the Resurrection
(with a seventeenth-century bell tower) at Gorodnya, a Sheremetev
estate Ivan IV confiscated and turned into a royal hunting lodge.

The churches built on estates near Moscow during the early part of Peter's reign signaled the new cultural direction. The Church of the Savior at P. B. Sheremetev's Ubory; the Znamensky church at Dubrovitsy (fig. 11), erected by Peter the Great's tutor, B. A. Golitsyn; and the Naryshkins' church at Fili (fig. 12) are among the few remaining exam-

11. Church of the Virgin of the Sign (constructed between 1690 and 1697/1704?) at Dubrovitsy, originally the votchina of I. V. Morozov.

10. Engraving of Peter the Great, based on a portrait of Peter painted by Gottfried Kneller in 1697. (Courtesy of the State Historical Museum, Moscow)

Russians must learn to act like Europeans. Hence he set out to force the Russian nobility to model itself culturally on the European example. Favors were showered on those who successfully negotiated the cultural transition from Muscovite to Westerner and, above all, on those whose initiative and energy were, like Peter's, directed to transforming Russia.

12. Church of the Intercession of the Virgin at Fili (1690–93), in the seventeenth century the suburban Moscow votchina of L. K. Naryshkin, Peter the Great's uncle.

ples of the turn-of-the-century style known as "Moscow baroque," the first challenge to traditional architecture. Peter himself attended the dedication of the Dubrovitsy church. Not surprisingly, a Sheremetev, two Golitsyns, and Alexei Volkov were in the entourage accompanying Peter on his first trip to Europe in 1697.

This voyage opened a new world to Peter and his companions. As they passed through the Baltic states and northern Germany, then on to Holland and England, they were as stunned by the stone architecture of Western cities as their hosts were by the Muscovites' odd appearance and lack of manners. The Russians left an English suburban villa, Sayes Court, in shambles following a three-month occupancy. John Evelyn, the outraged owner, presented his government with a huge bill for a destroyed lawn, smashed furniture, torn curtains, and family portraits that had been used for target practice.

The display of Muscovite barbarism should not have been surprising, for it was well known that Russians had nothing resembling the elegant town houses or stylish country seats of the Dutch, English, or French. At a distance Moscow had long dazzled European travelers, the gilded onion domes of churches gleaming and the ornate red brick walls and buildings of the Kremlin flaming in the sun. Yet on closer inspection Moscow appeared little more than a haphazard conglomeration of wooden buildings clustered around the Kremlin. The fiery images all too often became reality as a spark turned the heart of Russia's capital into a raging inferno; with the exception of the Kremlin, the buildings in Moscow had an air of impermanence. The general lack of interest in aesthetics is indicated by the fact that Moscow boasted stores of prefabricated parts for wooden houses so that in the event of fire, the simple dwellings could be hastily reconstructed. Although even Olearius had remarked on the Moscow magnates' personal retinues of hundreds of servants, their style of living was drab. Their houses, built to no particular plan, offered little in the way of comforts. For important events

their servants dressed in plain cotton caftans. Veal, capons, asparagus, grapes, and imported wines, soon to become staples of an aristocrat's dinner table, were virtually unknown. Most carriages and sleighs were functional rather than elegant (though bridles and saddles were sometimes decorated with precious stones).

Outside Moscow, nothing resembling European manor houses or patterns of country life was to be found. Suburban Moscow, to be sure, had a few wooden country residences, the most impressive of which were the two royal seats: Kolomenskoe, whose elaborate 250-room palace was constructed in the 1680s; and Izmailovo (fig. 13), the ancient Romanov family seat, which had a regular garden and a menagerie of wild animals. When the tsar began summering outside Moscow, his boyars gradually converted their simple farms into family summer houses—though they were only slightly larger than a peasant's house and seldom had more than one story. An engraving of Nikolskoe (fig. 14) in the 1660s shows a two-story wooden house with a shingled roof and small windows in the center of a large courtyard surrounded by a fence. Along the fence are the service buildings, and beyond it a wooden church. V. V. Golitsyn's Medvedkovo was more elaborate. Large wooden gates, carved and brightly painted, marked the entrance. The manor house had stoves of Dutch tiles and paintings and maps on the walls. D. M. Golitsyn's manor house at Arkhangelskoe at the turn of the eighteenth century consisted of three large rooms (with the traditional icons in the corner opposite the door) connected by granaries. The bathhouse was nearby, and off of the enclosed courtyard were various service buildings: a kitchen, cellar, icehouse, storehouse, and pantry. Arkhangelskoe also had two orangeries (rare at that time), in which lemons, oranges, figs, and oleanders were grown, and a large garden tended by a gardener, an assistant, and four apprentices.[7]

The area immediately beyond Moscow was a vast, sparsely settled wasteland, impenetrable during spring and

13. Ivan Zubov. Engraving of Izmailovo, the royal seat outside Moscow. 1726(?). (Tikhomirov, *Arkhitektura podmoskovnykh usadeb*)

late autumn, when dirt and log roads became impassable quagmires. Provincial outposts were nothing more than soldiers' settlements, though some old appanage towns such as Vladimir or Novgorod boasted a medieval kremlin or fortress at their centers. Like Moscow, all of these small towns were well endowed with churches and nearby monasteries, complete with palaces to house the visiting tsar and his retinue. But Russia at the dawn of the eighteenth century lacked Western Europe's long-established and stylistically varied architectural vocabulary for secular domestic structures.

Imagine, then, the Russians' surprise as they walked the streets of major urban centers like Amsterdam or London, and their astonishment at seeing even lesser cities like Utrecht or Bath that were well laid out, with tidy cobblestoned streets, elegant suburban villas and palaces, and a host of architectural styles, from Gothic to baroque. Before the turn of the century Vasily Golitsyn had been almost alone in his taste for Western elegance. Now, travel opened the eyes of a number of Petrine servitors to Western styles in architecture, furnishings, and town planning and to the concept of noble gentility. Peter Tolstoy, sent to

Venice to learn navigation, was overwhelmed. In a Polish noble's garden Tolstoy came across the "most marvelous of fountains" surrounded by palaces with exterior walls "of plaster of fine workmanship, like carved alabaster," and interiors "decorated with shells and great mirrors . . . and with other excellently made things, the likes of which are impossible to describe . . . fine stoves . . . excellent tables, fine armchairs, patterned pictures, and many other sorts of decorations."[8] The Moscow travelers soon discovered that in Europe an elegant table, refined personal be-

havior, and luxurious dress, furnishings, and interior decor distinguished the person of noble rank.

Peter lured the first European craftsmen and experts to Russia shortly after his return in 1698, in what was merely the beginning of a vast northward migration of European artistic talent. In 1701, initiating a sustained effort to enforce solid construction and regularity in city planning, Peter decreed that owners of lots in central Moscow must build masonry houses with facades situated directly on the street, as was customary in Europe, rather than at the back

14. Storn. Sketch of Nikolskoe, a seventeenth-century boyar estate near Moscow. To the right of the house is a large campaign tent. (Tikhomirov, *Arkhitektura podmoskovnykh usadeb*)

of a courtyard. He also issued numerous decrees to change Muscovite habits. In replacing the old Orthodox calendar with the Julian, for example, he ordered streets and homes decorated with fir branches for the New Year and demanded that "as a sign of happiness on January 1, friends should greet each other and the New Year."[9]

In 1703 the building of St. Petersburg, Peter's window on Europe and the new imperial capital, began. From the start it was intended to trumpet Russia's Europeanization to a startled world. Peter's use of outstanding foreign architects and artists and the speed with which his impressive new city arose on its swampy foundations were paradigmatic of Russia's eighteenth-century architectural revolution. To this day Russia's "Venice of the North" is a unique architectural museum, a period piece built from scratch according to the plans of such leading architects as Dominico Trezzini, Andreas Schluter, and Alexandre Le Blond. The immense proportions of Palace Square, bounded on one side by the baroque Winter Palace and further enclosed in the early nineteenth century by a semicircle of government office buildings, breathe by design a Western concept of imperium. The building of St. Petersburg and the transfer of court life to the new city symbolized Peter's determination to expand Russia's boundaries, to make the country a force in Europe.

Peter's courtiers were told what to wear, where to live, and how to behave in their new surroundings. All courtiers were obliged to build masonry houses of prescribed design, to devise heraldic coats of arms for their families, to shave their beards and abandon Oriental caftans for European dress, and to learn essential forms of European politesse such as dancing, fencing, and correct behavior. Noblewomen, heretofore secluded from male company, were commanded to appear at court functions in Western fashions. Early in his reign Peter introduced the European titles of count and baron to supplement the ubiquitous honorific "prince" and began to investigate hierarchies in other countries, such as Sweden and Prussia. The result was the Table of Ranks of 1722, which made lifelong service to the state not only compulsory for the nobility but the precondition for noble status.

Peter's intention seems to have been the creation of a clearly defined class of nobles comparable to other European elites. In Russia, however, membership in this elite, though facilitated by birth, wealth, and education, was to be confirmed solely through one's usefulness to the crown. Only by working one's way up one of the three service ladders (civil, military, or court) of the Table of Ranks—from the fourteenth rank, the lowest, to the eighth, which conferred hereditary nobility—could one lay claim to an estate. Nobles were not allowed to marry without passing a literacy test. In an effort to protect family fortunes, Peter decreed immovable property indivisible for all families regardless of status, noting that "the division of estates upon the death of the father causes great harm to Our state and state interests and brings ruin to subjects and the families concerned."[10]

Peter punished nobles for poor performance or laziness and rewarded (with titles, money, and land) those who distinguished themselves, setting a precedent that would continue throughout the century. The cumulative effect of all these decrees on the service class was to obliterate old distinctions between votchina and pomestie, aristocrat and service noble, and to reduce the significance of birth. Rank in service continued to determine status, but rank was now determined by merit. Only a hereditary noble could own land populated by serfs, yet anyone of talent might aspire to this title.

As a result the Petrine elite were a motley group. Some were from old families, some were parvenus. Peter's transformation of their dress and material surroundings inevitably created an expensive appetite for the stylish, the elegant, the novel. The ultimate measure of a noble's wealth remained the number of male serfs possessed, for their labor provided his or her chief income. But having money, costly possessions, and stylish mansions became

15

significant attributes of rank in the early eighteenth century. Fortunes were often acquired overnight, mostly from imperial largesse but also in more imaginative and dishonest ways. High Petrine officials used their positions for personal gain, sometimes accumulating great wealth. Princes Matvei Gagarin and Alexei Cherkassky made fortunes as governors of Siberia. As one Siberian official told Peter: "You, sire, have not bestowed sufficient salaries on your administrators so that here no one has villages, and even if a good person wanted to be honest, having no means of subsistence he is forced to nourish himself dishonestly."[11]

Prince Alexander Menshikov rose from nothing to become the foremost grandee of the Petrine period, embezzling enormous sums to add to Peter's lavish gifts. Inventories of Menshikov's property confiscated after Peter's death show that these gifts and his own profiteering from offices such as the presidency of the War College had enriched him by 90,000 serfs; 6 houses in Petersburg and others in Moscow and Ingermanland (to which he had honorary title and which produced a yearly income of 228,710 rubles); 4 million rubles in cash, with 9 million more in London and Amsterdam banks; 24 dozen silver table settings; and 4,000 pounds of gold service. In 1727 J. L. Lefort, Saxon minister to the Russian court (and nephew of Peter I's favorite, Francis Lefort), reported as exaggerated the rumors circulating that 20 million rubles' worth of goods had been confiscated from Menshikov as he traveled into exile in Siberia.[12] Whatever the real worth of Menshikov's lost fortune, it was sufficiently immense to create a number of family fortunes when awarded to new favorites. During the eighteenth century such redistributions of wealth occurred frequently. War, Peter's major occupation, was also profitable. Admiral Fyodor Apraksin made off with a large portion of the war booty he extracted from Charles XII. Peter granted Admiral Fyodor Golovin land, peasants, and the title of count for his naval victories; Boris She-

remetev was awarded 12,000 peasants and the same title for victory at Poltava.

Wealth and rank also accrued to Petrine entrepreneurs such as Afanasy Goncharov and Alexei Miliutin. In 1714, by imperial decree, Miliutin was allowed to found Russia's first factory for the manufacture of silks and brocades. Four years later Goncharov collaborated with a wealthy merchant to found a profitable linen and paper factory. By 1735 Miliutin had enough capital to build a trading shop on Nevsky Prospekt, the central boulevard in St. Petersburg; by 1736 Goncharov was able to buy out his partner. Their achievements were assisted and rewarded by the crown. In 1740 Miliutin was granted the rank of collegiate assessor, which conferred hereditary nobility. Goncharov was promoted to the same rank two years later. Goncharov, who had already built a masonry church on his property Polotnyany Zavod in 1736, now began construction of a lavish country residence there. By the end of the century Miliutin's grandson was a grandee who had two mansions in Moscow and another at Titovo, a handsome estate of one thousand souls, located on the borders of Kaluga and Tula Provinces.

The renowned Demidov family also got its start under Peter. Although the exact circumstances that led to the founding of this mining fortune are shrouded in legend, it is known that Nikita Demidov, the founder, began as a talented pistol maker in Tula. Apprised of Demidov's skills, the tsar gave him the right to run several weapons factories (to which state serfs were ascribed) in Tula and St. Petersburg and to extract iron ore in the Urals. In 1720 Demidov was awarded nobility and at his death left about ten thousand serfs and numerous houses to each of his three sons, thus laying the basis for the wealth of successive generations of Demidovs (see figs. 15, 98).

The rise to nobility of men like Goncharov, Miliutin, and Demidov was precisely what Peter intended: a first estate of talented, ambitious men. Upon Peter's death,

15. Salvatore Tonci. Portrait of N. N. Demidov, a grandson of the Petrine entrepreneur Nikita Demidov. Late eighteenth century. He is pictured in the Urals, holding a chunk of the mineral ore that made the family fortune.
(Courtesy of the Russian Museum, St. Petersburg)

Sheremetevs, profited from its application, few adopted it, and the old practice of giving equal shares to all heirs (including women), often ruinous to family fortunes as Peter had foreseen, again became accepted practice.

Russian nobles likewise viewed compulsory education as an insult to their status. After Peter's death nobles withdrew en masse from the state cipher schools, where they had been subject to corporal punishment by non-nobles. The preferred model for educating noble youths became (and remained) home tutoring, followed by training in a noble cadet corps school, which guaranteed entrance into an elite branch of the Russian military such as a guards regiment. Lastly, the Petrine concept of compulsory service for life was reduced first to thirty years and then to twenty-five, and the requirement of earning nobility subverted in practice. Nobles were enrolled in prestigious regiments as infants; by the time they actually joined them they had been automatically promoted several ranks. The cadet corps schools routinely graduated pupils with the rank of officer.

The elite had, however, internalized Peter's cultural goals. By the end of his reign nobility was synonymous with life on a grand scale. Peter did not oppose this trend, for despite his own simple tastes, he considered the manifestation of opulence prestigious for Russia and a stimulus to trade. The Spanish envoy to Peter's court reported: "I can attest that the court here in its luxury and grandeur surpasses the most wealthy courts. . . . Here everyone is richer than in Paris." A ball the envoy gave in 1728 cost him nearly seven thousand rubles, almost a quarter of his yearly budget, and he ended up having to pawn his diamond-encrusted gold Order of the Golden Fleece to pay for it. Within a generation, cultural westernization had become part of the Russian noble's self-definition. The ability to dance, fence, speak French, and demonstrate some familiarity with European art, music, and culture identified one as a member of the elite. All this cost

however, this concept was rapidly undercut, as a fierce reaction against Petrine compulsion and egalitarianism produced reversals of a number of his decrees. Many nobles viewed the law prohibiting the equal division of estates among heirs as a restriction on their hereditary right to their property. Although at least one wealthy family, the

money, and money continued to be showered upon those who enjoyed imperial favor. During the reigns of the luxury-loving monarchs who followed Peter, his niece Anna (1730–40), and his daughter Elizabeth (1741–62), Petrine standards of imperial largesse, court luxury, and official venality were quickly surpassed. Even Frederick the Great took note of this, writing, "The Russian minister Bestuzhev-Riumin is bribable to such a degree that he would sell the Empress [Elizabeth] herself if he could find someone rich enough to buy her."[13]

Peter's death initiated a prolonged period of court intrigues in which the stakes were enormous—the plotting culminating more often than not in the overthrow of the reigning monarch. Being on the wrong side brought ruin; being on the right side, vast wealth. Ivan Dolgoruky, for example, was a personal friend of Peter II, Peter the Great's grandson, who inherited the throne in 1727 upon the death of Peter's wife, Catherine. Dolgoruky managed to affiance his sister to the new young tsar and was awarded forty-four thousand serfs. But then, in a notorious reversal of fortune, when Peter II suddenly died in 1730, Ivan was ruined, lost everything, and died soon thereafter in Siberian exile.[14] The Russian noble, when not fearing ruin at the hands of the monarch, was often to be found begging for his supper. Mikhail Vorontsov, one of those who had helped Elizabeth seize the throne in 1740, had been richly rewarded with large estates, but their income could not offset the debts he incurred living at Elizabeth's court. In 1751, requesting yet another handout, he wrote Elizabeth: "We are all your faithful slaves. Without the grace and rewards from your Imperial Highness we cannot live. I do not know the family of a single house in the realm which on its own, without the rewards of the monarch's generosity, could sustain itself."[15]

Elizabeth was generous to her supporters. The Shuvalov brothers, Alexander and Peter, were both given the title of count in 1746, and Peter a property with 20,000 serfs, which brought him 200,000 rubles annually. The Buturlin family fortune was assured when Elizabeth's field marshal, Alexander Buturlin, was named count for his victories in the Seven Years' War and awarded 108,000 acres in Voronezh Province, on which he settled 15,000 serfs.[16] Elizabeth granted the largest fortunes to the Razumovsky brothers, sons of a poor Cossack. In 1742 she awarded Alexei (her greatest favorite and possibly her morganatic husband) lands near Mozhaisk and in Ukraine, in 1744 the estate of Perovo near Moscow, subsequently other confiscated estates, and finally an entire island in Petersburg. Alexei's brother, Kirill, lived almost as splendidly, with a house in St. Petersburg, staffed by about two hundred servants, and vast territories in Ukraine.[17]

During Elizabeth's reign St. Petersburg continued to develop, graced by the renowned baroque structures of Bartolomeo Rastrelli (whose name became synonymous with this style): the Winter Palace, Catherine Palace, Smolny Convent (fig. 16), and private mansions along the embankments of the Neva River. During the same period Russian grandees began constructing elaborate residences in outlying areas as well. The earliest Western-style estates were the suburban pleasure palaces that Petrine grandees like Menshikov erected outside the new capital city. By the reigns of Anna and Elizabeth no courtier could do without a palace along the road from St. Petersburg to Peterhof (the Russian Versailles), or near Tsarskoe Selo ("the tsar's village"), the imperial summer residence. Their playful names—Zabava (Amusement), the Naryshkins' whimsical Ga-Ga, and Menshikov's Favorite and Mon Courage—epitomized their chief function, lavish entertaining. Count Francesco Algarotti, an Italian envoy writing in 1739, was not impressed; he reported that the residences were shoddily built by slavish courtiers: "One sees clearly that they were built more in obedience than by choice. Their walls are all cracked, out of plumb, and remain standing with difficulty. . . . Elsewhere ruins make themselves, while in St. Petersburg they are built."[18]

The word *dacha* has been commonly used since the

16. Church of the Resurrection at the Smolny Convent, St. Petersburg 1748–64. B. F. Rastrelli, architect. The convent's Smolny Institute, founded by Catherine II, became Russia's premier boarding school for noblewomen.

nineteenth century to refer to a summer or vacation dwelling, whether palace or cottage. Its origin in the phrase *dacha imi* (meaning "given to them"), referring to lands the Muscovite rulers had doled out to their highest officials, makes it particularly applicable to these Petersburg suburban villas. The proximity of a Petersburg dacha to an imperial palace indicated its main function: to remind the ruler of one's presence and one's willingness to entertain him whenever possible, in the hope of reward.

Although the court had moved to St. Petersburg in the first decades of the eighteenth century, a few large residences were also being built in the environs of Moscow. Among the earliest was the Golovin mansion on the banks of the Yauza River. In 1714, intent on finishing his new

capital, Peter forbade all masonry construction in Moscow. This decree was rescinded in 1728, and around this time the Lyapunovs built Isady outside the city, on the right bank of the Oka River. The *piano nobile* of the two-story house sat on a rusticated base with small windows, which contained the service quarters. Pilasters decorated the main facade of the house, which consisted of a central section and two lateral wings. At about the same time a stuccoed brick manor house of similar design arose at Yasenevo, a crown estate Peter I had awarded to the Lopukhins, parents of his first wife. The estate house, now at the southernmost extent of Moscow, was a good two days' ride from the Kremlin when built. General Jacob Bruce's Glinki, constructed in the early 1730s, after his

17. View of the aviaries and duck pond at Kuskovo. Mid-eighteenth-century engraving.
(Courtesy of the Library of the Moscow Institute of Architecture)

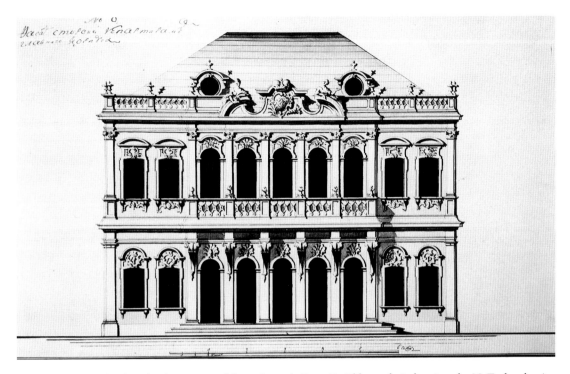

18. Baroque facade of Neskuchnoe, viewed from the park. From D. Ukhtomsky's drawings for N. Trubetskoy's estate on Sparrow Hills. 1753. (Courtesy of the Shchusev Museum of Architecture, Moscow)

retirement, was closer to the city center. This house was somewhat differently designed, perhaps because Bruce, of Scottish extraction, is said to have planned the house himself. The square manor house, whose main floor featured a front balcony decorated with paired columns, was separated from the service buildings and the stables by an impressive allée.

In Elizabeth's reign grand mansions proliferated. Alexei Razumovsky commissioned Rastrelli to design a grand house with extensive gardens at Perovo. In 1743 Count Peter Sheremetev, son of the Petrine field marshal Boris, married the richest heiress of the day, Princess Varvara Cherkasskaya; as a result of this union, he added her family's estate, Veshnyakovo, to his family's, Kuskovo, and in 1751 began transforming the modest hunting lodge built by his father into a magnificent country residence (fig. 17). Shortly thereafter, in 1753, the architect D. V. Ukhtomsky designed Neskuchnoe ("not boring") for Prince Nikita Trubetskoy on Sparrow Hills, above the Moscow River, with elaborate parterres in front of the house, belvederes and orangeries in the park behind it, ponds, and a menagerie.

Neskuchnoe's elaborate baroque facade (fig. 18) heralded a new age of splendor that was no longer confined to

19. Church of the Birth of the Mother of God at Podmoklovo,
the estate of Prince N. S. Dolgoruky. 1754.

Russia's two major cities. Almost due south of Moscow, on
the far side of the Oka River, an extraordinary Italianate
church was built in the 1750s on the Dolgoruky estate of
Podmoklovo (fig. 19). Located 75 miles south of Moscow
and 35 miles northeast of Tula, Podmoklovo is hard to

reach even today; at that time the journey from Moscow
took at least 3 or 4 days. Perhaps the Dolgoruky who
served as a Petrine envoy to Italy returned with the design
for this church. The rotunda, which was circled by an open
colonnade and crowned with a gallery of life-size sculptures, is a remarkable caprice for rural Russia of that time.

At virtually the same time Alexander Griboedov, a
retired commander of the Imperial Guards, was designing
another remote estate, Khmelita, near Vyazma, in Smolensk Province (figs. 20, 21). Records of a lawsuit against
him suggest that he may have acquired the fortune this
project required by bilking the other heirs of a common
ancestor out of their property. Over the next 150 years
Khmelita, like most Russian estates, had a checkered history. Initially it was the seat of two generations of luxury-
loving Griboedovs. In the early nineteenth century it
became the summer home of the family's most famous
member, Alexander, author of the biting comedy *Wit Works
Woe*. By the 1840s it had been abandoned to decay, but in the
1890s Vladimir Volkov-Muromtsov and his wife, Varvara,
acquired Khmelita and restored it as their family home.

In the 1750s the estate comprised ten thousand acres
with seven villages. Over the next thirty years an unknown architect supervised the building of a baroque palace, constructed of locally made brick that was stuccoed
and painted. As was customary, Griboedov also built new
churches—a brick church with two chapels for the family,
just beyond the house of the estate steward, and a wooden
church for the village. The plan of Khmelita (fig. 22) was
typical of most country estates until the end of the century. An impressive allée led through a triumphal archway
and across a large courtyard to the main entrance. The
main house consisted of an almost square central section,
extended by two long lateral wings, opposite which were
two large annexes. All these buildings were connected by a
wall that enclosed the parade square in front of the manse.
Two side entrances opened onto the courtyard from south
and north. At the rear of the house, an elegant split stair-

case curved down from the ballroom terrace to a formal garden with avenues of shady linden trees and two ponds linked by an artificial river that was spanned by a bridge. Beyond the bridge a road wound through an irregular park with a large artificial lake.

Numerous outbuildings surrounded the palace complex. To the north lay a horse-breeding stable and enclosed riding ring. On the south side were a large orangery, quarters for Griboedov's serf actors and a gypsy choir, and two smaller buildings, one of which was the estate office. Beyond the church were the artisans' workshops, and beyond them the cow and threshing barns, which formed two squares. The Griboedov lands extended for thousands of acres, encompassing serf villages, arable fields, forests, and

20. The mansion and parade courtyard of Khmelita, the Griboedov estate, under restoration in 1991.
(Courtesy of Viktor Kulakov)

21. Khmelita in 1992, after its restoration. (Author)

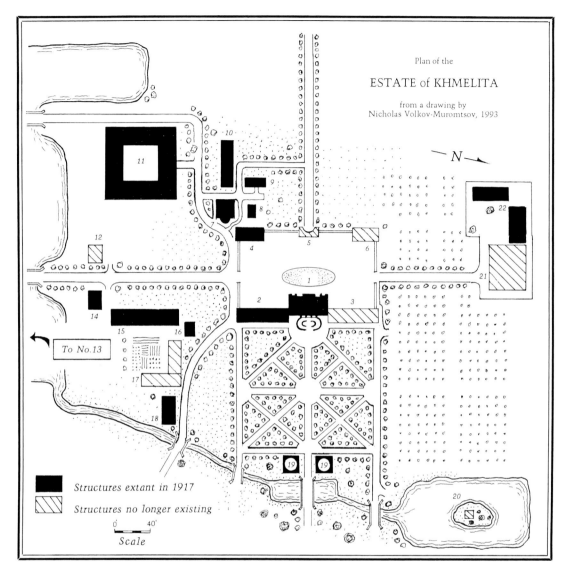

Plan of the

ESTATE of KHMELITA

from a drawing by
Nicholas Volkov-Muromtsov, 1993

N

To No.13

■ Structures extant in 1917

▨ Structures no longer existing

0   40'

Scale

22. Plan of the central estate buildings at Khmelita. (Author's collection)

1. Main house	7. Kazan Church (1759)	14. Blacksmith's shop	19. Garden pavilions
2. South wing	8.–9. Artisans' workshops	15. Orangery	20. Island pavilion
3. North wing	10. Artisans' living quarters	16. Estate office	21. Riding ring
4. South annex	11. Cow barn and stables	17. Housing for actors	22. Stables
5. Main gate	12. Oil mill	18. Outbuilding (post office,	
6. North annex	13. Threshing barn	20th century)	

pastures. The plans of estates varied greatly, depending on the amount of land, the idiosyncrasies of terrain, or a particular owner's preferences. But the main elements of the Khmelita estate complex—the imposing, stylish manor house, decorative service buildings and workshops, formal gardens, and large naturalized park—were ubiquitous and essential to the Russian estate. Together they constituted an enclosed, self-sufficient, idealized world of nature and art.

By the 1750s and 1760s the third generation of Russian nobles was descending on Europe for study, service, or pleasure. Venturing beyond London, they were struck by the magnificent country seats of the landed aristocracy. Whether Gothic or neo-Gothic, Elizabethan, baroque, or Palladian in style, these manors, surrounded by forests, rolling hills, and villages of tenant farmers, symbolized local power and prestige. This was the world to which the Russian noble began to aspire. England's aristocracy was widely envied for its independence and prosperity. Here, manor houses were material embodiments of lineage and standing. Within their walls resided family history and tradition, preserved in the family coat of arms above a fireplace or woven into an old tapestry, in the ancestral portraits crowding the walls, and in the treasures assembled by generations of family members. The feudal aristocracy represented in the greatest of these houses had ancient title to its lands, rights assured through contracts wrested from the sovereign, and local political power.

At mid-century the Russian nobility, by contrast, was an elite whose evolution had been determined by the crown's political needs and goals. The Russian noble's very existence, not to mention sustenance, continued to depend on retaining the sovereign's favor. The frequency of disgrace and confiscation of property is evidence of the point. By mid-century this phenomenon had created a second difference between St. Petersburg, the new capital, and Moscow, the old. Moscow tended to attract the disaffected or out of favor. This trend was to continue, until the nobility itself began to differentiate between the Petersburg courtier and the Moscow *velmozha*, or grandee. The latter usually owned a house in Petersburg but preferred Moscow, where he lived a life more or less independent of the crown. Moscow, with its rings of broad boulevards, became the city of the aristocracy; there, grandees inhabited not the formal mansions of St. Petersburg but urban estates set back from the street, with courtyards and large gardens, much like estates in the country. In a country with only two major cities, Moscow combined the attributes of Boston and Main Line Philadelphia. It was the city of old money, tradition, culture, and feeling, whereas St. Petersburg was the center of fashion and power, Russia's New York and Washington rolled into one.

Without more independence from the crown and security of person and property, the Russian noble, no matter how wealthy, could not aspire to the existence of an English lord. A major step in that direction was taken in 1762, when Peter III issued a decree freeing the nobility from service. One minor noble, Andrei T. Bolotov, recalled literally jumping for joy at the news, which he hardly dared believe, and hastening to submit his resignation. Until then, only the aged, retired noble who could not afford town life had lived in the provinces. Like Bolotov, numbers of lesser nobles for whom service had meant ruinous neglect of their small estates now hurried home, swelling the ranks of nobles living permanently in the country. Increasingly, wealthier nobles like Count Peter Sheremetev also took advantage of the decree, retiring from service to travel or live abroad, or sometimes creating a new life on estates they owned but previously had been able to visit only sporadically (fig. 23).

The next few decades, commencing with the seizure of power by Catherine II in 1762, inaugurated what has been called the "Golden Age of the Nobility." Catherine, a German princess, had come to Russia as a girl in 1745 to marry Elizabeth's heir, Peter III. Among the conspirators who helped Catherine seize power from her inept husband and who were appropriately rewarded were the dashing Orlov brothers and the young Princess Catherine Dashkova, niece of Elizabeth's chancellor, Mikhail Vorontsov. Although Catherine II (fig. 24) consistently presented herself as thoroughly Russian, her concept of nobility remained more European than Muscovite. Upon coming to power she reversed much of her husband's legislation but let stand his decree freeing nobles from compulsory service. In it Peter had expressed his expectation that the nobility would continue to serve out of a sense of noblesse oblige. In practice, the service concept was so ingrained and state salaries so necessary that few nobles abstained from service altogether. But Catherine, an enlightened autocrat, offered the nobility a new venue for activity. Focusing on

23. Count Peter Sheremetev's palace at Kuskovo, viewed from across the great lake.

24. D. G. Levitsky. Catherine as lawmaker, in the Temple of the Goddess of Justice. (Courtesy of the Tretiakov Gallery, Moscow)

responded by voicing concern about their insecure status, the deplorable state of local administration and justice, and rural lawlessness. In 1775, on the heels of the Pugachev rebellion, a widespread peasant jacquerie that proved the urgency of reform, Catherine restructured provincial government. The territory of the Russian Empire (by the end of Catherine's reign considerably enlarged through the incorporation of eastern Poland and Ukraine) was divided into 50 provinces. For each, Catherine designated a provincial capital, districts, and district capitals and appointed a host of new officials. Between 1775 and 1785 Catherine's building commission, which had planned the renovation of 200 older towns, designed 216 new towns, each with central official buildings of uniform, neoclassical style, and regulations governing all construction on the central streets. Finally, in 1785, on her fifty-sixth birthday, Catherine issued the Charter of the Nobility, which clarified questions of noble status and created provincial corporate institutions for the nobility.

During the eighteenth century the ranks of the Russian nobility swelled with foreigners from recently acquired territories and with those ennobled through service, causing it to become one of the largest groups of nobles in Europe. Historically, many Russian nobles were of non-Russian origin. The Yusupovs traced their roots to a Tatar prince, the Davydovs and Uvarovs to a common Tatar ancestor, the Korsakovs to a Corsican prince, and the Kantemirs to a Turkish pasha. Russia's enormous territorial expansion in the eighteenth century first brought in German nobles from the Baltic such as Count Ivan Ostermann and the notorious Count Ernst Johann Biron (Empress Anna's lover); then the Potockis, Czartoryskys, Razumovskys, and numerous other noble families from Poland and the Ukraine; and at the end of the century, Georgian princely families such as the Bagrations and Chavchavadzes. At the same time, the principle of ennoblement through service increased the numbers of both hereditary nobles and titled magnates such as the Shu-

the spread of enlightenment beyond the old and new capitals, Catherine envisaged her nobles as her culture bearers and governors in the provinces.

At her Legislative Commission of 1767 Catherine had elicited suggestions for improving her realm. Her nobles

28

valovs, Orlovs, and Potemkins, all of whom had been awarded enormous fortunes by the crown.

In 1767 the Master of Heraldry had confessed to the Legislative Commission that he was not certain of the exact qualifications for nobility. The Charter to the Nobility of 1785 was intended to reward Catherine's most trusted estate by clarifying who belonged to it and what noble status meant. The charter granted the nobility such long-sought rights as freedom from corporal punishment and arbitrary confiscation of estates and established special courts enabling the nobility to deal with its own affairs. In addition the charter required the nobility to elect "marshals of the nobility" from each district and province and to handle corporate affairs and maintain their books of heraldry.

What did all these changes mean for the Russian noble? By the end of the century, certain styles of life had evolved that to some extent approximated European models. The living patterns of the Russian aristocrat were much like those of his French counterpart until the reign of Louis XVI; the French spent most of their time at court, the source of power and wealth, and rarely visited their estates. However trapped he might feel at Versailles, a French aristocrat who chose to live in the country forfeited access to the generous pensions and court offices he needed. As one Frenchman commented, "A nobleman if he lives at home in his province lives free, but without substance; if he lives at court he is taken care of, but enslaved."[19]

Similarly, Russian courtiers who felt that their fortunes depended on attendance at court continued to winter in St. Petersburg, retiring to nearby suburban dachas only for the summer. Europeans visiting the Russian capital now took a more positive view of the habitations of the Russian nobility. A young Englishman wrote of Petersburg in 1788: "The palaces of the nobility are in general built in the highest style of magnificence and elegance. Many of them are superior both in size and elegance to anything I ever saw in England. They are all built of brick plastered over in imitation of stone, ornamented with pillars and every other embellishment of Grecian or Italian architecture."[20]

The English model of country life, discovered only recently by the Russians, was becoming increasingly popular throughout Europe. Even the French were infected by Anglomania, as reflected in their opulent country houses and luxuriant gardens. Take, for example, the Duc d'Harcourt, whose magnificent house a short distance from Caen boasted the "most beautiful English garden in France." In the late eighteenth century a sojourn there invariably included walks in the "delicious garden, hunts in game-filled forests, conversations with educated, spiritual men, women seductive of mind and body, dancing, music, and in addition, the charms of the old simplicity united with modern elegance." The Duc de Penthièvre was reported to have "only one distraction, to make varied visits to the numerous residences he possesses in many parts of the kingdom." The Comte d'Argenson displayed "a very active taste for English furniture and customs."[21]

By the end of the century a sizable number of Russian aristocratic families were likewise becoming increasingly Anglophile. Most were estranged from, or at least not intimately dependent on, court life, considered the area around Moscow their permanent base, and had substantial estates on which they spent long periods each year. Europeans were surprised by these oases of culture. In 1803 Martha Wilmot, of a distinguished Anglo-Irish family, went to Russia as the guest of Princess Dashkova (1743–1810), who some years earlier had toured Ireland as the guest of Lady Hamilton, Martha's relative. Now elderly, Dashkova spent most of her time on her estate on the Oka River, south of Moscow. Martha had been told (she later reported) that the princess "lived in a castle situated in a dreary solitude, far removed from the society of any civilized beings." Yet the day after her arrival at Troitskoe, about seventy miles from Moscow, she wrote her father,

25. Artist unknown. *Promenade at Ostankino* (detail). Trinity Church
(1678–83), on the left, overlooks the new neoclassical palace (1792–98).
(Courtesy of the Ostankino Museum, Moscow)

"This place is splendid. Her English taste provides, and she has realy [*sic*] created from rather a barren situation one of the most lovely and magnificent places that is to be found any where!"[22]

Yet the Russian noble's relationship to his lands and to the surrounding countryside in some respects remained very different from that of other eighteenth-century elites. Many Russian grandees had recently been given lands from the crown, sometimes in territories that were newly acquired and hence unrelated to their family roots. These properties became the site of fashionable new manor houses. Often, however, as at Ostankino (fig. 25) and Arkhangelskoe (fig. 26), a church representative of old Russian architecture was retained as a visual counterpoint to

the new mansion. From the 1760s a parade of traveling Russians found models in magnificent houses such as Blenheim, Twickenham, Stowe, and Chatsworth, the showplaces of eighteenth-century England. But the grandeur of these establishments was very much connected with the local roots and political role of the British peerage. Such manors therefore had both a private (family) and public (political) function. As Mark Girouard and others have pointed out, landownership and political power in England were inextricably entwined: the English country estate was a "power house," a structure emblematic of its owner's social and political standing.[23] In Russia the aristocratic estate had a public function, that of prestige-enhancing display (fig. 27), but patronage connections were still critical to obtaining a high position, and hence ambitious nobles were apt to shun the provinces. Russia's provincial towns, unlike those of Europe, offered little or no cultural advantages. So despite Catherine's intention of attracting the nobility to local affairs, service in the provinces (except as governor) remained a second-choice career for the ambitious noble, and a term as marshal of a noble assembly (except on the provincial level) had little prestige.

For this reason, the English attitude toward the estate was markedly different from the Russian. Karamzin noted the contrast while traveling through England in the 1790s: "Here they live in the country as if in the city, and in the city as if in the country."[24] By this he meant that aristo-

26. Church of the Archangel Michael (built in 1667) at Arkhangelskoe.

31

cratic Russian landowners typically spent most of the year living grandly in the city, much like Italian nobles, who preferred their town palazzi to their country houses but unlike the Austrian nobility, who maintained residences in Vienna but lived mostly in the country.

Transmission of land intact played a key role. The Esterhazys in Hungary, the Schwarzenbergs in Austria, or the Lobkowitzes in Bohemia had kept vast domains undivided over many generations, because in these countries primogeniture determined inheritance, and the sovereign's permission was required for sales of ancestral lands outside the family. The English, whose estates were subject to entail, likewise had a sense of roots in the countryside. They frequented London only for the short winter season, during which time, Karamzin observed with surprise, illustrious peers of the realm thought nothing of using rented carriages or walking around in shabby dress. The English country seat took precedence over the capital because it symbolized family and cultural traditions accumulated over many generations. All this was absent from the Russian scene, where hereditary lands were customarily subdivided among heirs and estates frequently changed hands.[25]

The initial connection of the Russian estate with national culture was even more tenuous. By the time of Catherine, the wealthy Russian noble had thoroughly in-

27. Artist unknown. The formal garden of a mid-eighteenth-century estate.
(Courtesy of the State Historical Museum, Moscow)

corporated the externals of Western European culture—language, dress, architecture, interior decor, and the fine and decorative arts—into daily life. The result was a melange of European styles: the French language and Parisian fashion reigned, but Catherine's Anglomania in architecture and landscaping and her taste for Wedgwood china or Sèvres porcelain influenced the building and buying patterns of the aristocracy. In designing and furnishing estates according to foreign cultural models, the westernized Russian nobility was, inevitably and consciously, expressing rejection of its native culture.

What was this culture, and where was it to be found? By the end of the eighteenth century the first stirrings of romanticism prompted some Russians to begin searching for a national culture; to a large extent, they discovered that "peasant" and "Russian" were synonymous. Thus, paradoxically, the creation of these Western oases in the countryside just as inevitably initiated the tortuous process of rediscovering and appreciating native culture. The estate provided a vantage point from which Russia's culturally Europeanized elite could observe Russia's other culture, the world of the Russian peasant. Peasants had preserved the links to Muscovy; their language, dress, art, and cultural outlook were unchanged from what they had been a hundred years earlier, whereas their master's were those of a foreigner.

In the pages that follow, I shall be examining different groups of these "noble foreigners," whose wealth determined their position in the steep pyramid of the Russian nobility. In the first rank were a handful of grandees, representatives of families like the Sheremetevs, Apraksins, Yusupovs, Kurakins, and Golitsyns, all of whom owned tens of thousands of serfs and numerous estates. These families had town houses and elegant dachas in St. Petersburg, but the individuals with whom I am concerned felt primary allegiance to Moscow, where they maintained both substantial city mansions and suburban or country estates. Beneath them in status were a number of very wealthy families (those with between one thousand to five thousand serfs) who might pass the winter in their town mansions but who spent a large part of the year on provincial estates. Included in this group were families like the Vyazemskys, Griboedovs, Buturlins, Yankovs, Miliutins, Kropotkins, and Bibikovs. The more numerous provincial elite (two hundred to one thousand serfs) constituted a third stratum. Social life for these families—the Davydovs, the Nikolevs, the Khvoshchinskys, and the Tuchkovs—revolved around provincial capitals, though on occasion they visited Moscow or even St. Petersburg for business or pleasure. Beneath them were Russia's legion of "small-estate" (*melkopomestnyi*) owners, among them the families of the writers Nikolai Gogol and Fyodor Dostoevsky.

Russia's cultural elite was drawn from all these strata, and indeed the lines between them are less clear-cut than this schema indicates. Occasionally, fortunes fell or rose, causing a family to move from one group to another. Prominent courtiers often retired to their estates to become patriarchal landowners and part of the provincial elite. For all these groups, the Russian estate, whether large or small, was in large measure a self-contained world. Regardless of his status elsewhere, on the estate the noble was supreme ruler of his serfs. Over the next century the various forms life took on the Russian country estate would reflect the noble's complicated relationship to autocratic, official Russia, to European culture, and to native tradition.

2

The Golden Age
of the Pleasure Palace

The fury to build is a diabolical thing; it devours money, and the more

one builds the more one wants to build; it is as intoxicating

as drink. —**Catherine II**

28. The main bridge at Tsaritsyno. Vasily Bazhenov, architect. (Author)

29. The church at Chesme Palace (1777–80), built to commemorate the naval victory of the Russians over the Turks at Chesme in 1770. G. F. Veldten, architect.

BETWEEN 1750 AND 1800, ESTATE building transformed the environs of Moscow and the Russian provinces as thoroughly as the swampy banks of the Neva had been altered during the preceding half century. Whereas Peter the Great had forced radical changes in habits on reluctant Muscovites, Catherine led a more willing generation. One Russian scholar terms Catherine a "totalitarian enlightener" in that she was determined to create an ideal country through legislation and example.[1] In her reign estate boundaries were surveyed for the first time; the provincial towns and roads that served these estates sprang up overnight at her command; and her decrees created a new provincial arena for noble activity.

This flurry of legislation had a strong impact on the Russian noble's sense of property and self, of space and place, while his concept of architecture as an expression of power and refinement was directly affected by what Catherine wrought on the outskirts of Russia's two capitals. For Moscow she commissioned two experiments in Russian neo-Gothic, Petrovsky Palace and the fairy-tale Tsaritsyno (fig. 28), where the architect Vasily Bazhenov (1738–99) fused Russian, Gothic, and Masonic motifs to create a fantastical and symbol-laden complex.[2] Near St. Petersburg arose her neo-Gothic Chesme Palace (fig. 29), after the model of Longford Castle, depicted in volume 5 of *Vitruvius Britannicus*, which Vasily Neelov, sent to England to study landscaping, may have brought back to his empress.

But Catherine's most ambitious projects were reserved for the twenty-square-mile area of Tsarskoe Selo, south of St. Petersburg, which became a laboratory of architectural experiments designed to enlighten her subjects. When completed, it contained four ideological worlds, all of which would be replicated on grand private estates. Her Chinese village illustrated the world of fantasy and caprice; the world of medieval melancholy was evoked by neo-Gothic structures. A "political garden" symbolized her ambition to gain the Black Sea (and eventually Constantinople) for Russia; it contained a lake replicating the Black Sea, dotted with Turkish, Russian, and Moldavian pavilions. Last, there was the model estate of Pavlovsk, complete with ornamental farms and vast poetic gardens (see fig. 63). These ideological worlds surrounded a central complex designed by the Scottish architect Charles Cameron that imitated the paradise of antiquity. It had a Palladian bridge identical to the bridge at the British estate Stowe, neoclassical pavilions, and luxurious Roman baths; this architectural ensemble expressed Catherine's desire for a unified arcadia of power, patronage, and intellect, a place where Caesar, Mycenas, or Cicero would feel equally at home.[3]

Like Catherine's experiments, the best private-estate architecture abounded in echoes of the classical world rediscovered by Enlightenment thinkers and patrons of the arts throughout Europe. In the 1760s Catherine initiated a stylistic shift in architecture away from Elizabeth's flamboyant baroque to the more restrained, less highly ornamented (and less expensive) neoclassical style that would dominate Russia's architectural vocabulary until the late 1830s, a style that had been in vogue for some time in Europe. By the 1760s the grand tours of numerous Russian aristocrats had left them smitten with Italy's classical ruins and Britain's treasury of houses and gardens.[4] Catherine herself was a connoisseur of Italian architecture and English style. Although she never visited England, by the early 1770s she had amassed an extensive collection of illustrated works on English country houses and gardens. In addition the 952 pieces of her Wedgwood Frog service depicted 1,244 views of the English countryside, featuring both famous and lesser known country seats.[5]

Architectural historians subdivide the half century of Russian neoclassical estate building into early, ripe, and late stages, yet certain cardinal elements unite the grand estate houses of this period. Among them were a facade with little ornamentation; massive pillars, often supporting a large portico, which announced the main entrance;

and a belvedere or, less commonly, a rotunda. The main house (a Palladian cube or a rectangle) was usually flanked by two or four dependent pavilions—sometimes free-standing, sometimes connected by a covered colonnade—for service, servants, or guests (fig. 30). This group of buildings faced a formal courtyard, while the rear facade of the main house opened onto a poetic garden and park. These Russian palaces were built in a spirit reminiscent of Blenheim Palace, designed by Sir John Vanbrugh in the 1690s as a triumph of movement and drama, combining "castle airs" of the English past with new Italianate motifs such as belvederes to celebrate the Duke of Marlborough's military successes. A century younger, the Russian structures were statements about the sense of identity of Catherine's grandees. Nobles in the depths of the Russian countryside imitated their wealthy neighbors, and in this manner, for nobles of Catherine's era, *le bon goût* rapidly became synonymous with Palladian proportions, pillared porticoes, and a naturalized garden filled with fanciful caprices or commemorative monuments.

30. Aerial view of the Goncharovs' Yaropolets, now a sanatorium. Built in the 1780s, it belonged to the parents of Alexander Pushkin's wife. The design is sometimes attributed to I. V. Egotov. (Author's collection)

The theatrical, playful side to Russian estate architecture can hardly be overestimated. The fact that estate design (unlike urban building) was unregulated made it ideal for combining in startling fashion architectural forms and styles that were traditionally distinguished. The estate complex was, in effect, a stage set on which the triumph, confidence, and enlightened ideals of the Catherinian era could be paraded. Taste was demonstrated by neoclassical design and decor, but the spirit behind these houses was not the refined statement of Lord Burlington's Chiswick House. Like the "prodigy houses" of Elizabethan England such as Hardwick Hall, these Russian mansions were built to impress, to serve as sites for regal entertainment and lavish public display. Some owners were Catherine's "eagles," the men who had helped her seize power, led her troops to victory, or shared (however briefly) her bed. They were copiously rewarded with land, serfs, and cash, which they hastened to reinvest in estates worthy of an imperial visit. Others were simply men of taste and great wealth who wished to have a residence commensurate with contemporary standards.

A small circle of highly talented architects served these aristocrats. One cannot speak of significant regional differences in estate architecture, for grandees inspired by the same examples often used the same architects to design country mansions hundreds of miles apart. In the race for lucrative imperial and private commissions, foreigners competed with a host of talented Russian architects. The Russians included Vasily Bazhenov; Karl I. Blank (1728–93), considered the best Moscow architect in the 1760s; Matvei F. Kazakov (1738–1812); Ivan E. Starov (1743–1808), who designed Nikolskoe (fig. 31) for Prince Sergei Gagarin, near Moscow; and Nikolai A. Lvov (1751–1803), Prince Alexander Bezborodko's protégé and the designer of Gavrila Derzhavin's Zvanka, Illarion Vorontsov's Voronovo, and numerous estates near Torzhok. Charles Cameron (1740–1812) designed Pavlovsk for Catherine's son, Paul, and worked on Baturin, the showplace of Kirill

Razumovsky. The eminent Italian architect Giacomo Quarenghi (1744–1817) designed the English palace at Peterhof; Lyalichi, for Catherine's favorite Peter Zavadovsky; and possibly Nadezhdino, for her son Paul's close friend Alexander Kurakin. Other foreign architects at work on both crown and court commissions included Adam Menelas, designer of exotic pavilions at Tsarskoe Selo and N. G. Repnin's Yagotin, in Poltava Province, and the Frenchman la Motte, who designed Pochep for A. K. Razumovsky.

Moscow Estates

Near Moscow, where older estate houses existed, the new aesthetic prompted a flurry of remodeling. Between 1765 and 1787 the old house at Kuskovo, Count Peter Sheremetev's suburban estate, was renovated under Karl Blank's direction, with the assistance of Pavel Argunov (1768–1806), a talented serf architect belonging to Sheremetev. We know from a French engraving that the earlier house had an additional story; its thrust was vertical rather than horizontal. It was in many respects an old-fashioned, relatively simple boyar mansion, not suitable for the elaborate entertaining Sheremetev had in mind.

The new eighteenth-century house is one of a precious handful of original houses extant today. For the most part one is confronted with a kaleidoscope of shifting shapes: estate houses might be renovated by new owners, accidentally burned or abandoned, then rebuilt or restored, or simply left to crumble. The renovated Kuskovo has an impressive center portico supported by twelve Corinthian columns, the outer ones paired (see fig. 23). A circular driveway enclosed within a white wall and announced by seated lions leads to the reception rooms on the first floor, demarcated by white balustrades in front of the portico and along the entire facade. Two lateral jetties with columns balance the portico but do not protrude sufficiently to disturb the serenity of the facade.

Inside, the rooms fall into the three categories com-

39

31. The park facade of the manor house at Nikolskoe-Gagarino, built between 1774 and 1776 according to the designs of I. E. Starov. The house is now a mental hospital for children.

mon to the classical estate house: public reception rooms, private living quarters, and service areas. The suite of parade rooms on the first floor forms the enfilade or procession of grand reception rooms typical of the Russian pleasure palace. The enfilade, which emphasized the house's public function, could be easily adapted from town to country and realized on different scales, from the palatial to a modest suite of connected rooms. This element of Russian neoclassical estate architecture derived from the French example (Palladio's villas, by contrast, being characterized by a square plan) and was one of the most persistent features of Russian domestic architecture well into the nineteenth century.[6] Mirrors strategically placed along

the enfilade emphasized movement from one space to another, and a mirror or window at one end sometimes extended the view.

At Kuskovo the enfilade occupies the entire main facade of the house, while the ballroom (fig. 32) is located in the center of the opposing garden facade. The ballroom has the white-and-gold decor typical of palatial great halls, with seven large windows on the park side (three of which are French doors opening to the garden). On the opposite

32. The ballroom, or white hall, of Kuskovo. Ceiling painting by Louis Jean-François Lagrenée the Elder.

40

wall seven mirrors identical to the windows reflect the parterre of the park into which the room seems to flow. The ballroom's dimensions are also enlarged by the huge ceiling painting executed by Jean-François Lagrenée the Elder (1725–1805), framed by arabesques and the orders of St. Andrew, Alexander Nevsky, St. Anne, and the White Eagle, all of which were awarded to Peter Sheremetev.

At approximately the same time as Kuskovo's renovation drew to an end, Nikolai Golitsyn (1751–1809), recently returned from his grand tour, decided to update the large wooden Petrine manor house at Arkhangelskoe, his suburban Moscow estate. The design his French architect, Charles de Guerne, produced had typical Palladian elements: a portico supported by four massive Corinthian columns over the main entrance, and a central corpus connected to pavilions by open colonnades. Such courtyards intentionally resembled the huge open-air halls of antiquity. As at Kuskovo, an enfilade of staterooms ran along the entire main facade of the house, and the oval, pillared ballroom opened to the garden. A musicians' gallery extended around the entire upper portion of the oval hall, which was crowned with a belvedere. On either side of the great hall were suites of staterooms, similar in design, which emphasized the stylistic unity of the house.

In the 1790s Nikolai Petrovich Sheremetev, heir to his father's enormous fortune (2,228,500 acres in 17 provinces

33. The manor house at Pekhra-Yakovlevskoe (1783–86), an estate owned by the Golitsyn family from 1591 to 1828. Karl Blank, architect(?). The building is now a biological institute.

and 210,000 serfs), embarked on a remodeling of Ostankino (see fig. 51), a Sheremetev estate north of Moscow. His ambitious goal was to transform Ostankino into a palace of the arts, with a theater rivaling the best in Paris, where his famous serf troupe would be able to perform the European operas he loved. In designing Ostankino, Sheremetev drew on the talents of the foremost architects of the day, Starov, Blank, V. F. Brenna, and E. S. Nazarov, as well as on the skills of his serf architects P. I. Argunov, G. E. Dikushin, and A. F. Mironov. The profusion of exterior pillars and pilasters, neoclassical friezes and statuary, and a belvedere made the remodeled Ostankino more elegant and modern than his father's Kuskovo. Inside, the enfilade of reception rooms runs the length of the main facade; at the rear of the house, the theater occupies the central area usually taken up by the ballroom. Two opulent pavilions connected by corridors to the central corpus demarcate the extremities of the main house; from the pavilions, low corridors and service areas enclose the front courtyard on three sides.

Estates of Moscow Province

Kuskovo, Ostankino, and Arkhangelskoe, all marvels of their day, are still in relatively good repair. Other once-grand pleasure palaces near Moscow have either crumbled away or been altered beyond recognition. The mid-eighteenth-century baroque estate house of Dubrovitsy, for example, originally had two diagonal wings, the earliest known example of this style. Catherine's favorite Grigory Potemkin bought the estate in 1781 and began remodeling it in neoclassical style, but then sold it to the treasury. Catherine's last favorite, A. M. Dmitriev-Mamonov, completed the renovations, but the estate house, now an agricultural institute, has undergone so many renovations that it has entirely lost its original character.

Only ruins remain of the Apraksins' Olgovo, a once-elegant estate to the north of Moscow remodeled in the

34. The central part of the 240-foot main facade of Gorenki (1777–?). A. Menelas, architect(?). Owned by the Razumovsky family from 1747 to 1822, it now serves as a hospital.

1780s and 1790s under the direction of the Italian Francesco Camporesi.[7] The substantial masonry house built by the luxury-loving field marshal Sergei F. Apraksin in the 1750s had a huge, two-story great hall with choir lofts supported by baroque Corinthian columns and a large rectangular

43

35. The manor house (park facade) of the Volkonskys' Sukhanovo, where Leo Tolstoy wrote parts of *War and Peace*. Architect unknown. Now a vacation spot for members of the Union of Architects.

reception room divided by pillars, furniture, and plants into four discrete areas for tea, games, music, and relaxation. To this massive rectangular corpus Camporesi added two lateral galleries on rusticated arches for more entertaining space, uniting the wings (one for married house servants, the other for unmarried) with the main house. From the galleries two staircases similar to the Cameron galleries at Tsarskoe Selo descended to the park.

Estate houses around Moscow, however united in design elements, are startlingly different in feeling. The main houses at Valuevo (which A. I. Musin-Pushkin acquired from Peter Tolstoy in the 1740s) and the Golitsyns'

Pekhra-Yakovlevskoe (fig. 33) are connected to two flanking wings by covered colonnades, creating an ensemble that is plastic, light, and graceful. Gorenki, a nearby estate, uses the same design principles, but in far more powerful fashion. Built by A. K. Razumovsky around the 1770s (and perhaps designed by Menelas), Gorenki has the massive proportions of a city estate, which in the countryside appear almost overwhelming (fig. 34).[8] The three-story central house has two huge lateral wings, from which extend curved colonnades two stories high, ending in cubic pavilions facing a lake. Estate houses without such colonnades to lead the eye away from the core to pavilions or into the landscape seem more solidly and serenely located. The large main house at the Volkonskys' Sukhanovo (fig. 35), visible from afar yet nestled into the landscape, demands the undivided attention of travelers on the post road from Moscow. West of Moscow, the Golitsyns' Petrovskoe, though smaller in scale, breathes a similar serenity.

Several houses near Moscow are outstandingly original. At the turn of the century Nikolai A. Durasov, a general, was so delighted when he received the coveted Imperial Order of St. Anna that he commissioned a mansion for his estate, Lyublino, in the star shape of the order. His architect, I. V. Egotov (a former student of both Bazhenov and Kazakov), designed a central rotunda with four rectangular chambers radiating from it and connected to each other by semicircular colonnades (figs. 36, 37). A huge statue of St. Anna crowned the belvedere. Completed in 1803, Lyublino produced a stunning effect on Catherine Wilmot when she accompanied Princess Dashkova to "an entertainment" there in 1806. "The House . . . looked like a Marble Temple from the first story being supported by white Columns excepting the Center part which rises in a high Dome & serves as a Banqueting Room the vaulted Ceiling of which is most beautifully painted with Loves & Graces, Apollo & the Muses, Aurora & the Hours &c. &c. &c! All the Company were assembled under the open Col-

onnades which stood in flights of Marble Steps cover'd with Arabian and Persian Jasmines!"[9]

N. A. Demidov's mansion, Petrovskoe-Alabino (1776–80), now a majestic ruin (see fig. 228), was in its day equally startling (fig. 38). Kazakov designed it as an imposing cube topped with a large cupola, its facades ornamented with large pillars and pilasters and surrounded by four identical free-standing pavilions. A third departure from the norm was V. G. Orlov's elegant Otrada (meaning "comfort"), whose red brick facade accented with white stone insets and columns rose boldly above the Lopasnya River.

The Nashchokins' Rai-Semenovskoe, to the west on the Nara River, rivaled Otrada in grandeur. Its two-story oval hall, with a choir gallery mounted on columns of false marble, made one visitor liken it to an Italian villa. Like Arkhangelskoe, the Stroganovs' Brattsevo, and many other country mansions, Rai-Semenovskoe was crowned with a belvedere from which one could see the countryside for miles around. Later two huge halls were added to the main house for balls and theatricals. By the late nineteenth century Rai-Semenovskoe, like many other palatial residences, had the air of a neglected white elephant, but its typically eighteenth-century interior was intact. The present century has been far less kind to this estate. The manor house is unrecognizable, and the estate church of which Nashchokin was justly proud is a strikingly picturesque ruin. The tombstone of Nashchokin's son Pavel, a close friend of the poet Alexander Pushkin, lies neglected in the main courtyard, turning its back on the completely altered house, totally overgrown gardens, and ruined church.

Provincial Mansions

Like mushrooms after a heavy rain, Palladian mansions sprang up in remote areas as well. Catherine II led the way, commissioning Starov in the mid-1760s to design the palace of Bogoroditsk, east of Tula, for Count Bobrinskoy, her illegitimate son by Grigory Orlov. At about the same time Nikolai Tishinin, living on his estate Tikhvinskoe far to the north, in Yaroslavl Province, was eliciting plans from his godfather in St. Petersburg, the renowned engraver Mikhail Makhaev, for a fashionable renovation of his house and estate church and for grottoes and pavilions for his garden. In advising his godson on these structures, Makhaev stressed the importance of their being designed "without much ornamentation, in the now-fashionable Italian style, which our all-merciful sovereign deigns to

36. The main facade of Lyublino. Designed in 1801 by I. V. Egotov, it is now an oceanographic institute. (*Stolitsa i usadba*, no. 29)

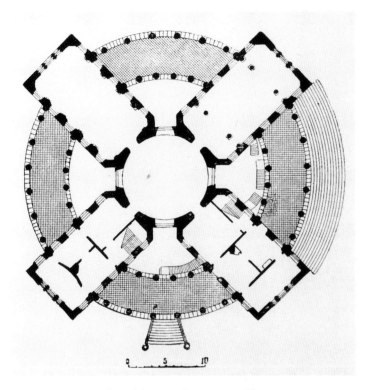

37. Plan of the main house at Lyublino.
(Tikhomirov, *Arkhitektura podmoskovnykh usadeb*)

favor."[10] As the conquests of Catherine's troops greatly expanded the territory of her empire, mansions began to appear far to the south. In 1776 Catherine granted Field Marshal P. A. Rumyantsev five thousand serfs and a huge tract of land (confiscated from the Polish Czartoryskys) in the new province of Chernigov. Rumyantsev hired Ya. N. Alekseev the following year to supervise the building of Gomel, a magnificent house probably designed mainly by Starov, with K. I. Blank as consulting architect. Construction on the high riverbank of the Sozh began sometime prior to 1780, and by 1782 Rumyantsev was already pondering furnishings for some of the rooms. Not far from Gomel was Lyalichi, another remote estate attributed

to the seemingly ubiquitous Quarenghi. Like Gomel, Lyalichi, awarded to Peter Zavadovsky (Catherine's former lover) in 1775, took almost two decades to complete. In November 1800 Zavadovsky proudly wrote Semen Vorontsov, Princess Dashkova's brother then serving as ambassador to England, "A masonry house has been built which is miraculous in these parts and would be remarkable in the English provinces, not for its massiveness, but for the beauty of its facade's pure proportions."[11] The house was indeed a very large variant of a classic Palladian villa, with an imposing facade, a high rusticated ground floor supporting the *piano nobile*, and a third story of private apartments. On the park side, a massive six-columned Corinthian portico projected into the park; two low semicircular wings led to orangeries on the right and left, which marked the entrance to the park. Inside, a magnificent grand staircase led from the ground floor to the Catherine Hall, which was two stories high, columned, and crowned with a cupola. Lyalichi, a tribute to Catherine's generosity, was completed only in 1796, after Emperor Paul had ascended the throne. Jealous of his mother's former favorites, he expressed displeasure at the height of the mansion. In response, Zavadovsky is said to have cleverly (and judiciously) terraced the grounds around the main house to make it appear lower.

Hundreds of miles to the southeast, in the Sumy district of Kharkov Province, was the eighty-seven-room palace of Khoten, built for the Kondratievs around the same time as Lyalichi. Its virtually identical main and park facades, two upper stories of nearly equal height, and rusticated first floor have led scholars to attribute it to Quarenghi despite the absence of concrete evidence. Khoten's relatively simple exterior concealed a magnificent interior. Its vestibule, for example, was executed in Tuscan style, with columns and pilasters dividing it into three parts, each with a simple but elegant cornice and rusticated walls. In typical Quarenghi fashion, the grand staircase led from the central portion of the ground floor to the

38. N. A. Demidov's mansion house at Petrovskoe-Alabino (1775–76), the design of which is usually attributed
to M. F. Kazakov and occasionally to Vasily Bazhenov. (Tikhomirov, *Arkhitektura podmoskovnykh usadeb*)

piano nobile, on which most of the reception rooms were located, with others above them on the garden facade of the house.

In Saratov Province, several hundred miles northeast of Khoten, Grand Duke Paul's close friend Prince Alexander Kurakin built a similar palace. In the 1770s Kurakin had traveled with Paul and his wife throughout Europe. Exiled in the 1780s from court because of an incautious remark about Catherine's favorite Grigory Potemkin, Prince Kurakin retreated to his Saratov estate, Borisoglebskoe, which he renamed Nadezhdino (Hope) to express his desire for a return to favor. After living a few years in a

wooden house there, he decided to build a palace (fig. 39). Again, the architect may have been Quarenghi, though in a letter of 1794 Alexander insisted that the interior arrangements were his own idea and that "all three facades are done according to my ideas." Kurakin had seven hundred thousand bricks made for the main house and about the same number for the outbuildings. The massive three-story main house, with a high rusticated first floor supporting the piano nobile and a small third floor, rose majestically on a high riverbank of the Serdoba. Moving the house to this "mountain" was, Kurakin admitted to Paul, a "fantasy, which cost me rather dearly." But, he continued, "[the project] has succeeded beyond my expectations, and the pleasure it gives me repays me well for all the expenses."[12] The main house was flanked by two horseshoe-shaped service wings that ended in large pavilions. In the middle of each of these horseshoes were triumphal entry gates. Inside the house a grand staircase led from the first floor to the reception rooms, ranged in two enfilades separated by a short service corridor. A circular staircase hidden inside a thick wall communicated with servants' quarters on the third floor (where Alexander, a bachelor, is reputed to have lodged his harem).

More certain than Quarenghi's design of Nadezhdino is Charles Cameron's hand in the design of Baturin for Kirill Razumovsky. The mansion, in Chernigov Province, southeast of Lyalichi, was finished in 1803, shortly before Razumovsky's death. Like Pavlovsk, Cameron's other chef-d'oeuvre, it was spacious without appearing massive, its rooms elegantly proportioned and not overwhelming. Like Lyalichi and Nadezhdino, Baturin's reception rooms were above a high rusticated ground floor with service quarters. The private living apartments were on a third floor, while the two-story lateral wings had many small rooms for staff. In Kiev Province as well, grand houses proliferated, as evidenced by Matussov (fig. 40), built for Ivan Orlov, a Cossack general, and designed by Bartolomeo Rastrelli (according to family legend); and by houses on two of Prince Potemkin's many estates in this area, Belaya Tserkov and Kamenka (both inherited by his nieces).

39. Artist unknown. Lithograph of Prince A. B. Kurakin's Nadezhdino.
(Courtesy of the State Historical Museum, Moscow)

40. Mariamna Davydova. The park facade of the manor house at Matussov, designed, according to family legend, by B. F. Rastrelli. Watercolor. 1920s. (Courtesy of Alona Vassiloff)

Some of these provincial palaces decayed with startling speed after their owners died or moved away. At Gomel, construction had proceeded by fits and starts for more than a decade, possibly because Rumyantsev was simultaneously building a second palace at Kachanovka, to the south. Gomel was completed only in 1796, the year Rumyantsev died. That August he complained that the palace was poorly roofed and that "most of the stucco has fallen off, and the brick itself is being damaged."[13] Kachanovka likewise seems to have declined rapidly after the field marshal's death. In 1802, after a visit to Kachanovka, Alexander Kurakin wrote his brother: "The way in which everything is falling into ruins makes the heart bleed," an ironic remark in retrospect since his own Nadezhdino would soon be abandoned by its owner and fall into similar disrepair.[14]

Throughout Russia, Dutch, Oriental, and Gothic touches provided a theatrical element to many estate ensembles. At Voronovo, I. I. Vorontsov built a Dutch house (fig. 41) to outshine the one at Kuskovo; the Chinese decorative motifs on the balconies of Vorontsov's Dutch house were probably copied from illustrations in a popular book by the English Halfpenny brothers. The Dutch house, like Kuskovo's Italian house (fig. 42) or Arkhangelskoe's Caprice, was an elegant playhouse, a miniature mansion where intimate gatherings requiring fewer servants could be held.

The Gothic was used mainly as a decorative accent, to provide contrast with the main neoclassical structures.[15] At the Golitsyns' Petrovskoe, for example, the service buildings were pseudo-Gothic. The Goncharovs' Yaropolets had Gothic gates, walls (fig. 43), and decorative farm buildings surrounding a neoclassical house and church. At another Goncharov estate, Polotnyany Zavod, the factory (which produced paper for Russian currency up until 1917), stables, and the three gates to the estate were Gothic contrasts to a neoclassical mansion. Bazhenov's remarkable Gothic church at Bykovo (fig. 44) has survived, as have the elaborate Gothic stables, also possibly designed by Bazhenov, at D. I. Buturlin's Marinka (see fig. 74). Here, however, the Gothic main house has vanished, as have other estate buildings, among them a theater.

After the war of 1812, as romanticism displaced the rationalism of the Enlightenment, the pseudo-Gothic became even more popular, as M. D. Bykovsky's remodeling of Sukhanovo's servants' quarters and priest's residence (see fig. 89) in the 1820s indicates. In the 1830s the search for a national architectural style began, spearheaded by the "Cottage" palace Nicholas I commissioned in St. Petersburg. Its style reflected the invention of a Russian Gothic vocabulary, expressed most eloquently at Marfino. This estate, rebuilt at the very end of the great age of estate architecture, is the sole surviving complex near Moscow to display the Gothic in both manor house and outbuildings (fig. 45). Marfino was originally a neoclassical estate famous for the lavish entertainments of its owner, Count Saltykov. It was burned by the French in 1812; Saltykov's heir began reconstruction in 1822 but died nine years later, leaving Marfino to his daughter, Countess Sophia V. Panina. She chose the young Bykovsky to continue the work, and he designed a remarkable structure that resembled, according to contemporaries, the grandiose fairy-tale castle of Fata-Morgana. With its towers, bastions, Gothic windows, huge griffons and, above all, the magnificent bridge across the main pond (see fig. 78), Marfino was one estate owner's response to the nationalism currently inspiring dachas designed as palatial versions of the peasant log house.[16] A second, equally striking monument to Russian

41. The Dutch House at Voronovo, designed in the 1760s by Karl Blank.

architectural fantasy to have survived to the present day is the palace at Alupka, in the Crimea. Built for M. S. Vorontsov in the 1830s and 1840s, its architecture boldly combined Tudor, neo-Gothic, and Oriental elements.

Several features of the grand Russian estate house are noteworthy. First, its design and furnishings clearly reflect its function: the entertainment of throngs. The great hall for balls or banquets, invariably two stories high, usually pillared, and often of immense proportions, dominates the reception rooms, which overpower the lone visitor in their scale. The enfilade connecting them promotes touring the house rather than settling down in a comfortable nook, as do the elegant but uncomfortable furnishings. Although some rooms are invitingly small, on the whole the impression conveyed by the magnificent suites is intentionally one of splendor, as befitted their function. They were built for short periods of public display, not for prolonged private comfort.

Second, the Russian estate house diverged in some regards from its European model. The ubiquitous divan room, characterized by low comfortable sofas lining the walls (the younger Rostovs' favorite retreat in *War and*

42. The Italian House (1754–55) at Kuskovo. This miniature palace, designed for small gatherings, contained a gold-and-white reception room, oak-paneled study, and art gallery. Yury Kologrivov, architect. (Author)

43. A section of the Gothic walls at the Goncharovs' Yaropolets. Beyond the wall is a two-story park pavilion overlooking the Lama River.

Peace), is not found in Europe. Russian estates frequently lacked a library. At Kuskovo the glassed-in shelves of the library displayed Sheremetev's porcelain collection, not books. Sometimes the library was relegated to the second floor, which usually contained the family apartments; a world apart, these rooms were often architecturally undistinguished and smaller in dimension, with lower ceilings and simpler furnishings than the public rooms. Last, Russian country mansions were less of a contrast to city dwellings than was the case in Europe by the end of the eighteenth century. Count F. A. Tolstoy's Ivanovskoe, in fact,

was an exact replica of his Moscow house. In the Moscow region this was particularly pronounced, since many town dwellings there were laid out on the estate plan; but even in St. Petersburg the room arrangement of Gavrila Derzhavin's town mansion, for example, was remarkably similar to that of his country estate.

In a letter to his brother, Prince Alexander Kurakin likened his retreat to Nadezhdino to a Roman senator's withdrawal to his country villa. "Remember how they lived in ancient Rome: never in demeaning idleness, always either in active service to the fatherland or in com-

44. The pseudo-Gothic Vladimir Church (1789) at Bykovo, the estate of M. M. Izmailov. Vasily Bazhenov, architect.

45. The manor house at Countess S. V. Panina's Marfino, reconstructed in neo-Gothic style by M. D. Bykovsky between 1834 and 1846. Currently a sanatorium. (Author)

plete, far-removed solitude, in service to themselves, providing the spirit with new forces, the mind with new ideas and abilities."[17] The neoclassical estate house certainly had plentiful features intended to evoke antiquity: triumphal arches, colonnades, porticoes, great Roman halls, and allegorical statuary. In fact, however, Kurakin's life at Nadezhdino was not one of solitude, of self-imposed rustication. Both his house and his life in it imitated the court environment from which he had been banished.

Like the court, the great aristocratic household offered little or no privacy. Personal servants slept on pallets outside their masters' doors or sometimes in their bedrooms; guests were often bedded down equally haphazardly throughout the house and wings; and daily dinner was a large affair. Catherine's aristocrats, probably on the example of the elegant "Hermitage" Catherine added to the Winter Palace, sometimes fled this throng for private refuges. Peter Sheremetev built a "House of Solitude" at Kuskovo, where he could indulge his passion for reading and escape his constant visitors. A wooden structure on a stone foundation, it had simple planked exterior that concealed a suite of comfortable rooms: pantry, anteroom, living room, bedroom, luxurious boudoir, dressing room, office, and three other rooms all opening onto a narrow service corridor.

At the end of the century Peter's son Nikolai Sheremetev created a more modest refuge at Kuskovo out of a one-story wooden laundry building. In the dining room (which could seat thirty) two cabinets held English porcelain and crystal. The living room had a plain pine floor and items not usually found in a palace drawing room, such as an inlaid chessboard. Nikolai's personal suite of rooms included a bedroom with a water closet, dressing room, and study. A passageway from the study led to the female half of the house, which had its own entrance and vestibule, his wife's bedroom, and three maids' rooms.[18]

Interior Decoration and Furniture

By the early nineteenth century the great country palaces of Catherine's reign were attracting flocks of visitors who marveled at their proportions and elegance. But D. I. Sverbeev's comment upon touring Rai-Semenovskoe in the 1820s indicates a major change in attitudes. Noting that the palace could not have been comfortable, he opined that Nashchokin lived there only for show.[19] The show was considerable, the interior of the Russian country mansion fully matching its exterior splendor to create a luxurious, harmonious whole. Three aspects of Russian interior decor are particularly evident. First, in imitation of European practice, the evocative neoclassical motifs of the house itself were carried through in more elegant detail on interior floors, walls, and ceilings, as well as in furnishings (fig. 46). Using decorative techniques such as *faux marbre*, grisaille, bas-relief, and *trompe l'oeil*, artists reinforced the main aesthetic theme, antique mythology, while also incorporating more modern honors owners had earned, such as Sheremetev's awards or Durasov's Order of St. Anna. Second, Russian woodworkers, renowned for their skill, produced marvelous effects in parquet floors, marquetry tables, and carved wood that was then gilded or bronzed. Third, the natural world, either real or imagined, played a special role in Russian interior design. Exotic plants and hothouse flowers filled estate drawing rooms; paintings of outdoor scenes enlivened walls; painted, inlaid, or carved fruits and flowers adorned furniture.

In England by the early eighteenth century, the decorating and furnishing of the country house had evolved into a high art, supported by a "regiment of artificers," as the noted architect and interior designer Robert Adam called the masters of fine and decorative arts executing his designs.[20] Working at the direction of the architect, they supplied the high-quality brickwork, sculpting, wood carving, plastering, and decorative painting these houses demanded. Furnishings reflected an owner's wealth and taste. Antiques, the trophies of countless grand tours by noble scions, were casually displayed. Chippendale and Sheraton had become the leading furniture makers, and Sir Joshua Reynolds or Thomas Gainsborough the most sought-after portraitists.

In a remarkably short time, Russian estate owners were able to fashion similar country environments, using much the same methods. Initially much was imported. The Parisian silversmith Roettiers became fashionable when Catherine ordered a silver service from him for Grigory Orlov; Sèvres porcelain became the rage when in 1778 Catherine commissioned a service of eight hundred pieces decorated with cameos. Josiah Wedgwood had cast an early eye on the Russian market but in 1772 commented acerbically, "The Russians must have Etruscan, and Grecian vases about the 19th century. I fear they will not be ripe for them much sooner, unless our good friend Sr. Wm. Hamilton should go Ambassador thither & prepare a hot bed to bring these Northern plants to Maturity before their natural time."[21] Although a different ambassador was appointed, his wife displayed Wedgwood wares on her table and reported that they received the "highest approbation" from Russian nobles. She suggested that Wedgwood open a showroom in St. Petersburg and personally delivered samples to Catherine, thereby undoubtedly procuring the or-

46. The central hall of Lyublino, with ornamental pilasters, friezes depicting scenes from Greek mythology, and coffered ceiling, all executed in trompe l'oeil.

der for the famous Frog service. By the end of the century, Wedgwood pieces were common in Russian drawing rooms, as were his cameos set into Russian furniture.

Less renowned foreigners also conspired to profit from the Russian appetite for foreign luxuries. Shortly after arriving in Russia in 1779, James Meader (commissioned by Catherine to design gardens at Peterhof) formed an art partnership with another English gardener, John Bush, who was then working at Tsarskoe Selo. In one letter home Meader asks for "new, good prints which are finely engraved," as they "sell here at an enormous price. . . . They cannot come to a better market, for they are purchased with avidity." In another he notes, "Good landscapes will please. I wish you would chuse me some fine impressions and if you see any others should be glad of them." Still later, he asks for fine prints of ships.[22]

Russian aristocrats were able to purchase foreign goods through relatives in the diplomatic corps and friends abroad. In the 1770s V. G. Orlov, a passionate horseman, asked a friend serving in London to buy saddles, saddle-girths, stirrups, and the like, as well as fire pumps, lanterns, carriages, and woodworking tools for Otrada. He requested that a friend in Leipzig hire him a good coachman and gardener. From people in Paris he summoned a lady's hairdresser; from the Russian consul in Livorno, flower seeds and Tunisian and Italian doves; from his Lyons banker, wine and clothing.[23]

But as early as the 1780s the Russian demand for imports slackened in some areas. Renowned furniture makers such as Christian Meyer, Roentgen, and Pavel Spol had established elegant shops in St. Petersburg and Moscow, thereby making the importation of furniture unnecessary. In these workshops numerous Russians, both freemen and serfs, were apprenticed to learn the art of sophisticated cabinetry. By 1794 the Russian furniture-making guild was the largest in St. Petersburg, with 124 master craftsmen, 285 journeymen, and 175 apprentices. Other branches of the decorative arts were coming into their own. The Impe-

rial Porcelain Factory was beginning to have competition from private factories, and sophisticated textiles and tapestries were being woven domestically. Russian artistry in stonecutting was stimulated by the discovery in the 1780s of deposits of new varieties of jasper, quartz, and especially lapis lazuli and malachite. Workmen in Tula, a metal-working center, started producing decorative furniture and furnishings in iron, steel, gold, and silver.

The wealthiest Russians were also now commonly spending six to eight of their formative years abroad, during which time they became connoisseurs and collectors. V. N. Zinoviev, for example, born in 1755, left Russia at the age of twelve to study in Leipzig and Dresden, where he was impressed with the art gallery, the number of talented craftsmen, and the high level of intelligence of the towns-people. He also traveled to Italy and England. At twenty-eight he again made an extensive European trip, developing an "ardent interest in art" in Rome. The sizable Russian colony in Paris, which included Saltykovs, Shu-valovs, and Prince Vladimir Golitsyn and his wife (who were living abroad to educate their children), welcomed Zinoviev, and the Koshelevs invited him to visit their rented villa near Tours.

Zinoviev then toured England, visiting the Russian ambassador Semen Vorontsov (Princess Dashkova's brother and formerly the ambassador to Venice) in London and the estate of a Mr. Dickenson, near Leeds.[24] Russian aristocrats in England now made it a practice to tour the great country houses. In 1770, for instance, Princess Dashkova visited Claremont, Cobham, Longleat, Wilton, and Blenheim; some decades later Fyodor Rostopchin (governor-general of Moscow in 1812) spent six weeks at Blenheim. One traveler's enthusiastic words capture the impact of English connoisseurship on Russians: "How many treasures in paintings and antiques are scattered throughout the country houses! For a long time now the English have had a passion for travelling in Italy and buying up everything magnificent, ancient or modern, for which that country is famous. The grandson increases the grandfather's collection, and a painting or statue, which artists once admired in Italy, is buried forever in a country castle."[25]

It is difficult to assess the extent to which Russian connoisseurs followed this example. One memoirist describes her grandfather and his brother as ardent collectors who brought back from Europe "Rembrandts, Van Dycks, Reubens and other famous masters."[26] Because of this her father became a connoisseur "in the cradle" and built a large picture gallery for Mikhailovskoe, his estate in Zvenigorod district of Moscow Province. By the early nineteenth century some Europeans were extremely impressed by the results of Russian purchases of European art: "One would think that Russian magnates had gathered up all of Europe to create their remarkable collections," wrote one Englishman.[27] With a few well-known exceptions, however, the value of many vaunted Russian collections is unknown, as no archival records exist to document them: observers may well have been admiring skillful copies, not originals.

Only a few grandees like the Sheremetevs and later the Yusupovs had workshops of first-rate furniture makers, professionally trained painters, and serfs highly skilled in other specialties at their service. But virtually all aristocrats kept on hand craftsmen who could stucco, carve, gild, paint, or practice other arts important to the upkeep of the country house. By contemporaneous Western standards, these large staffs of artisans were anomalous. In Europe skilled workmen were hired for a particular job and traveled from house to house. In Russia a large number of estate serfs practiced arts and trades simply to satisfy their masters' appetites for luxurious surroundings.

This combination of artistic talent and imported luxury produced palaces decorated and furnished in accordance with the latest tastes and highest standards of European elegance. Throughout the reign of Catherine, the prevailing style in interior decor and furnishings was, as in Europe, Louis XVI. Furniture was delicately carved, painted, and gilded; interior motifs were invariably neoclassical, executed in the polychromatic tints evocative of Pompeian frescoes. All these elements are apparent in the Sheremetevs' Kuskovo and Ostankino and the Yusupovs' Arkhangelskoe, the three best-preserved Moscow pleasure palaces, whose furnishings (largely original) and sophisticated decor rival those of Russia's imperial palaces.

Kuskovo

At Kuskovo (see fig. 23) one enters the staterooms from a vestibule whose strict classicism announces the house's stylistic theme. Its wooden walls are stuccoed and painted to resemble veined white marble; lining the walls are paired pilasters, also stuccoed and painted to resemble green marble, alternating with niches holding large alabaster vases with gilded, papier-mâché trim. Beyond the vestibule is the blue drawing room, its walls upholstered in blue brocade and draped with a variety of antique Flemish tapestries. Their scenes of leafy groves, allées, pavilions, fountains, and distant views add depth to the room and echo the park landscape outside. The furnishings are French gilt, with French girandoles and a Russian chandelier. Next to it is the music room, with Chippendale furniture and a specially designed table with eight music stands for chamber-music octets. Here on display is the famous marquetry table the serf master craftsman Nikifor Vasiliev executed in the 1780s from a French engraving of the park and palace (see fig. 177).

The adjoining crimson drawing room (fig. 47), the most elegant room of the palace, has Russian furniture of the 1760s, French portraits by Nicholas Benjamin de la Pierre, a dazzling parquet floor with a star design, huge mirrors framed by garlands of gilt flowers, marble busts of Boris and Anna Sheremetev, and an Italian-made organ that played operatic arias during receptions. Off the drawing room are two game rooms—the card room, with its intimate, comparatively severe decor and walls hung with imperial portraits, and the billiard room, decorated in shades of green, with Russian and Italian wall and ceiling paintings.

In contrast to most eighteenth-century Russian palaces, which used the great hall for banquets, Kuskovo has a palatial dining room. A unique recessed alcove, imitating a trellised summerhouse entwined with grapes, holds an elaborate wooden china cabinet surmounted with a bust of Alexander the Great. On the walls, ornamented with gilded stucco, hang family portraits of Sheremetevs and of the former owners, Alexei and Maria Cherkassky. The state bedroom on the same floor (fig. 48), its baroque decor

47. The crimson drawing room of Kuskovo. Pavel Spol's workshop designed the housing for the elegant organ (left); its tunes included the overture to Monsigny's opera *The Deserter*, which was performed at Kuskovo.

48. The state bedroom at Kuskovo, with original stucco and wood carving from the 1770s and a parquet floor of birch and black-and-grey oak from the 1780s.

49. The divan room at Kuskovo. Through the door is the library, its vitrines filled with porcelain.

balanced by the restraint of the classical gilded furniture, replicates a similar bedroom in the Sheremetevs' Petersburg mansion on the Fontanka. The bed alcove (a French feature characteristic of Russian mansions) contains a bed made by Spol in 1790; doors on either side lead to the service corridor and a commode. In Kuskovo's art gallery, triple-hung paintings cover the entire wall area. Most are copies of works by Dutch, German, and Italian artists, although the Sheremetev portraits here are originals executed by two of Sheremetev's talented serfs, Ivan Argunov and his son Nikolai.

Along with these formal reception rooms, there are smaller rooms for daily activities: a private dressing room, divan room (fig. 49), library, and a study (fig. 50) paneled in oak and furnished with Petrine antiques. Two family bedrooms are also on the first floor: Peter Borisovich's has walls and furniture of blue-and-white brocade and a plain wood-plank floor (which was covered by a carpet), and Nikolai Petrovich's, rose-striped silk wall coverings and a planked floor.

Ostankino

Nikolai Petrovich Sheremetev intended Ostankino (fig. 51) to surpass his father's Kuskovo in elegance and grandeur. King Stanislav Ponyatowski of Poland described it glowingly in his diary. "The first-floor rooms seem a bit narrow, but all the rooms of the piano nobile are of sufficient height and noticeably well-proportioned. . . . As to the cabinetry, the gilded mirrors, the window and door fittings, the parquet—all was of the very best work and in all of this it would be impossible to find anything closer to perfection. . . . If I were to begin to enumerate the paintings, bronzes, and marbles which are to be found there, I would create a whole catalogue." Count Jacob Sievers, a leading statesman of Catherine's reign, was similarly overwhelmed. "On the first story everything gleams with gold, the marble, the statues, the vases. One would think that this must be the extent of the owner's possessions, but

50. The study at Kuskovo, with eighteenth-century oak paneling and Russian still lifes.

then you go up to the piano nobile and are astonished by the sight of new, no less regal magnificence." In 1801 an Englishman termed the palace a "fantasy reminiscent of one of the Arabian nights. With respect to splendour and magnificence it exceeded anything which the richest imagination of man can give, or which the most daring fantasy of the artist might draw."[28]

At Ostankino a low hall lined with columns ends in a grand staircase (fig. 52) that leads to the parade enfilade. The mansion served almost exclusively as a showcase for theatrical performances and summer entertainments, often for the reigning monarch, and its sumptuous interior decor reflects this. The walls of the vestibule are paneled in crimson silk framed by carved and gilded wood; chairs and console tables, similarly carved and gilded, line the walls.

Sparing no expense, Nikolai Sheremetev ordered for the next room of the enfilade, the blue salon (fig. 53), an elaborate parquet floor from the Petersburg shop of the German master Taude and gilded classical furniture from Spol's workshop; in the estate workshops Sheremetev's talented serf master I. S. Mochalin produced the four carved gilded lamps of the salon. Two Egyptian figures support its entablatures, topped with classical urns flanked by sphinxes. The ceiling of the salon is elaborately painted and decorated; on one side a small loggia, intended for an orchestra, is supported by massive pillars of faux marbre. In the al-

51. The main facade of the Ostankino Palace (1792–98), designed by the architects F. Camporesi, G. Quarenghi, and P. Argunov. (Author)

52. The grand staircase at Ostankino.

cove beneath the loggia are bronze-framed Wedgwood medallions of Peter I and Catherine II. Between the windows of the blue salon stand mirrors and console tables with malachite tops created by the Russian carver Yakov Dunaev. The room of honor features a larger-than-life portrait of Paul I done by Sheremetev's serf N. I. Argunov and displayed in a gilded frame from Spol's workshop. From this room one enters the magnificent pillared portrait gallery, whose blue wallpaper anticipates the blue of the spectators' hall in the theater. The ceiling of the gallery is covered with a French geometric wallpaper in which red and blue predominate; the three sections of the ceiling are each accented by a massive Russian gilt-and-glass chandelier with flowered rod.

Ostankino's elegant ballroom was equipped with hidden machinery that could transform it in one hour into a theater (see fig. 104). Today the original machinery that produced such special effects as waterfalls, lightning, and thunder rests silently in the wings. To transform the ballroom into a theater the false ceiling at the stage end of the hall was removed to allow the raising and lowering of sets, and the flooring at the other end of the hall taken up, revealing the seats of the parterre and the orchestra pit. The large white "pillars" in the stage end of the ballroom, constructed of painted cardboard and mounted on rolling bases, were moved into position as stage props. Panels on either side of the stage swung open, revealing mirrors that projected light to the very back of the stage. The main level of the theater, above the parterre, was reserved for important guests, with the count's loge in the center. Ostankino even had a "paradise," a gallery high above the parterre from which serfs and actors not in the production were permitted to watch a performance. At intervals along this gallery were special vents that enhanced the acoustics of the theater.

Elegant galleries (fig. 54) led to magnificent salons for entertaining at either end of the mansion. The Egyptian pavilion was used for banquets and concerts. With its lyre-backed chairs and doors executed in Spol's workshop, intricate parquet floor, bas-relief frieze of winged griffons under the cornice, and Corinthian pillars and pilasters of green-flecked marble against pale yellow walls, it is rivaled

53. The blue salon at Ostankino.

only by the Italian pavilion in elegance and stylistic complexity. The Italian pavilion, used for formal receptions, is designed as a large salon with reception chambers in each of the four corners. The salon has two fireplaces rather than the customary stoves, which, however practical in a northern climate, did not produce the charming yet cozy effect of a fireplace. Marble pilasters line the walls, the door surrounds are elaborately carved, and the doors themselves are painted and gilded with cameo insets. Eleven types of wood, including white birch, ebony, rosewood, and two varieties of walnut, were used for the extraordinary parquet floor P. I. Argunov designed.

Arkhangelskoe

Arkhangelskoe (fig. 55) is one of the few private estates in Russia that might with some certainty be styled a "treasure house." Prince Nikolai Yusupov, who bought the estate from Golitsyn in 1810, clearly viewed it as such. "Arkhangelskoe is not run for profit," he declared, "but is a source of expense and joy," meaning that he felt it his

54. The gallery leading to the Egyptian pavilion at Ostankino.

55. Entrance gates to Nikolai Yusupov's Arkhangelskoe.
Designed by S. P. Melnikov in 1817.

obligation to buy what was rare and superior.[29] A mere two years after Yusupov's purchase, Napoleon's troops inflicted extensive damage on the house and grounds. Undaunted, Prince Nikolai undertook repairs and renovations, enlisting the services of two leading Moscow architects, Osip Beauvais and Yevgraf Tyurin, assisted by some of Yusupov's serfs. In 1820 the whole palace had to be redecorated yet a third time after a ruinous fire destroyed the interior.[30] Because Arkhangelskoe was designed to display Yusupov's extensive art collection, only a few rooms are as richly decorated as the rooms in the Sheremetev estates. Despite the late date of the second renovation, the interior decor reflects Yusupov's eighteenth-century tastes (with the exception of the Empire-style furniture). The vestibule, entered from the elegant portico, has pilasters painted in faux marbre, between which are recessed niches with copies of antique statues. The ceiling and areas above the portals and niches are enhanced by fine grisaille swans, palm fronds, and wreaths. Half-columns with Corinthian capitals frame the doorways leading into an antechamber and the oval hall, the center of the house. One's eye is immediately drawn to the paired marble columns with Corinthian capitals and to the finely carved entablature. Similar pilasters against the curved walls support the musicians' gallery. Large mirrors between the pairs of columns enlarge the space, while three large French windows look onto the park. At the center of the cupola (painted to imitate caissons) is the painting *Cupid and Psyche*, executed by Nicholas de Courteille in the 1820s.

Among other important rooms along the enfilade (fig. 56) are the imperial room, hung with portraits of emperors, the state bedroom, its alcove set apart by four massive columns, and two rooms dedicated to the French painter Hubert Robert, which are linked by a gallery of antiquities. Whereas in the imperial room and state bedroom the furniture is gilded, the Empire chairs in the oval hall and Hubert Robert rooms are veneered in the Karelian birch peculiar to furniture of Russian manufacture.[31] The Hubert Robert

56. The enfilade at Arkhangelskoe.

rooms, octagonal in shape, are reminiscent of lanterns. Each wall holds a large canvas of an imaginary classical landscape; to look out upon the park from an intervening window is to add a third landscape to the view. The connecting gallery, with grisaille paneling and molding, is a perfect setting for Yusupov's collection of classical sculpture, mounted on pedestals along the walls. The Tiepolo room displays Yusupov's Italian paintings, including two gigantic Tiepolos; the study has tiers of paintings lining its walls and elegant pieces of Empire furniture. The arms of the poplar settee are black-and-gilded carved sphinxes; the backs of the matching poplar armchairs are formed by the necks of two black swans with gilded beaks. The last important room, the state dining room (fig. 57), is a vast hall with Egyptian-style decor and wall paintings, in which Yusupov's porcelain collection was displayed.

Arkhangelskoe, like Kuskovo or Ostankino, was designed mainly for public display and used predominantly in summer. But it also had three so-called winter rooms; these private quarters for the prince, in their simplicity and smaller scale, resemble the living room and study of a more modest country estate of the period. A wooden staircase painted in faux marbre leads upstairs to the library and other living quarters.

Provincial Interiors

In contrast to these three estates, whose art and furniture collections have been extensively inventoried and remain relatively intact, little information exists for the furnishings of other grand estates. We know that Zavadovsky placed an order with the St. Petersburg Academy of Arts for various bas-reliefs for Lyalichi in 1795, for the relatively

57. The state dining room at Arkhangelskoe.

modest price of 184 rubles, 75 kopecks. Archival photographs of the remarkable neoclassical ornamentation on the ceiling of the Hall of the Four Seasons and of the bower effect achieved in the painting of the cupola over the central columned hall bear out two eyewitness accounts of Lyalichi's lavish interior. Count P. I. Shalikov wrote in 1803 of "marble busts, statues, superb paintings and mirrors" in all the rooms, and we know that at least in 1805 a portrait of Zavadovsky by the artist J.-B. Lampi hung in the house, because Zavadovsky mentioned it in a letter to A. R. Vorontsov.[32] One visitor was shocked to find a naked sleeping Venus hanging in Zavadovsky's study alongside his wife's portrait!

In 1813, a year after Zavadovsky's death, a French doctor who spent the spring there described being led into the great hall: "[It was] decorated with marble statues and historical paintings, among them a portrait of Cardinal Richelieu. . . . I counted more than a hundred rooms. . . . In the so-called Apollo hall hangs a full-length portrait of Catherine II in a magnificent frame with the imperial crown. The other hall, the Lucullan, was hung with Gobelin tapestries depicting mythological scenes, a gift from the Empress. . . . Practically everywhere there were paintings by the best masters; their worth is estimated at a hundred thousand rubles."

Again we must question whether these "best masters" were originals. He found the furnishings luxurious but a bit old-fashioned. One investigator claimed to have evidence that Gobelin tapestries, bronzes, Sèvres porcelain, paintings, statues, and furniture had been obtained for Lyalichi from the Trianon and that the house once contained a desk belonging to Marie-Antoinette, with marquetry work and bronze decorations and Sèvres medallions painted by François Boucher (later acquired by the Louvre Museum), as well as a bed owned by her (later sold to the Kensington Museum).[33] Unfortunately, none of these claims are verifiable.

Similarly, we have a general inventory of 1813 for Znamenskoe-Raek, designed for General Glebov by Nikolai Lvov (see figs. 199, 200). An enormous number of paintings were simply counted up ("In Peter Fedorovich's half 138, in the oval [hall], 260, in Dmitry Fedorovich's half 250"), as was an assortment of furniture. The listing for the oval living room, for instance, included "2 marble and bronze tables with mirrors, 2 small triangular tables of simple wood, on which there are 2 vases of faux marbre, 2 bronze chandeliers with crystal pendants," and so on for the other rooms.[34] In most instances, however, even such general inventories either were never made or vanished; thus we have little idea of the original furnishings of a given house, its provenance, or how long it remained there.

In the eighteenth century, there being little perceived difference between a grandee's country and city life, palatial furniture was moved to town for the winter. Since furnishings were stylistically international at that time, they would also have fit well in an aristocratic residence in London or Paris. The furniture in most estate houses, by contrast, was eclectic in style, more Russian in appearance, and old-fashioned compared to that of the pleasure palace. In the remoter provinces, essentially the same style—Russian Empire—prevailed for over half a century. New pieces might be added to the main reception rooms, but estate interiors were rarely renovated; hence the estate lacked the stylistic purity of the palace. Moreover, Russian Empire in a palace setting like Arkhangelskoe preserved the grandeur, monumentality, and magnificence it had in Europe. On most estates, however, the interpretation of this style was simpler, more fanciful in form and decoration, lighter, and more comfortable.[35]

Certain pieces of estate furniture were ubiquitous. One was the "barrel" or "trough" chair, shaped like the French gondola armchair but with a solid wooden back fashioned by fitting vertical pine staves together, then covering them with a mahogany, Karelian birch, or poplar veneer. In the 1820s this simple silhouette became more complex; sometimes the back or sides were pierced or dec-

58. An early nineteenth-century reception-room ensemble of Empire sofa, pedestal table, and barrel chairs executed in Karelian birch veneer at Arkhangelskoe. (Photo by Anne Odom)

orated with carving. The main reception room of an estate commonly contained one or two ensembles—each consisting of a sofa, a pedestal table (usually oval), and two chairs (fig. 58)—usually aligned on one side of the room. Mirrors in mahogany frames above console or card tables and secretaries and cabinets with square or paw feet were also pervasive touches. This furniture was produced in Moscow workshops, in provincial towns, or by estate craftsmen working from pattern books or actual pieces of furniture.

Elizaveta Yankova's memoirs, which chronicle a half-century of Moscow and provincial life, contain observations about the furnishings of houses near Moscow that provide some idea of the varying levels of elegance at the end of the eighteenth century. She and her husband owned slightly under one thousand souls, whereas her parents had owned five thousand. By birth a Rimsky-Korsakov with a Tatishchev grandmother, and related by marriage to Gagarins, Meshcherskys, Volkonskys, Shcherbatovs, and Tolstoys, Yankova was acutely aware of social distinctions. At Bobrovo, her Tatishchev grandmother's estate where she lived as a child, the old-fashioned furniture, which she described as "very nice and solid," was constructed of boxwood covered with black leather held in place with gilded studs. Only the windows in her mother's sitting room were curtained. At Rozhdestveno, Dmitry V. Golitsyn's estate, Yankova noted his "simple furnishings: birch furniture, upholstered with ticking, with no gilding or silk." By contrast Yankova describes Countess Anna Orlova-Chesmenskaya's Neskuchnoe as lavishly appointed "for a private person." Silver services and crystal were a sign of luxury. During her grandmother's day there was no silver at Bobrovo, only tin; her father bought the first silver for her sisters' weddings. Yankova was therefore impressed by the place settings at a wedding dinner Countess Orlova gave for her niece: "Everything was of silver; the place settings were gilded, and the dessert knives and forks were gilded with carnelian handles." Orlova gave the young couple the entire service, which Yankova estimated at over forty place settings.[36]

Paintings and photographs of the Apraksins' Olgovo chronicle the alterations to its furnishings as successive generations with different sensibilities lived there.[37] In the days of Field Marshal Apraksin the baroque great hall emphasized the martial exploits of family members, expressing the pride of this Catherinian eagle. Semicircular plaques above the windows, illuminated by two massive crystal candelabras, held fanciful depictions of heroic Apraksin ancestors in high relief on a red background, with the words "killed," "died from wounds" and other military tributes. A huge portrait of the field marshal hung on one wall, with the gold inscription "Patri Optimo." Columns of rose-colored faux marbre supported choir lofts decorated with imposing alabaster vases; beneath the lofts stood marquetry tables. Save for one long table, the great hall was relatively empty, undoubtedly to facilitate the circulation of footmen during the Apraksins' legendary entertainments.

For twenty-five years Olgovo was the center of Elizaveta Yankova's social life. When her convivial host Sergei S. Apraksin (son of the field marshal) died in 1827, his widow (born a Golitsyn) abandoned refined simplicity for a more grandiose atmosphere. The great hall and reception rooms were now filled with magnificent dark Empire furniture decorated with gilded swans. Apraksina bought expensive French card tables, marquetry cabinets, and an inlaid Italian mosaic table said to have cost the huge sum of thirty thousand rubles.[38] Serf master craftsmen fashioned wooden objects, such as candelabras, clocks, and vases gilded or painted to resemble bronze or porcelain (even Sèvres azure), for the new decor. By the 1840s, paintings reveal, the vases on the choir lofts had been replaced by busts, lighter and more detailed, and small chairs and Japanese vases on pedestals had been added to break up the emptiness of the great hall. The walls and columns were now pale green, which along with the lighter furniture altered the triumphal, martial feeling of the original hall.

Photographs from the 1880s show the great hall now cozily cluttered with furniture. Cabinets had been placed between the columns, and a huge buffet, an enormous pierglass, and an English grandfather clock added. Elsewhere, pieces of furniture recalled the history of the house. From S. S. Apraksin's day there remained an Empire couch upholstered in red brocade, its arms supported by massive griffons; this piece was possibly commissioned for a visit Count Apraksin anticipated from Catherine II. A pair of carved wooden candelabras was markedly similar to a pair at Ostankino. In the state bedroom the refined form of a huge bed of Karelian birch, almost certainly made by serfs, flanked by similar armchairs with swans and tapestry seats, reflected the skill of Apraksin's master craftsmen. Less successful but very typical was a secretary made for the Chinese gazebo in the park. French in form, with numerous pigeonholes, it was decorated with rather crude

gold arabesques meant to resemble Chinese characters. Like most estate houses, Olgovo teemed with ancestral portraits, paintings of other Apraksin estates, and landscapes.

Over the large drawing room, the owners' winter apartments—consisting of a bedroom, study, and private chapel or oratory—had typically eclectic, utilitarian furnishings in the 1880s. The bedroom contained a huge bed from the 1850s, chairs of serf manufacture, a fairly crude armoire with an abundance of drawers and compartments, and an elegant pier glass. In the study stood an inlaid table, a desk, and chairs copied from a French model by serf craftsmen who, though faithful to the decorative details, had changed the proportions.

On most estates during the reign of Nicholas I the quest for comfort, a concept completely out of character for the status-conscious noble of earlier epochs, became the norm. Empire furniture competed with lower, softer furniture, just as the fancy two-story hall and elegant but cold reception rooms were abandoned for smaller, cozier rooms. The enfilade was interrupted by closing doors and placing bureaus or étagères in front of them. The enormous interest in Orientalia, which, after Napoleon's campaigns, inspired sphinxes and other Egyptian motifs, waned; now, in the wake of the Russian conquest of the Caucasus, the divan room was likely to be furnished with low, wide, soft ottomans, and the smoking room with low divans and racks of long-stemmed Turkish pipes. Turkish shawls for women and long Oriental dressing gowns and caps—even an occasional fez—for men replaced the raised waist dresses and nipped frock coats of the Napoleonic period. The popularity of the Gothic at this time prompted some furniture in this style but rarely on the estate, where the ubiquitous Empire style continued to predominate.

Valuable antiques were still to be found on estates in the early twentieth century. In 1910 the gentleman scholar Baron N. N. Vrangel listed the following inventory of such pieces he had seen: "17th-century Italian cassones at Bogoroditsk, along with an outstanding Dutch cupboard with Peter the Great carved in relief . . . two amazing cabinets with Wedgwood medallions at Nikolskoe (Moscow province); Petrine chairs at Polotnyany Zavod and Bogoroditsk; remarkable [bronze and porcelain] at the Moscow Sheremetev estates and Arkhangelskoe, superlative clocks at the Golitsyns' Petrovskoe, and Saxony porcelain in Bogoroditsk."[39]

But by this time most such pieces had been sold or moved to the city for safekeeping. What remained were the comfortingly familiar furnishings associated with estate life: an eclectic mix of mahogany, poplar, and birch furniture, handsomely decorated stoves, soft ottomans, endless racks of pipes, collections of old weapons, and charmingly clumsy family portraits, an old-fashioned look most estate owners had come to cherish.[40]

3
Tatyana's Garden

THE PARADOX OF ESTATE PARK DESIGN

The site of a garden should be considered the canvas on which the garden's creator paints

his picture. . . . My gardens have nourished my mind and heart, and have given me not only emotional

and physical but even spiritual pleasure.—**A. T. Bolotov**

IN HIS STORY "MISTRESS INTO MAID" Alexander Pushkin introduces us to Grigory Muromsky, a "real Russian grandee" who has fallen on hard times. On his one remaining estate he is busily squandering the remnants of his fortune on an "English garden." The gardening revolution of eighteenth-century England, inspired by the overgrown ruins of Rome and Naples and by a new feeling for untrammeled nature, set in motion a vogue for informal, picturesque landscaping that swept across Europe, altered garden design in the United States, and reached Russia in the reign of Catherine II as the harbinger of a later, more pervasive aristocratic Anglomania. As Muromsky's landscaping suggests, by the early nineteenth century the English, or irregular, garden had become a universal form for the Russian country estate, its basic motifs carried out on whatever scale a landowner could afford.

It therefore comes as no surprise that in *Eugene Onegin*, written between 1823 and 1830 and published in 1833, Pushkin describes the Larin garden in conformity to this canon. Its features are catalogued only briefly, yet its romantic, natural, and poetic attributes seem meant to reflect the very qualities of his heroine, Tatyana. As a moonlit landscape to which Tatyana is drawn on the sleepless night during which she composes her artless letter to Onegin, and as the refuge to which she flees when he arrives in response, this garden seems emblematic of Tatyana's instinctive Russian virtues, to which Pushkin opposes Onegin's city-bred, imported moral deficiencies.

Pushkin specialists may wish to stop here, for my theme, though neatly encapsulated in these contrasts, concerns a broader problem: the cultural predicament of the Russian elite of Pushkin's age, torn between imported norms that dictated the form and content of the estate park and the nativist impulses of the romantic age (fig. 59). Throughout his novel, Pushkin seems to have employed images of nature and noble responses to nature to expand on the romantic theme of the city (particularly St. Petersburg) as foreign, artificial, and morally corrupting and

of country life as native, natural, and restorative. Not all of these images ring true, for good reason. As a highly cultured member of the Petersburg aristocracy Pushkin was conditioned to a different, far more condescending view of rural Russia. Nonetheless Pushkin's images, like the real gardens of his time, suggest a filtering of, and contrast in, sensibilities toward nature that culminate in a paradox. On one level of realization the English garden seems to have expressed the desire of Russian aristocrats for an immediate and natural relationship with their surroundings; on another it was an emphatic reminder of their ambivalence toward rural Russian reality.

Pushkin wrote the third chapter of *Eugene Onegin* while living at Mikhailovskoe, his family's small estate in Pskov Province. The garden of the Vulfs' small Trigorskoe, a neighboring estate that he visited almost every afternoon, seems the most likely inspiration for the features Pushkin attributes to the Larin garden: flower beds, meadows, little bridges, an allée to the lake, a grove, lilac bushes. Clearly its scale was far more intimate than that of some grand English parks he is known to have visited with pleasure, such as Pavlovsk, Ostafievo (which belonged to the poet Prince Peter Vyazemsky), or Yaropolets (the estate of his father-in-law, Nikolai Goncharov). Significantly, the Larin garden appears to lack the decorative structures almost invariably found in such gardens. Even Pushkin's grandfather's modest Petrovskoe, for example, had a grotto pavilion (fig. 60).

In fact, the type of garden with which Pushkin associates Tatyana—a simple and small landscaped area surrounding the modest house of a provincial landowner—differed greatly from the park of a Russian grandee. The country estate was an aristocrat's arcadia, an environment in which to express his sensitivity to nature in elaborate and highly contrived fashion. He began by selecting the most advantageous site for the manse (one where it would stand out from its surroundings yet blend in as the new esthetic demanded). He built magnificent orangeries and

59. Artist unknown. The house and park at Akhtyrka as they appeared in Pushkin's days. Of this elaborate estate, belonging to the Trubetskoi family, only the church has survived. (Courtesy of Shchusev Museum of Architecture, Moscow)

60. Grotto pavilion at Petrovskoe, Pushkin's grandfather's estate near Mikhailovskoe.

hothouses whose bounty within the house vied for attention with the decorative floral motifs on the walls, furniture, and floors of the interior. Last, he lavished enormous attention and funds on his gardens and park.

In the 1790s Karamzin marveled at England's "vast greenhouses . . . where fruits and plants have been gathered from all parts of the world."[1] He appears not to have been aware of the gardening mania that had produced comparable greenhouses in Russia by that time. These well-heated, often elaborate orangeries that doubled as winter gardens were sometimes attached to the house, but more often they were large separate structures. At Kurakino, Prince Alexei Kurakin's estate in Orel Province, the orangery was a long stone building containing pear, apricot, and cherry trees. Catherine Wilmot wrote her sister of promenading in the Troitskoe orangery in December, and Prince Kurakin entertained in his orangery in the dead of winter, delighting his guests with tropical birds that flew around it.[2]

In defiance of Russia's short growing season and inhospitable clime, aristocrats also lavished attention on more utilitarian hothouses and forcing beds, proud of being able to produce throughout the year an abundance of fresh flowers for every room and fruits for their table. The English gardener Meader, fresh from Syon House, near London, was not impressed with Russian greenhouses, which he found "great heavy clumsy buildings," but noted that the Russians "raise Peaches, Nectarines, Cherries, Pineapples etc. in the fruit way, and in others Cucumbers, Sallads etc."[3] Kurakino had two hothouses for pineapples and open-air forcing beds for melons.

By the late eighteenth century Russia was a player in the international trade in exotic plants. The aristocrat's park might contain Lebanese cedars, Siberian pines, and American elms, and his hothouses rare tropical flowers. Russian aristocrats competed in collecting specimens from abroad, whereas foreigners wanted Russian rarities. Meader responded as best he could to requests from the Duke of Northumberland and the gardeners at Kew for Siberian plants and seeds but told his importuners to "look at a map of the Russian Empire and you will see that Siberia is a vast distance. . . . Few people travel to that country except criminals and soldiers."[4] Luckily for Meader, two English gardeners in Moscow promised him seeds and plants from the renowned botanist Baron P. A. Demidov (see fig. 98) in Moscow. In the 1780s the gardens and greenhouses of Demidov's estate, Neskuchnoe (now Gorky Park), which stretched from house to river in a series of terraces, contained 4,500 types of plants. Apprised of the Russian taste for exotica, one enterprising Englishman, John Fraser (1750–1811), who had established himself in Charleston, South Carolina, in the 1790s, sold a number of North American specimens to Catherine II. Empress Maria Fedorovna, wife of Paul, was also a passionate gardener who gathered plants from all over the world for Pavlovsk.[5] When Fraser returned to Russia in 1797–98, she placed a large order with him; one can only imagine his disappointment when, after Paul's death in 1801, Alexander I refused to honor the commission.[6]

By the early nineteenth century the most renowned suburban Moscow orangeries and gardens were on the sightseer's agenda. In 1822 one tourist described the Kuskovo orangery (fig. 61) as "the best in the Moscow area," noting that sales from it brought in more than 8,000 rubles annually.[7] But pride of place must surely go to the Razumovskys' Gorenki, 15 miles from Moscow. It featured an enormous botanical garden, which Robert Lyall in 1825 described as "one of the most magnificent in the world"; directed by a Dr. Fischer, the garden cost between 70,000 and 100,000 rubles a year to maintain. According to Lyall, one could take "a fine promenade through a gallery 910 feet long, including at each end a commodious forcing house . . . made doubly agreeable by the sweets of orange and lemon groves, as well as the quantities of peaches and apricots produced." Between 9,000 and 10,000 types of plants were represented, including all known varieties in the Russian empire, as well as specimens from Europe and America. Gorenki had 11 hothouses in 6 separate buildings, with a combined facade of 1,148 feet. "Here are enjoyed Asiatic pleasures in the rigorous climate of Russia— walks amidst woods and groves of tropical vegetation even when the cold is . . . 35 degrees below zero" (fig. 62).[8]

Plants were an important component of interior decor. Reception rooms were filled with an abundance of potted plants; wrought-iron railings twined with climbing plants served as room dividers; and trellissed bowers, somewhat elevated above floor level, afforded a sheltered corner for the mistress of the house. The Marquis de Custine guessed that this custom had been imported from Asia, and it struck him as so attractive that he expressed hope it would spread to Paris.[9]

Beyond house and orangery lay the elaborately natural English garden, whose neoclassical temples, summer- houses, and belvederes echoed the architecture of the house. In 1772 Catherine the Great officially endorsed the transition from the French formal style in landscape archi- tecture to the English garden, sending Voltaire an impas- sioned denunciation of formal gardens: "I am at present madly in love with English gardens, with curved lines, gentle slopes, lakes formed from swamps, and archi- pelagoes of solid earth, and I profoundly despise straight lines. I hate fountains that torture water in order to make it

61. The conservatory at Kuskovo, designed by Fyodor Argunov and built between 1761 and 1763.

62. The winter garden at the Tarnovskys' Kachanovka, Chernigov Province. The fashion for tropical vegetation persisted to the end of the imperial period. (*Stolitsa i usadba,* nos. 40–41)

take a course contrary to its nature; in a word, Anglomania dominates my plantomania." Catherine hired leading European and Russian architects and gardeners to transform the outbuildings and grounds of Tsarskoe Selo into a garden paradise in which she described herself taking walks "which would make the most determined walker in London tremble."[10] In 1779 Meader was brought to Russia to design the English park for the new English Palace Catherine planned for herself at Peterhof. A number of artists, including Charles Cameron, V. Brenna, P. Gonzago, and A. Voronikhin, worked on the design of the grounds of Pavlovsk, one of the most exquisite expressions of the blending of neoclassical architecture with a large English park into a harmonious whole (fig. 63). By the 1790s Catherine's mania for gardens was being celebrated in court panegyrics acclaiming "Felitsa" (as Derzhavin dubbed the empress) for creating a veritable paradise around her new

palaces. These imperial edens served as inspirations and models for the court nobility, who either used the same architects or their protégés for their parks or hired their own European gardeners. In analogous fashion, the provincial gentry drew much of its notion of landscape design from the gardens of nearby aristocratic estates.

Some sophisticated Russian nobles had anticipated Catherine's enthusiasm for the new style. During a trip to England in 1764 Ivan Shuvalov raved about English gardens in a letter to M. L. Vorontsov and offered to assist him in designing one for Kimora, Vorontsov's estate in Tver Province. "The gardens are beautiful, in a taste completely different from others; . . . the whole art consists of making it conform to nature. It seems to me that this is better," he wrote.[11] During this period, numerous other Russian nobles toured the great English gardens such as Lord Temple's Stowe, Alexander Pope's Twickenham, and Horace

Walpole's Strawberry Hill. But their reactions were not uniformly enthusiastic; some were taken aback by English naturalness. In 1771 Alexander Kurakin (who visited Blenheim, Thursby, Hagley, and Chatsworth) wrote a bemused account of his impressions of the new taste in gardens: "Everything is bizarre and conforms to the strange taste they have adopted. Everywhere there are nothing but vast prairies on which are scattered hills, groves, flower beds, fields, groups of trees, isolated trees, or sometimes, stone monuments of an antique architecture. . . . One is undeniably struck with the novelty of the view. At every step the scene varies. All is contrast. . . . One finds in these country estates everything of the most agreeable sort which nature aided by artifice can offer, and that which is

63. The Temple of Friendship in the garden of Pavlovsk, designed by Charles Cameron.

the result of artifice appears to be that of nature." Kurakin attributed the unusual style to the desire of the English to "distinguish themselves from other nations" and criticized both the lack of shade in their parks and "the expenses which are entailed by work such as erecting hills where formerly there were nothing but plains."[12]

Yet Kurakin, like most of his contemporaries, eventually became a convert. Two decades later, exiled to Nadezhdino (fig. 64), Kurakin turned his energy and substantial resources to re-creating the grand English parks he had seen both abroad and in St. Petersburg, where the Pavlovsk park was particularly influential. Other aristocrats did likewise, as the craze for the English garden gathered momentum. In 1794 Kurakin, delighted with his new garden, boasted to Paul that "120 yards behind my courtyard is my new English garden, which is almost finished, thanks to strong arms and much care; it is five versts [or about three and a half miles] in circumference. There are no pines, and

64. Artist unknown. Engraving of Prince A. B. Kurakin's Nadezhdino, Saratov Province. Late eighteenth–early nineteenth century. (Courtesy of State Historical Museum, Moscow)

practically no birches; one sees only oaks, lindens, elms, etc. The most temperate climates cannot produce a more pleasant woods: from the morning until evening and even during the night I hear the song of the nightingale there and the warbling of a multitude of different birds."[13]

The great Russian gardens such as Kurakin's at Nadezhdino were designed to produce the four levels of association—historical, allegorical, philosophical, and picturesque—which were common to the carefully planned garden tour of Stowe, Chiswick, or Twickenham. In England the Belt Walk, or Circular Walk, which began and ended at the house, had been introduced in the early eighteenth century. Charles Bridgeman contributed the idea of the "ha-ha": a ditch, sometimes concealing a high wall, which created an invisible boundary, allowing the surrounding countryside to become an integral part of the park scenery. In England ha-has soon replaced fencing as a means of restraining animals such as deer or sheep, which did not belong in the lord's pleasure grounds yet contributed visual interest to the landscape. Bridgeman also initiated an emphasis on water in the landscape. He was followed by the talented William Kent, whose landscapes imitated the idealized landscape paintings of Salvator Rosa, Nicholas Poussin, and Claude Lorrain; by Lancelot "Capability" Brown, a follower and expander of Bridgeman's ideas who added a lake to the grounds of Blenheim; and by Humphrey Repton, master of the picturesque. By the end of the eighteenth century the designs of these giants of English landscaping had transformed much of rural England (at great expense) to meet the new sensibilities of the English aristocracy toward nature.

Although none of these renowned English landscapers seems to have worked in Russia, other foreign experts did, throughout Catherine's reign and beyond. John Bush, from Hanover, and Meader were hired by Catherine to work on the gardens of Tsarskoe Selo and Peterhof, respectively, but they probably also took on private commissions. Bush, like the architects Rastrelli and Rossi and the theater de-

signer Gonzago, never left Russia; he and his son worked together on Pavlovsk and later Elagin Island (a private estate owned by the Elagin family until Alexander I purchased it for his mother). One contemporary ecstatically called Bush "not simply a gardener, but an artist with respect to horticulture."[14]

Meader stayed in Russia from 1779 to at least 1787, and his letters home reflect a growing demand among the Russians for English gardeners. At one point he notes that one John McLaren is staying with him and posits that when Prince Orlov returns from Poland he will hire McLaren "at 200 pounds per annum." In another letter he notes that "the Nobles who have been in England are so much enraptured with the English pleasure gardens that they are cried up here. This has set them all gardening mad. Any of the Nobility will give 100 pounds pr Ann for an English gardener." Meader himself had been solicited a number of times, and he was anxious to prevent Russia from being overrun with second-rate English gardeners, "lest one scabby sheep spoil the whole flock."[15]

Foreign experts were well compensated. In 1786 the "foreign gardener" at Kuskovo, Peter Wrack, was receiving the largest salary of anyone on the staff: 700 rubles, plus goods worth 317 rubles, such as candles, feed for two horses, and firewood.[16] Count Nikolai Sheremetev's detailed instructions of May 1797 to his English gardener at Ostankino, Roman Robert Manners (who had been there since 1791 and who was undoubtedly also handsomely paid), indicate a substantial interest and personal involvement in his garden. "In the large garden keep the paths and meadows clean and make them perfect, and add decorations as you see fit, I leave it to your judgment; if it is necessary to cut down old trees, tell me first and don't begin without this." Sheremetev wanted Manners to use his large staff of serfs efficiently:

The gardening assistants, pupils, and workers
are under your command and should be obedient,

as I have informed them all. One must supervise these men well and always be with them while working; in summer they should come to work no later than 4 A.M.; when the weather is bad and it is not possible to work in the garden, then the students should be taught to draw so that their time not be wasted, and the workers set to work appropriate for the weather, carrying gravel, cleaning up any mud. Make me a note regarding the number of workers needed for the little paths begun beyond the garden in the grove by the Kamenka River, and what you need for them.[17]

Clearly, English ideas had an enormous influence upon the design of the great Russian parks, particularly insofar as the "garden of artifice," a garden (such as Pope's Twickenham) containing a number of exotic or allegorical structures, was concerned. In Russian landscaping, however, one rarely finds Capability Brown's virtual obliteration of the distinction between estate park and the countryside beyond it. Great Russian estates and their gardens were enclosed worlds within a family's vast domains. Their separateness from their surroundings might be announced by imposing entrance gates to the main drive (figs. 65, 100) or by an obelisk engraved with the words

65. The gryphon-adorned entrance gates spanning a moat at the Golitsyns' Kuzminki.

"Boundary of the World."[18] Within this enclave was an area of limitless fantasy. The view beyond the park was important. From the windows of his new eighty-room manse situated on a high elevation, Kurakin observed that he could see the river, a magnificent lawn, a lake over one mile long, villages, plains, and forest. But the allegorical re-creation of his sentiments within the garden proper overshadowed the view in significance. "I was agreeably surprised by four charming pavilions built at my instigation from English drawings which Prince Sergei Golitsyn furnished. I have just had them all built as temples; I have given names to all these temples and to all the large and small walks in this delicious garden. On each path one will find several posts with writing which furnishes its name, so that everyone who passes can be filled to overflowing with the ideas and the sentiments which correspond to it. These names give me pleasant and interesting reminiscences: they indicate the nature of my feelings and the people who are in my heart."[19]

Faithful to the sentimentalism of the age, Kurakin named his temples Harmony, Patience, Friendship, and Truth (his Temple of Friendship being, of course, a tribute to Paul's temple at Pavlovsk). Other garden structures included gazebos, summerhouses, and a gallery designed as a "receptacle of eternal feelings." Allées and paths meandering among these structures were named for the tsarevich, for Kurakin's brother Alexei, and even for some house servants. The names of other paths catalogued his sentiments in exile: Pleasant Enjoyment, Solitude, Difficulties Overcome, Spiritual Tranquility, Memories of Past Consolations, The Constant Friend. It may have been true, as one visitor to Nadezhdino in 1848 concluded, that Kurakin was a "true lover of nature," but clearly this garden was primarily an elaborate stage set for its owner's emotions.[20]

Olgovo's eighty-acre park similarly abounded with the caprices of its owner, many designed by the Apraksins' resident architect, Francesco Camporesi. They included a Temple of Virtue, erected by the unfaithful Sergei Aprak-

sin in homage to his wife's fidelity, an obelisk and triumphal gates honoring his friends Stroganov and Golitsyn, a series of ponds with humorous names, artificial ruins (which no wealthy landowner in those times could do without), a delicate Chinese gazebo, and a Turkish minaret. Beyond the park stood decorative miniature structures housing the kennels, a paper factory, and a carpet factory.

At A. P. Nashchokin's Rai-Semenovskoe, the terraces of the English garden cascading down to the river overflowed with eye-catching whimsies: temples, a Chinese pagoda, artificial ponds, and two grottoes (one of which was connected to a nearby temple by an underground passageway). Beyond the garden was a menagerie that contained, among other animals, wild goats and merino sheep. A regular garden lay on the other side of the mansion, bordered by a meadow named for Nashchokin's wife, Elizaveta, beyond which was another pond.[21] By the late eighteenth century, grand Russian re-creations of the English garden on crown and private estates were widespread. In the early nineteenth century, Russians were touring these estate parks, as earlier generations had toured the originals in England, and publishing ecstatic accounts of their impressions, which helped popularize the English approach to landscaping.

The work of Andrei T. Bolotov (fig. 66) provides a link between the grand estate and the world of the more modest estate owner. Bolotov was both a serious agronomist (a field to which he made important contributions) and a passionate gardener. In his memoirs his highly sentimental reaction to nature surfaces in frequent rhapsodic digressions about his surroundings, the weather, or a view that matches his current mood. The type of landscaping improvements Bolotov was recommending in the 1780s to educated landowners of limited means (meaning few serfs) such as himself were more typical of the provincial estate. In 1764, when Bolotov retired to his modest estate of Dvoryaninovo, the first improvement he had ordered, to

66. A. T. Bolotov. Self-portrait in his study at Bogoroditsk. 1789. (Bolotov, *Zhizn i priklyucheniya Andreya Timofeevicha Bolotova*, frontispiece)

the dismay of his serfs, was the planting of a large regular garden. In his memoirs he describes this as a threefold mistake: first, because he used foreign books that were not written for the Russian climate; second, because regular gardens were too difficult to maintain; and third, because, as he put it, "unfortunately, at that time there was not yet any concept of other types of gardens; for regular gardens were the only customary ones, and everywhere in the greatest of fashion." Ultimately he would have to redesign his garden to fit his new esthetic. Bolotov's conversion to the irregular garden occurred when he read C. C. L. Hirschfeld's enormously influential *Theorie der Gartenkunst* in 1784. Up to that time, he confessed, he had been devoted to the designs of André Le Nôtre, first head gardener of the Tuileries and then designer of the elaborate formal gardens of Versailles. After reading Hirschfeld, Bolotov wrote (with a hint of Anglophobia), "[I] became completely disenchanted with them and discovered a taste for the new gardens, called irregular or natural gardens, for it would be sinful to call gardens of this type English gardens."[22]

In eleven years the prolific Bolotov produced eighty illustrated articles on landscape gardening (fig. 67) for the two Moscow periodicals he edited, *The Village Dweller* (1778–79) and *The Economic Magazine* (1780–89). In 1784, his reputation for innovative landscaping ideas growing, Bolotov was hired to work on the gardens at Bogoroditsk, the crown estate of Catherine's illegitimate son Alexei Bobrinskoy, near Tula. The contrast between Bolotov's literary endeavors and his designs for Bogoroditsk highlights the differences in the landscaping required for the small and the great estate. On the one hand, his fifteen articles on the irregular garden (borrowing heavily from Hirschfeld) aimed at inspiring and guiding the transformation of the small landowner's environment into a natural paradise.[23] Bolotov stressed that relatively simple and inexpensive alterations, such as winding rather than straight paths, the channeling of water where possible, variety in plantings, and attention to alternating light and shade along the garden walk, would maximize the owner's pleasure from seemingly untrammeled nature. On the other hand, Bolotov's elaborate relandscaping and building as steward of Bogoroditsk reflect the particular spirit behind

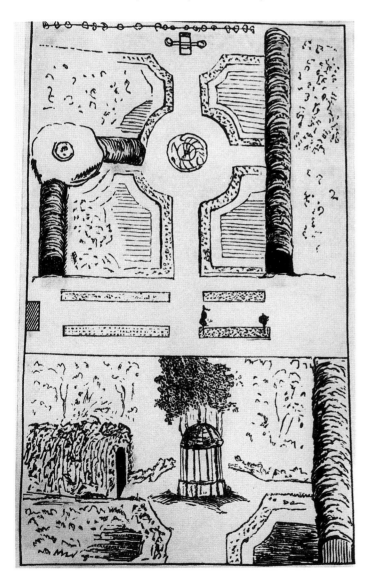

67. A. T. Bolotov. Design for formal gardens near a manor house. 1780s. (Likhachev, *Poeziia sadov*)

the first generation of aristocratic English gardens in Russia, designed as grand showplaces, "pleasure gardens." In them, one might enjoy the picturesque charms of apparently natural surroundings, without necessarily feeling that identity with nature characteristic of the romantic period.

Elaborate fountains and geometric pools had been essential for the old-style formal garden; in the new, water figured even more prominently—this time in the form of irregularly shaped ponds or lakes, brooks, streams, and waterfalls. As early as 1750 a natural lake at Kuskovo had been greatly enlarged for landscaping purposes. Lakes such as this one enhanced the house by reflecting its image, provided such amusements as boating (the wealthy favored elaborate Italian gondolas) or bathing, and added to the picturesque elements in the park. At Bogoroditsk, Bolotov's first task was to locate a spring and raise it at its source to facilitate the creation of the mandatory cascades and waterfalls. Ordered to move masses of earth, brigades of peasants resculpted the territory of the garden and created ponds, reservoirs, and canals. In the late eighteenth century such large-scale earthworks were carried out on many estates; the result was a reshaping of the local terrain to include from one to five or more ponds (some with picturesque islands) connected by canals. Despite long absences from his own Dvoryaninovo, Bolotov managed to create there a series of four cascading ponds, which have survived to the present.

An equally artificial but seemingly natural look was achieved by plantings. In England Humphrey Repton had returned flower beds, banished by Brown, to favor. Hence, close to the house one might find geometric parterres and flower beds that complemented the classical proportions of the mansion; beyond this circumscribed area the visitor would likely be struck by raw nature, contrasts of hue and light, and picturesque views at every turn of a winding path or at the end of an allée. Broad meadows, perhaps containing a few large old trees, contrasted with wooded

87

68. A. T. Bolotov. *View of the Bathing Landing, Waterfall, and Midday Bench.* Bogoroditsk. Bolotov designed other locations in this park specifically for morning and evening enjoyment. Watercolor. (Courtesy of the State Historical Museum, Moscow)

glades and dense forest; the shores of ponds and lakes were planted with a variety of bushes and trees carefully selected for size and hue. When Bobrinskoy's lieutenant arrived to inspect Bolotov's work, he was impressed by the overnight transformation of the garden. In only a few months Bolotov's workers had successfully transplanted many large trees to achieve the desired effect. Bolotov, an avid amateur painter (fig. 68), had planned the garden by tracing its natural contours on a pane of glass, on which he subsequently superimposed his planting scheme. Echoing Pope's famous dictum "Consult the genius of the place in all," he stressed that he had let the terrain dictate what the

best plantings should be; beyond that, virtually any rearrangement was possible.[24] Moreover, he had spent little money. The irregular garden was, in a serf-owning society, less expensive to create and to maintain than a formal park, because the major expense, labor, was free.

The most common buildings in such gardens were the "stone monuments of an antique architecture" that Alexander Kurakin had seen in England. These shrines, usually columned round or rectangular structures resembling small Greek temples, were popular in that they embodied the four levels of association mentioned above. Their execution varied, from elaborate stone temples containing copies of Greek or Roman statues, designed by such leading architects as Vasily Bazhenov and Nikolai Lvov, to simple wooden gazebos placed at a spot that afforded a particularly impressive view. Close association with the ruling family was celebrated in the garden. Arkhangelskoe boasted a temple to Catherine II (fig. 69), while at Sukhanovo an obelisk commemorated a visit by Alexander I. At Troitskoe, Princess Dashkova's estate, Catherine Wilmot described a "winding walk among the birch trees" as the princess's favorite "because of its leading to the Monument of Granite erected on a Mount and dedicated to the remembrance of the [day] Catherine ascended the throne!"[25]

But much of the garden was intended to be simply picturesque. Although the profusion of strategically placed statuary common to the regular garden had vanished, an occasional statue was to be found in the new gardens—no longer featured, however, as the centerpiece of a geometric lawn or flower bed, but secreted as a random delight. Most estates of any pretensions had hermitages or grottoes. The canon for their construction varied; among the wide-ranging examples were Kuskovo's elaborate baroque building with a shell-encrusted interior (figs. 70 and 71); Arkhangelskoe's recessed niche at the base of the Italian stone terrace; Valuevo's stone grotto beneath the hunting lodge (fig. 72); Sofievka's cavelike grotto; and the pavilion

69. Temple to Catherine II at Arkhangelskoe. (Author)

grottoes of Mikhailovskoe and nearby Petrovskoe. At Troitskoe, behind the monument to Catherine there was "scooped a Hermit's Cell furnished with moss and rocky seats."[26] These conceits were the owner's private refuge. In 1770 Bolotov paused en route to Moscow at the estate of Count Golovin; the count's overseer told him that Golovin closeted himself in the grotto whenever he was at the estate. At Bogoroditsk, Bolotov took particular delight in his design for a grotto that was carved into a hill containing veins of brilliantly colored marble.[27]

Foreign and exotic elements, particularly Oriental and pseudo-Gothic garden structures, abounded. In 1771 a small appendix to Sir William Chambers's *Dissertation on Oriental Gardening* (1757) was published in Russian, aiding the spread of Chinese bridges, teahouses, and pagodas. At Tsarskoe Selo, the Italian architect Antonio Rinaldi designed a pagoda for Catherine as part of a Chinese village, and Vasily Neelov a caprice in the form of a Chinese summerhouse and a bridge of four arches supporting a Chinese pavilion. Turkish motifs also appeared in Russian gardens,

70. The grotto pavilion at Kuskovo (1755–61). Fyodor Argunov, architect. Its baroque exterior was designed to suggest water cascading down the sides from a fountain. (Author)

71. *Facing page*: The shell-encrusted interior of the Kuskovo grotto.

72. The hunting lodge (ca. 1800) at Valuevo, the estate of A. I. Musin-Pushkin.
Beneath it is a grotto constructed at the end of the nineteenth century.

largely because of Catherine's victories over the Turks, which she commemorated with a pavilion in the style of a Turkish mosque for Tsarskoe Selo. The Chernyshevs' Yaropolets, near Moscow, had a similar mosque-pavilion with two minarets dedicated to the Treaty of Kuchuk-Kainardzhi. A bas-relief Genoese sculpture of Christ, which Field Marshal Yury V. Dolgoruky had removed from the city gates of Cathay, graced another monument in the Yaropolets garden.[28]

In 1782 Abbé Jacques Delille, in his widely read and very influential poem "Les Jardins, ou l'art d'embellir les paysages," warned against an excess of exotic garden structures:

Their use I grant, but be it not abus'd;
Far from the garden cast that heap confus'd
. . . .
Kiosk, pagoda, obelisk and dome,
Drawn from Arabia, China, Greece and Rome,
In one small spot, profusely-barren, hurl'd
Each quarter of the wide-extended world.
There should no idle ornament be seen,
But each delight should wear an useful mein.[29]

In their fascination with the garden of artifice, Russians tended to disregard this advice, seeking out the exotic. Tombs in the garden added an air of poetic melancholy.

Cameron's pyramid tombs at Tsarskoe Selo for Catherine's favorite greyhounds were early examples of this fashion in Russia.[30] One of Lvov's pyramidal tombs, constructed of unhewn boulders, still exists at Mitino, in Tver Province. Not to be outdone, Bolotov scrupulously designed a "so-called melancholy scene" for Bogoroditsk. From a winding path the visitor gazed down upon a small overgrown clearing, in the middle of which stood, "on a small hillock, a black pyramid, with white inscriptions on it, looking like some sort of tombstone."[31] At the Chernyshevs' Yaropolets a number of marble tombs with mysterious Arabic inscriptions were scattered randomly about the garden, a gift from Dolgoruky, who had brought back a whole Turkish cemetery as war booty, part of which he placed in the garden of his own estate, Znamenskoe-Gubailovo. Family mausoleums also contributed to the park atmosphere. The grandiose mausoleum at Sukhanovo (fig. 73), flanked by family tombs, stood in the section of the park devoted to ancient memories. In the same spirit the Goncharovs constructed a handsome mausoleum in their Yaropolets park honoring their ancestor Peter D. Doroshenko, a seventeenth-century Cossack hetman. Legend has it that their new son-in-law Alexander Pushkin provided the idea.

As has been mentioned, pseudo-Gothic outbuildings such as stables (fig. 74), quarters for house serfs, and orangeries introduced another exotic and picturesque element. Contrived ruins in the park were another dramatic

73. The Volkonsky family mausoleum (1813) at Sukhanovo. Designed by D. I. Zhiliardi or A. G. Grigoriev.

touch. Bolotov painted a rock scree more than one hundred feet long and visible from the main road to Bogoroditsk, creating the illusion of a ruined monastery complete with towers and windows.[32] Ruined arches over garden drives or ruined columns were even easier to create and remained popular well into the first half of the nineteenth century. An 1840 painting by P. A. Gerasimov of Meshcherskoe, in Moscow Province, suggests the ruined Gothic folly of many an English park.

Although such ruins in the later period added a romantic note to the park, Bolotov's trompe l'oeil monastery seems more related to the spirit of play and surprise that characterized the most impressive pleasure gardens in the 1770s and 1780s. These gardens marked a transition in style from the baroque to the romantic. However naturalized in their landscaping and plantings, they retained playful elements that in England had been eliminated by the late eighteenth century. The renowned garden of Kuskovo sported a "fire-breathing dragon" and shams (see fig. 103): life-size and lifelike painted wooden depictions of Spanish cavaliers and French peasant girls, intended to surprise visitors walking through the birch grove.[33] At Bogoroditsk, Bolotovdesigned a grassy hillock surrounded by a moat. Visitors who ascended the artificial hill found themselves trapped when water suddenly gushed out from a hidden

74. The stables at D. I. Buturlin's Marinka, designed in the 1780s, possibly by Vasily Bazhenov.

reservoir. A "rescue" was effected when a servant lowered a drawbridge.[34]

By the end of the century Bolotov's articles were being overtaken by a number of translated and original works. These broadened the market for the English garden beyond his provincial readers and provided precise instructions on how to create it.[35] In 1792 the *Universal Gardener, or Detailed Dictionary for Rural Amateurs and Lovers of Botanical Pleasure Gardening* was published in St. Petersburg, followed by N. P. Osipov's *New and Complete Russian Gardener* the next year. Lvov's project for an elaborate allegorical park for Count Bezborodko's estate on the Yauza River was published in 1799, as was a *Collection of New Thoughts for the Decoration of Gardens and Dachas in the English, Gothic, and Chinese Style* (published simultaneously in English, French, and Russian in Leipzig and Moscow). All these works were lavishly illustrated. *The Universal Gardener*, for instance, offered three or four variants for each particular concept, such as a temple, grotto, or pavilion. The landowner need only select the preferred model for his architect to copy (figs. 75, 76, 77).

The republication in 1818, almost twenty years later, of I. Lem's *Sketch of Various Buildings of Ancient and Modern Times, such as Temples, Houses, Gardens, Statues, Trophies, Obelisks, Pyramids, and Other Decorations* indicates the continuing importance of the European model for Russian landscaping. This work possibly provided inspiration for the allegorical elements of Fyodor Melnikov's plan for an English garden at Ostafievo. This design, done in 1821, softened and romanticized the previously rather formal setting of the house. In front of the house, a large semicircle with a straight drive along the facade was to be broken up to make room for two asymmetrical parterres that flanked a circular approach to the main entrance. Behind the house, on the garden side, paths were to be made more irregular, open spaces enlarged, and a whole panoply of evocative outbuildings and statues added. The extant large formal garden was to be demol-

75. The Temple of Venus (early nineteenth century) above the lake at Sukhanovo.

ished. Melnikov envisioned an oval lawn, dotted with a few isolated trees and a statue of Flora, extending from the park facade; to the right and left, asymmetrically placed, two circular beds of summer flowers were to be planted, but "without statues." Beyond the central lawn would stretch the "Field of Mars," with a statue of Hercules. A

95

76. The rotunda "Milovida" at Marfino, an unusual octagonal design with a Doric colonnade inside the lower part and a statue of Apollo above. Attributed to N. A. Lvov.

extreme of the park a new pavilion would be erected. Up to this point Melnikov's plan harmonized well with the iconography of the European romantic garden, as did his suggestion for a "ruin, of destroyed Athens or Rome" midway along the return circuit to the house.

By the first decades of the nineteenth century, the Russian aristocracy's impetus for a more romantic, less contrived look in gardening had undoubtedly been stimulated by European art and literature, such as the paintings of Hubert Robert or Jean-Jacques Rousseau's descriptions of nature in *Julie, ou la nouvelle Héloïse.* Melnikov's plan suggests some general changes in landscape architecture throughout Russia that coincided with the apogee of Russian classicism in architecture in the first third of the nineteenth century.[36] Embodying the new romantic attitude toward nature, these alterations tended to make park design more informal. The ceremonial drive from gate to house, for instance, became a meandering way parallel to the house facade rather than an imposing straight avenue perpendicular to the main entrance. Parterres shrank. The picturesque became the overwhelming consideration in landscape design. The park ceased to be a stage set for the house, which was now more naturally integrated into the landscape.

Yet in Russia these changes did not amount to a total surrender to the romantic impulse. Melnikov's plan called for a pleasure grove (complete with games or tricks to surprise the visitor) within the triangle formed by the Oracle of Delphi, the pavilion at the other extreme of the park, and the lower end of the woods. For this landscaper, at least, the playful elements of the eighteenth-century garden had not been entirely subsumed in the quest for romantic intimacy and the picturesque as they had in England. Perhaps for this reason Vyazemsky, romantic poet par excellence, never executed Melnikov's plan.

This difference from the European pattern suggests that for the Russian aristocracy life in the countryside was still not entirely "natural" and that their attitude toward it

dense woods would border the right side of this field. Beyond the woods, winding along the shore of the main pond of the estate, Melnikov traced a path for the philosophical wanderer that would lead to the grotto and, beyond it, to the Oracle of Delphi at the end of the park. At the opposite

differed from that of the English. As we know, Alexander Kurakin tried to liken his enforced exile to Nadezhdino to the spiritually refreshing, voluntary interlude that a Roman senator might seek at his country villa. Yet as soon as he could, Kurakin hastened back to Petersburg and civilization. (Within a few years Nadezhdino's gazebos and pavilions were being used as pigsties and the park as a pasture, as Kurakin's angry correspondence with his steward reveals.) The court aristocracy and, indeed, any family with sufficient means to support a major residence in either St. Petersburg or Moscow looked upon the country estate as essentially a summer residence and source of winter supplies, though by the 1820s some families were spending longer periods there. The aristocrat's experience of country life was therefore vastly different from that of the typical permanent resident, whether a noble of modest means or an individual who had been compelled by economic misfortune to live in the country. Pushkin succinctly portrays this contrast in "The Shot." The narrator, languishing on his modest country estate, hears exciting news: a wealthy countess is coming to visit a neighboring estate that she owns but has seen only once before, the first

77. Pavilion on an island in the lake at Bykovo. Attributed to Vasily Bazhenov, it is an outstanding example of late eighteenth-century Russian garden architecture.

year of her marriage. "The arrival of a wealthy neighbor," he writes, "is an important event for country dwellers. Landowners and their house servants talk about it for two months beforehand and three years afterwards."[37]

Those banished to estates or forced by economic misfortune to live there often shared this narrator's attitude of superiority to ordinary provincials. But the early nineteenth century also marks the appearance of increasing numbers of well-to-do landowners who were voluntarily spending most of their time in the provinces, who had created European surroundings for themselves in the Russian countryside, and who were thoroughly Anglophile in their habits. Natalya Grot says that her wealthy uncle had an "exquisite garden" at his estate, comparable to the "most cultivated refuges of Europe," and characterizes him as a "confirmed Anglomaniac."[38] Such men played billiards and whist and enjoyed their elegant parks and stocked fishing ponds. They also hunted avidly, boated, and swam. In a word, they aspired to the healthy, active, outdoor life of the English gentry, to which the natural estate park was well suited.

But for the Russian landowner there were dangers and anomalies in the English model. Later in his story "Mistress into Maid," Pushkin points out that Muromsky's Anglophilia was not exhausted by his English garden. "His riders were dressed like English jockeys. His daughter had an English governess. His fields were worked according to the English method: 'but Russian grain does not grow according to a foreign system.'"[39] Most landowners (including Pushkin's family and neighbors) had heavily mortgaged estates partially because of the craze for expensive pavilions or follies. Neoclassical temples or Gothic ruins in England, moreover, even if recently constructed, connected the garden to a specific and native cultural past, to Roman or medieval Britain. In the Russian context such self-conscious gestures were doubly foreign. Certain aspects of landscaping in England, even if romanticized, provided a link with the true rural population, the peasantry.

A hermitage might be designed as a woodsman's hut or shepherd's thatched cottage. The ha-ha, which separated the estate park from surrounding fields by a depression so unnoticeable that it provoked an exclamation of surprise, expressed the ease that the English lord felt with his rural neighbors. In England far more than in Russia, peasant villages were part of the estate; they might be moved or redesigned (as was the entire village of Milton Abbas, first by Sir William Chambers, then by Capability Brown) to become part of a picturesque setting.[40]

Russian owners of large estates often copied foreign ruins but rarely sentimentalized Russian rural life in their gardens. In fact, they cut themselves off from it by physical barriers which, inevitably, created psychological boundaries as well (fig. 78). Throughout rural Russia today, along with lakes or ponds and the remains of decorative walls, one can see traces of *vali*, the sometimes sizable earthen ramparts that customarily surrounded the estate's pleasure grounds. Only house serfs in European dress and exotic animals such as llamas were freely admitted into the territory within these boundary markers. Although the peasant fields, villages, and forests across the water or beyond the boundaries remained part of the estate landscape, the vali, like the ponds, were physical reminders of the divide between the Europeanized owner in his idealized setting and his Russian serfs in their villages. Serf labor alone had made the creation of these often elaborate estate parks possible, yet in Pushkin's time little reminder of the real rural Russia existed within the park. Even the few birch-log cottages and *fermes ornées* inspired by Catherinian models were so idealized as to increase, not lessen, the distance from the village.

By contrast, in the smaller country gardens of provincial nobles such as Pushkin's fictional Larins, the absence

78. The Russian Gothic bridge and colonnade spanning the lake at the main approach to Marfino, designed by M. D. Bykovsky in the 1830s.

of foreign elements and the more intimate scale prompted an emotional immediacy to nature that fit the romantic mood. Pushkin's sensitivity to this, coupled with his own experience, leads him to emphasize contrasting responses to nature in his story of the provincial miss and Petersburg dandy. He begins by stressing the difference between Onegin's boredom in the country and Tatyana's identification with her surroundings. As narrator, Pushkin seems to side with Tatyana: "The village where Eugene was bored was an enchanting nook." Elsewhere Pushkin expresses his own apparent love of the countryside. "I was born . . . for rural tranquility. . . . Meadows! My soul is devoted to you," he exclaims, underscoring the difference between Onegin and himself. Tatyana's lengthy adieu to hills, forests, and nature itself as she leaves for Moscow gives Pushkin an opportunity to show his heroine at one with nature, talking to groves and meadows "as with old friends."[41]

Tatyana's and Eugene's gardens are texts for their psyches. Pushkin reads in Tatyana's garden the attributes of his heroine: its simplicity and intimacy, the meadows and lawns (open spaces from which nature can be perceived), woods and fragrant bushes (which create a sensory immediacy), make this garden the mirror of the poetic, emotional, and natural Tatyana. Onegin's lack of response to nature as a representative of the *grand monde* is clear from the moment he arrives at the charming, old-fashioned country house, perched on a hillside above a stream. In contrast to Tatyana's intimate and beloved retreat, Onegin's garden is "huge, overgrown." As the "refuge of pensive dryads" it has romantic qualities that our author notes but that the new owner entirely ignores, as he does the garden itself. After a mere two days, Pushkin tells his readers, Eugene lost interest in the view of fields and the "gurgling of the quiet stream"; by the third, "groves, hills, and streams occupied him no longer." If he had any regrets at leaving the countryside, we do not learn of them. After his departure the educated, even bookish Tatyana, trying to fathom Onegin's character, feels she must read the text

of his surroundings: "I will look at the house, at this garden."[42] Appropriately, Tatyana finds clues to Eugene's character in his books, but not in the neglected garden.

The polar opposition of responses to gardens and the Russian countryside in *Eugene Onegin*, for all its ironic overtones, highlights the cultural problem that the English garden personified: how could, or should, an educated, Europeanized Russian relate to rural Russia? Some Russian aficionados were defensive about the fact that the English garden in which they delighted could be made to appear natural but was clearly not native. As we have seen, Bolotov did not even like the term *English*, in spite of his passion for the style. In one of his first articles on the irregular garden, he had (somewhat mysteriously) warned fellow landowners that it was, in some respects, unsuitable for Russian "moral characteristics" and advised them to avoid blind imitation, to make their gardens truly their own.[43]

By Pushkin's time the English garden had for some time contributed to estate culture by providing wealthy nobles like Pushkin's friend Prince Vyazemsky with a whole new raison d'être, an escape from superfluity in the model of the English gentleman farmer continuously relandscaping his world. Yet, like Bolotov, Pushkin had reservations about noble Anglomania. We also know that his own mood in the country alternated between boredom (an acute sense of exile that he ascribes to some of his narrators and protagonists) and true romantic rapture with nature, which makes it hard to distinguish those attitudes in his writing truly identifiable with his own.[44] As author of *Eugene Onegin* Pushkin may distance himself from Eugene's Byronic ennui in the country, but elsewhere his fulsome praise or overblown images of nature hint at mixed emotions and a possible preference for something more civilized.

Consider, for instance, Pushkin's description of Lensky's final resting place, which is a lexicon of romantic symbols. The sophisticated courtier Kurakin, one recalls, had boasted of the absence of pines and birches, the trees most evocative of the Russian countryside, from his "*jardin délicieux.*" Pushkin himself proposed a fittingly stylish mausoleum for Doroshenko in the elegant Yaropolets park. Yet the grave of Lensky, the ardent (and wealthy) noble

79. A bower bench at Pushkin's Mikhailovskoe.

young poet, is to be found between two ancient pines near a peasant village, a natural, romantic setting in which it is almost indistinguishable from its surroundings. Marked by a simple stone, the grave lies by the edge of a stream. Although once, Pushkin hazards, friends might have met in moonlight to weep together over the grave, now it is all but forgotten, its sole visitor a grizzled shepherd who sits on the stone and sings while weaving his bast sandals.

The images of Tatyana's garden in the context of *Eugene Onegin* are strikingly unequivocal by comparison. They seem meant to evoke, however briefly, the immediate relationship with nature that romanticism demanded, and through this immediacy to suggest the genuine harmony with rural Russia to which generations of Russian intellectuals would aspire (fig. 79). It is hardly surprising that Pushkin and his contemporaries were on the whole more at home in the isolated, often theatrical, and ultimately foreign English garden of the grandee than in a Russian village. Certainly Pushkin was aware of the difference between the two. But for others of his generation the physical separation of the grand estate from rural reality, and the romantic perception of nature through the prism of the huge, artificially natural garden of the country house may have produced a psychological distancing from, or an idyllic myopia toward, their real surroundings, a distancing that was ultimately of some consequence. It was this sort of myopia, for instance, that allowed the Slavophile of the 1830s to feel at one with rural Russia and its inhabitants while, in fact, observing them from a safe distance.

4

A Private Princedom

THE HOUSEHOLD AND ITS PASTIMES

It is really astonishing, but the number of servants is dreadful. Think of 200, 300, and often

400 servants to attend a small family. A Russian Lady scorns to use her own feet to go upstairs,

and I do not Romance when I assure you that two Powdered footmen support her lily

white elbows and nearly lift her from the ground, while a couple more follow

with all manner of Shawls, Pelises, etc. . . . If a fair one gently calls, four or five footmen are ready

in an antechamber to obey her summons.—**Martha Wilmot**

A WEALTHY RUSSIAN LANDOWNER'S COUNTRY estate was a small kingdom. During its golden age the country estate closely resembled Sir Henry Wotton's description, a century earlier, of "Every Man's proper Mansion House" as "the Theatre of his Hospitality, the Seat of Self-Fruition . . . a kind of Private Princedom, nay, to the Possessors thereof, an Epitomy of the Whole World."[1] This princedom included an enormous number of people. Aside from the aristocrat's immediate and extended family, there were numerous house serfs and their families, professionals of various kinds (architects, doctors, tutors, governesses, and dancing, singing, riding, and drawing masters), serf entertainers, and a number of other individuals who, sometimes understandably, sometimes mysteriously, ended up living with the family for an extended period.

Household Serfs

The sheer mass of the estate household would strain modern credulity were it not for the consistency with which the figures are confirmed in documents of the period. In 1804 Catherine Wilmot's maid, Eleanor Cavanaugh, wrote her father from Princess Dashkova's Troitskoe: "There is 200 servants that lives in & out of the House."[2] When Ellen Southey Poltoratsky arrived at her husband's estate Avchurino, not far from Troitskoe, almost half a century later, she found no fewer than forty "inmates: impoverished male and female cousins, neighbors fallen on lean days, pensioned-off agents, doctors, tutors, and governesses" awaiting her on the steps of the mansion. Behind them was massed an enormous crowd of servants. Elizaveta Yankova termed two hundred servants "normal" for a well-to-do household. This is echoed in Turgenev's story "The Estate Office," when the clerk on duty says that his mistress has "not so many" house serfs, only "about a hundred and fifty or so."[3] The numbers tended to swell over the years, as faithful servants retired but were retained and others married and had children.

The Russian grandee felt a patriarchal obligation toward his house serfs, who unlike his village peasants were entirely dependent on him for room, board, and clothing. Kirill Razumovsky said of his staff, "I don't need them, but ask them if they need me." When Alexei Kurakin disapproved of his brother Alexander's "superfluity of servants" at Nadezhdino, Alexander retorted, "It is much easier, my friend, to talk than to act: if you could be here, I'd find it very interesting to see who of this number you would dismiss, and what form and style of life you'd suggest for me."[4] Shortly thereafter, the tables were turned on Alexei. His parents and brothers died, and he inherited their staffs, including his brother Stepan's choir (reputedly the best in Moscow). By 1820, eight hundred house servants and their dependents were living at Kurakino; an entire new village was built for them. Supporting the superannuated retainers and their families was an inherited obligation, but Kurakin did not dismiss any of the others. Some were useful in running his estate, others were decorative and appropriate to his status, and the extra singers and musicians he kept for his enjoyment.[5]

Although this was an extraordinary situation, the overabundance of house serfs explains their extraordinarily specific responsibilities. More than one landowner had a man who was responsible solely for holding his pipe and giving it to him to smoke; one mistress kept maids who were each in charge of one particular garment; many retained special cooks for the annual duty of making pancakes at Shrovetide. This bewildering swarm (as foreigners perceived it) customarily occupied separate male and female servants' wings and had their own kitchen or kitchens, cooking and laundry staff, and bathhouse.

The entire household staff of Russia's wealthiest families was diversified by function and status. The family's numerous offspring had their own retinue. Wet nurses from the village, distinguished from other servants by their traditional Russian dress, tended infants. In addition, there were *nyanyas* and *dyadkas* (female and male nannies) for young children, and governesses, tutors, and art and music teachers for older children (fig. 80). The adults required ladies' maids and valets, hairdressers, scribes, tailors and dressmakers, architects and artists. Personal attendants included decorative pages, lackeys, and the costumed three-man "bouquet" that adorned an elegant carriage: a blackamoor and two tall footmen dressed as hussars or Cossacks. Key figures were the housekeeper, steward, butler, cellar keeper, and chamberlain, who supervised a staff of over one hundred lesser servants. In addition a very wealthy household might have as many as a hundred individuals who provided entertainment: dwarfs and fools, a choirmaster and singers, dancers, actors, and musicians.

At the bottom of the household hierarchy were the ordinary house serfs who cared for the household furnishings, did the laundry, and staffed the kitchen (fig. 81). A partial inventory of Razumovsky's staff at Baturin mentions three silver polishers, seventeen laundresses, eleven kitchen apprentices, two apprentice embroiderers, an apprentice baker, and an unspecified number of apprentices to the two confectioners. There were also scullery maids, window washers and furniture polishers, stove stokers and cleaners, and those young men who, as Alexander Dumas reported in astonishment, were to be found skating majestically across acres of parquet floors, buffing them to a high gloss with the felt pads on their feet. Above these invisible

80. Young Princess Elizaveta Golitsyna having tea with her governess at Dolzhik while the housekeeper and laundresses look on. (Courtesy of Mrs. E. Zinovieff)

81. The kitchen wing at Kuskovo.

helpers were servants with greater responsibilities, such as Baturin's "manager of the linens" and three chefs. The grounds and stable staff made up a separate group. At Baturin, Razumovsky had numerous gardeners, two surveyors and assistants, and over forty grooms, in addition to stable hands, huntsmen, kennel keepers, coachmen, and so forth.[6]

Above these were the personal attendants of the family, dressed in keeping with their positions. Martha Wilmot described Princess Dashkova's lackeys as "in general dress'd much like English Sailors, one or two in white linnen jacket and trowsers, but of a day that company is expected their liverys are Superb, all embroider'd with lace."[7] Some personal attendants had quarters near the person they served and uniquely privileged positions. The nanny was allotted her own apartment and in most instances was treated entirely as a member of the family. She was responsible for a child's upbringing until he or she began to be educated; her devotion, frequently to several generations of the same family, made her a much-loved figure, comparable to the fabled mammies of our Old South. Housekeepers and chamberlains, who managed the male and female servants under them, were likewise in positions of special trust, and often these positions were passed down from generation to generation.

Fools and dwarfs (fig. 82), maintained in many households as late as the 1840s, were a different privileged category. Anachronistic by contemporaneous Western stan-

105

82. Artist unknown. Portrait of Prince P. A. Rumyantsev-Zadunaisky's dwarf. 1840s. (*Stolitsa i usadba*, no. 57)

he passed by; amused, he sent her one hundred rubles. Matryoshka called her mistress "Lizanka" and took her to task for letting her large staff eat her out of house and home and steal from her. Said Matryoshka, "You think that you're the mistress because you sit there with folded arms and receive your guests: well, you're our servant, and we're your masters: you gather the dues from the peasants and give it to us, and nothing's left for you!" Another woman's fool, Polya (who walked around proudly in beaded slippers, one of which read "Polya," the other "Dura" [fool]), was devoted to her mistress and slept in her room. After the latter's death she was so disconsolate that a small hut was built for her at her mistress's favorite spot in the garden, and there she kept vigil until her own death. Yet a third, a male, was so beloved by his family that they outfitted him with his own horse and carriage. In Moscow he drove out, gaily costumed, to the promenades of the nobility, with garlands of flowers around his neck, and amused passersby with his loud renditions of sentimental folk songs. Fools were part of the owner's personal retinue: they ate at the master's table and traveled with the family. Because the position conferred special status, some house serfs sought it out. One memoirist recalls a house serf who came up with a specialty to ensure himself the job. His master would give him someone's name, and he would immediately invent a half-nonsense, half-clever string of words associated with it. Since this took some talent, the memoirist opines that the serf was probably more clever than those he amused.[8]

In the hierarchy of serfdom on the estate, house serfs were more exposed than were village peasants to an owner's vagaries. This may explain why, according to Martha Wilmot, "the Russ Peasants usually look upon it as a misfortune to have a child taken to the House of a Noble." Some occupied ambiguous or anomalous positions in the families that owned them (fig. 83). On a whim, a serf child might be taken from its parents and perhaps raised and educated with the master's children as a companion, only

dards, they played a role rather like that of the wandering *yurodivy*, or holy fools: they were permitted the most familiar treatment of their masters, and for their brashness petted and cosseted. Countess Elizaveta Orlova's fool, Matryoshka, paraded around heavily made up in cast-off finery that she begged from the countess's friends. Once she called out "Bonjour, mon cher!" to Emperor Alexander I as

to have nowhere to go as an adult. Shortly after Martha Wilmot arrived at Troitskoe, she was presented with eleven-year-old Pashinka as her own property! Pashinka cried the entire first week, despite "her fine Clothes, her dolls, etc. etc.," but she eventually got used to her new position.[9] Serf children who showed artistic talent were often identified at a young age and given special training. Some, despite their serf status, were on intimate terms with their noble patrons. Others suffered from capricious masters, who might turn on them and strip away their privileges or who refused to grant them freedom. Housemaids, considered fair game by males of the noble family, were bedded on a regular basis and often gave birth to illegitimate children who were sometimes raised and treated as nobles, sometimes not.

In life and in literature some of these unions ended in marriage. Vasily Davydov, a leader of the Decembrists' Southern Society, grew up at Kamenka, in Kiev Province, where his liaison with the serf girl Alexandra Potapova produced six illegitimate children. They were legally married after his disapproving mother's death, just before his arrest and exile, and had seven more children in Siberia. Fyodor Lavretsky, hero of Ivan Turgenev's *A Nest of Gentlefolk*, is the son of Ivan, a refined, wealthy noble, and the maid Malanya, "a very pretty girl with clear gentle eyes and delicate features. . . . She loved him as only Russian girls can love—and she yielded to his love."[10] Ivan marries Malanya, infuriating his father. (Then, in a gesture typical of Russian antiheroes, having played out his sense of duty, he abandons Malanya and "detestable country life" for St. Petersburg.)

A similar real-life union that took place at roughly the same time as this literary episode caused a notorious scandal. The secret marriage of Count Nikolai Petrovich Sheremetev, the wealthiest noble of his day, with the serf Praskovya Kovalyova (see fig. 109), the diva of Ostankino's operatic troupe, deserves a digression, because no better illustration of serfdom's anomalies exists. The marriage was the culmination of a lengthy liaison that undoubtedly resulted from Praskovya's unusual talents and upbringing. Born in 1768 to a blacksmith on the Sheremetevs' estate Berezino, in Yaroslav Province, she was taken into the Sheremetev household at the age of seven for special training. Praskovya became fluent in several European languages, studied music and voice, and soon had the makings of a star. She debuted on the Kuskovo stage at eleven and

83. Ivan Argunov. Portrait of Annyushka, the Kalmyk ward of Countess Varvara Sheremeteva, holding a portrait of her benefactor. 1767. (Courtesy of the Kuskovo Museum, Moscow)

became Kuskovo's leading operatic soprano, performing under her stage name Zhemchugova, or "The Pearl" (Sheremetev named all his divas after jewels).

When Nikolai Petrovich took over the troupe from his father in the 1780s, Praskovya became one of a pleiad of "girls in my house" (as Nikolai termed his stars in letters to his accountant) who were in constant attendance, traveling with him to St. Petersburg for the winter and back to Kuskovo in the summer. As Nikolai was a bachelor, the group may well have constituted a harem. Several times a year the girls received bonuses of 30 to 50 rubles; twice "The Emerald" was given an expensive jeweled necklace. By the late 1790s Nikolai clearly had a special interest in Praskovya. In December 1797 she received the largest Christmas bonus (250 rubles) of the seven girls in Petersburg. On September 10, 1799, Sheremetev ordered that "Parasha" receive annually 100 rubles' additional salary for "trifles such as slippers"; a month later, he ordered her salary raised by an additional 560 rubles.[11] At some point during this period she received her freedom.

Praskovya's marriage to Nikolai Sheremetev took place secretly at a small Moscow parish church early in 1801, shortly before Paul's assassination. The following year a son and legitimate heir was born; Praskovya, already weak from tuberculosis, never recovered from the birth and died early in 1803. A late portrait by the Sheremetevs' talented serf painter Nikolai Argunov (who knew Praskovya well), one of the most sensitive studies of Russian portraiture, shows her ill, with luminous sorrowful eyes, a sparkling miniature of her secret husband around her neck (fig. 84).

Nikolai Petrovich survived her by six years but ceased his theatrical activities entirely, either from grief or from his renewed role at court. One can imagine the difficulties this passionate union of unequals, both of whom were unwell, created. Praskovya's grandson Sergei wrote that she had to deal with enemies among the "innumerable people who constituted the domestic staff of a [wealthy] land-owner of that time."[12] Virtually no one would receive them, and apparently the deeply religious Praskovya never considered her earlier sinful relationship absolved by marriage. Before she died, she raised her husband's concern for the well-being of his serfs and was instrumental in the founding of the Sheremetev almshouse in Moscow. Some of Praskovya's serf friends achieved special status in her house, particularly her best friend, the ballerina Tatyana Shlykova (see fig. 110), known as "The Garnet," who became an intimate confidante of Praskovya's descendants. Sergei Sheremetev remembers visiting Shlykova at Ulyanka, their Petersburg dacha, where she occupied the rooms that had belonged to her former master, Nikolai Petrovich, and served her guests tea on blue English porcelain plates he had given her.[13] She also had her own apartments in the Sheremetev Petersburg mansion, on the embankment of the Fontanka River, as did other old retainers.

The Greater Household

Professionals formed an intermediate rung of the household hierarchy. Architects and artists (sometimes serfs, sometimes freemen), family doctors, tutors and governesses, dancing instructors and choirmasters, might all be present at the lower end of the dinner table, along with children. Most salaried dependents maintained a respectful distance even when they and their families lived with the noble family for many years; others were close confidants. V. A. Bakarev, an architect at Kurakino for eight years, had detailed knowledge of Alexei Kurakin's life and financial affairs. The talented Italian architect Camporesi lived at Olgovo, the Apraksin's suburban Moscow estate, until his death, designing buildings and acting as master of ceremonies for the Apraksins' lavish entertainments.

84. Nikolai Ivanovich Argunov. Portrait of Countess Praskovya Kovaleva Sheremeteva in a red shawl. 1801–02. (Kuskovo Museum, Moscow, Courtesy of Kyra Cheremeteff)

The pages of Russian novels and memoirs are sprinkled with the figures of superannuated tutors and governesses who customarily lived out their lives with the family of their pupils. Hence the bitterness of the German tutor in Tolstoy's *Childhood, Boyhood, and Youth* when he is dismissed, his charges having reached the age for formal education. After a touching scene with the old man, his master decides to change his mind. At Avchurino (figs. 85, 86) Ellen Poltoratsky found three pensioned-off English compatriots: a Mr. Jennings, who had been Sergei's father's agent, and two former governesses of her sister-in-law's children.

Such elderly individuals joined with others in the household to form a large indeterminate category of persons who were neither family members nor, properly speaking, household staff. This plethora of unaccounted-for household members imparted a medieval quality to the aristocratic estate. Nobles down on their luck simply moved in with a wealthy neighbor. Many poor provincial noblemen attached themselves to the "court" at Nadezhdino while Kurakin was there and stayed on after he had left. The term that memoirists most often use for such a person is *prizhivalets*, frequently translated as "hanger-on"; this accurately describes the financial dependency of

85. Sh. Rebu. *The Old House at Avchurino.* Watercolor. 1846. Rebu was the resident drawing master for the Poltoratskys. (Courtesy of the State Historical Museum, Moscow)

86. Watercolor by a niece of Ellen and Sergei Poltoratsky. The church at Avchurino.
The Poltoratsky family and peasants are shown leaving church after a service. 1840s.
(Courtesy of the State Historical Museum, Moscow)

such individuals but not their actual status in a wealthy household, regardless of how they came into it.

In literature this class of people is generally portrayed as pathetic, vulnerable, and humiliated, most strikingly in Turgenev's play *A Provincial Gentleman*, written in 1848. The main figure, an elderly gentleman taken in at the age of twenty by the father of the current mistress, is mocked by two coarse neighbors who try to force him to sing and act the fool, as, they assume, he had in the old days for his

benefactor. Memoirs offer quite a different picture, portraying the support of poor nobles as a widespread, customary form of private charity. Chances are a family would have been thought poor or stingy were not some extraneous people living at its expense. One memoirist has left a vivid account of two such men who lived with her family in her youth. She had no idea how either had come to be in the household, but each had his own quarters, both were treated with great respect, and one hunted with her father.[14] Wealthy landowners often supported a number of young people who were, in effect, wards, perhaps indigent young noblemen or noblewomen or the illegitimate offspring of a relative. The father of the memoirist M. S. Nikoleva, for example, took in Elizaveta Eismond, the daughter of the steward of a neighboring estate, who lived with them for many years and studied with the daughters of the family.[15]

Patterns of Residence

In the late eighteenth century, for much of the year most grand Russian estates were sparsely furnished and uninhabited save for a skeletal staff of servants. When the family arrived from the city in late spring or early summer, the house came to life. Smartly liveried lackeys, their hair powdered and the family crest on their buttons, and well-dressed maids stood at attention in the reception rooms or waited elsewhere to respond to the summons of a bellpull. Other servants moved invisibly through the house, eschewing the parade enfilade and grand staircase for the narrow service corridors and circular staircases that allowed them to pass unnoticed from service to reception or living areas. In the autumn at least half the house was shut up—even when a family stayed on into the winter. A large portion of the household, including the upper levels of servants—personal maids and valets, cooks, and agents, as well as some of the extraneous dependents who served as companions—moved with the family back and forth between city and country, along with much of the furniture.

Staff members likewise accompanied noble landowners on business trips. Alexei Kurakin, a high government official at the turn of the nineteenth century (he served as procurator general under Paul I, as governor-general of Little Russia, and then as minister of the interior under Alexander I), traveled between Kurakino, south of Orel, and St. Petersburg several times a year, accompanied by his staff. Nikolai Sheremetev also traveled frequently from Moscow to St. Petersburg and back, taking his household with him.

As the nineteenth century progressed, the residency pattern reversed itself to some extent: a number of wealthy families began spending most of the year on their estates rather than in the city. The Poltoratsky routine in the 1840s illustrates this shift from the earlier pattern of exclusively summer occupancy. During the eighteen years Ellen Southey Poltoratsky spent in Russia (1842–60), she lived mostly at her husband's estate Avchurino, on the Oka River, south of Moscow. Almost every year, however, she made a trip to Moscow, St. Petersburg, or one of her husband's several other estates. Her husband, Sergei, spent much time away from Avchurino on business but considered it home nonetheless.

The Russian aristocrat has been likened to a stockholder with a diversified portfolio. Very wealthy families usually owned estates in three or more provinces, city mansions in St. Petersburg and Moscow, and sometimes houses in provincial capitals as well. In many cases they developed an attachment to, and preference for, a particular estate and would occupy this one regularly, usually during the summer and fall, but sometimes year-round, while their others remained empty.

Allegiances changed with generations, and with them, estate occupancy. Vodolagi, for example, the Dunin family estate in Kharkov Province, was visited by Alexander I and for one generation was brimful of the activities of a large, bustling family in permanent residence. After the death of the strong-willed matriarch who had presided over this household, the land was divided up among her heirs and the house left unoccupied. Other grand provincial houses, among them Alexander Kurakin's Nadezhdino, the Stroganovs' Khoten, and the Griboedovs' Khmelita, were similarly abandoned, either because the heirs preferred city life or were enmeshed in debt or discord.

The well-documented history of Sheremetev preferences among their many estates can serve as an example. Sergei Sheremetev claims that his father, Dmitry, son of Nikolai and Praskovya, "never especially liked Kuskovo." At one point in his life Dmitry "fell in love with Ostankino," but the family spent most summers at their Petersburg dacha Ulyanka, leaving Kuskovo virtually abandoned. Dmitry's first wife brought it briefly back to life in the mid-1840s, but after her death there, the family never returned.[16] At the end of the nineteenth century Mikhailovskoe, the estate where Sergei's mother had grown up, had become the family estate of this branch of the Sheremetevs, as Pokrovskoe was for the descendants of Nikolai Petrovich's brother Vasily, or Bolshye Vyazemy for one branch of the Golitsyns. Thus, to say that the Russian aristocrat had the mentality of an absentee landowner distorts the picture. The small number of very wealthy individuals who owned over half of Russia's serfs may have had little or no contact with most of their peasants, but they did have personal links to the serf population of the estate where they preferred to live, particularly to the household staff.

Daily Life

The letters and journals of Martha and Catherine Wilmot, written between 1803 and 1808, provide a detailed picture of life on these estates. The Wilmots were related to Princess Catherine Dashkova's great friend Mrs. Hamilton, who suggested that Martha (fig. 87) visit Dashkova (fig. 88) at her estate Troitskoe, south of Moscow. Dashkova, estranged from her daughter, took an immediate and lasting fancy to Martha (whose portrait she had painted no fewer than seven times!), showered her with attention and presents, and would not hear of her leaving. Martha spent five years (1803–08) in Russia, and her sister two (1805–07). The Wilmots spent portions of both winter and summer at Troitskoe and accompanied the princess when she traveled.

87. Artist unknown. Portrait of Martha Wilmot, painted in Russia during the first decade of the nineteenth century. (Wilmot and Wilmot, *The Russian Journals of Martha and Catherine Wilmot*, frontispiece)

Troitskoe was evidently a magnificent mansion, purportedly built to Dashkova's design and even with her participation. It is poetically described as "a sprig of Lily of the Valley, that is, the white stucco'd House is shaded with a dark spreading Forest of seven miles breadth." In a letter to

88. D. Levitsky. Portrait of Princess Dashkova. The princess gave this portrait to the Wilmot sisters as a keepsake. (Courtesy of the Hillwood Museum, Washington, D.C.)

for it is really magnificent. . . . The floors are all inlaid with different Colour'd Wood as is most of the Furniture. Now pass into the 2nd Drawing room, 'tis lovely! . . . Never mind the Suite of Rooms which follow, they are only Bed Chambers. But 'tis worth while going upstairs again to the Library which contains I know not how many thousand volumes in half a dozen languages. . . . The room commands a view of all the encircling Country and is supported by pillars each of which is in itself a little Library. Upstairs again is the Apothecary's Hall etc. etc.[17]

Around the manor house was a "little town" of buildings: a theater, a riding school, an infirmary, the stables, the steward's house, a guest house, a building for "a gigantic English Bull," four houses for servants, and a "Bath Establishment in the Shrubbery" (figs. 89, 90, 91). The Wilmots had their own apartments in a detached wing of the huge house. Catherine Wilmot noted that there was a "system of each person having a seperate [sic] little establishment," run by chambermaids who were in charge of the provisions for each: these included not only personal bedding but "saucepans, candles, candlesticks, tea and coffee. . . . I might lock my Castle door . . . and . . . have provisions to keep the Citadel a week in flourishing health."[18] In 1807 Martha's "establishment" consisted of four or five rooms.

Troitskoe's elegant and extensive appointments were hardly unique, for Catherine's grandees (among whom one must count Dashkova, though she was out of favor during much of the reign) had built extensively south of Moscow. Mikhail N. Krechetnikov, appointed viceroy of Tula and Kaluga, erected Mikhailovskoe on the Pakhra River between 1776 and 1784. Bolotov described it as a palace "practically identical to our Bogoroditsk." He wrote: "[Krechetnikov] lived there like an English lord. . . . Behind the house was a regular garden with a multitude of gazebos and various little houses, and before the house a

her sister Alice, Catherine Wilmot invited her on an imaginary tour of the interior.

I don't believe I ever walk'd you up stairs! Whisk the tail of your gown then, again, over your Shoulders and ascend these stone stairs. At the top of the 2d flight turn to your left into the Antechamber. Those are all the old pictures of the House of Daschkaw & Worontzow. Now enter into the Drawing room, or rather public looking Ball room,

89. The priest's house at Sukhanovo, remodeled in this neo-Gothic style by M. D. Bykovsky in the 1820s.

90. The male servants' quarters at Aleksino, the Baryshnikov estate. An identical building for female servants faces it. (Author)

broad expanse with several ponds, and beyond them I saw the Pakhra River, and beyond it and on both sides a handsome forest and groves."[19]

For all their elegance these mansions could be surprisingly comfortable, as the Wilmots found Troitskoe. In winter the large stoves in the corners of each room, stoked and lit early in the morning (fig. 92), offered more heat than a fireplace and retained it well after midnight; the double-paned windows and thick walls also kept out the cold. Shortly after Catherine arrived, the Wilmots awoke one day to find a crew of twenty men building a temporary covered walkway from their wing to the main house for their convenience in winter. At Troitskoe and in Moscow as well "a bearded Slave but more frequently a well powder'd Lackey" walked around with a charcoal censer (made in Tula) that burned perfume to freshen the air. In summer the Wilmots were well supplied with ice from the princess's icehouse, stocked each winter with large blocks cut from the river. Martha wrote home that "the weather is scorching, but there are contrivances for cooling as well as

91. Eighteenth-century neo-Gothic servants' quarters at the Golitsyns' Petrovskoe.

Au petit jour en hiver.

92. Mariamna Davydova. Stoking the stove in a bedroom at Matussov. Watercolor. 1920s.
(Courtesy of Alona Vassiloff)

heating the rooms, and we eat Ice whenever we chuse."[20] During hot spells, windows and doors were opened wide. There being no screens, paintings and other gilt-painted furnishings were shrouded in gauze and beds were covered with netting to keep off flies.

In winter Martha Wilmot's day began when a maid arrived with a chunk of ice for her morning ablutions. Scrubbing her face with ice, she opined, was intended to produce the rosy cheeks obligatory for Russian women, which otherwise would have to be painted on. At 9:00 A.M. they assembled for coffee; at 1:30 or 2:00 the dinner bell summoned them to a lengthy meal; tea was at 6:00; and a "prodigious hot supper" was presented at 9:30 or 10:00 in the evening (fig. 93). Dashkova, the Wilmots tell us, prided herself "on the produce of her Farm, Dairy, Gardens, Hot Houses, Pineries," and a bewildering array of dishes was daily set before them.

Honey with fresh Cucumbers is a favorite dish, preserved Dates, Apple bread, young Pig & Cold Cream, Egg Paties eat [*sic*] with soup, another Soup made of Fish, & every sort of Sallad. . . . With your roasted meat you must eat Salt Cucumbers, & then Caviare made of the roe of Sturgeon. Fish soup do you chuse? Fowls? Game? Vegetables? raw Apples from the Crimea? or the Siberian Apples? or the transparent Apples? or the Kieff sweetmeat? or honey comb? or preserved rose leaves, or pickled plums? In the name of goodness eat no more, for in six or seven hours you will have to sit down to just such another dinner under the name of Supper![21]

The Wilmots spent their mornings informally. "What with lounging or talking or music or walking most frequently a couple of hours are spent Lord knows how!" Wintertime troika excursions into the snowy forest brought them face to face with "Wood cutters who look like Satyrs . . . & whose endless Beards, clogg'd in snow and lengthen'd by icicles, crackle in responsive measure to their Hatchets'

93. K. A. Trutkovsky. *Postprandial Repose.* 1840s. The old housekeeper, butler, and other servants on an anonymous estate are depicted resting after dinner. (*Stolitsa i usadba,* no. 35)

117

strokes." Princess Dashkova, although old and infirm, was endlessly active. "She helps the masons to build walls, she assists with her own hands in making the roads, she feeds the cows, she composes music, she shells the corn . . . she is a Doctor, an Apothecary, a Surgeon, a Farrier, a Carpenter, a Magestrate, a Lawyer." Summertime brought early-morning swims in the river and walks through the extensive park. Martha often set off for a "little Chinese Temple," her face covered with gauze netting to ward off the "swarms of Gnats and Wasps."[22]

Bolotov observed a similar daily pattern (which he confidently describes as English) during a weekend he spent at Krechetnikov's Mikhailovskoe in 1784: "Numerous other guests came, and all of them and I spent the day as is done in England. In the morning we all gathered to drink tea with him; at the same time a large round table was placed in the hall for breakfast, and here we drank tea. Then, up to dinner we were free to walk and promenade where we wanted to and do what we wanted. And when a bell rang to let us know that the dinner table was ready, all hastened to it and were rewarded with a copious and elegant dinner." Like the Wilmots at Troitskoe, Krechetnikov's guests spent much time touring his park, which Bolotov, the expert, naturally considered inferior. "After dinner we spent the rest of our time in uninterrupted promenading together along the ponds and through the groves, went across the river, and there, in a tent which had been erected, drank tea. Then we rode with him to his paper factory, walked through his insignificant English garden and so forth. In a word, we spent this whole day in satisfaction."[23]

On all estates this routine was punctuated by celebrations and excursions. On December 4, 1805, Princess Dashkova celebrated her name day jointly with Catherine Wilmot, commencing with a solemn mass said in the great hall. "After this Ceremony was ended everybody of every description press'd forward to offer their Congratulations and presents. Peasants in tribes lined the Hall, each with a large loaf of Bread cover'd over with a heap of Salt which they offer'd as their homage and some a little plate of Apples to enhance the tribute."[24] The following day there was a church service, followed by a "great Dinner" accompanied by much champagne and numerous toasts, music, and card playing. The guests departed late the next afternoon. For Christmas the household traveled to Moscow for an exhausting round of parties; in the summer they traveled there again on business and at the end of August set out for the venerable St. Sergei-Trinity Monastery, northeast of Moscow, and points beyond.

Travel

The Wilmots were amazed by the caravan that accompanied the princess on these trips, by accommodations en route, and by the Russian roads. In July 1804 Martha Wilmot and the princess set out for Dashkova's estate Krugloe in Poland, accompanied by five maids, fourteen male servants, twenty-seven horses, and three dogs. Ahead of them traveled the kitchen, with the butler, two cooks, and the food. "[The kitchen] sets forward an hour before the rest to prepare, to find a shelter, light a fire to dress dinner which is afterwards serv'd on silver dishes with plates, spoons, wine Glasses etc. . . . So compleat a service and so clever for the purpose I cou'd not have conceiv'd, for it is all pack'd into a Trunk of very small dimensions, and yet the service is large enough for six or seven people with all the elegance of a feast."[25] Two baggage carts followed the kitchen, one with "a trunk which when open'd becomes a Bedstead in which is found Bed, Pillows and every comfort to court Sleep." The three passenger carriages consisted of an English coach, a *lineika* ("a sort of long Jaunting Carr for six people on four wheels with a top like the roof of a coach and a sort of petticoat to keep off rain"), and a calèche. The Wilmots described another traveling coach, the *kibitka*, as "a large Cradle, in which three or four people lie or sit with great ease." Winter travel was often easier, for sleigh runners replaced carriage wheels, and frozen riverbeds became roads. But Catherine Wilmot wrote of one winter trip from Moscow to Troitskoe, in a caravan of eight conveyances, as a nightmare owing to the "rocks of frozen and refrozen snow over which you must drive. . . . In these dreadful holes one is sometimes rooted for 20 minutes at a time, the miserable Horses falling with the exertion of pulling one out & lashed up again & again by dozens of People & servants who aid in supporting either side of the Carriage."[26] En route, the princess and her companions often stayed in the houses of other nobles. On one occasion, however, no accommodations being available, her men unfurled a tent Martha found most magnificent. On another night they slept in their carriage.

By 1803, when Martha arrived in Russia, Princess Dashkova was elderly and infirm and left her beloved Troitskoe only for brief periods. Most aristocrats, by contrast, preferred life in town for most of the year but by the last quarter of the eighteenth century had established the pattern (which persisted until 1917) of quitting Moscow for the summer. The *déménagement* could not occur until the flooding and mud brought on by the spring thaw had subsided; such conditions made most roads impassable during that period. From mid-May to September or later, Moscow became a ghost town as noble families and their retinue deserted it for their summer estates. These migrations were complicated by logistical concerns, involving large numbers of people, numerous carriages, the preparation of food for the journey, and the packing of bedding, linens, furniture, luxury goods unavailable in the country, and all sorts of personal possessions. One memoirist recalls, "I remember once there were a hundred carts to carry off our household goods. . . . Provisions bought in town which had to last the entire summer also were in the caravan: tea, sugar, coffee, candles, and various trifles, because you couldn't buy anything in our district town other than tar and soap, and the post arrived only once a week."[27]

Alexander Herzen (1812–70), who describes himself as "passionately fond of country life" in his brilliant mem-

oirs *My Past and Thoughts*, recalls his childhood eagerness mounting as the annual trip to Vasilievskoe drew near: "Little by little there seemed more ground for hope; provisions began to be sent off, sugar, tea, all sorts of cereals, and wine—and again there was a pause; then at last an order was dispatched to the village elder to send so many peasants' horses by such and such a day—and so we were going, we were going!"[28] The lower levels of household staff left about a week before the family, making the trip on foot. The anarchist Prince Kropotkin (1842–1921) recalls, "When we saw a file of servants marching along one of our streets, we knew at once that the Apukhtins or Prianishnikoffs were migrating." On the road these large groups of men, women, and children, "dressed in all sorts of impossible coats, belted with cotton handkerchiefs, burned by the sun or dripping under the rain, and helping themselves along with sticks cut in the woods, certainly looked more like a wandering band of gypsies than the household of a wealthy landowner."[29]

Before departing from their home in Moscow, the family gathered together for the leave-taking ritual: a few moments of silence in the drawing room, with everyone seated. If the family had a house chapel, their priest might hold a special service before the journey. Then the family climbed into a number of spacious *dormeuses* (traveling coaches drawn by six horses), infants and small children traveling with their wet-nurses and nannies, older children with their tutors and governesses. Other household members traveled in a number of smaller vehicles, with carts of provisions and baggage bringing up the rear. The family took with them food and a cook, bedding, and any other supplies necessary to be self-sufficient en route. Either relays of horses were sent ahead to await the arrival of the carriages, or, if traveling a long way by a post road using hired horses, the family would send someone ahead to arrange for horses with the various stationmasters.

Memoirists portray these childhood trips as one big adventure, "an inexhaustible source of enjoyment," in

Prince Kropotkin's words. "The stages were short, and we stopped twice a day to feed the horses. . . . In big, animated villages, and after a good deal of bargaining about the prices to be charged for hay and oats, as well as for the samovars, we dismounted at the gates of an inn. Cook Andrei bought a chicken and made the soup, while we ran in the meantime to the next wood, or examined the yard of the great inn." En route there were amazing sights: "files of loaded carts, groups of pilgrims, and all sorts of people." Kropotkin's French tutor told them stories of the Napoleonic wars fought over the territory they were passing through, "as if he himself had taken part in the battle." Kropotkin traces his first love of nature to the impression made by a pine forest beyond Kaluga toward the end of their journey. "The sand in that forest was as deep as in an African desert. . . . Immense red pines, centuries old, rose on every side, and not a sound reached the ear except the voices of the lofty trees. In a small ravine a fresh crystal spring murmured, and a passer-by had left in it, for the use of those who should come after him, a small funnel-shaped ladle, made of birch bark, with a split stick for a handle."[30]

Arrival at the estate was a magical moment. Kropotkin writes: "At last we caught sight of the willows which marked the approach to our village, and all of a sudden we saw the elegant, pale yellow bell tower of the Nikolskoe church."[31] Herzen describes the welcome: "In the village by the big house, approached by a long avenue of limes, we were met by the priest, his wife, the church servitors, the house-serfs, several peasants, and Pronka, the fool."[32] Often, after being greeted ceremoniously by the waiting staff, the family would go to church for a service of thanksgiving. Then all dispersed to their quarters, the immediate family going to the main house, others to wings or garden pavilions.

Childhood Amusements

In the late eighteenth century, an aristocrat's children (treated generally as miniature adults) were allowed no

more freedom in the country than they had enjoyed in the city. At General G. I. Bibikov's Grebnevo, east of Moscow, magnificent gardens surrounded the large stone mansion. Its huge ponds were dotted by islands with summerhouses to which visitors were taken by boat for tea. Like other lavish estates it probably had an allée of games (for adult amusement as much as for children): swings, carousels, lawn bowling, and the Russian form of cricket. But Bibikov's wife would not let her daughters walk in the gardens without permission, and even then only when attended by their governesses and two lackeys in livery.[33]

By the 1820s, however, childhood was coming to be viewed as a special stage of life, and country life as different from city life. For the young the regimentation of the city disappeared on the estate, where a variety of special amusements awaited them. A Bibikov granddaughter recalls wandering with her tutor at her grandparents' estate, Staro-Nikolskoe, to collect flowers, grasses, and colored stones and fossils from the stream.[34] At Vasilievskoe, Herzen roamed along the long shady allées, played on the white sand and among the reeds along the riverbank, and consumed "all sorts of vegetables," bounty from their stooped old gardener. Every evening his father allowed him to fire a small cannon, "an operation which of course entertained all the servants, and grey-haired old men of fifty were as diverted as I was." He played with serf boys and read a bit but "was much more interested in a hare and a squirrel which lived in the loft near my room."[35] One strict father relaxed with his children in the summer, taking them to watch the haymaking or to gather mushrooms, and even into the huge underground root cellar, stocked to the ceiling, where they could sample whatever they wanted. In the evenings he played games with his children in the great hall. On August 1, the day of the saint to which their church was consecrated, the whole family attended the service, then went to the village priest's house to feast on pastries, tea, mead, and pickles (fig. 94).[36] Sergei Sheremetev recalls chasing geese and ducks into the Kuskovo

94. Mariamna Davydova. The Lopukhins paying a visit to the house of Father Agathon, the priest at Matussov. Watercolor. 1920s. (Courtesy of Alona Vassiloff)

At the Kropotkins' Nikolskoe, family parties were organized, which sometimes involved "picking mushrooms in the woods, and afterward having tea in the midst of the forest, where a man a hundred years old lived alone with his little grandson, taking care of bees" (fig. 95). In *Childhood, Boyhood, and Youth* Tolstoy describes a similar tea party after a day of hunting:

When we reached the Kalina woods we found the carriage already there and, surpassing all our expectations, a one-horse cart in the middle of which sat the butler. We could see, packed in straw, a samovar, a tub with an ice-cream mould and various other attractive-looking packets and boxes. There could be no mistake: it meant tea out of doors, with ice-cream and fruit! . . . To drink tea in the woods on the grass, and where no one had ever

lake, feeding the fish in the pond near the Dutch House (which his mother converted into a bathhouse), and taking boat rides with his mother. A descendant of the other branch of Sheremetevs speaks of a "sort of original and sweet disorder, an accidental quality to the life" during his childhood at his family's estate Pokrovskoe.[37] I. A. Raevsky recounts that when his mother was away at one of their other estates on business, the servants "never refused us anything." He recalled that "in the fall we'd go shoot blackbirds in the garden with our tutor, or collect all the [fallen] leaves from the linden allée and drag them into the fields. . . . In winter we'd put three or four sledges together and go sledding; sometimes with the help of the house servants we made a snow house and then turned it to ice by pouring water over it. On winter evenings we gathered by the stove in the great hall and drank *sheeten* [a drink of hot water, honey, and spices]; usually one of us had to recite French or Russian verse from memory."[38]

95. Mariamna Davydova. Picnicking in the woods near Kamenka. In the foreground, Lev Davydov courts Mariamna Lopukhina. On the right, a friend returns from mushrooming. Watercolor. 1920s. (Courtesy of Alona Vassiloff)

121

drunk tea before, was the greatest of treats. . . . A rug was spread in the shade of some young birch-trees and the whole company disposed themselves in a circle. . . . Gavrilo, the butler, having stamped down the lush green grass around him, was wiping plates and taking out of the box plums and peaches wrapped in leaves. The sun shone through the green branches. . . . A light breeze fluttered.[39]

Young nobles, accompanied by tutors, made long excursions around the estate. Kropotkin remembers going to the village where his former nurse lived. "There was no bound to her joy when I came to see her. Cream, eggs, apples, and honey were all that she could offer; but the way in which she offered them, in bright wooden plates, having covered the table with a fine snow-white linen tablecloth of her own making . . . and the fond words with which she addressed me, treating me as her own son, left the warmest feelings in my heart."[40]

Hunting

From the late eighteenth to mid-nineteenth century and beyond, hunting, an expensive and time-consuming sport, was the primary daytime pastime for men. One poor noble's diary for 1778 records his peregrinations between the estates of richer nobles near Moscow for daily hunting in late April and May. At Shabolovo, the estate of Prince Peter Prozorovsky (whose brother owned Lyublino), the diarist and Prince Dolgoruky flushed a fox but did not manage to shoot it. At Vlasovo, twenty miles away, the group bagged four hares on April 26, nineteen on the 28th, six on the 30th, two hares and some snipe on May 1, and seventeen hares two days later.[41] The wealthy Golitsyn clan owned a network of villages and estates in Moscow and surrounding provinces—among them Bolshye Vyazemy, Rozhdest-veno, Gorodnya, Lopasnya, Dedevshino, and Kamarichi. The male Golitsyns, particularly Nikolai and Alexander (sons of Mikhail), and their cousins Vladimir and Alexei

(sons of Boris) were all passionate hunters who not only coursed together but exchanged dogs, horses, and huntsmen. In December 1779 Nikolai (the owner of Bolshye Vyazemy) asked his cousin Vladimir to order two hunting carriages for himself and his friend Peter Prozorovsky: light two-seaters, with harnesses that blinkered the horses (so that they would not be startled by shooting). Correspondence between Vladimir, also a friend of Prozorovsky, and his brother Alexei shows their intense preoccupation with selecting and training the best dogs for their kennels. Six days before his death, in November 1792, Alexei, aged sixty, sent a long and detailed letter to Vladimir. "As concerns my hunting this fall, not only I but all our hunting brothers had very little pleasure because of the great drought and defoliation. . . . My preparations for the hunt are the usual, although I have never had fewer men or dogs. . . . For spring, if they live, there will be 73 dogs. . . . Your piebald harriers are at my place. I will take care of them as you wish, not putting them in with any others." Alexei was clearly a connoisseur of hunting dogs, as revealed in the following passage: "I watched the gray bitch Prince Alexander Mikhailovich [Golitsyn] gave you. . . . The houndkeepers said that she jumped adroitly along with my dogs at the first snowfall. . . . Yes, and you sent Agrenev to ask how well the bitch that Prince Prozorovsky gave you jumps. I haven't seen her. But Isaika from Yaroslavl came to Gorodnya [Natalya Petrovna Golitsyna's estate in Tula] with six harriers which had been given to you and a little bitch he said Koshkin gave you—he didn't leave her with me but took her to Gorodnya. I saw her, but she doesn't seem particularly special." The last part of the letter shows us dogs and huntsmen being moved from province to province, estate to estate: "Agrenev told me that in addition you were given four hounds in Kaluga, and that your men were traveling together with some of Efim Durnov's men and dogs from Yaroslavl, and that they had all gotten ill. I told Argenev to bring these rotters and all the dogs to Rozhdestveno. . . . We will try to cure them, and they won't get drunk. . . . And if God permits it to be spring I will bring them to you, shaped up, for they have been completely spoiled."[42]

After Alexei's death, Nikolai, as trustee of his estate, sent Vladimir a list indicating the estate villages in which Alexei's various horses, hounds, and houndsmen were located. "In the village of Uskoe, 14 borzois and 5 puppies; in the village of Pistsovo, 5 borzois, 54 hounds, and 16 hound puppies. The chief group of horses is in the village of Borki: 23, among them mountain, Kazakh, and Kirghiz."[43]

Boys were initiated early into this consuming male activity, and their progress and behavior closely watched. In *Childhood, Boyhood, and Youth* Tolstoy recalls one of his first hunts. The preparations for the afternoon's coursing for hares began before dinner, with his father's instructions to his steward Yakov concerning "the carriage, the dogs and the saddle-horses—all in great detail, each horse being mentioned by name." After dinner the carriage, "with a serf boy perched on each of the springs," approached, followed by the huntsmen with the dogs and behind them the coachman on one saddle horse, leading Tolstoy's ancient pony. "And now we heard papa's footsteps on the stairs; the kennel-man rounded up the hounds; the huntsmen with the borzoi dogs called them in and mounted their horses. The groom led a horse up to the steps; papa's leash of dogs who had been lying around in various picturesque attitudes rushed to him. . . . Papa mounted his horse and we set off." The whipper-in and his assistants were responsible for flushing out game from cover or putting the dogs on the scent of a hare. Tolstoy remembers his shame when, distracted by beetles and butterflies, he let a hare escape and was reprimanded by his father's whipper-in: "I would rather he had hung me to his saddle like a hare."[44]

Yanuarius Neverov had a similar experience at the age of thirteen at Veryakushki, near Arzamas, in Nizhegorod Province, the estate his father managed for the wealthy P. A. Koshkarov. It being Neverov's birthday, Koshkarov, a passionate hunter, gave him a pair of borzois and assigned him a huntsman, "since every male is supposed to like hunting."

When we got to the grove Koshkarov got out of his carriage and onto his horse, showing every hunter where he should stand with his pack, and the hounds were sent into the grove. They immediately found a hare and began to follow it. All the hunters eagerly followed their baying; I'd brought my book with me and did not even notice the hare run right by me; nor did I pay attention to my groomsman, who needed my assent to loose my pair of borzois. Koshkarov got so angry that if my uncle Peter hadn't grabbed me he would have beaten me, and he ordered my pair of borzois taken away.[45]

Bears and wolves were also popular targets (fig. 96). At Belaya Tserkov (in Kiev Province), owned by Count Branicki, a group set off on a crisp February afternoon in 1828, bound for a small forest to shoot wolves. The night before, Branicki's men had enclosed a large area with "strong rope nets about seven feet high." The hunters, huntsmen, and dogs entered the area, the huntsmen following behind the barking dogs and traversing the whole area to drive the wolves toward the sportsmen.[46] The novelist Alexander Dumas describes a different method of wolf hunting, which involved tethering a young pig to a troika and riding through the snow with the hope that its squeals would attract a pack of wolves. Dumas thought this risky, for if the horses were startled they might overturn the troika, exposing the hunters to the pack.

Tolstoy, a passionate huntsman, understandably portrayed this side of the aristocrat's life in his novels. In *War and Peace*, hunting for hares and wolves is carried out on a grand scale at Otradnoe, the Rostovs' estate. The party of eight hunters and the Rostov family start off with about 130 dogs (40 of which are borzois), numerous whippers-in,

96. Bear hunting in Novgorod Province. (*Stolitsa i usadba,* no. 8)

huntsmen, and grooms. During the hunt, male pride and passion is at a peak: the Ukrainian huntsman Danilo gets furious at Count Rostov for letting a wolf slip, and the hunters vie over the abilities of their prize dogs. When the dogs of Nikolai, his uncle, and a neighbor compete for a hare, their masters can barely restrain their emotions. When Nikolai's uncle's dog finally catches the hare, the uncle exclaims delightedly, "There's a dog for you! He outstripped them all."[47] In *Anna Karenina* Constantine Levin is an avid hunter; Oblonsky finds him in a Moscow hotel with a peasant from Tver, measuring the skin of a bear he had just shot, and they spend an hour talking about bear

hunting. Later Levin shoots snipe with Oblonsky, spending the night in comradely fashion in a peasant's hut.

There were exceptions to the general passion for hunting. Alexei Kurakin had loved the sport in his youth, and his sixty-thousand-acre estate of Kurakino had abundant wild game, including "snipe, woodcock, double snipe, wild ducks, teals, grebes, and geese . . . blackbirds, bustards, and nightingales."[48] Yet Kurakin permitted his neighbors to hunt at Kurakino only once a year, and then under the eagle eye of his head huntsman, Egor, a master shot capable of hitting two birds simultaneously. (Egor bagged up to seven hundred birds a year for Kurakin's table.) Sergei Poltoratsky frequently let his neighbors hunt, dine, and spend the night at Avchurino, as hospitality demanded, but never hunted himself.

Quieter Pleasures

For landowners like these, estate life offered other sources of enjoyment. The library at Avchurino held rare manuscripts (including Nikolai Karamzin's annotated copy of Russia's earliest chronicle, used for his *History of the Russian State*). Poltoratsky, a passionate bibliophile, added to its collection a complete set of the early years of "Moscow News" and some first editions of Pushkin's works inscribed to him by the author. For a gentleman farmer like Alexei Kurakin there were architectural improvements to be made to his house, churches, and villages; supervision of the farming and various enterprises on the estate; and

the selection and breeding of livestock. A horse and cattle fancier, Kurakin spent seven thousand rubles on an English stallion named "Olen" and one thousand rubles on a prize cow that became "the apple of his eye."[49] The fashion for imported livestock was widespread. At Lyubizhi, in Tula Province, Raevsky's invalid father loved to inspect his favorite horses or to sit in the garden admiring his English cows and calves as he drank milk from his favorite goat, Mashka. His wife, like many aristocratic women, took a keen interest in her gardens. She particularly enjoyed planting exotic varieties such as perennial jasmine, which her husband bought for her in Petersburg.

Both boys and girls received art lessons as a matter of course, and amateur painting, portrayed in many estate drawings, was a favorite occupation on the estate (fig. 97). Visitors frequently drew a scene (or composed a verse) for

97. Artist unknown. *On the Estate* (detail). 1814. (Courtesy of the State Historical Museum, Moscow)

the album of a young lady of the estate. A typical quiet evening was spent playing cards, usually Boston (a type of whist), to the accompaniment of the estate's serf musicians. On other occasions family members or guests might sing or play the clavichord or harp.

The household usually planned the return to town when the first "snow road"—a frozen river—became solid enough to support the weight of the carriages. When the Poltoratskys set off for Moscow in the late autumn of 1852, Ellen, the English nurse Miss Gibson, and the two youngest children occupied an enormous green sleeping carriage, its eight wheels having been exchanged for sledge runners; Sergei Poltoratsky and a couple of male retainers followed in a smaller coach; his valet, the cook, and two maids rode in a large hooded sledge; and behind them followed four enormous wagons with the family's luggage and provisions. The size of this caravan, somewhat reduced in comparison to Princess Dashkova's a half-century earlier, is the only significant measure of change in the habits of the aristocratic household. As before, furniture such as the beds and mattresses brought from Moscow to the country would be readied for the return trip. The aristocrat's estates continued to supply his city household with food for the winter. In the fall enormous convoys of carts arrived from the country carrying fruit preserves of all kinds, compotes, wines, and liqueurs. One memoirist recalls oats, flour, buckwheat, butter, and frozen dressed fowl arriving in Moscow from their distant estate in the steppes, while from their suburban Moscow estate they got dried mushrooms, firewood, and hay. Another remembers a mass of provisions—"Jam, figs, dried, cured meats, fruit and berry conserves, pickles . . . flour, vegetables, butter and bran"—being sent to Moscow on a string of sledges.[50]

Literary sources are virtually all we have to rely on for the details of aristocratic country life during the golden age of the estate. Among visual sources, informative paintings such as the "conversation piece" popular in late seventeenth- and eighteenth-century Europe (an informal portrait of a family in front of its country seat) are few in number. In the first half of the nineteenth century artists typically immortalized their patrons' neoclassical mansions and grounds by painting them in grandiose but static, iconographic fashion, using human figures only as decorative, subsidiary elements (see fig. 59).[51] Portraiture does not close the gap, for aristocrats were most often posed formally in court dress or military uniform, their imperial decorations prominently displayed. There are, to be sure, a few exceptions. Levitsky's magnificent portrait of the wealthy, powerful, and independent P. A. Demidov, painted in 1773 (fig. 98), shows him in an imaginary temple, wearing an informal dressing gown and cap, attire usually worn at home. His watering can, book, and potted plants indicate his main passion, botany, while in the background we see the outlines of the magnificent Moscow foundling home he endowed. Bolotov, an artist as well as author, chose to draw himself not in his gardens at Bogoroditsk or Dvoryaninovo but at his desk at Bogoroditsk (see fig. 66); Masonic symbols—a pyramid and a compass—reflect a dangerous allegiance he takes pains to deny in his memoirs. To my knowledge, there is no portrait of Krechetnikov at Mikhailovskoe or of Dashkova as mistress of Troitskoe.

The absence of Russian conversation pieces indicates not only that genre painting came late to Russia but also that few eighteenth-century aristocrats felt personally attached to their estates. Dashkova's passion for Troitskoe was exceptional. Alexander Kurakin hastened to court from distant Saratov once Paul I came to the throne and rarely visited Nadezhdino thereafter (though he wrote angry letters to his steward about cattle grazing in his elegant park). Kurakin, a vain man known as the "Diamond

98. D. G. Levitsky. Portrait of P. A. Demidov, grandson of Nikita. 1777. (Courtesy of the Tretiakov Gallery, Moscow)

99. V. L. Borovikovsky. Portrait of A. B. Kurakin. 1801–02.
(Courtesy of the Tretiakov Gallery, Moscow)

Prince," was painted possibly more often than anyone else of his generation, and to this we may owe another exception: the unusual, rather clumsy portrait (probably by his resident artist) of Kurakin seated, Nadezhdino gleaming on a distant hillside.[52] Borovikovsky's portrait of 1801–02 (fig. 99) is both artistically superior and more characteristic. In it Kurakin emphasizes his courtier's role. Paul's bust is shown to his left, while the cloak of the Order of Malta Paul commanded is on the right. Paul's Mikhailovsky Fortress, not Nadezhdino, appears in the background; the ribbon and Order of St. Vladimir Kurakin had just received from Alexander I bedeck his court costume. For Kurakin, one must conclude, the Nadezhdino period was an interlude. During it, like most of his peers, he used his princedom as an alternative setting for the theatrical display that, as will be seen, was characteristic of aristocratic estate life.

5

Emerald Thrones and Living Statues

THEATER AND THEATRICALITY ON THE ESTATE

There I revel in deception,
Evoking a golden age;
In verse and in prose I am distinguished,
I, a young tsar of dreams.
—Ivan M. Dolgoruky

FROM THE REIGN OF CATHERINE until the emancipation of 1861, serf theater was a major source of entertainment for rural Russia. Estate theater markedly differentiated the Russian estate from its European model and, for that matter, from the plantation life of the American South. Palatial estates like Kuskovo and Ostankino were famous for their troupes of actors, musicians, and dancers, but even minor landowners prided themselves on being able to field a violinist or two for guests. Master and serf also collaborated in theatrical rituals or elaborate displays. Some of these were clearly an exaggerated form of the entertainment and display of wealth that characterized estate life elsewhere in Europe.[1] But overt role playing also served private ends: some estate owners masqueraded as autocrats, while others created a fantasy world for their own pleasure.

The theatrical continuum thus encompassed serf performances, elaborate displays of hospitality, theatricality in the material culture of the estate, and the theatricalization or ritualization of private life. Yury Lotman's important essays on the semiotics of Russian culture provide insights into the cultural roots of noble theater and theatricality. By the late eighteenth and early nineteenth centuries, Lotman contends, the process of Westernization had produced a Russian noble who was deliberately "acting" the part of a foreigner. Art invaded life: role playing, or the restructuring of life on a theatrical or literary model, became normal cultural behavior.[2]

Lotman sees the estate as one of numerous stages on which the noble indulged in self-revealing semiotic behavior. What happened on that stage, and in provincial theater generally, reflects not only the cultural attitudes of the Russian nobility but also significant anomalies in its sociopolitical evolution in comparison with other European elites. No other elite behaved in the same way, partially because no other elite faced comparable problems of cultural identity. But other factors stimulated and played into the theatrical continuum, chiefly the institutions of autocracy and serfdom, which made Russian estate owners at once the most dependent and the most powerful of European nobles. The Russian noble's problems of status and self-definition were as much bound up with these native elements as with the fact that he was adapting to a European cultural model.

Serfdom was the economic and social precondition for estate theater proper, as well as for much estate theatricality. Serfs built, decorated, and sometimes even designed estates whose exteriors, interiors, and surrounding gardens had multiple elements of theatricality (fig. 100). A few late eighteenth-century estates were little more than stage sets on which grateful recipients of land and serfs from Catherine the Great built large houses and hosted a lavish week of entertainment for the empress, only to leave the area, allowing the instant estate to fall into disrepair.[3] On virtually all sizable estates, theatricality was expressed in design or decor. Lyublino was a theatrical embodiment of Durasov's pride in his new award. Ostankino, a theater built to resemble a Palladian manor house, had false windows on the facade. The main house at Kuskovo was constructed of wood carved to resemble stone; its grotto was fancifully embellished to suggest water cascading from a fountain on the roof. Two estates owned by Golitsyns had extraordinary examples of theatrical architecture. The main entrance to the stable courtyard at Kuzminki doubled as the music pavilion (fig. 101). With its triumphal arch framed by two life-size, rearing bronze horses (sculpted by P. Klodt and poured in Golitsyn's own factory) and its four massive Doric columns supporting a gallery in the center of which are statues of Apollo and his muses, the pavilion dominates the view from the house. Musicians were stationed on the gallery level; guests assembled to enjoy concerts in the semicircular hall below, which projected into the stable courtyard. One wonders

100. The elaborate stone entrance gates to Marfino suggest an enchanted realm. (Author)

101. The music pavilion and stables at Kuzminki, viewed from the house. Lithograph by F. Benois, from an album of drawings by J. Rauch. 1841. (Courtesy of the State Historical Museum, Moscow)

whether Golitsyn horses performed here, as they did in the "round court" at Trostyanets (in Poltava Province), a huge Russo-Byzantine coliseum (fig. 102). The serf performers, perhaps costumed in classical tunics like Karl Bryullov's equestrian vaulter (see fig. 116), lived in the bastions of the court; their horses were stabled along its walls, and above the stables were spectators' loges.

Inside estate houses, skilled painters wrought marvels of deception on walls and ceilings, creating pillared halls and arcadian bowers. The park outside was deliberately designed as a stage set, each contrived vista planned to create a particular emotion in the viewer. The different parts of the garden were, in effect, emotion-provoking

scenes in a play. The use of props such as shams (fig. 103)— lifelike renditions of foreigners or of peasants in holiday dress picturesquely grouped around a genuine haystack— increased the sense of theatricality.[4] Estate parks also contained sculpted and live fantasies. Mythical griffons adorned the Marfino landing; sphinxes guarded Kuzminki's gates, and stone lions Arkhangelskoe's ballroom doors. Many estates had menageries of live wild or rare animals and aviaries of exotic birds.

These theatrical elements of house and garden, though European in conception, were executed with the exuberance and exaggeration characteristic of late eighteenth-century Russian design. Their abundance indicates the skill and speed with which the Russian elite assimilated this model, following the empress's taste for allegory and spectacle. For theater the nobility took its cues from imperial performances at the Hermitage Theater and the Chinese Theater at Tsarskoe Selo. "Not a week passes but there is a *féte* [*sic*] at the Hermitage," reported one English visitor in 1790. In another letter he described a "grand play" the empress had written:

> It is a tragedy with chorusses, like the ancients, with a kind of Greek music: there are no less than thirty personages in the play; two emperors, and the rest of proportionate rank; the suite consists of *six hundred* people, who are all to be upon the stage at once: it must be a marvelous sight, I think. This morning, as I was looking out of the window, I saw the *clouds* and the turrets of Constantinople going to the theatre, in a cart. It was acted on Tuesday, before the Empress, at her private theatre; and on Sunday will be exhibited to the profane.[5]

This was probably the lavish production *Oleg*, staged to celebrate the continuing Russian victories over the Turks. Its three acts contained Russian dances and games, Greek choruses, dancing, scenes from Euripides' dramas, and a stage rendering of the Olympic games, all against suitable backdrops. In act 3, Oleg, having been richly entertained by the Byzantine emperor, nails his shield to a pillar,

102. The round court, or coliseum, designed in pre-Petrine style in the 1840s, at the Golitsyns' Trostyanets.
(*Stolitsa i usadba*, no. 54)

104. Interior of the Ostankino theater, viewed from the stage. For performances the flooring was removed to reveal the parterre.

thereby inviting his successors to return to Constantinople.

Undoubtedly Catherine's main purpose in such extravaganzas was to publicize her ambitions and military triumphs to the south. The aristocracy, using serf performers, emulated her lavish productions in the private theaters of their St. Petersburg and Moscow mansions and on many estates. The Sheremetev serf troupe, formed by Peter Borisovich (1713–1788) in the 1760s to perform both

103. A sham depicting a peasant girl with watermelon. Oil on wood. (Courtesy of the Kuskovo Museum, Moscow)

in his Moscow house theater and at Kuskovo, was the most impressive of its time. By the early 1770s it was ranked on a level with the Petersburg court theater and considered far superior to the leading theater company in Moscow (whose English director, Maddox, complained about the competition). Peter Borisovich's son Nikolai (1751–1809) surpassed his father in his passion for theater. When given the troupe in the mid-1770s he immediately began plans for a theater large enough to accommodate the French and Italian comic operas he had fallen in love with during a trip abroad. The wooden theater at Kuskovo (supplementing its open-air theater), with a stage larger than that of the

Royal Swedish Theater or the Dresden opera house (though smaller than the Paris Opera), was completed in 1787.

In the 1790s, Sheremetev created the slightly smaller but more technically complex Ostankino theater (fig. 104).[6] A Parisian correspondent sent Sheremetev both detailed set designs and information on the latest theater

105. Costume sketch for the heroine of a Sheremetev production. 1770s. (Courtesy of Kyra Cheremeteff)

106. Sketch for a hero's costume. 1770s. (Courtesy of Kyra Cheremeteff)

technology, from which, using a French architect and his own serf architect A. F. Mironov, Sheremetev worked out his plan for the Ostankino theater-palace complex. Foreign artists created sets and costumes, and a host of special teachers trained the troupe. Sheremetev clearly relished the prestige Ostankino brought him. A few years after the theater was completed, he wrote, "Having achieved a great thing, in which my knowledge and taste is visible, which is worthy of amazement, and which the public has acclaimed, I will forever peacefully enjoy my productions."[7] Inventories done in 1810–11 by the guardians of his young son Dmitry listed seventy trunks of costly costumes (figs. 105, 106); seventy-six trunks, cartons, and boxes of props such as banners, weapons, animal skins, and masks; and three trunks of sheet music.[8]

Many other aristocratic estates, among them the Goncharovs' Yaropolets, the Saltikovs' Marfino, Nashchokin's Rai-Semenovskoe, Orlov's Otrada, and Count F. A. Tolstoy's Ivanovskoe, had separate theater buildings, all of which have disappeared. At Otrada the theater director was Orlov's serf musician L. S. Gurilev, whose son became a noted composer (fig. 107). Understandably, Catherine's eagles were among the most avid impresarios. At Shklov (in Mogilev Province), Semen Zorich (Catherine's lover from June 1777 to May 1778) retained the poet Timeon de Salmorain as resident playwright. After two years, de Salmorain billed Zorich for 14,158 rubles. Among the expenses listed were 200 rubles for items a maid had stolen and, he asserted, handed over to Zorich's hairdresser. De Salmorain requested 2,400 rubles for his wife's singing, clavichord playing, and costumes (for which, he claimed, Zorich at one time had promised her 10,000 rubles). For his own work on comedies and operas he requested a mere 800 rubles. Given the chaotic state of Zorich's finances, it is doubtful that de Salmorain was paid.[9]

Other provincial estate theaters were hardly less lavish. Like Kuskovo, Marfino boasted two theaters. Ballets, pastorales, and vaudeville were performed in the open-air theater situated about a mile from the main house, more

107. Count Orlov-Davydov's gypsy chorus performing at Semenovskoe-Otrada in the 1860s.
(*Stolitsa i usadba*, no. 48)

complicated dramatic works in the enclosed wooden theater in the formal garden. I. D. Shepelev's theater in Vladimir Province, near Murom, was only slightly smaller than the Marinsky theater in St. Petersburg and was lighted with gas rather than oil lamps—an unusual feature for the 1830s.[10] The Melgunovs at Sukhanovo and S. S. Apraksin (fig. 108) at Olgovo, near Moscow; the Povalo-Shvikovskys, Nakhimovs, and Brovtsinys, of Smolensk Province; I. O. Khorvat, of Kursk Province; and the Kurakin brothers on estates in Saratov, Tver, and Orel Provinces all had serf theaters with sets, costumes, and performers of high quality; their well-equipped troupes were capable of performing European and Russian plays, ballets, opera, and burlesque. Some serf actors and actresses from these troupes became well known, because they also commonly performed in provincial capitals or in house theaters in the capitals.

In his theatrical undertakings the noble was both emulating the autocracy and asserting his own power. For centuries Russian rulers had employed theater to educate and discipline their subjects, from Ivan the Terrible's Oprichnina to Peter's mock-emperors and patriarchs, Anna's ice-palace weddings, and Elizabeth's court spectacles and male attire. Catherine's lavish theater productions at the Hermitage and the simple Russian dress she sometimes affected had a similar pedagogical purpose: to inspire her courtiers to follow her lead in introducing new ideas and manners through theater and spectacle. In 1776, for instance, the new viceroy of Kaluga Province, Mikhail Krechetnikov, was instructed to build a theater that would "bring people together, for the spread of social life and politesse."[11] Imperial decrees established similar provincial theaters in Tula, Kharkov, and Penza. In taking part in theatrical productions the local nobility, it was hoped, would pick up the more refined manners of the capital. The poet and statesman Gavrila Derzhavin, posted to Tambov as governor in 1786, found the nobility there "so crude and unsociable, so to speak, that they did not know how to dress, walk, or behave as a nobly-born person should." To civilize them he organized "theatrical presentations by amateurs, young nobles of both sexes," especially on official holidays.[12]

By the turn of the century the lesser nobility was participating with zest in these local productions, while some wealthier nobles had become impresarios, creating for the countryside troupes of serf actors and dancers whose skills sometimes rivaled those of imperial artists. Count S. M.

108. Artist unknown. Portrait of S. S. Apraksin. Late eighteenth century. (Starikova, *Teatralnaya*)

Kamensky and Prince A. A. Shakhovskoy, like I. D. Shepelev, ran serf performances in well-appointed theaters complete with parterres, loges, piani nobili, and galleries. Kamensky spent huge sums on this consuming hobby. He once sold five hundred serfs to buy a few skilled actors from another owner; on another occasion he offered twenty thousand rubles for the renowned serf comedian Shchepkin.[13] The count's theater loge was equipped with a book for noting any errors on stage and with whips, which he used on offenders during rehearsals. The serf-owning noble's propensity for imperial imitation is amply illustrated by the fact that Kamensky's actors were uniformed and given court ranks, which rose or fell depending on their performances. In 1827 this troupe presented eighty-two productions: eighteen operas, fifteen dramas, forty-one comedies, six ballets, and two tragedies. The serf actresses were kept in haremlike seclusion and closely guarded, and Kamensky clearly reveled in their erotic bondage.[14] M. D. Buturlin recalls that when he was a young hussar stationed in Orel, he tried to arrange a secret rendezvous with Kamensky's prettiest star after seeing her perform. Alas, the lackey to whom he entrusted his billets-doux betrayed him, an enraged Kamensky threatened to write his father, and the affair was nipped in the bud.[15]

Prince Shakhovskoy's troupe not only performed in Nizhni Novgorod but also went on the road. At the annual Makariev fair, using a makeshift theater, it presented nightly operas and ballets to a rapt audience of one thousand, at Moscow ticket prices. According to contemporaries Shakhovskoy's pride in his troupe was as immense as his profits, and the quality of repertory and performance far above Kamensky's. Shepelev's serf opera was trained in a special school on his estate and performed to the music of a fifty-piece orchestra of salaried musicians. Shepelev himself taught the female singers (selected for beauty as well as for voice), beating them with a huge cane when he was displeased.

In addition to these serf troupes performing in provincial towns, there was a host of private estate theaters whose numbers can only be estimated. As late as 1858, 1,396 landowners owned an average of 2,200 serfs each, more than enough to support a staff of serf performers. Given the frequent references to noble aficionados in memoir literature, it is reasonable to assume that in the heyday of the estate several hundred presented serf theater regularly.[16] In 1805 F. F. Vigel saw the troupe of the stage-struck P. V. Esipov perform an opera on Esipov's estate Umatovo, thirty miles from Kazan, and reported that the acting was "no better and no worse" than usual in the provinces. One memoirist recalls that the theater of her grandfather G. I. Bibikov, at Grebnevo, had "every sort of decoration" in its wings. The masters he hired to teach music and dancing to his children also instructed his serf orchestra and ballet dancers. His wife, even when very pregnant, would get down on her knees to pin flowers to the skirts of her husband's ballerinas in order to please him.[17] In a not uncommon progression, some Grebnevo musicians were later freed and went on to become renowned artists.

At Princess Dashkova's Troitskoe (in Kaluga Province) there were about twenty-five hundred serfs and a separate theater building. The Troitskoe troupe, drawn from the ranks of the house serfs, was amateurish in comparison to troupes such as Kamensky's or Shepelev's. Yet accounts of the weekly performances praise the Troitskoe acting and Dashkova's substantial investment in sets, costumes, and special effects. Martha Wilmot wrote her mother delightedly, "We have a little theatre here, and our laborers, our cooks, our footmen and chambermaids turn into Princes, Princesses, Shepherds and Shepherdesses etc. . . . and perform with a degree of spirit that is quite astonishing." Martha's Irish maid was even more impressed by the spectacle to which she, along with all the other maids, was treated: she wrote her father about entering "the finest Play House the world ever seen" to see a play that had "a Dragon! and Kings! and Birds! and a Witch! and loads of music! and Flames, and ladies and gentlemen in gold and diamonds dancing, not on the ground at all hardly, and the beautiful noise! and smoke! and plenty of pleasure of all kinds! Ogh, says I, clapping my hands, 'Mary Nugent and Kiff wou'dn't believe the sight I seen!' "[18]

On lesser estates the theater might be little more than a large empty room, and the repertory correspondingly unsophisticated. Sometimes riding rings doubled as theaters. Bolotov trained a troupe of children to perform dramas such as Kheraskov's *The Ungodly Man* in his living room and had amateur musicales virtually every day. One memoirist recalled, "There was not a single wealthy landowner's house where an orchestra did not make a din, where a chorus did not sing, and where a stage was not erected."[19]

Foreigners sometimes remarked on an expensive (and relatively rare) Russian entertainment: the forty-man horn orchestra, in which each man produced one note. The horn players had no other duties, and such orchestras were bought and sold for large sums. One observer noted that some players, when asked their names, responded with the note they played, and one must assume that they learned by rote. Martha Wilmot, although rightly shocked at the "value placed on men in this country" if such was their sole responsibility, enjoyed the concert she heard at Prince Alexei Orlov's.

Serf troupes and horn orchestras distinguished Russian estate theaters from anything in Western Europe, as did the estate's role as a source of entertainment for the entire community. Imitating imperial festivals, owners of large estates in the environs of Moscow and St. Petersburg sponsored public spring and summer festivities, causing traffic jams as a parade of carriages streamed out from the capitals. Alexei Orlov-Chesmensky was famed both for the racetrack at his palace outside Moscow and for summer garden parties that anyone with "decent dress and a respectable appearance" (as one visitor put it) could attend.[20] The Kuskovo archives contain a small piece of paper with gold lettering announcing that "in the village of Kuskovo a promenade is planned for Sundays and Thursdays this summer and fall for all who wish to come. On June 28, 29, and August 1 everyone is also invited." Kuskovo festivities featured open-air theater (on Sundays, operas with ballet), outdoor games such as lawn bowling, boating in exotic gondolas on the great lake, and spectacular midnight fireworks (figs. 109, 110).[22] A poster of May 11, 1828, similarly invited the public to the estate theater of Suryanino, in Orel Province, to see a variety performance by the serfs of Peter and Alexei Yurasovsky and

109. Artist unknown. Portrait of Praskovya Kovalyova (whose stage name was "Zhemchugova") as Eliana in Gretri's opera *Samnite Weddings*. 1780s. (Courtesy of Kyra Cheremeteff)

110. Nikolai Argunov. Portrait of the serf ballerina Tanya Shlykova
(known as "Granatova") in costume. 1789.
(Courtesy of Kyra Cheremeteff)

their sister Alexandra. The presentation would include a three-act pantomime ballet entitled "The Virtuous Algerian" (featuring "battles, marches, and great spectacles" that had "delighted audiences in St. Petersburg and Moscow"), a potpourri of dances, a conjuring act, and choral music. Guests were invited to a supper in the garden after the performance.[22]

For almost half a century aristocratic country estates served, in effect, as regional amusement parks. The Kuskovo garden contained a "fire-breathing" dragon, a labyrinth, and a casino. At Kibentsy, owned by D. P. Troshchinsky, marshal of the nobility of Poltava Province, the host threw gold coins into a huge vat filled with water. Guests and clowns then took turns trying to collect them all: if a diver missed some, he had to throw them all back.[23] Yankova, waxing nostalgic about the Apraksins' Olgovo, with its theater, musicians, balls, and fireworks, said that "their whole life was one of constant gaiety and prolonged revelry."[24]

Not surprisingly, some noble enthusiasts were unable to keep up the pace. In the 1840s Baron von Haxthausen described the fate of a Nizhni Novgorod impresario: "Many years ago . . . a wealthy bachelor landowner built a theater on his estate, trained a select group of his serfs to become musicians and actors, and had them perform plays and operas. Later he moved to Nizhni, built a theater there, and extended invitations to his friends and acquaintances. Extravagance gradually became his ruin; he began charging admission and ended as the concession director of his own company!"[25] Alexei E. Stolypin, of Simbirsk Province, likewise ruined himself on theater. Inspired by his daughters, who played the major tragic roles in his productions alongside serf actors, he sent a maid to a fashionable French dressmaker in Moscow, apprenticed a boy to the best hairdresser, and set up a "whole factory" for costumes and props. The serf actresses' dresses were made from Stolypin's daughters' castoffs, while the actors' costumes were adapted from fancy dress of dandies who had lost fortunes gambling during Carnival; Stolypin snapped them up the first day of Lent at a Moscow consignment store. Stolypin's woes began when he took the troupe to Moscow in 1801. After three years of lavish entertaining, he was broke and had to sell his troupe and nineteen musicians to Maddox's theater.[26] In the 1820s Vasily Obreskov, a bachelor with the same ruinous passion, converted his estate house at Ponezhskoe, Kostroma Province, into a theater, bought promising serfs from neighbors, and trained them. In search of a larger audience he expanded to

Kostroma. The troupe, Kostroma's first, performed in a converted leather factory; later it also performed in a rented house in Yaroslavl. Obreskov died in 1830, forty thousand rubles in debt.[27]

The nobility's passion for theater was closely related to a tendency toward spectacular ritual and display that, like theater proper, imitated imperial practice (fig. 111). One historian notes that Catherine the Great's penchant for "pageants, triumphal arches, processions, illuminations, fireworks, food, and above all, drink" was a "belated echo of the political use of court spectacle . . . in much the same way and with much the same objects as Louis XIV."[28] Catherine's visit to Moscow in June 1787 for the twenty-fifth anniversary of her accession to the throne occasioned artillery salutes, the building of a triumphal arch, orchestra concerts, a masquerade ball, and banquets. "In the course of all these days," said one writer, "Moscow rang with the triumphal peal of bells."[29]

On Catherine's wide travels throughout her reign she was always royally received. In the spring of 1767, returning from Kazan along the Volga River, the imperial barge paused briefly at the estate of Bartsovka (in Kostroma Province), which belonged to the Kozlovskys, the parents of General A. I. Bibikov's wife.[30] Catherine landed at the dock, which had been covered with red cloth, and was greeted by Bibikovs, Kozlovskys, and their peasants. After church she sat down in the shade of a tree, with little three-year old Sasha Bibikov cockily positioned in her lap. Taken with the boy, she made him a standard-bearer of the Semenovsky Guards.[31]

Anticipating similar favors, grandees spent enormous amounts on regal entertainments. In August 1775, on a trip to Moscow, Catherine visited General P. A. Rumyantsev's estate Troitskoe-Kainardzhi, then feasted at Kuskovo. On the table before her stood a golden cornucopia that bore her cipher made out of "quite large diamonds"; the table was covered with an "innumerable amount of crystal dishes . . . decorated and enriched by

111. D. G. Levitsky. Portrait of E. N. Khrushcheva and E. N. Khovanskaya (aged eleven or twelve) performing at the Smolny Institute, which schooled young noblewomen in the arts emphasized at court. 1773. (Courtesy of the Russian Museum, St. Petersburg)

precious stones of various types and colors, extraordinarily valuable."[32]

For the silver anniversary of her reign in 1787 Catherine made a renowned trip to the newly incorporated Crimea. The so-called Potemkin villages—house facades that the imperial barge *Dniepr* glided past—were but one of numerous special effects Grigory Potemkin and others devised to delight Catherine. At various stops she was greeted by battalions of "Amazons," by fantastic fireworks (such as Mount Vesuvius erupting or her cipher inside a revolving circle of color) and by endless choruses sung by spotless, colorfully garbed local peasants. The foreigners who sneered at the sham villages missed their significance in the larger context of Russian theatricality of this era: they were programmatic, allegorical, and viewed as such (at least by Russians), with no less delight. Wherever the imperial cortege agreed to stop, grandees entertained: Rumyantsev welcomed Catherine at Vyshenki, on the Dniepr, and Sheremetev again at Kuskovo. This time special entrance gates to the estate had been built, bearing elaborate statuary, inscriptions, and allegorical paintings referring to the conquest of the Crimea and other feats of Catherine's reign. As she entered, the liveried Kuskovo servants stood along the roadside in pairs, strewing flowers in her path.

Catherine's two visits to Shklov cost her former lover Zorich dearly. For the first, in May 1788, Zorich sent to Saxony for special china costing fifty thousand rubles. Noble amateurs performed a pantomime in her honor, during which the elegant sets were changed seventy times. After dinner there was a fireworks display of fifty thousand rockets, months in the making. For her second visit, the following year, Zorich staged a jousting match in a specially constructed amphitheater with four entrances, its periphery decorated with green boughs, military emblems, trophies, and knightly banners. The guests sat along the walls, and the distinguished judges in a center pavilion. When the jousting began at 2:00 P.M., four teams assembled, and at a signal, one cavalier from each team advanced to the center, to be loudly applauded for his artfulness, skill, or courage. After a trumpet sounded the end of the games, the guests went into the orangery for dinner and from there to the theater, where the students of Zorich's

Shklov cadet school staged a small Russian comedy and his ballet troupe performed an allegorical ballet to choral accompaniment. Festivities climaxed with a ball, at which Eloise de Salmorain and others sang an ode to Zorich, the local sovereign, lauding his mercy and beneficence.[33]

As this episode suggests, the lavish, ritualized public and private celebration of authority the crown encouraged throughout this period inevitably filtered downward. Greater nobles regularly entertained lesser nobles. In 1767, to celebrate the convening of the Legislative Commission, Count Zakhar Chernyshev spared no expense in giving the local nobility he represented a feast followed by fireworks on his estate Yaropolets. Catherine's lieutenants arrogated imperial ceremonials for themselves. Krechetnikov, for instance, ordered cannons to be fired and all the Kaluga church bells to be rung when he attended services in the cathedral. Just as imperial birthdays and anniversaries occasioned holidays, he designated certain days for fireworks, balls, and masquerades in his honor.[34]

The tradition of theatrical extravagance outlived Catherine. For a visit by Paul to Ostankino, Nikolai Petrovich created a spectacular effect. He had a number of trees in the wooded grove that led to Ostankino sawed nearly all the way through, and stationed a man next to each. As Paul drove along the road to Ostankino, at a given signal these trees were pulled down. The effect was that of raising a curtain to reveal the full panorama of Ostankino—church, pond, palace, and garden. Paul, no stranger to theatricals, was amazed by this display of Sheremetev's ingenuity. (Nikolai Petrovich also screened off from view the homely dwellings of the house serfs to the left of the palace with a row of trees that were still standing a century later.)[35] Some three decades later the Golitsyns celebrated the 158th birthday of Kuzminki with a dinner for 136 guests, followed by public festivities for 5,000.[36]

Large public festivals on private estates occurred in England as well, but for quite different reasons. Some were charitable or educational. At Petworth, for instance, in

May 1834 Lord Egremont hosted a famous public dinner for six thousand of the poor, followed by fireworks for ten thousand. Coke's annual sheepshearings at Holkham, his model agricultural estate, attracted up to seven thousand attendees of all classes.[37] Yet only a few important family events, such as the birth or coming-of-age of an heir, or the death of an important family member, were occasions for festive or solemn public display.

In Russia, foreign observers were struck by the frequency of lavish entertaining, by its theatrical detail, and by the tinge of vulgarity associated with Russian magnificence. The notoriously debauched connoisseur Nikolai Yusupov entertained male friends with excellent ballet in the elegant Arkhangelskoe theater (figs. 112, 113); at a wave of his cane, the ballerinas would strip naked on stage.[38] General Nashchokin had a serf sentinel permanently on watch for visitors to Rai-Semenovskoe. When a carriage was spotted in the distance his musicians would be ordered to climb up into the Chinese tower and surprise the guest with a sudden burst of music as he or she passed through the entrance gates. Robert Lyall, the object of such

112. Exterior of the theater at Arkhangelskoe.

a fanfare in 1825, noted that Nashchokin severely punished a sentry who missed an arriving prince.[39]

Banquets called forth extravagant display. At his suburban Moscow estate Mikhalka, Orlov astounded William Coxe by producing a profusion of exotic fruits for dessert, including a small Astrakhan melon that had traveled, Coxe reckoned, one thousand miles by carriage.[40] The assembled guests picked fruit from cherry trees in full leaf at either end of the table. Martha Wilmot called the typical banquet, with its procession of fifty or sixty dishes (which meant four hours at table) downright fatiguing; but she could not help being impressed by a dinner at Alexei Golitsyn's in the dead of winter that featured asparagus and all sorts of fruits, including "grapes as large as pigeons' eggs."[41]

Foreigners noted that Russian largesse was more a way of life than a purposeful or occasional activity. Madame de Staël commented that Russians "are much more hospitable than the French."[42] Lyall went further: "So strong is the passion for entertaining company among the Russian nobles, that were it possible to find the means of supporting it, and to obtain a succession of guests, every day would be spent as they spend Sunday; and indeed some of the richer individuals keep open table throughout the year." Nashchokin, reported Lyall, customarily sent out invitations for Sunday to all nobles within twenty or thirty miles of his estate. They would begin arriving around 11 A.M. for the service in the estate church forty yards from the house, to which they were ceremoniously driven in a lineika. At noon, the guests were served a light repast of *zakuski* (hors d'oeuvres such as meat-filled pastries, smoked fish on bread, and pickled mushrooms) and vodka. They then dispersed to play cards or take a walk. At 3:00 came a dinner of French and Russian dishes accompanied by fine wines, followed by more cards, walking, riding, or a nap until 6:00, the hour for tea. Theater or dancing filled the evening, and supper was served at midnight, after which the guests either went home or retired to guest quarters.

113. The Arkhangelskoe stage with a trompe l'oeil curtain by the Italian
set designer and architect Pietro Gonzaga.

"Such," Lyall observes, "is a pretty general picture of the manner in which the hallowed day is spent by the nobles of the Russian empire. Those who are rich become hosts, and those who are poor form the guests."[43]

For Russian nobles on all levels, lavish hospitality was not merely a source of pride, it was a way of life, the obligation of a civilized person. Contrasting Russian to English habits in the 1790s Karamzin noted that "with us the rule is: 'Always be a guest or receive guests.' An Englishman says, 'I want to be happy at home, and only now and then have witnesses to my happiness.'"[44] Although not all nobles could entertain on the grand scale, all felt obliged to feed and entertain swarms of visitors, whose very presence was considered a compliment.

The frequency and duration of theatrical festivities and entertaining in the provinces support Lotman's view that a general impulse to theatricalize life pervades this period. At Nadezhdino (see figs. 39, 64) Prince Kurakin used his serfs to create a complete parody of a court, including a serf police chief and other officials. Life at Nadezhdino was governed according to strict rules of etiquette inscribed in a printed sheet titled "The order and regulations for the manner of life here in the village of Nadezhdino." Kurakin, resplendent in a silk camisole and

145

brocade or velvet caftan with bejeweled fastenings and proudly wearing his dazzling imperial orders, reigned over a host of circling servants and a crowd of nobles, the poorer of whom often stayed for months at Nadezhdino without ever seeing their host. He had a special staff of servants whose only task was to oversee the transformation of ordinary life into "weeks, months of gigantic celebrations." The guests who stayed at I. O. Khorvat's pleasure palace of Golovchino weeks on end— "stuffed and drunk," according to one visitor—marveled at his romantic fantasy "Keingrust" (No Sorrow) in the forest, an artificial hill with a spiral stairway and numerous gazebos, crowned with a large summerhouse in which they were served fresh crayfish.[45]

Often (as in the case of Kurakin) noble fantasy celebrated or drew on imperial ritual. As has been noted, nobles customarily built triumphal arches or erected monuments to commemorate an imperial visit to their estate. But one country noble whose estate was not so honored nonetheless decorated the entrance to his estate with a triumphal arch and ordered his serfs to gild a number of carriages. A young male serf was dressed in uniform, a young female in a fancy dress, and then, seated in one of the carriages, they reenacted the festive entry into Moscow of Emperor Alexander I and his wife, complete with a "suite" of costumed house serfs. The landowner led the procession and rang the bells.[46] Prince D. V. Golitsyn, who was raised in prerevolutionary France and served as governor-general of Moscow in the 1820s, treated his Rozhdestveno as a "toy," Yankova tells us. He refashioned the service buildings into a ferme ornée stocked with foreign breeds of decorative cattle. In a special room of one of the buildings his wife treated guests to milk and jam, served by the head milkmaid garbed in foreign costume.[47] At Aleksino, in Smolensk Province, the cowsheds were similarly hidden behind a decorative facade called the Fyodorev fortress (fig. 114).

Theatricalization based on royal theater or church ceremony (as Kurakin's crosses and the processional bell ringing suggest) did not exhaust the models upon which the Russian noble could draw. One noble periodically aligned his serfs, each holding sprays of branches, on either side of the road from his estate house to the village and ordered that they throw the branches at his feet as he passed between them, in imitation of Christ's entrance into Jerusalem.[48] V. V. Golovin drew on folk theater in ritualizing daily life at Golovino. The master and his servants staged daily performances, with a set script and gestures for morning and evening. Golovin himself was actor, playwright, and spectator.[49] Drawing on pagan peasant traditions similar to those that inspired Golovin's ritualistic incantations, another noble exorcised evil spirits nightly by assigning a serf woman to walk around his house shaking a rattle.[50]

The noble's usual costume while at the estate, the dressing gown rather than the court or military uniform, symbolized the "otherness" of the milieu. Kurakin's caftan was an elaborate version of a pre-Petrine costume. Some nobles preferred even more exotic alternatives. Shepelev, the Vladimir impresario, succumbing to the early nineteenth-century fashion for orientalism, strode about in a Turkish robe, gold-embroidered skullcap, and slippers, his voluminous pantaloons made of forty arshins (about thirty yards) of silk. Turkish carpets, furniture, and huge, fragrant tropical plants decorated his private apartments.[51]

Like exotic costume or decor, unusual house serfs—not only blackamoors (popular since Petrine times and in vogue in England at that time) but hunchbacks, dwarfs, and non-Russians—increased the estate's theatricality. Miss Wilmot noted an evening's entertainment that consisted of three children, aged five, eight, and nine, who danced charmingly for the company; one was a Kalmyk, one a Circassian, and one an Indian.[52]

Nobles theatricalized events on the estate by borrowing easily accessible elements of court ritual such as fanfares, processions, and parades. At Koshkarov's Veryakushki, in Nizhni Novgorod Province, hunting was transformed into an elaborate pageant. The master of the hunt, in full costume, announced the event from the porch, blowing his horn for a prolonged period. At the sound, the stable master gathered the horses, the huntsmen led out the dogs, and the hunters (Koshkarov's lackeys, who also made up his orchestra and choir) donned their "picturesque costumes," mounted their horses, and lined up. Koshkarov got into a trap (behind which rode the stable master, leading his riding horse), the horn sounded again, and the cavalcade set off, singing lustily. The return from the hunt was carried out just as ceremoniously.

Even Koshkarov's hunting dogs were trained to entertain. After food was poured into a trough, the huntsman sounded his horn, and the kennel gates were opened. The borzois ran out single file and sat in a line in front of him without touching the food. At a second signal, out ran the harriers, who emptied the trough and ran "in good order"

114. The "Fyodorev fortress" at Aleksino,
a decorative facade from the 1790s concealing the cow barns.
Attributed to Vasily Bazhenov. (Author)

back into the kennel. Food was then prepared for the borzois; at a third signal they threw themselves on it, then returned to the kennel in the order they had come out. Trumpet music was played throughout the ceremony.[53] Koshkarov reigned over this performance from an armchair placed in front of the long feeding trough, his guests seated nearby on chairs and benches.

Lastly, some nobles structured estate life in a manner that reflected the passion for military ritual of Russian autocrats, from Peter the Great to Nicholas I. The young noble's experience of a regimented, regulated life in military service often gave rise to an attempt to re-create on his estate a similarly ordered and planned universe.[54] Numerous memoirs testify to this impulse. Peter Kropotkin's father, for instance, issued two sets of military "marching orders"—one to his major domo and one to his wife—for the annual déménagement of servants and family from town to country. "To the Princess Kropotkina, wife of Prince Alexei Petrovich Kropotkin, Colonel and Commander," read the commands enumerating all the stops on the five-day journey. The function of these orders was clearly ritualistic in that Prince Kropotkin often read them aloud to the family some days after the specified departure date had passed. The family sometimes left Moscow in the afternoon, not at 9:00 A.M. as designated, throwing off the whole schedule. But, says the son, "as is usual in military marching orders, this circumstance had been foreseen"; one paragraph commanded the princess to deal as best she could with unexpected changes "in order to bring the said journey to its best issue."[55]

Some landowners, not content with regimenting the daily routine, went so far as to create drill units made up of their serfs. On his estate Shchelnikovo, Field Marshal Gudovich (1741–1820), a hero of Catherine's Turkish campaigns, tried to organize the harvesters like soldiers. They were lined up in long straight rows and given orders to swing their scythes in unison to the field marshal's commands. Predictably, after every mowing a number of peasants had cut legs. Luckily for the mowers, Gudovich was soon recalled to duty in the Caucasus.[56]

Baron Vrangel's anecdote concerning a landowner of the 1850s illustrates the theatrical extremes possible on the estate. This Russian eccentric built not one but six or seven small, spacious houses on his estate, each decorated in a different international style: French, Spanish, Chinese, and so forth. The houses were staffed with harems of serf girls dressed in styles appropriate to each house; the owner (a bachelor) lived now in one, now in another, presumably changing his own cultural persona with each move. In his garden the landowner must have fancied himself in ancient Rome, for here, pedestals supported classical "statues" that were, in fact, nude males and females. Their bodies painted white, these living sculptures remained motionless in classical poses while the owner enjoyed his garden. Eventually "Venus" and "Hercules" conspired: Venus threw sand in the owner's face and Hercules leapt off his pedestal and clubbed the tyrant to death.[57]

The cultural and social impulses behind the theatrical continuum on the Russian estate were complex, and its psychological dimensions are difficult to assess, despite the abundance of memoirs. The historical significance of estate stages and the estate-as-stage is far more apparent. Without estate theater the great dramatic tradition that developed in Russia would clearly have been delayed, if not diminished. Private theaters both developed thespian talent and encouraged play writing. Serf artists were among Russia's first professional actors, dancers, and singers, in spite of their legal status (fig. 115). Visiting authors were often asked to produce something for an estate theater, as Karamzin did at Marfino in 1803, writing the rustic comedy *Exclusively for Marfino*, in which he played the owner (Count P. S. Saltykov), V. L. Pushkin a night watchman, and F. F. Vigel the steward. The considerable expense of estate theater and theatricality is also obvious. The vast quantity of cheap or free labor that serfdom afforded made theatrical productions appear "free," when, in fact, for many a family they were ruinous.[58]

The estate's theatrical continuum validates yet also challenges Lotman's assertion that the noble perceived town and country as distinctly different semioticized stages for theatrical behavior. On the one hand, there is no question that those aristocrats who treated their estates as pleasure grounds were trying, in their celebratory style of life, to get away from routinized urban hierarchy and rituals into some sort of carnival world. Lesser nobles also deliberately created a different routine or atmosphere on their estates. But festive behavior on the estate often took its cues from imperial revels, and some nobles introduced into this private sphere the type of hierarchical, militaristic order of Russian life elsewhere.

The observation that the Russian nobility stretched "from the foot of the throne into the peasant's hut" has often been used in discussing the glaring disparities of wealth in this class. This remark acquires cultural significance in the light of estate theater and theatricality, which were based mainly upon court practice but also borrowed from popular culture and peasant tradition. In some ways estate theater drew lord and serf closer: the cultural gap between them lessened because serfs were educated and trained for performing, sometimes alongside nobles. But the theatrical continuum also highlights anomalies of the lord-serf relationship. In the last analysis serf actors were trained slaves. Sheremetev may have freed and married one of Ostankino's operatic stars, but this choice on his part, as much as Kamensky's whips and Yusupov's cane, proved the absolute power of lord over artistic serf.

Little is known of the serf's attitude toward estate theatricality. The comments of guests reveal that peasants who were hastily transformed into liveried footmen be-

115. Nicolas de Courteille. Portrait of Nikolai Yusupov's serf actress Anna Borunova in rehearsal. 1821. (Courtesy of the Arkhangelskoe Museum)

hind every chair for a showy banquet were not always trained to serve properly. But there is no way to know whether most enjoyed or resented being pressed into entertainment duties or considered their owners' dramatic behavior unusual. One group of Princess Dashkova's peasants seemed delighted when she appeared with her Irish friend Mrs. Hamilton and suggested that they rename their village Gamiltonovka, in honor of the visitor.[59] By and large serfs seem to have collaborated in the staged aspects of estate life, perhaps because they had to or perhaps because of the long-standing tradition of hospitality that, like Orthodox ritual, informed both noble and peasant culture.

Although a passion for and pride in estate theater is writ large in memoir literature, we know little more of the landowner's attitude toward his theatrical life than we do of the serf's. This is primarily because, as Lotman points out, behavior that to cultural outsiders seemed "theatrical" did not seem so to those who had been brought up in the fashion of the Russian noble, who rehearsed the cultural and social roles he would use in later life. To him these roles were unremarkable, a part of normal behavior. But we can assume that to some extent the theatrical continuum described above must have been compensatory. Theatrical activities modeled on court practice psychologically reinforced the noble's identity with the autocracy; the role playing gave him a sense of power and an enhanced self-image possible only in the arena he entirely controlled: his estate.

In the early twentieth century a number of gentleman scholars, including G. Lukomsky, the painter V. A. Vereshchagin, the art historian I. Grabar, and the author and memoirist Baron N. N. Vrangel, began to investigate the many theatrical aspects of Russian estate culture, a way of life they were the first to proclaim unique. In one article Vrangel offered a hypothesis about the psychological impulse behind estate theatricality: until the 1820s, Russian nobles, he said, had been "playing grown-ups" on their estates.[60] From the context of the article it is clear that Vrangel was pointing to a culturally childlike Russia compared to an adult Western Europe, an immaturity reflected in the noble's exuberant imitation of Western culture. But the evidence points to a more organic and deeply rooted parent-child relationship, based on dependency and imitation: that of autocrat and noble.

This relationship was reflected first in the fact that the estate was not an organic outgrowth of local landownership and power. Although an estate might be used for the enhancement of prestige, the noble's real chances for wealth and position remained tied to a presence at court. The ill-defined, sometimes tenuous nature of noble status in Russia, even after Catherine granted her Charter to the Nobility in 1785, certainly contributed to the noble's eagerness to use his estate for theatrical display. Since one could lose noble status through unbecoming behavior, proving nobility by acting noble assumed a particular importance. Just as the French grandee at Versailles used role playing and conspicuous consumption to maintain his status in the eyes of his peers at court, and as the English landed gentry used hospitality to maintain local prestige, some Russian theatricality was directed toward a pragmatic concern for status.[61]

But for Russians, acting noble had an additional cultural connotation: the autocracy demanded that they behave like Europeans. As Lotman has pointed out, the ideal was not to *become* a foreigner but to *act* like one.[62] The westernization of the Russian elite, though initiated by fiat, within a few generations had produced a Russian nobility that used the externals of Western European culture as important components of its self-definition. Yet literary satires of foppish Russian Francophiles and eccentric Russian Anglomaniacs warned Russians of the dangers of overplaying their European roles. On the self-contained world of their estates nobles could, if they wished, ignore these cultural pressures and fashion a role suited to their psychic needs. Ironically, although they lacked real political power in the world beyond their estates, on them Russian nobles had more absolute power than their peers elsewhere. A theatrical reshaping of this private world was a personal response to the official restrictions and controls of the world of official Russia. Estate theatricality went both ways: it could reinforce the noble's image of himself in his roles of cultured European and Russian office holder, or it could engender a fantasy that implicitly or explicitly rejected this imposed image by countering it with carnival, or with ritual or costume of a different rank or nationality.

In trying out alternative identities, the Russian noble can be said to have been playing grown-ups. But his desire to play in such a fashion still does not fully explain the enormous investment in estate theater and theatricality. Lotman posits a general blurring of the lines between theater and everyday life in late eighteenth- and early nineteenth-century Russia that seems significant. For the Russian elite well into the nineteenth century, life itself was a form of theater, in which *chin* (rank) determined one's role, costume, and lines. A Russian critic pointed to the ridiculousness of the Table of Ranks, whose categories embraced not only the military and bureaucratic hierarchy but teachers, doctors, and actors. "Why not forty-one classes instead of fourteen? Fourteen, when in reality there are but twelve. . . . The relation between the rank and the functions is quite arbitrary," he wrote in the 1840s.[63] So schooled were people in these chin roles that when Khlestakov, Gogol's impostor "inspector general," is mistaken for one of another rank, he uses verbal cues to discover what rank he is thought to be and changes his own lines to fit the new role. Russian life-as-theater was both well known and predictable, yet it could result in the fantastical or improbable. As Khlestakov's temporary success or the instant fortunes of imperial favorites, raised from obscurity to enormous wealth, illustrated, role playing could effect radical transformation.

Beyond outright theatricality, many ritualized aspects of estate life such as the carefully ordered household hierarchy, assignment of living spaces, dining procedures, and forms of address substantiate Lotman's life-as-theater model: such cultural markers defined the roles of everyone on the estate stage. But estate theater could also blur real-life distinctions. Serf cooks became princesses, footmen became princes, nobles became stewards. A mixed set of actors—serfs and their owners—played to similarly mixed audiences. One sophisticated theatergoer, who during a journey in 1820 saw performances in the provincial capitals of Orel (where he visited Kamensky's theater), Tula, Nizhni Novgorod, and Saratov, criticized both nobles and serfs for poor acting and heaped scorn on nobles who, as he put it, "spend all their money on the passion to have a theater on their estate in which they themselves play, and for the most part serfs applaud whether or not the master plays well," terming the money squandered both "comical and sinful."[64] This Russian insider's critical stance was unusual in a society driven by the theatrical impulse. Outsiders were more apt to note the social ironies of serf theater. In the 1840s a serf performance in Nizhni Novgorod provoked Baron von Haxthausen to ruminate, "What a vast conflict in feeling this must evoke. From their earnings in this, the freest of all arts, as in the lowliest trade, they have to pay dues to their masters."[65]

Some of the repertory of provincial theater bolsters Lotman's assertion that the distinction between what was happening on stage and in real life virtually disappeared in this period. Shakhovskoy's popular comedy of 1808, *Semi-Noble Enterprises*, for example, is a play about serf theater on an estate. In it a resident poet and acting instructor are preparing an allegorical play to celebrate the betrothal of the landowner's daughter—a ballet with dialogue, featuring Minerva, Juno, the Muses, Graces, naiads, and dryads. By the fourth act, despite feverish preparations, the whole production has become a fantastical shambles. Some actors are drunk, a groom who was to dance in the ballet has been bitten by a dog, and the female dancers have been overcome by heat while cooking blinis. In a final farcical twist, the theater itself collapses.[66]

Although farce was one mainstay, provincial theater also relied on elaborate, allegorical celebration and reenactment of real-life events in the way that Shakhovskoy's play-within-the-play depicts. Such productions called for spectacular effects and cast important personages in multiple roles as characters, spectators, and sometimes actors. Before their very eyes, their existence or exploits in real life were transformed through allegory and allusion into those of classical or mythical heroes. Great spectacles like *Oleg*, or Potemkin's celebration for the birth of Grand Duke Constantine in 1779, or his even grander fete to celebrate the capture of Ismail in 1791 were models for lesser productions. For these famous occasions Potemkin's palace and garden became a theater, and the costumed guests were drawn into the action. Battles were reenacted on the estate lakes, a grotto modeled on the mountains of the Caucasus served as the site for supper, and choruses of maidens in Greek tunics entertained. Guests were transported to other countries and times as they entered various parts of the house decorated in Turkish, Italian, and Indian style, or they went out into the park's arcadian groves and Elysian fields complete with young Olympian wrestlers.[67]

Potemkin was both producer and costumed participant, just as Catherine II was both audience and dramatis persona. Her subordinates in the provinces found themselves in similar positions. To celebrate the arrival of E. P. Koshkin, Krechetnikov's successor as provincial viceroy, Vasily Levshin and Ivan Kartseli wrote *Rejoicing Kaluga and Tula: A Prologue,* casting a nymph, the Oka River, Vulcan, Mercury, and the people of Kaluga and Tula, along with the viceroy, in leading roles. In the opening scene, against a backdrop representing a gloomy wasteland with an amphora containing the springs of the river, the nymph sings a lament about Krechetnikov's death. Vulcan tries to comfort her, predicting that "a hero will come." Soon enough, after an elaborate ceremony, Mercury flies on-stage heralding the arrival of the new viceroy.[68] One wonders how Koshkin felt watching his theatrical alter ego appear in the company of mythical gods to transform life in Kaluga. Was art invading life, blurring the distinctions in such a way as to suggest that life itself was a masquerade?

Ivan Dolgoruky's poem "My Theater" speaks of "reveling in deception," of the allure of remodeling life on stage that many an aristocratic impresario must have felt. Dolgoruky himself described one of his plays, *The Magic of Love* (staged in 1799), as an extraordinarily complex production, designed to amaze viewers by a series of "miraculous events." He continued: "Gods constantly fly down from above and up from below, earth and sky are in movement, forests spring up, buildings move, and imps issue from the ground like sprouts from seed. Everything . . . is evoked magically. The final enchantment [comes when] suddenly the palace of Venus is presented, and Cupid appears seated on an emerald throne."[69]

The death of Alexander I, in 1825, and the abortive uprising in December of the same year by the Decembrists (as this group of idealistic young nobles who sought a liberalized regime came to be known) signaled the close of the heroic period of provincial theater and theatricality represented by Dolgoruky's fabulous spectacles. Perhaps appropriately, by 1825 numerous great estate houses were also empty shells, abandoned by their inhabitants. The nobility's sense of limitless means and romantic literature, the wellsprings of this period of theatrical splendor and fantasy, had both succumbed to a merciless realism. By the 1840s, Lotman suggests, art began to draw on life, and life to reject literary models.[70] By mid-century, in any case, few nobles could still afford the streams of cupids, nymphs, satyrs, Turks, Persians, Greek gods, and equestrian vaulters (fig. 116) that had flooded the prosceniums of provincial stages. The age of playing grown-ups was ending. Midway through Nicholas's reign signs of a more economical privatization of estate life were evident; the

116. K. P. Briullov. Sketch of an equestrian vaulter. 1820s.
(Courtesy of the Russian Museum, St. Petersburg)

search for a national Russian architectural style was beginning to transform estate architecture; and with the exception of Baron Vrangel's neighbor, extremes of estate theatricality were yielding to a more refined taste and manners.

At court and among the intelligentsia, however, theatrical display and a theatrical consciousness continued strong. The court continued to stage elaborate masquerades, and the Marquis de Custine described Nicholas I as a "great actor" (a reputation Alexander I had as well).[71] Small wonder, then, that the aristocratic elite still viewed its life and behavior through the prism of theater. Like the fabulist Krylov, who earlier had commented that "this world is nothing other than a capacious building into which a great multitude of masked people have been gathered," the Decembrist poet V. F. Raevsky, in his last poem, written around 1846, warned his daughter about the deceptive brilliance of high society. It is all a masquerade, he told her, in which men wear "masks and theatrical costumes, and are not what they seem."[72]

Although serf theater subsided under Nicholas and vanished with emancipation, estate theater and theatricality left a rich legacy. This unique form, which both educated and entertained several generations, laid the groundwork for Russia's rich theatrical profession. On an amateur level it remained a staple of estate life to the end of the old regime, as the plot of Chekhov's *Seagull* attests. At Matussov, in Kiev Province, Nikolai Lopukhin (director of the Imperial Theater) arrived each summer in the 1880s and 1890s to stage elaborate productions starring his numerous relatives.

Estate theatricality, played out on two alternative stages, also had a lasting impact on Russian culture. One stage had pandered to official Russia through imitative, sometimes spectacular pantomime. The other stage had been, in effect, an embryonic theater of alienation, employing transforming costume, speech, and behavior to express disaffection from reality. This type of theatricality became a characteristic response of the Russian who felt psychologically oppressed, alienated from, or enraged by his surroundings and circumstances. Well-known later types—the bearded Slavophile in peasant dress, the nihilist of the 1860s whose costume, language, and manners owed much to literary models, the phony revolutionary Nechaev, the Populists of the 1870s—might all be considered heirs to the theatrical model of life the noble impresarios and amateurs of this earlier epoch established.

153

117. F. P. Tolstoy. *Hunting.* Silhouette. Ca. 1818. (*Stolitsa i usadba,* nos. 12–13)

II
The Patriarchal Enclave

I don't know why our learned men

Call them slaves!

. . . .

On this unchangeable foundation

Rests Holy Rus.

—Alexander Bakunin

6
Nests of Gentlefolk

PATRIARCHY IN THE PROVINCES

"Truly, if this is a specimen of the barbarism of the interior, which Western Europeans

discuss, and for which Peterburghers warn the uninitiated to be prepared, it is barbarism of a very

agreeable kind," I said to myself.—**Mary Ann Pellen Smith**

FROM THE EIGHTEENTH TO THE early twentieth century, the phrase "patriarchal Russia" had two very different meanings. For liberal intellectuals and some aristocrats, it was a pejorative term for the large group of struggling, often ignorant, and uncultured provincial landowners in Russia. Here, however, I use it in the positive sense, as most landowners, rich or poor, themselves did. To them patriarchal Russia connoted the traditional outlook, sense of responsibility, and close involvement in estate management they considered the strengths of their class. If the aristocratic estates celebrated in sometimes frivolous fashion their owners' sense of cultural power, the patriarchal estates celebrated their piety, attachment to duty, and traditionalism. The patriarchal estate embodied and maintained the fundamental values of the old regime to such an extent that up to 1861 many landowners used patriarchalism as a justification for serfdom and, thereafter, for the continued existence of a noble landowning elite.

Aristocratic and patriarchal Russia coexisted and interacted in the countryside. Wealth and estate occupancy distinguished the grandee summering in the country from a true provincial, but grandees who retired to their estates tended to adopt patriarchal values, while provincials with pretensions (Andrei Bolotov, for example) tried as best they could to copy aristocratic life. Based on established patterns of social intercourse and domesticity, the life of patriarchal Russia was a seemingly immutable existence, tranquil to the point of monotony. By the 1820s, the serenity of estate life had been jarred twice—by the Pugachev rebellion (1773–75) and by Napoleon's invasion of 1812. The ensuing decades brought the first stirrings of a transition from an essentially medieval way of life to a commercially driven one, culminating in the emancipation of the landowner's "living wealth." Yet despite the changing social and cultural complexion of the countryside, for all the ominous portents of derelict pleasure palaces, most landowners retained a sanguine and insular worldview. This view, and the patriarchal way of life associated with it, survived in many respects until 1917.

The Social Mosaic

Provincial Russia was extremely status conscious. Transient aristocrats who brought a steady influx of sophistication and culture to the provinces from the capitals topped the provincial hierarchy. Their sporadic visits to their estates were great local events, their retirement to a particular region affected the tone of life there, and the new tastes and habits they introduced became part of country living.

The aristocracy also had considerable economic clout locally. Until late in the imperial period, Russia's towns, small in population and limited in resources, functioned mainly as administrative outposts of the central government. Their slow growth has been attributed to their inability to compete commercially not only with Moscow but with the large estate, whose cottage industries and privately owned villages diverted income from urban centers. One historian even asserts that in Russia "there were neither towns nor artisans' corporations in the Western European sense." Manorial serfs could hawk wares or services in town without being taxed as citizens, thereby undercutting urban production and trade. As a result, up to the emancipation, Russian industry "preserved its patriarchal character as the side occupation of the agriculturalist."[1]

Provincial landowners sought close connections with local grandees for the economic as well as social and cultural advantages. In his memoirs of his family estate Sutoki (in Smolensk Province), Sergei Glinka recounts the workings of aristocratic patronage in the late eighteenth century. His family's two "benefactors" were the absentee landowners and courtiers L. A. Naryshkin and M. F. Kashtalinsky. In St. Petersburg Naryshkin sang the praises of Sutoki's jams, honey cakes, liqueurs, and cheeses and procured orders for them. From the Glinkas he once ordered one thousand honey cakes fashioned with his crest on them; even Grigory Potemkin bought Sutoki's liqueurs. Kashtalinsky's contacts helped the Glinkas and their neighbors when they came to Petersburg on business: he housed them and shepherded their petitions through the courts. When Kashtalinsky returned to the province, "he brought court life with him to his Smolensk estate."[2] According to Glinka, Kashtalinsky was an attentive neighbor who sought out the needy and helped them financially, until he was undone by gambling. The estates of transient aristocrats like Kashtalinsky became focal points for surrounding areas, as did those belonging to wealthy, well-educated, and traveled nobles who had retired to the provinces. Some estates provided entertainment, others assistance and reading materials for poorer neighbors; their inhabitants' dress and manners were studied and copied.

Beneath the small pinnacle of these absentee courtiers and Moscow grandees was a stratum of the lesser elite: well-to-do families of the old nobility like the Engelhardts, Rimsky-Korsakovs, Yankovs, Griboedovs, or Kropotkins, who had houses in Moscow but summered in the country; and the wealthiest of the provincial elite like Nikoleva's family in Smolensk, the Chicherins and Baratynskys in Tambov, or the Davydovs in Kiev Province. Below them were a mass of less-cultured provincials and small-estate owners and, finally, a group who were noble in name only.

Concern about status flavors many memoirs and appears early in legal documents.[3] In the reports that Catherine's Legislative Commission of 1767 received from the nobility of each province concerning conditions in their area, for example, there were a number of requests either for more limited access to the ranks of the nobility or for some legal differentiation among the members of this wide-ranging estate. In partial response to this evidence of noble insecurity, the Charter to the Nobility of 1785 distinguished six categories of hereditary nobles. By law, however, all categories retained the same fundamental rights, including that of owning populated estates. In practice families of ancient birth often sneered at nobles of recent origin and Muscovites looked down on provincials, but rank and wealth, cultural level and behavior, determined family status as much as these formal distinctions.

Behavior patterns indicate a clear consciousness of one's position in the pecking order. Social superiors were deferred to; inferiors were lorded over. The wealthy landowner P. A. Shipov, of Kostroma Province, says a contemporary, was renowned for greeting people with a degree of cordiality commensurate with the number of serfs they owned.[4] In Kaluga Province, Yankova's grandmother (daughter of the famous historian Mikhail Tatishchev and wife of a Rimsky-Korsakov), very much the grande dame, made her social inferiors enter Bobrovo from the back porch off the maids' quarters.

Speech patterns also indicate widespread consciousness of social status. Russian, like French, has two modes of address, a familiar *thou* and a formal *you*. *Thou* was used with children, servants, and social inferiors, *you* between equals, by children with their parents, and to superiors. Wealthy nobles routinely used *thou* with lesser nobles. When Bolotov met the rich absentee landowner Prince Gorchakov, with whom he was embroiled in a boundary dispute, the prince, appearing "proud and pompous," used the familiar form with Bolotov and did not invite him to his estate, Zlobino.[5] Yankova's grandmother used *thou* to an inferior noblewoman she thought had said something insulting about her: "How dared thou speak ill of me? Dost thou know who I am, and who thee be?"[6]

The status hierarchy affected the lives of the nobility in various ways, most obviously in their marriage prospects and social life. In Moscow of 1763 Bolotov speaks of balls and masquerades to which only the "upper class" was invited.[7] Peter Rimsky-Korsakov (Yankova's father), a Tula landowner, was "a complete nobleman . . . [who] received every noble as his equal, though of course he wouldn't have given his daughters to just anyone." In Moscow Rimsky-Korsakov and his daughters were also beneath the top social level and therefore not on the guest list for the 1787 Kuskovo festivities honoring Catherine II. They did not know Sheremetev, his daughter explains; despite her entreaties Rimsky-Korsakov, a proud man, would not allow her to join the public crowd of spectators. On another occasion Rimsky-Korsakov was snubbed by Prince Peter Dolgoruky, the newly appointed governor of Tula. During a courtesy visit by Rimsky-Korsakov the prince acted very haughtily and did not ask him to sit down; as a consequence Rimsky-Korsakov never had anything to do with the prince again, even though Dolgoruky's estate was in his district.[8]

In Smolensk, a long-settled region, Nikoleva's family was part of what she calls the local beau monde. It included the Rimsky-Korsakovs; the Golubtsovs; the Baryshnikovs, of Aleksino; the Engelhardts, of Pokrovskoe (fig. 118); and Ivan Gedeonov. But Gedeonov, though married to a princess, ignored the necessary social distinctions and fraternized "with nobles of the second level, who although possibly good people, in terms of their spiritual attributes were not really counted as society." Middling nobles, Nikoleva explains, lacking "good education, manners, and worldly amiableness," educated their sons for low-level jobs in the civil service, but their daughters were barely literate and engaged in weaving and spinning, pastimes considered inappropriate for a noblewoman. And Nikoleva mocks the copycat behavior of the Rimsky-Korsakovs at Ushakovo, not far from the Nikolevs' Pokrovskoe: "They always tried to imitate richer relatives in habits, manners, possessions, and social group. . . . If they noticed something new [furniture, handiwork, or dress] they immediately did the same, though frequently unsuccessfully. They knew nothing about music, but sent their untalented house servant to study. . . . Rimsky-Korsakov was very content if his musician, at his order to 'play something else,' played the same tune on lower or higher keys."[9]

In the 1820s, Nikoleva's family, residing at rural Pokrovskoe, had to be wary, she says, of the company they kept, for there were many "so-called small-estate nobles," the lowest stratum, living nearby. "What to say of their education? Most had not gone beyond the Psalter and breviary, and the women were even worse. One must add to this their various superstitions. . . . Their unceremonious behavior with newly arrived neighbors was intended to

118. Recessed alcove painted as a bower at the Engelhardts' Pokrovskoe. (*Stolitsa i usadba*, no. 28)

show that they were on the same level. I remember one person (it is hard to call her a lady), Agafya Bibikova, who had no other distinction than belonging to the noble class, and based her right to acquaintance with my father on that alone. At every occasion she proudly proclaimed, 'I am a noblewoman.'" Bibikova owned only twenty souls. Nearby lived a Princess Glinskaya, who, convinced that "somewhere in the world there was a Prince Glinsky to whom she was related," was insulted if someone did not call her by this title. The German traveler Kohl recalls coming across nobles reduced to being stewards, doctors, or "even menial servants in houses of wealthier individuals of their own class . . . [and who] will not fail from time to time to exclaim haughtily, 'I am a noble!'"[10]

Other nobles confirm the pattern of avoiding poorer neighbors. One says, "We had little intercourse with our neighbors; they were all poor people and even lower in rank. Probably they were intimidated by my father's rank and wealth."[11] Most of Elizaveta Yankova's neighbors in Tambov were poor landowners, with little education or manners. She was shocked by the way one noblewoman swore at her maids in front of Yankova's children. When Elizaveta remonstrated, the woman merely replied, "Why do you pay attention? These aren't people, they're animals, scoundrels."[12]

Status was marked by gentility in toilette and clothing, the way one kept one's house, and the behavior of children and servants. Yankova's descriptions of her in-laws suggest that she felt she had married down. Her husband's elder sister, she says, had been a good friend of the young Princesses Dolgoruky. But later, on her estate of Teploe, in Tambov Province, she "became a lazybones, ceased being a lady, cut her hair, did not do it up, dressed any old way, [and] her face became wrinkled." Moreover, at her house "the entryway was full of cats; . . . in the antechamber the lackeys and maids played cards and shouted; the furniture was dusty, and the cats shredded the flowers and plants." Yankova also describes her brother-in-law's

slovenly family life at Petrovo, in Tula Province. A limited man whose wife's education was "poor even by the standards of the day," he hired a gypsy troupe to teach his daughter dancing, and socialized with the village priest. Elizaveta and Dmitry were horrified by maids who ran unceremoniously across the living room and by the general disorder at Petrovo.

A noble's status could be improved through altered behavior or by an advantageous marriage. Dmitry and Elizaveta insisted that the gypsies be fired, and when the family went to Moscow, Elizaveta urged her brother-in-law to spend enough money to live in a fashionable part of town. Meanwhile Elizaveta's brother Nikolai (well bred and educated but not particularly wealthy) married up. His father having died, he became friendly with the haughty Prince Peter Dolgoruky (whose estate was in the same district as his Pokrovskoe) and wed his daughter Maria Petrovna. Elizaveta scornfully describes Maria as "short, hunchbacked, with a potato nose and crooked fingers. I couldn't believe my eyes!." Her father's high rank, however, earned her the distinction of an appointment as Fräulein (the court title for a lady-in-waiting) to two empresses.[13]

Under most circumstances, only nobles of a certain breeding could hope for such an advantageous marriage. One poor Kursk noble candidly described looking for a wife in the 1760s. "I wanted a highborn wife, but my clothes and manners weren't right. I didn't have city habits or . . . expensive, fashionable clothes, and when I noticed that the well born were somewhat contemptuous I decided to look for someone with manners and behavior like my own."[14] Grigory Osipov was far luckier. The son of a village priest, he met the wellborn Maria Samoilova on a trip to St. Petersburg, married her, and through his wife's relatives got a good civil service position in Tobolsk. Osipov subsequently became governor of Smolensk, earning respect and a small fortune in this post. He ended his career as a hereditary noble and bought the village of Gnezdilovo, where his father had served as priest.

Cultural pretentiousness sometimes attracted ridicule. Sophia Engelhardt, a sophisticated observer, tells an anecdote about the art connoisseur Nikolai S. Mosolov, who let a neighbor send his serf painter to copy a painting in Mosolov's renowned collection at Zhernovka (in Tula Province). When the copy was finished, the delighted landowner exclaimed, "Who would dare say which is the original!" to which Mosolov coldly replied, "They *will* dare." Engelhardt scoffs at this provincial's uninformed opinions on poetry and at his commissioning for his grotto a wooden statue of a hermit with a book in his hands. "It is hard to understand middling people's desire for things completely alien not only to their understanding but to their inborn inclinations. One must conclude that it comes partially from envy."[15] Descendants of old noble families likewise scorned the nouveau riche. Yankova ridicules the Obolyaninovs, recipients of three thousand souls from Paul I. Obolyaninov was smart but "did not know any foreign languages and in general did not like anything foreign."[16] According to Yankova, Obolyaninov lavished attention on flowers at his lavish estate Gorushki, while his wife let her many dogs (who had their own maid) rule the house.

By the 1840s, even far-removed areas had oases of sophistication and cultivation. Boris Chicherin insisted that "Russian literature has portrayed the old life of landowners one-sidedly and wrongly; it has left out what was appealing. It has described Orzhevka, but not Mara or Lyubichi."[17] In the steppe area where he grew up, on the border of Penza and Saratov Provinces, and where by 1837 his clever father had acquired enough capital to buy the handsome estate of Karaul, social life centered around two magnates' estates.[18] At Zubrilovka (built by Catherine's field marshal S. F. Golitsyn and inherited by his second son, Fyodor) there were "endless parties. . . . [Golitsyn's] doors were open to all; there was always a crowd of all types for dinner." Bekovo, fifteen miles to the north, along the Khopra River, was owned by A. M. Ustinov, a passionate gardener with a magnificent orangery. On his name day and during his village's annual fair, "the huge house was filled with a multitude. . . . For several days there was dancing, fireworks, and feasting," with guests from Penza and Moscow.[19]

But the cultural magnet was the Baratynsky estate Mara, which Paul's wife, Maria Fedorovna, had given her favorite lady-in-waiting, Abram Baratynsky's wife. The gardens of Mara had "ponds, cascades, a stone grotto with a hidden path to it from the house, gazebos, little bridges, and artfully laid-out paths." Abram's eldest son, the poet Evgeny Baratynsky, spent long periods there with his youngest brother, Sergei, who inherited Mara and transformed it into a cultural fantasy. A remarkably talented man, Sergei Abramovich traveled in bad weather over poor roads to tend the sick for free. He also "made fireworks, engraved in bronze, made complicated musical instruments," designed architectural structures, and composed music. "Over the grotto in the ravine . . . Sergei Abramovich built a delightful summer residence to which he moved with his whole family for several weeks or even months. Below, next to the spring, was a bathhouse . . . shaped like a gothic tower, reached by a handsome bridge. . . . On family holidays the woods were full of lanterns of various colors and Bengal fires burned, which gave everything a fantastical appearance. Choruses from classical operas were presented here; and in winter Sergei Abramovich even put on whole operas that the family performed."[20] Nikolai Krivtsov lived at nearby Lyubichi. Raised with his Decembrist brother on the family estate Timofeevskoe, in Orel Province, Krivtsov traveled abroad as a young man and knew all the Moscow intellectuals. He served in England and then as governor of Tula and Voronezh. Unable to get along with corrupt provincial officials, Krivtsov was denounced and demoted, after which he retired to Lyubichi, near Umet, the modest estate of Boris Chicherin's grandfather B. D. Khvoshchinsky.[21]

At Lyubichi, Krivtsov's Anglomania produced a "charming oasis where one could find all the comforts and all the elegance of a cultivated life." There "he built a large manor house without the caprices of the old Russian nobility, but with all the comforts of English life, furnished with taste, with a cozy and comfortable living room with a large and elegant fireplace, a dining room on one side, a large library, handsome orangeries connected to the house, and extensive service buildings. Not far from the house was another building that was somewhat of a fantasy: a tall tower of handsome design, with a flag flying over it which dominated its surroundings, reminiscent of an English fortress." From its top Krivtsov surveyed the territory and drew up plans for an elegant park. He also built an estate church with a large English-style priest's residence. A man of modest means, Krivtsov carefully calculated every detail so that he would not waste his money. The result was "elegant simplicity. . . . Enchanted by English life, he took from it what would fit into the Russian context and what the cultivated man needed." Among the "remarkable collection of intelligent and educated people" living in this area was Chicherin's father, whose elegant manor house at Karaul Krivtsov helped design.[22]

Not far from the cultivated world of Lyubichi was the village of Orzhevka, the realm of a family of old-fashioned landowners (fig. 119). The two Martynov brothers and their sister jointly owned the village, and each had a manor house nearby. Ivan and Avdotya were uneducated but very hospitable, the stock characters of Russian novels. On Ivan's name day, crowds of people came to Khilkovo, his estate, for feasting, theatricals, music, and balls that lasted until sunrise. Ivan's brother Sergei was another prototype for Russian authors—a miser who cheated women at cards, slyly turning zeros into nines on the tally sheet.

In Smolensk Province the social mosaic was equally complex. As elsewhere, members of the social elite were all related through generations of intermarriage. V. I. Lykoshin states that at Kryukovo, his uncle's estate, life was lived "on a grand scale . . . with all the luxurious wonders which at that time one could see in aristocratic houses." The same was true of Bogorodskoe, which belonged to Lykoshin's grandfather, and of Khmelita, where Alexei F. Griboedov, "a hopeless lover of amusement," lived "magnificently, without calculating the costs." The young Lykoshins invariably spent Sundays there with Griboedovs and assorted cousins, organizing "parties de plaisir" and amateur theatricals, taking walks around the countryside, participating in Alexander Griboedov's pranks, or listening to recitals by his sister, a harpist and pianist of some renown.[23]

At nearby Kholm the aristocratic and very hospitable Daria Uvarova (having dissipated her fortune to such an extent that Alexei Kurakin, her brother-in-law, became its manager) lived in a refined if modest fashion. While visiting, the Lykoshins often encountered her two Paris-educated sons, Sergei (later minister of education) and Fyodor. Lykoshin remarks that Kholm provided "schooling in good form—'comme il faut'—for our childhood." Fyodor Uvarov subscribed to all the "best foreign journals and literary works, which he willingly shared with neighbors."[24] Nikita Panin, exiled by Alexander I to nearby Dugino, frequently visited Kholm, as did Stepan Khomiakov (wealthy father of the renowned Slavophile), who owned a neighboring estate of five thousand serfs.

The Lykoshins mingled with this elite but, being relatively poor (though of ancient lineage), were clearly not one of the first families of Smolensk Province. Their estate Kozulino was near both the wealthy Baryshnikovs' Aleksino and the Engelhardts' Ovinovtsina, but neither family appears to have received them. Every summer they traveled to Grigorievskoe, another of their estates, expressly to be near the Griboedovs at Khmelita, camping out in an assortment of outbuildings as there was no manor house.

Memoirists provide fleeting glimpses of other well-educated landowners, "superfluous men" who, unlike Krivtsov or Baratynsky, could not find a role commensurate with their talents. Some vented their anger in sarcas-

164

tic speech and small acts of defiance, much like Chatsky, the hero of Griboedov's *Wit Works Woe*, who, like many of these individuals, had views too liberal for Russia of the 1830s. Others, though wealthier than Turgenev's "Hamlet of Shchigrovo district," were equally out of touch with their surroundings. One such man, "smart, but in a light, sarcastic way," entertained his neighbors by composing satirical verses. As a youth, he had amused himself by staging amorous advances toward his sisters' governesses in an effort to force his parents to dismiss them. Natalya Tuchkova-Ogareva writes that "his whole life went by like this; he recognized that society could not respect him and therefore constantly acted with bravado." Another had an "original cast of mind, unusual energy and rare independence of character." Of him the same memoirist says, "Had he been born in the West, he would have had one of the most outstanding roles in public life, but with us at that time there was no place for such personalities."[25]

The lament for wasted talent is a common refrain. Pavel Katenin, a man of remarkable personality and intellect, was a landowner with three hundred souls. N. P. Makarov, another memoirist, comments, "Had he been born and lived in England or in France, he would have become one of the greatest orators in Parliament, a new Mirabeau. At home he shone like a brilliant firework which vanishes, leaving behind it nothing other than a momentary flash and smoke, which immediately evaporates without a trace. Yet had he gone into the theater, he would have been a tragedian of genius, a second Garrick." At the peak of a potentially brilliant military career "unpleasantnesses" forced Katenin to retire to his estate, where he was "condemned to a fruitless and aimless exis-

tence."[26] He turned his argumentative genius against his country neighbors and ended as a drunken, dirty, cynical, and ignored eccentric. As Alexander Herzen wrote in 1859, "The Onegins and the Pechorins were perfectly true to life; they expressed the real sorrow and breakdown of Russian life at that time. The melancholy type of the man who was superfluous, lost merely because he had developed into a *man*, was to be seen in those days not only in poems and novels but in the streets and the villages."[27]

The cultivated Krivtsovs and the spleen-filled Katenins were the two faces of the educated provincial stratum. Beneath it were the old-fashioned landowners Russian literature ridiculed, represented by the Martynovs at Orzhevka. Lower still on the scale of wealth, underrepresented in literature but numerous in life, were small-estate landowners like the Dostoevskys, who owned Darovoe, in Tula Province. In the mid-eighteenth century the Khotyaintsev family had owned most of the land and villages near Darovoe, but over two generations the property was divided among numerous heirs or sold off. By the 1830s all the estates of the area were extremely small, and its villages owned jointly by a number of people. P. P. Khotyaintsev's residence at Monogarovo, the only true manor house, was the social center of this little world, and his brick church (erected by a Khotyaintsev in 1763) drew peasants and landowners from the entire area. The town of Zaraisk, on the road to Moscow, was the economic center. Landowners and peasants went to fairs, posted their mail, visited the apothecary, and summoned the doctor from Zaraisk. Kashira, a district town, was the administrative center. In its court Dostoevsky's father conducted his protracted land disputes with an heir of the original owners of Darovoe.[28]

Provincial Architecture and Decor

The evolution and outward appearance of Russia's provincial "nests of gentlefolk" (to use Turgenev's memorable phrase) mirrored the social mosaic (fig. 120). Although

119. L. K. Plakhov. Portrait of A. S. Strumilov and his family. 1842–43. Strumilov, a typical, old-fashioned landowner, wears the traditional at-home dressing gown. (Courtesy of the Tropinin Museum, Moscow)

120. The estate house at Spasskoe-Lutovinovo, belonging to the family of Ivan Turgenev. (Author)

121. The living room of Petrovskoe, the estate of Pushkin's grandfather. Note the icon corner (upper left).

with little furniture: a chair or two, a table in one corner, and icons on the walls. Linen-covered walls with hunting scenes or landscapes painted by not very skillful serfs were a sign of luxury.[30] But a new status-conscious architecture slowly invaded the countryside. In his memoirs Bolotov proudly lists the rooms of the single-story house he built for his family at Dvoryaninovo in the 1770s, providing the inventory that distinguished a manor house from a large peasant dwelling. Although small, the house contained a "servants' room, a hall, a living room, bedroom, dressing room, dining room, nursery, maids' room, a quiet study for myself and another for my mother-in-law," as well as closets and a pantry (fig. 123).[31]

These "homely landowners' houses of our grandfathers," with their planked sides and shingled roofs, imitated the architecture of the palace (fig. 124). "Onto the more ingenious of these buildings four columns with a triangular pediment above them were glued, so to speak, to

mansions did exist, the world of most of Russia's landowners was one of mezzanines rather than of grand two-story halls, of icons in living rooms as well as in bedrooms (figs. 121, 122), of homemade furniture and finery produced by family seamstresses, not purchased from the fashionable French shops on Moscow's Kuznetsky Bridge —that is, a world of piety, tradition, and superstition.

Vasilievskoe, the fictional nest of gentlefolk where Turgenev's hero Lavretsky was born and to which he returns, was a typical mid-eighteenth-century nobleman's nest: small, built of pine, and more solid than it looked. Before the great age of estate building, even the houses of wealthy provincials were barely distinguishable from peasant huts. Most had two rooms, only one of which was used in the winter. They were low to the ground and sheltered rats and mice that jumped on the beds as soon as the candles were extinguished.[29] In the late eighteenth century, when palaces first appeared in the provinces, most landowners' houses still consisted of a few small rooms

122. Mariamna Davydova. Icon corner in the bakery at the Orlovs' Matussov. Watercolor. 1920s. (Courtesy of Alona Vassiloff)

this gray background. Among the better-off, these columns were plastered and smeared with whitewash, as were their capitals; with the less wealthy landowners the columns were made of skinny pine logs without any capitals. The ceremonial entrance porch, with a huge wooden awning hanging outward and two blank side walls resembling a vast sentry box, was open in front."

The interiors replicated the enfilade and the clear division between public and private space found in the mansion. "From the entrance porch there was a door into the privy . . . and therefore the entrance into the house was not always distinguished by its fragrance. Beyond the entrance hall . . . was a long great hall . . . with numerous windows on two walls and therefore as light as an orangery. At the far end there were two doors; the first, always low, led into a dark corridor, at the end of which was the maids' room and a back exit to the courtyard. The other door, large and as high as the top of the windows, led into the drawing room; a door the same size led from the drawing room into the study or master bedroom, in the far corner of the house."[32] Another memoirist notes that the same arrangement held true in town and country: a porch with two privies (one for masters, one for lackeys), a smelly entrance hall filled with a crowd of lackeys, then the high-ceilinged enfilade of great hall, living room, and divan room, study, or master bedroom, in which the air was cleaner. Other bedrooms, dressing room, and maids' room were on the opposite side, facing the courtyard.[33] These small rooms had significantly lower ceilings, which sometimes allowed for a second story or mezzanine. A narrow staircase

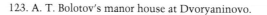

123. A. T. Bolotov's manor house at Dvoryaninovo.

124. Main facade of Petrovskoe, the estate of Pushkin's grandfather.

in the corridor led to this second floor, where the nursery was invariably located and sometimes the family bedrooms as well.

These little houses grew in haphazard fashion over several generations, sometimes beginning as the village elder's house that would be enlarged by a family settling on an estate. One memoirist describes his family's Tula manor house as "a long, wooden structure, with a shingled roof, with additions extending from it without any symmetry."[34] Buturlin calls a similar house, the Chernyshevs' Tagino in Orel Province, "extremely original." It began as a small one-story wooden house, to which were added "as they were needed" enfilades of rooms and corridors on both sides, "without any symmetry or unity in external architecture. . . . From the outside the whole thing looked like a sort of factory; the inside was a labyrinth," which confused guests.[35] A Smolensk landowner (whose family house had only three rooms with small windows) confirms that "in those days real houses were created . . . as a family grew; they were outside the rules of architecture."[36] Most were one story, though the owner might add a mezzanine for additional space (as the Yankovs did at Gorky in 1806). Alexander Vereshchagin's family estate Pertovka, in Novgorod Province, was characteristic: a gray wooden house with a mezzanine fronting on a courtyard. Across from the house were the service buildings: servants' quarters, two kitchens (one for the family, the other for the servants), and beyond them the bathhouse, stables, and other outbuildings.[37]

Interior decor and furnishings distinguished families of substance and taste from others. Raikovo, the Bakunin estate (fig. 125), for example, appears to be a modest, one-story house from the outside. Yet an interior painting shows a columned great hall with elaborately decorated ceiling. Wrought-iron trellises bedecked with live vines section off part of the room, as do screens between the columns. By the early nineteenth century, cultivated Russians were sensitive to genteel furnishing. The poet Con-

125. Artist unknown. Raikovo, an estate of the Bakunin family. Watercolor. First half of the nineteenth century. (Courtesy of the Alexander Herzen Museum, Moscow)

stantine Batyushkov takes us inside two houses of remarkably different character. In one entryway he finds a group of crude, ragged, and drunken servants playing cards. "The rooms had no wallpaper, the chairs no cushions, on one wall life-size Russian tsars were depicted, and across from them, Judith holding the bloody head of Holofernes on a large silver platter, and a nude Cleopatra with a large viper—amazing productions of the house painter. Through the window we can see a laid table on which there is *shchi* [cabbage soup], *kasha* [buckwheat cereal] in earthenware mugs, mushrooms, and bottles of *kvass* [a fermented drink]." Batyushkov then comes across a "small wooden house with a picket fence, a clean courtyard planted with lilacs, acacias and flowers." The scene inside contrasts sharply

with his description of the previous house: "at the door we are met by a proper servant not in rich livery but in a simple, clean dress coat. . . . The rooms are clean, the walls painted by an artful brush, and underfoot rich carpets and a lacquered floor. Mirrors, lamps, armchairs, divans—everything is elegant and appears to have been made by the god of taste himself" (fig. 126).[38]

Interspersed with these small houses were those of wealthier proprietors. The Struiskys' Ruzaevka, in Penza

126. P. Bezsonov. Portrait of a lackey sweeping. 1836. The peasant portrait on the wall is a tribute to Bezsonov's mentor, A. G. Venetsianov. (Courtesy of the State Historical Museum, Moscow)

171

127. The living room of Ivan Turgenev at Spasskoe-Lutovinovo.

Province, had two richly furnished drawing rooms with family portraits crowding the walls. Veryakushki, in Nizhni Novgorod Province, likewise had a proper vestibule, a huge great hall, billiard room, divan room, other drawing rooms, and a number of bedrooms on a single floor. So did the house in which Ivan Turgenev grew up, and in which he wrote the novel *A Nest of Gentlefolk*, though this wealthy landowner's residence, in Spasskoe-Lutovinovo, located in Orel Province, was smaller and simpler than the neoclassical house it had replaced after a fire in 1838. In the 1870s Turgenev described the structure to his friend Gustave Flaubert: a wooden house sheathed in planks and painted a pale lilac, with an ivy-covered veranda and green tin roofs (fig. 118). (Reconstructed in 1976, the house appears much the same today and contains original furniture rescued from a second fire that again destroyed the house.) The spacious drawing room (fig. 127), dining room, game room (which Turgenev, a masterful chess player, called the casino), study, library, bedrooms, and servants' rooms were all on one floor. The furnishings were typical: spoon chairs veneered in poplar and birch, oval Empire tables, large glass-fronted cabinets, and stiff, high-backed sofas, also veneered.

In most districts there were also mansions owned by courtiers who either never visited them or who lived there only in summer. Krasnoe Selo, two hundred miles east of Moscow, in Ryazan Province, described as a "summer retreat," had an expansive enfilade of great hall, a dining room that sat fifty, an English boudoir and state bedroom, a study, and a library; adjoining the library was a private suite of rooms for the countess and her staff.[39] Even in the early nineteenth century, however, numerous wealthy families were living year-round on remote estates and raising large numbers of highly educated children far from a major city. The high cultural tone of life on estates like the Dunins' Vodolagi, the Davydovs' Kamenka, or the Chicherins' Karaul attracted visitors from the city rather than the reverse.

In Russia, where sexual roles were sharply delineated, it was not unusual for large estate houses to be divided by gender. Krasnoe Selo was so divided; at the ends of the two halves of the main house were square towers about fifty feet high, from which different flags were flown to signal whether master, mistress, or both were in residence.[40] Memoirists speak of going from the "half" of the house ruled by a woman to their father's or grandfather's "half." Veryakushki, P. A. Koshkarov's estate near Arzamas, had a "woman's side" with its own living room and suite of bedrooms for female family members and servants. In larger houses, adult family members might have private suites of rooms, in effect apartments, the males on one side, the females on the other. Guests spending the night were assigned rooms on one side or the other, according to sex. One young female guest who got up in the middle of the night in an unfamiliar house mistakenly returned to an empty bed in the male half. In the morning the young man into whose room she had blundered gallantly asked her parents for her hand, realizing that she was compromised.

Provincial living rooms (figs. 128, 129), one memoirist insists, were "always identical."

> In the two piers between the windows there hung mirrors, and beneath them card tables. A sofa, clumsy, huge, with a wooden back and arms (sometimes of mahogany), stood in the middle of the bare opposite wall; in front of the sofa was a large oval table, and on both sides, symmetrically aligned, rows of clumsy chairs. . . . All this furniture was stuffed with nut husks and covered with white calico to protect the material under them (though frequently this was only very thick, unbleached hempen cloth). At that time there was not a trace of soft furniture; but in the bedroom frequently there stood a semisoft sofa covered in green oilcloth, and in the corner a small étagère with the owner's best tea service, the grandfather's intricate goblets, little china figurines and similar knick-knacks. . . . Both internal corners of the living room were cut off by two stoves (not always tile, frequently brick); their backs radiated heat into the hall and bedroom.

Another memoirist agrees that "little imagination, taste or money was spent on decorating rooms."[41]

A more elaborate country house might have reception rooms with painted walls and ceilings and furniture evocative of the pleasure palace (fig. 130). Yankova recalls gilded and white furniture at Lamonovo, her grandmother's suburban Moscow estate. The reception rooms of the wealthy were likely to be fussily overfurnished with possessions accumulated by several generations of inhabitants. The living room of one Tula estate contained Empire-style mahogany-veneer furniture upholstered in brocade, large Voltairian armchairs, old mirrors with bronze clocks in front of them, large bookcases, and étagères filled with porcelain figurines. Garlands of flowers bordered the top of the living room walls; the ceiling was covered with similar designs as well as allegorical medallions. Portraits of ancestors crowded the dining room walls, and a family tree and crest hung over the stairwell.[42] At Mangushevo (which had a two-story great hall) Shompulev recalls his great-grandfather's study, which held collections of arms, coins, crystals, and precious stones, as well as the horns and bones of various animals. Dmitry Miliutin's father's study at Titovo was completely lined with books; the doors to the study were painted with trompe-l'oeil bookshelves, which sometimes confused guests.[43]

By the mid-nineteenth century, estate houses held family relics. At his grandmother's estate Vasilievskoe, Lavretsky (hero of *A Nest of Gentlefolk*) found "little slim-legged divans upholstered in glossy grey damask, frayed and sagging . . . a vivid reminder of the days of Catherine the Great," family portraits, icons, and a dusty wreath of immortelles that his aunt had made. A memoirist describes a similar treasure trove: "There was a lovely frame with the cipher of Catherine II beautifully created out of artfully chosen insects, beetles, and butterflies . . . [and] several pictures made from shells. . . . There was a caftan of antique French work, blue velvet with a wide border embroidered in gold and with large jeweled fastenings." What looked like a "small inlaid bureau with decorative fittings" upon closer inspection by their serf musician turned out to be an instrument with seven pedals "producing the tones of a harp, bells, guitar, flute, etc."[44]

Patriarchal Values and Behavior

In its ideal form the patriarchal estate was a miniature version of the Slavophile dream, a polity ruled by benevolent autocrats who were stern but attentive to their subjects' needs. Literature and memoirs powerfully convey two opposing images of the patriarchal estate. One is of a harmonious kingdom ruled by a caring master, the other its opposite—the harsh domain of a frustrated despot or

128. Artist unknown. The living room of Bogdanovskoe, the Filosofov estate. The bare planked walls and parquet floor were typical of such estates at that time. Ca. 1850. (Courtesy of the Museum of Art, Pskov)

cruel tyrant. The possibility of these polar extremes explains the furious debate that the ownership of serfs engendered. Many Russian writers considered this kingdom a paradigm for Russian backwardness, something to be done away with along with serfdom. Others agreed that serfdom was morally unacceptable yet argued that the patriarchal estate represented the best of Russian tradition—that which, in fact, was uniquely Russian. Still others saw serfdom as a system ordained by God for the benefit of the peasant.

Most memoirists fall into the second category. They give a clear picture of how life was supposed to be, praising patriarchal norms and highlighting deviations in the areas of greatest concern to landowners: estate management, the moral upbringing and economic welfare of family members and peasants, and maintenance of their family's status in the surrounding community. Written almost exclusively by the provincial elite, these memoirs describe landowners who were more involved with the running of their estates, more concerned about their peasants' welfare, and less ignorant and brutish than fictional landowners, but with the outlook typical of their class.

Up to the 1820s one often encounters the approving phrases "he had a broad nature" or "he lived openly." Like the aristocrat, many a provincial landowner of this period did not distinguish between public and private life. He was expected to be endlessly hospitable and to display a certain indifference to how much this way of living cost, particularly if he was a marshal of the nobility. Yankova says that in the 1780s it was customary at Bobrovo to have a constant stream of visitors and thirty people or more for every meal. Everyone arrived not only with his or her own servants but with personal bedding (as Wilmot observed with amazement) and stayed not just several days but sometimes for weeks, months, or permanently. Yankova quotes her father: "He is my neighbor, a fellow noble; I am obliged to receive him joyfully. A guest who mocks his host at table is a swine, but a host who does not respect and entertain his guest is a beast."[45]

Dmitry Miliutin's father, born in 1780, shared this view. Life at his Titovo, in Kaluga Province, was appro- priately lavish and ultimately ruinous. "Hospitality, love of company, and all those habits that accompany a broad nature made him go beyond the limits his material posi- tion prescribed." At Miliutin's estate "the manorial econ- omy was run on a grand scale. . . . There was every type of

129. Artist unknown. The door into the living room at Pushchino, the Strekalov estate.
First half of the nineteenth century. (Logvinskaya, *Interior*)

workshop, among them one for carriage making: everything was maintained that was considered necessary for a decent life and for getting credit. The worse one's financial affairs were, the more necessary to cover it up. . . . Father loved to live lavishly; he had great respect among all his neighbors, and often many came to us. Some stayed several days." Hunting, a major pastime for the provincial nobility (fig. 131), was not neglected at Titovo. Dmitry recalled that "my father was a passionate hunter: he had the best kennel in the area (borzois and hounds), and a whole staff of huntsmen, beaters, whippers and so forth, uniformed

and trained. The Titovo stud farm was also renowned. Sometimes the hunt was undertaken on a grand scale, neighbors who brought their own dogs participating; many people were invited; the ladies rode out in carriages to watch the shooting of hare, foxes, and wolves."[46]

Only a few memoirists were critical of this customary extravagance. On his estate Koshuno (about 17 miles from Smolensk), the retired courtier S. Yu. Khrapovitsky "became in a full sense the father-landowner to his villagers," says S. N. Glinka. Khrapovitsky did not indulge in balls, imported wine, costly clothes or carriages, or the expen-

130. Artist unknown. An estate interior of the 1820s, showing two noblewomen reading and doing needlework. A third, at her writing table, converses with a young officer. A nobleman smoking a Turkish pipe enters at left. (Courtesy of the State Historical Museum, Moscow)

131. E. F. Krendovsky. *Gathering for the Hunt.* 1836.
(Courtesy of the Tretiakov Gallery, Moscow)

"walked around leaning on a thick stick; if he saw something amiss, he shut himself in his study and prayed, and then, having calmed down, tried to figure out how much the peasant was at fault. . . . He either cudgeled him with his stick or lectured him until he sweated; he never whipped anyone, even for a grave mistake." Her grandfather's household was a pious one. Although lenient toward his peasants, he did not hesitate to whip his children, especially for inattention at prayers. "During vespers, which not only the whole family but the house servants had to attend, if anyone whispered or glanced around, he got furious. Sundays at the mass in the closest village he also watched everyone."[48]

Yury Golitsyn's daughter likewise portrays her profligate father as a model manager of his estate, Saltyki:

> He was strict but straightforward: [the peasants] never worked more than three days a week for him; if the steward tried to make them do more when he wasn't there, he would get very angry. The poor and sick were never abandoned or left without help. If someone fell ill, Father went to him with the assistant doctor (also a serf). . . . He fed all his people excellently. . . . From each of [the three servants' quarters] on the courtyard, daily at noon the dinner was brought for Father to try; if something was not right, he would summon the housekeeper and steward. Some people said that he was spoiling his peasants, but father answered, "I live for people, not for dogs!"[49]

When Golitsyn, deeply religious, discovered that few of his peasants knew their prayers or the commandments, he insisted that they study and pass his examination before being allowed to marry.

Landowners spent considerable time on estate maintenance and building (hence the ubiquitous family architects). Sergei Nikolev, a wealthy Muscovite by origin, settled in the Smolensk countryside around 1800 to raise his

sive passion for hunting. (Glinka notes, "Terrible to say, at that time a good hunting dog was worth 500 or a thousand rubles; even worse, sometimes peasants were traded for dogs.") Instead, he ran a school for the children of the local impoverished nobility and had an excellent library.[47]

One memoirist portrays her grandfather as the ideal master, insisting that his peasants at Zheleznovka (in Ryazan Province) "knew no serfdom other than the fatherly hand that guided them." She remembers that he

large family. Says his daughter, "He loved running things and was a good practical agronomist."[50] Although Pokrovskoe was dilapidated when Nikolev arrived, he gave it new life by building a large two-story house, a masonry church with two bell towers, two orangeries, a five-room pavilion, and another for the visits of his sons who were away in service. Like Golitsyn, Nikolev tended to his peasants' needs, building a hospital and dispensary, which he ran with the help of his eldest daughter and a serf woman who knew how to let blood and give vaccinations. On feast days Nikolev personally welcomed village elders to his house with wine and meat pies, while the family nanny dispensed mash and beer to other villagers.

Like grandees, the patriarchal elite retained massive household staffs. Although house serfs were a small percentage (slightly under 5 percent) of Russia's enserfed population, on estates where families resided, they constituted about 20 percent of the serf population. Dmitry

132. A. A. Kalashnikov. *The Kitchen.* Lithograph from a painting by G. A. Krylov(?). 1826–27.
(Courtesy of the State Historical Museum, Moscow)

Miliutin, after enumerating the most important serfs in the Titovo household, says that "to list all would be impossible," noting that "the specialization of occupations and obligations bordered on the ridiculous." Kropotkin says that in Moscow his family, which consisted of between eight and twelve individuals, had a staff of fifty; in the country they had seventy-five, which was considered none too many. Among them were four coachmen, three cooks for the masters and two for the servants, twelve footmen, and uncountable girls in the maids' room. At Bobrovo, Yankova recalls, her father had "his master craftsmen of all kinds: cabinetmakers, smithies, carriage makers. . . . The table linen was spun at home, and beyond that there were linen weavers; he had his own pastry chef. There were an abundance of servants in the room, so that a man with a platter stood behind every chair when dinner was served." Vereshchagin acknowledges that in the 1850s his family's staff at Pertovka was smaller than that on most estates of the wealthy: two coachmen, a cook, a gardener, two lackeys (who were also tailors), a furniture maker, a few weavers, and five maids.[51]

The wives of these patriarchs were household managers and mothers, roles that defined their existence. At Titovo, while Miliutin conducted his business or went out hunting with his friends, his wife supervised the staff of house servants with the help of her housekeeper, Maria Petrovna, the steward's wife. At the Nikolevs' Pokrovskoe the housekeeper was Fedora, who had managed family affairs for two generations. Summoned to remote Nerchinsk as nanny to Nikoleva's mother, a motherless infant, Fedora "became everything" in the household of her owner. When he died, she took her young charge to Tobolsk, over twenty-six hundred miles away, where Nikoleva's mother eventually married a wealthy bachelor. When the Nikolevs retired to Pokrovskoe, Fedora was in charge. "In her hands were the storerooms, provisions, and preparations for the house; everything depended upon her; she just went to the mistress to get permission for some undertaking and then

masterfully did it. Despite all these responsibilities she practically single-handedly brought up all the children of her masters, so that all of us except my sister Elizaveta were obligated to her for growing up in the fear of the Lord, with respect for our parents, and all without any noticeable physical defects." At the nearby Rimsky-Korsakov estate, Ushakovo, one Dukhonina fulfilled the same function. "She did everything: helped run the place, watched the children, sewed for the family, and managed to learn everything, even music; and since the masters themselves were poorly educated she selected the teachers, first seminarists and then a governess, so that she managed the whole house and was more mistress than the real one." Such housekeepers, whether serf or free, had great authority and lived on intimate terms with the family (fig. 132). Shestakov describes Nadezhda Semenovna, the housekeeper on their Smolensk estate, as "mother's alter ego . . . [who] ruled over all the servants; everyone feared and respected her."[52]

Preparing to become household managers themselves, older daughters took on substantial responsibilities. At Pokrovskoe, the four elder Nikolev daughters divided jobs up among themselves. Their father, who liked a good dinner, ordered it in the morning, selecting from "three big cookbooks." A normal dinner consisted of five dishes, with twelve or more for holidays. His wife and daughters were each responsible for carrying out a particular branch of the domestic operations.

Ekaterina Sergeevna made 140–170 pounds of jam, Elizaveta took care of the domestic fowl [up to 1,000, of several different types]; Elena looked after the spinning and weaving of linen, of which we annually produced up to 500 arshins [about 390 yards], from the very finest, as good as Holland linen, to homespun. Nadezhda Sergeevna, aside from healing the sick and running the apothecary . . . supervised the maids' work . . . sewing tulle

133. F. M. Slaviansky. *On the Balcony.* A family portrait depicting a well-to-do noble couple, their children, and an elderly nanny. 1851. (Courtesy of the Russian Museum, St. Petersburg)

bags and making lace according to my sister's lessons. . . . My mother with the help of Fedora readied all kinds of food. Even our candies were made at home; we had very good pistachio nougat and bonbons made from roses.[53]

Childhood on the Estate

Most noblemen spent their early years, and noblewomen most of their lives, on an estate. Until the early nineteenth century young children "led separate lives," says Yankova. They were raised almost exclusively by wet nurses and nannies, who periodically presented them to their parents. Obedience and courtesy were beaten into them, if necessary. "We never said, 'Why are you angry with me?' but rather, 'How did I anger you?'"[54] By the 1820s, however, in most families there was a new appreciation of childhood as a special stage of life and of the mother's role in upbringing. In 1820 Gerakov approvingly noted a provincial countess who was educating her daughters herself. Abram Baratynsky's wife and Dmitry Miliutin's mother considered their children's education their foremost responsibility.

In most memoirs, childhood on the estate is represented as a golden age and mothers as saintly beings. A recent study calls this a mythologizing of parents and childhood, modeled on Tolstoy's idyllic descriptions in *Childhood* (1852).[55] Yet the young Russian noble, cosseted by droves of attentive serfs, did in fact lead a happy, relatively carefree childhood existence. The nursery world was one of Russian custom and peasant beliefs imparted by wet nurses, devoted nannies, and maids, universally recalled as loving, superstitious, and sometimes rather childlike figures. The nanny (fig. 133), usually a serf who had sometimes raised several generations of the same family, taught her charges the rudiments of the Orthodox cosmology, also imparting a good deal about visions and evil spirits to instill obedience. She supervised the child's daily routine and first prayers and taught him or her to kiss the icon over the bed morning and night.

Although as a rule the noble child was pampered and indulged, a few exceptional parents (perhaps influenced by Rousseau's *Emile*) insisted on a spartan regimen designed to promote physical health and fearlessness. One father ordered the nanny not to stay with his children until they fell asleep and to have them do everything they could for themselves, including mending their clothes and shoes.[56] Labzina's widowed mother (the ideal of female piety and service, who taught her children to read and write while devoting her energies to healing sick peasants) raised her daughter to be strong and skillful. Labzina ate coarse food, went without a fur jacket in winter, and took a walk every day of the year, regardless of the weather. In summer she swam before breakfast, then studied the Scriptures. Her mother, she says, did not want her to be afraid of anything. "At 11 I could swim across a large, deep river without any help, I worked in the garden, planting and watering. . . . My mother worked with me, and never made me do anything she didn't do herself."[57]

Beyond the nursery boys and girls encountered the segregation by sex characteristic of nineteenth-century Russia. Women raised girls, and men boys, with gender-specific goals in mind. As one pedagogue noted, "For boys, the goal of education is the whole world, for girls—the home."[55] Girls usually stayed at home with governesses, while boys, after a few years with tutors, were sent off to boarding school and then began their service careers, coming home only for visits until they retired from service. The education of Nikoleva and her eleven siblings illustrates this pattern. Her eldest brother, Sergei (twenty-three years her senior) studied at Moscow University's boarding school for nobles and then entered the army; he did not see his family for nine years. At the age of forty, at his ailing father's request, he retired and moved home. The second brother, Alexei, was sent to the Cadet Corps and became aide-de-camp to Prince Repnin. The third brother studied at home, as did seven of his eight sisters (one attended the Smolny Institute, the most prestigious school for noblewomen in St. Petersburg).

The nanny's replacement by the first governess or tutor marked the cultural divide between a Russian infancy and a European adulthood. Given the task of eradicating traces of the Russian nursery, one Swiss governess taught her charge to say the Lord's prayer in French instead of Russian and forbade her to kiss the icon above her bed. The nanny's fairy tales and fantastic visions were replaced by moral fables, in which children's virtue was tested and evil punished.[59] The quality of these teachers was extremely varied. Some played with their charges and were well liked. Nikoleva's favorite tutor, a handsome Frenchman, was so attached to the family that years later, upon seeing her sisters in Moscow, he burst into tears. Others were at times purposely or pathologically cruel. Tutors and governesses ate with their charges and insisted on proper speech and manners.

In some families social contact with serf servants was prohibited after infancy, lest the young noble's language and habits be corrupted by peasant speech, prejudices, and superstitions. The inability of most tutors to speak Russian forced young nobles to learn a foreign language in short order. One memoirist notes that as a small child she rarely saw her older sister and even more rarely spoke with her, chiefly because the sister spoke only French or English, while the younger children spoke only Russian.[60] Some nobles became fluent in several languages at an early age. Princess Dashkova, the Wilmots observed, was "unconscious whether she speaks French, English or Russian, and mingles these in every sentence."[61] Before the age of six Natalya Grot could read in two languages.[62] Up until 1812, memoirists confirm, the Russian elite spoke their own language poorly. Ekaterina Bakhmeteva, raised at Vodolagi, in Kharkov Province, spoke French exclusively and had only seven lessons in Russian, from a Ukrainian priest who mispronounced the words. Dmitry Miliutin says, "In Russian society of those days [French] was used practically exclusively. . . . By five I was reading French children's books. Mother gave us lessons for a couple of hours every morning." Only later did Miliutin study Russian.[63]

Correct behavior was no less important than mastery of foreign languages. Boys were whipped, girls generally only shamed for behavioral lapses. At the age of ten

Ekaterina Bakhmeteva, seeing her cousin's infant being suckled by the wet nurse, announced that she would nurse her own child. (In *War and Peace* Natasha Rostova makes a similar decision, considered improper for the well born.) To shame Ekaterina, her governess dressed her in the costume of a wet nurse and invited everyone to come laugh at her.[64] When Sophie Kovalevskaya overslept, her governess brought her to dinner with the word "lazybones" tacked to her back.[65] Children, especially girls, were to be satisfied with everything, to submit unconditionally. A moralist advised parents "early on to teach their daughters to subjugate their own will to the will of others. This will assure them a happy life."[66]

Most male memoirists went from home to a cadet corps school or a boarding school, the harsh regimes of which undoubtedly intensified nostalgia for their estate childhoods. Although most women stayed home, they were surprisingly well educated in certain areas, primarily those that made them more marriageable. Piety and charity being desirable female virtues, a girl's education included large doses of religious readings, often formal religious instruction, and handicrafts (fig. 134). Adolescent noblewomen frequently emulated saintly females and sometimes became intensely religious; others took the veil, as does Liza, heroine of *A Nest of Gentlefolk.* Although some girls studied history, geography, literature, and elementary mathematics, deportment and drawing-room graces such as playing the pianoforte or harp, singing, drawing, and dancing were the centerpieces of a noblewoman's upbringing. Social training also dominated the curricula of female boarding schools, where students were theatrically rehearsed in worldly conduct. "The teacher met them in the big recreation hall. 'Now, dear,' she said, turning to a student, 'In your house a guest is sitting—a young man. You must go in to him to pass some time—how do you do that?' Afterward the girls pretended to accompany the guest, to give their assent to the mazurka, to sit down to play the piano at the request of a cavalier,

to meet and spend time with a grandmother or grandfather."[67]

This upbringing produced a marriageable young lady, or more accurately, a well-trained child. Ekaterina Samoilova, mother of General Nikolai Raevsky (the famous hero of 1812) by her first marriage and of the Decembrist Vasily Davydov by her second, was so young when she married that she played with dolls when her husband was away.[68] The only alternatives to marriage were to devote oneself to good works within one's family, to become a governess or teacher in an institute for noblewomen, or to live in a nunnery. Matchmaking was, in consequence, a major concern of noble parents. "My daughters won't become governesses! They are not dowerless, I'll take them to Moscow," exclaimed one provincial noble. His efforts to expose them to suitable husbands during the Moscow "season" failed, however; when they returned home, he married them off to neighbors.[69]

Two fathers often agreed upon a marriage after a couple of visits by the suitor; consulting the proposed bride was merely a formality. Bolotov negotiated on his own behalf with the widowed mother of a young girl he barely knew. (The widow being smart, and only a few years older than he, he calculatingly planned to win her as a housekeeper along with the bride.) By the 1830s and 1840s mutual attraction was more of a factor, but parents still controlled the process. Yankova turned down one of her daughter's suitors "because he had little money and seemed an empty-headed person," a decision she later regretted.[70] Of course, a love match did not necessarily ensure a happy marriage. In the 1840s the dashing young Yury Golitsyn mounted a romantic campaign for Ekaterina Bakhmeteva's hand, but his subsequent infidelity caused her great unhappiness.

Russia's early feminists sensed their second-class status even as children. Nadezhda Durova evaded her female destiny by disguising her sex and enlisting in the army; her courage during Napoleon's invasion earned the admiration of Alexander I.[71] The less fortunate Maria Tsebrikova, later a noted feminist writer, describes being torn during childhood between her mother's social aspirations and her own intellectual ambitions. She outshone her brothers in mathematics, but when she was twelve her father declared, "Logarithms are not for girls." She notes, "This wounded my vanity, all the more since my [male] cousins, my childhood companions, teased me, 'Where do you think you're going, girlie; you won't understand!'" Her "aesthetic" education, as she puts it, now took over, the intent being to transform her into "an interesting and gracious product for the market in brides." Once or twice a week she had dancing lessons with other children and at holiday times learned special dances. "The most unbearable were the minuet with its curtsies, the kachucha with its twisting and bending, and when we were 12—the balletic *pas de châle* and *pas de couronne.*" Young ladies were also taught how to walk, enter a room, bow, sit down, stand up, pick something up, offer something, and the like. "Daily a large percentage of time was spent on superficialities. . . . The goal was to prepare us to shine at balls, to please." The lessons ended when one turned fifteen and started going to evening parties.

Tsebrikova's parents, faced with a daughter of independent mind, warned her of a distant female relative who had read atheistic books and gone insane. The real story, says Tsebrikova, was somewhat different. "She was barely taught grammar, while her brothers studied in the cadet corps. Some rich neighbors came for the summer with a whole troupe of governesses and governors; one had pity on the able young girl who passionately wanted to learn, and worked with her. Success came swiftly. That winter the student progressed on her own. . . . She used her neighbor's library and read the encyclopedists; her childish faith was destroyed, and life appeared so dark—the life of the serfs, a life of idiocy and tyranny. She went out of her mind from one disturbing thought: why are all the best people suffering, and the evil ones happy? Where is justice?"[72]

Yet most female memoirists appear to have accepted their parents' values and contentedly describe the affective side of a provincial upbringing —the warm relations with nannies, parents, and governesses (figs. 135, 136). As adults these compliant daughters of the gentry managed estates prudently, acted as caring mistresses to their serfs, raised literate and properly socialized children, and survived their arranged marriages. In a later, more liberal age some had the tools to pursue intellectual interests if so inclined.

Male Tyrants, Female Viragoes and Victims

For all their idiosyncrasies, the patterns of estate life described thus far fit the behavioral norms of provincial life, norms that allowed for wide discrepancies of wealth, education and, consequently, status. There were, however, notorious deviations throughout provincial Russia. Some landowners were eccentric or tyrannical, in the manner of Aksakov's old Bagrov in *A Family Chronicle* or Tolstoy's Prince Bolkonsky in *War and Peace.* Bedding the occasional housemaid was normal, but some landowners sexually exploited female peasants beyond accepted limits. Others created ritualized existences on their estates.

The wealthy P. A. Koshkarov, already introduced, in many respects exemplified patriarchal ideals. At age seventy he spent the morning at Veryakushki hunting or on business matters—perhaps looking over reports from the estate steward, stable master, gardener, and others—then had dinner and a nap, and spent the evening listening to music or playing cards. Like most wealthy landowners of this period, Koshkarov had an orchestra and chorus for entertaining; when guests were present, there frequently was dancing. Koshkarov's peasants considered him a kind and just master and were well off in comparison to their neighbors. Although there was no school in the village, Koshkarov's male and female house servants were not merely literate but well versed in literature and the arts. Koshkarov prayed morning and night and made sure that

135. Artist unknown. Daughters reading in a family room opening onto the second-story balcony of a modest estate house. 1830s. (Courtesy of the State Literary Museum, Moscow)

his house serfs attended church regularly. Koshkarov, who never married, had illegitimate children, but he obtained noble status for them and enlarged and protected the property that one day would be theirs (that is, property he had acquired; the family estate would go to his legal heirs, his brothers). Koshkarov, however, also took advantage of the landowner's limitless authority within his domain and in doing so exemplified the gulf between the public ideal and certain private behavior. This lavish host, music lover, hunter, and pious patriarch was also a tyrant and erotic adventurer.

134. An unusual portrait of a mistress doing handicrafts, executed in fine beadwork and embroidery. Mid-eighteenth century. (Courtesy of the State Historical Museum, Moscow)

Koshkarov's house was, as already noted, physically divided into male and female halves, the latter containing his harem of twelve to fifteen pretty serf girls. The male half included the entry hall (decorated with hunting horns and weapons), a huge great hall, pantry, billiard room, divan room, and the so-called "brothers' rooms" for Koshkarov's sons. The women's half began with a living room, which was actually a neutral room, because males and females mingled here. From this living room, one door led to the great hall and another to Koshkarov's bedroom (in the women's half); these two doors were guarded by a lackey and a harem member, respectively. Female servants could not step into the great hall, nor could lackeys enter the bedroom. Koshkarov's bedroom had no bedroom furniture and served, in effect, as a second living room for his family and harem. Beyond it was the obligatory study (unfurnished save for various housekeeping equipment), and beyond the study Koshkarov's personal privy. Off the study lay the room of his former mistress, Natalya Ivanovna, mother of his illegitimate daughter and seven sons, and beyond it the huge maids' room for the harem, partitioned into several separate little chambers.

In the household hierarchy the widely respected Natalya Ivanovna occupied the rung below Koshkarov. Next came Feoktista Semenova, Koshkarov's secretary, accountant, and manager of his household. (Some speculated that she was his daughter, others that she had replaced Natalya Ivanovna in his bed.) A handsome and lively peasant, Feoktista, though educated entirely at home, was erudite and played the piano excellently. Feoktista's mother managed the harem, made up of girls selected from Koshkarov's peasant families and moved to the manor house. Koshkarov's peasants apparently welcomed this honor, which brought with it a dowry, European clothing, salaries, gifts of money on holidays, and education. Harem members read to Koshkarov and played whist with him, so as a rule they were unusually well educated; the older girls were expected to instruct newcomers. The memoirist Yanuarius Neverov fondly recalls a Nastasya, who taught him his letters and had him copy and memorize verses of Pushkin and Zhukovsky.

The master retired to bed in ritualized fashion. After supper, at Koshkarov's signal the girl on duty would loudly announce to the lackey, "The master is pleased to go to bed." The family immediately retired, and the lackeys carried a simple wooden bed from the male half into the middle of the neutral living room. Then the door to the great hall was closed for the night, and the harem brought Koshkarov's bedding from his "bedroom," as well as their own pallets, which they arranged around his bed. Meanwhile Koshkarov read his prayers while one of the girls held a candle for him. The girl on duty for the night undressed him; once he was in bed, she sat in a chair across from him and told fairy tales. She held a piece of cloth in her hands with which, on command, she rubbed his back or feet. For Russian landowners this was perhaps not as strange as it appears today: in *Dead Souls* the serf-owner Korobochka offers similar services to Chichikov, who is spending the night. "Maybe, father o' mine, you're used to having somebody scratch your heels at bedtime? My dear departed husband could never fall asleep without that."[73] One might also note that the whole routine, with its fairy tales and attentive females, mimicked the nursery.

When Koshkarov awoke, the girl on duty informed the lackey on guard at the door of the great hall, "The master has ordered the shutters opened," and went off to sleep. The half-hour during which Koshkarov dressed and washed was the worst period of the day. All the girls' sins of the previous day were punished by his slaps or whippings. One had been looking with too much interest at the lackey on duty; another had come back flushed from delivering the master's orders—any pretext was used. After his morning prayers Koshkarov resumed his patriarchal role.

Clearly Koshkarov's private property, the girls were strictly chaperoned at all times, forbidden any contact with male servants, and closely supervised during visits from male relatives. Their duenna took them to church, walked with them in the garden, and even supervised their trips to the privy across the courtyard. Whether from his own sense of propriety or because his memories were those of a young boy, the memoirist only hints at the sexual demands on these girls. Once a week the harem accompanied Koshkarov to the bathhouse; a girl who tried to hide herself from shame would be beaten. On occasion, for male guests only, the girls were brought out to sing innocent-sounding songs full of double entendres. Koshkarov also liked off-color stories. Neverov remembers a tale of seduction, allegorically cast as the capture of a fortress, which ended: "Finally the enemy invaded the fortress and torrents of blood flowed, while from the rear bastion there was a shot."[74] (To the titters of the household, this tale was read to a pious old woman as a newspaper account of a recent military campaign.)

After a certain period the girls were retired and married to one of Koshkarov's equally well-educated lackeys. Those who failed to live by the rules of the harem had their finery confiscated and were returned to their family in disgrace or, if they had committed serious violations, were severely punished. Such was the case when Fedor, a lackey, attempted to elope with Afimya, a maid in the harem. An enraged Koshkarov ordered a massive manhunt, and by the following morning the couple had been captured. After being brutally whipped, Afimya was chained by a spiked collar to a huge wooden block for one month. Fedor was beaten in front of Koshkarov until he could no longer cry out; horse dung was then thrown in his face. The memoirist does not know the fate of Fedor, who may have died or been sent away, but he later saw the demoted Afimya "in simple peasant dress sweeping the courtyard."[75]

Koshkarov's eroticism and cruelty were not unique. Filipp Vigel says that respectable women rarely visited the estate of Peter Esipov, a bachelor "whose sensuality knew no bounds." During an evening at Esipov's, Vigel encountered a group of attractive women who turned out to be the stars of Esipov's serf theater troupe. At dinner they seated themselves between the male guests rather than along one side of the table, as was customary. The "beauties" on either side pressed Vigel to drink and to kiss them, "neighbor to neighbor." Astonished, he wrote: "At the far end of the table there sat, can you believe it? Esipov's actors and musicians, that is, his servants, who took turns getting up from the table, serving us, and then sitting down again. They say that in Scotland the custom existed of master and servants of one clan sitting at a single table; one can see something patriarchal in that, but here, what kind of patriarchality! This saturnalia, bacchanal, continued long after midnight."[76]

D. N. Filosofov's conduct with his serf harem at Bogdanovskoe (fig. 137), in Pskov Province, inspired his daughter-in-law to become one of Russia's first feminists. Ivan Zaitsev reports that his father, a serf painter, was ordered by his master to produce erotic scenes, which were kept locked up because they were "disgusting and unpleasant."[77] V. A. Shompulev describes orgies involving housemaids and drunken guests in the great hall of Lev Roslavlev's manor house in Saratov Province. The estate with the "living statues," described by Wrangel, had a torture chamber, as did Struisky's Ruzaevka, in Penza Province. Struisky, who served as governor of Penza for a time, incongruously called the dusty top-floor study containing whips and chains his "Parnassus." Before becoming an impassioned poet (publishing his works at his own expense), Struisky had amused himself with law by interrogating and torturing his serfs, arguing for both the prosecution and defense, and then pronouncing sentence.[78]

The absolute power of landowner and paterfamilias put females and serfs in similar positions. Both were completely dependent, and both were expected to demonstrate obedience, service, and Orthodox piety. Fathers and husbands took for granted their right to control female property and destinies and, when they chose, to abuse women, who had little recourse. Anna Labzina's memoirs offer a case in point and a glimpse into the psychology of the late eighteenth century. Raised on a small farm somewhere between Ekaterinburg and Chelyabinsk, Anna lost her father at an early age. When Anna was thirteen, her incurably ill mother decided to secure her daughter's future by marrying her to Alexei Karamyshev, who had been raised and educated by Anna's father and was already a renowned scientist. Karamyshev exerted his authority over his young bride immediately, sometimes preventing Anna from being with her suffering mother. Shortly after the marriage Alexei's niece joined the household. One evening Anna innocently reported to her nanny that the young woman was happily asleep in her husband's arms. Karamyshev banished the nanny, forced pious Anna to eat meat during Lent, filled the house with his gambling and

136. Exterior view of Filimonki, an early nineteenth-century estate house in Empire style, with a second-floor balcony.

order to lead a "peaceful, secure life until the end of my days on my estate."[80] As late as 1836 the Law Code read, "A woman must obey her husband, reside with him in love, respect, and unlimited obedience, and offer him every pleasantness and affection as the ruler of the household."[81] This explains the harrowing and prolonged ordeal of a Tambov noblewoman in the 1850s whose abusive husband had similarly married her to get control of her property.[82] She finally fled from her husband's estate back to her own, where her sister and niece were living. The three women kept careful guard against the husband. On Christmas Eve of 1852, on their way to visit their brother, the husband waylaid their sledge with his band of serfs, threw the coachman and lackey into the snow, and took his wife home. Thereafter he treated her as if she were a disobedient serf, threatening to send her to the stables for a beating, to dispatch her to Siberia and, finally, to send her to a distant estate as a maid of his former mistress.

137. Artist unknown. The divan room of Bogdanovskoe, the Filosofov estate. (Courtesy of the Pskov Art Museum)

drinking friends, and continued to bed his niece. When Anna became severely ill from these traumas, her mother-in-law stepped in, and for a time Karamyshev reformed, though his periods of good behavior did not alter Anna's image of him as tyrant. One of the many extraordinary elements to this tale is the fact that Karamyshev repeatedly told Anna he loved her and desired her happiness. She had promised to obey him and did, until his death some twenty years later.[79]

Legally, an abused wife could not leave a tyrannical husband. In August 1768 Alexandra Krotkaya, a noblewoman, petitioned the empress and the Holy Synod for a legal separation. She asserted that her husband had never loved her and had married her solely for the estate that was her dowry; that he had mistreated her from the start and treated his serf mistress as his wife; and that her submissive behavior had not aroused his pity but increased his lascivious instincts to the point where he was seizing her peasants' wives and underage daughters and raping them. Alexandra asked merely to separate from her husband in

138. Main facade of Sergei Aksakov's Abramtsevo, where Aksakov wrote *A Family Chronicle*. (Author)

Three months later the victim escaped again. Defying the governor's order to return to her husband, she used the pretext of ill health to remain with her brother while her case dragged through the courts for several years. Not until 1856 was she given legal permission to live apart from her husband.

Sergei Aksakov's description of the tyrannical Mikhail Kurolesov in *A Family Chronicle*, written at his estate Abramtsevo (fig. 138), was based on the real-life trials of his father's second cousin once removed, who married a fortune hunter named Kuroedov. Aksakov's narrative, more fact than fiction, combines features of all the preced-

ing tales of female victimization. Kurolesov, who married Parasha Bagrova for her one thousand serfs, treated his wife very well, reserving his licentious behavior for a distant estate. Arriving there late one night, Parasha caught her husband and his cronies carousing and fondling women. The next morning her husband beat her and threw her into a dungeon, declaring that he would not free her until she had turned her estates over to him. Parasha was freed only five days later, when her cousin arrived with armed serfs. She had refused to believe ill of her husband until she had proof, and now she refused to prosecute Kurolesov (who shortly thereafter was murdered by his serfs). In most such cases, noblewomen reacted with the passivity and self-sacrifice bred into them.

But female landowners were also known to deviate from the norms of piety, service, and submission. Empowered by estate ownership in a society that in other respects treated them as property, some women developed patterns of behavior that in the mildest instances were capricious and in the worst outdid the men in sadistic cruelty. "Saltychikha," the nickname for Darya Saltykova, whose misdeeds occasioned a notorious court case during the eighteenth century, became a synonym for cruelty. Saltykova, of ancient lineage, owned more than 600 souls in three provinces. Over the course of a decade, enraged by improperly cleaned floors or linens, she put to death 139 serfs, mainly young girls. Saltykova personally beat some; others were sent to the stables to be flogged. One woman had her hair burned off her head; others were drowned.[83]

So legendary was Saltykova's cruelty that a century later, tales of her cannibalism circulated among local peasants. They insisted that she had brought young girls to Moscow from her estates to be fattened up. She then slit their throats, ate their hearts, and sent the bodies to the countryside to be secretly buried by the village priest (who was condemned along with Saltykova).[84] Although this account sounds too much like a fairy tale—the wicked queen of "Snow White" (well known in Russia) springs to mind—to be entirely credible, Saltykova's sadism is unquestionable. After a six-year trial, she was given a death sentence, but Catherine commuted this to lifelong incarceration in a Moscow nunnery. Another woman who flogged a serf to death in 1772 was merely jailed for three months.

More frequent and usually less publicized were random instances of physical or psychological abuse by female landowners. Ivan Turgenev's mother was infamous. Her neighbors claimed her villagers spread venereal disease because she encouraged her steward to take advantage of her serf girls. Turgenev's tale "Mumu," based on his mother's misdeeds, tells the story of a feeble-minded peasant who drowns himself when his mistress forces him to get rid of a stray dog he has adopted. The unfeeling mistress of Turgenev's sketch "The Estate Office" may be another portrait of his mother. Other landowning women exploited their serfs for profit. Anna Neklyudova, wife of the governor of Tambov and Vladimir Provinces in the 1820s, forced her seamstresses to embroider items for sale hours on end. She kept them alert by putting Spanish fly (a blistering agent) on their shoulders and prevented them from running away by tying them to their chairs by their hair.[85]

Occasionally, ill-treated serfs had their revenge. One landowner of the 1840s who slapped her maids continually and had her house serfs cruelly flogged set out one day with her coachman, lackey, and maid. A short distance from the estate the coach unexpectedly stopped in a birch grove. The two young men jumped down, cut some thick switches, hauled their mistress out of the carriage, whipped her senseless, and brought her home half dead. They were sent off to the army for their crime but went with no regrets. Their shamed mistress fled the provinces for Moscow.[86]

Were these viragoes simply sadistic by nature, or did the intoxication of their freedom from the Russian woman's traditional subordination set off some inner process leading to tyranny? In one instance, the psychological strain of defying social norms brought its own punishment. In the 1840s Ekaterina Shishkova so terrorized family and staff on her large estate Ernovo (Ryazan Province) that her younger children cried upon seeing her. She had serfs flogged in the stables or sent to Siberia for minor offenses, and she doubled her peasants' dues when she needed money. Any woman her husband glanced at was immediately sent to some distant estate and married off. Troops were constantly being summoned to Ernovo to put down peasant revolts against Shishkova (whom contemporaries called "Saltychikha" because her tyranny was reminiscent of the legendary Saltykova's).

One day, hearing that Yermolai, her cook, had been talking about her, Shishkova flew into a rage and ordered him and his family to Siberia. In return the old man loudly cursed her, shouting that while Siberia would be hard for him, her black soul would rot in hell. Curses in Russia were serious business. One day shortly thereafter Shishkova retired to her bedroom and remained there until her death, subsisting on only black bread. She was mute for the first twelve of her sixteen years of mysterious seclusion, but toward the end of her life her ability to converse rationally convinced witnesses that she had not gone mad. She frequently summoned the priest, and her self-imposed penance was clearly an attempt to absolve her crimes.[87]

Other matriarchs practiced milder forms of tyranny or favoritism. Avdotya Martynova put a special bottle of wine in front of Nikolai Krivtsov (whom she particularly respected) when he came for dinner without offering her other guests anything. Maria Passek made her adult daughter spend hours on her knees in front of her, begging for forgiveness. She punished maids by tying them to chairs with very thin thread; they dared not move for fear of breaking it. Passek favored certain relatives at dinner by putting various types of food in a dish, stirring it with her finger, and having a lackey place it in front of the favored person, who was obliged to eat it all and then come up to the head of the table to thank her. Passek would become enraged if the favorite did not comply.[88]

Like any system of unlimited power, the patriarchal estate and family provided ample opportunities for abuse. Mild abuse was obviously frequent, and the notorious cases I have cited make for exciting and disturbing reading. Possibly these viragoes and tyrants were the inevitable products of a system that subjected most females to lives of total subordination and most males to harsh military discipline and a delayed adulthood.[89] But abusive landowners like Koshkarov, Karamyshev, Shishkova, and Saltykova were a small portion of the total, as were highly cultivated landowners like Krivtsov or the Uvarov family. Although few estate owners may have lived up to the patriarchal ideal, the majority stayed within accepted bounds of behavior, practical considerations as much as social opprobrium restraining them from willfully wasting their living wealth. The misdeeds of a minority of serf owners received attention precisely because such iniquities proved the evils of the system.

7
Town and Country

THE RHYTHMS OF RURAL LIFE

In autumn [of 1825] the tsar traveled to the Crimea through our unpretentious Elnya. All the nobility gathered

to greet him. . . . One average lady had a very nice orchard, and knowing that the tsar's path lay

through her estate she went out to meet him with a platter full of plums. The tsar, seeing this,

ordered a halt and took one plum. "Take them all!" the landowner shouted in ecstasy, and poured the

whole contents into the tsar's carriage. The tsar smiled, drove on, then stopped and

ordered his suite to remove the plums. —**Maria Nikoleva**

IT IS CURIOUS THAT FEW Russian landowners sat for portraits in traveling clothes, considering how frequently they took to the road (fig. 139). Landowners seem, in fact, to have been continually on the move. Accompanied by their families and retainers, they traveled regularly to their neighbors and to district towns or provincial capitals for both business and pleasure (fig. 140). Even those living on remote estates occasionally journeyed to Moscow or St. Petersburg. Until the mid-nineteenth century these excursions were difficult and often dangerous. In the 1760s the nobility of Pskov Province reported that lawlessness and fear reigned: "The nobility and people of every rank of Pskov county suffer extreme ravages from brigands, thieves, robbers, and other kinds of criminals, which stops very many of the nobility from living on their estates, for the protection of their lives from wicked torment. . . . Those living in the provinces . . . are compelled for the defense and protection of themselves and their homes to keep up three or four times the normal number of household servants."[1] Provincial Russia reverberated with the reassuring sound of night watchmen beating on their tin boards and calling out to one another as they patrolled the manor-house grounds. In the late eighteenth century Andrei Bolotov, constantly on the road, sometimes took along armed serfs dressed up in military uniforms to frighten off highwaymen.[2] The grandfather of the anarchist Bakunin, attacked by brigands on a trip, single-handedly fended them off with a plain wooden board.[3]

In addition to outlaws, some provincial nobles were the scourge of their neighbors and passersby. Aksakov's semifictional Kurolesov, with his band of marauding serfs, recalls the notorious real-life Struisky, whose men waylaid travelers across his domain. Struisky interrogated them, then threw them into his jail, where some languished for years. In Kharkov Province one noblewoman amused herself by attacking merchants on the highway with her gang of robbers. Her brother tried to force her to mend her ways; finally, after catching her in the act, he buried her alive in a

139. F. F. Schwede. Portrait of E. T. Lazareva in a velvet traveling cloak and lace cap. 1844. (Courtesy of the Russian Museum, St. Petersburg)

brick wall.[4] This situation improved very slowly. It found its way into memoirs and literature such as Pushkin's "Dubrovsky," in which a Russian Robin Hood conducts raids on the highway from a hideout in a large forest. As late as the 1830s memoirists recall arming themselves to cross certain areas of central Russia.[5]

Throughout this period, despite difficulties and dangers, Russian nobles were intrepid travelers. In the 1730s, well before the arrival of carriages with springs, Yankova's grandmother commuted several times a year from her estate Bobrovo, fifteen miles from Kaluga, to her Moscow house. When her son was to join the Semenovsky Guards, she personally escorted him the hundreds of miles to St. Petersburg. She regularly dispatched couriers from Bobrovo to St. Petersburg with letters for him or winter provisions.

As in eighteenth-century England, the wealthy traveled in their own carriages, accompanied by a suite of vehicles that included "an open carriage with eight seats, drawn by eight horses, then an enclosed traveling carriage, a barouche, two hooded carts [*kibitkas*], and lastly a huge wagon decorated with an ancestral coat of arms."[6] The retinue was made up of the family's own Cossacks, a hus-

140. Trading rows dating from the late eighteenth century in the provincial capital of Rostov. Such rows of shops, under a common roof, were the commercial center of almost every Russian city and town. (Author)

sar, and a group of soldiers. Lesser nobles went by post, renting horses and carriages to take them from one post-station to the next, usually eleven to seventeen miles apart. Each verst (roughly a kilometer) was marked with a white wooden column eight feet high, with black numbers at the top indicating the distance from the last station on one side, the distance to the next on the other (fig. 141). At each station the traveler presented a government document on which his route, rank, and title were inscribed. The higher the rank, the more horses to which he was entitled. Because official couriers could requisition horses without waiting their turn, the number of horses at a station was frequently inadequate for the demand. As one might expect, quarrels between groups of travelers ensued, the person of the highest rank usually winning.

Partially for this reason, displays of rank while traveling were customary. By law, rank determined whether one was legally entitled to be drawn by six, four, or only two or three horses. Up to the 1840s an aristocrat was easily identified by the number of horses drawing his or her carriage, the crest on its side, and the livery of the servants on the box.[7] (Afterward, Yankova lamented, crests on the outside of carriages and fools inside them became less common, as lavish display went out of fashion.) Even short trips to nearby estates called forth a festive parade of carriages, the landowner's entourage containing numerous servants, his fools, and his favorite dogs (fig. 142).

For much of the imperial period any trip, long or short, was as difficult as it would have been in early eighteenth-century England. In 1702 it took fourteen hours for Prince George of Denmark to travel forty miles to Petworth, the house of the Duke of Somerset; the last nine miles took six hours. But by mid-century, the advent of the turnpike and the smooth paving invented by Macadam, not to mention better-sprung carriages, transformed travel in the English countryside. These advances took almost a century to get to Russia. In the 1770s the Reverend William Coxe described Russia's main highway, from St. Petersburg to

141. Mariamna Davydova. On the road at twilight. Watercolor. 1920s. (Courtesy of Alona Vassiloff)

Moscow, as a wooden *chaussée* formed by tree trunks that were anchored at the ends, overlaid with boughs, and covered with sand or dirt. "When the road is new it is remarkably good; but as the trunks decay or sink into the ground, and as the land or earth is worn away or washed off by rain, it is broken into innumerable holes. . . . The motion of the carriage is a continual concussion, much greater than I ever experienced over the Roughest pavement."[8]

Other highways might be extremely wide but barely passable. When an imperial party was scheduled to pass, scores of peasants were set to smoothing out the central part of the road, which was then reserved exclusively for the suite; lesser mortals, confronted with the ravines, boulders, and mud of the periphery, sometimes found adjacent fields better going. The road from Tula to Moscow, one of the most heavily traveled in the country, according to Bolotov, was full of deep ruts that turned into mud traps. In the 1820s Gerakov, heading north from Kiev, remarked

142. Aristocrats arriving at Stolnoe, in Chernigov Province, the estate of L. A. Musina-Pushkina and, later, the Kushelev-Bezborodkos. Early nineteenth century. (*Stolitsa i usadba,* no. 35)

of the highway to Nezhin, "The great poet Dante, describing the roads of hell, never experienced one like this."[9] The Marquis de Custine, en route eastward from Moscow to Nizhni Novgorod in 1839, recalls that his horses sank in mud up to their knees and refused to pull the carriage over the huge rocks and logs in their path (fig. 143).

In the first half of the nineteenth century traveling with hired carriages and horses from stage to stage was so difficult, says one memoirist, that it explains why provincials rarely went as far as St. Petersburg. Those on the road usually tried to complete their journeys as quickly as possible, traveling around the clock in enclosed sleeping carriages. Sometimes bad weather brought an unexpected delay, forcing a party to stop at one of the notoriously poor inns in Russia. En route to Odessa, Count Mikhail Semenovich Vorontsov (the nephew of Princess Dashkova) and his wife (née Branicka) spent a February night at a "miserable post-station." "The room . . . was scarcely habitable. It was but very imperfectly warmed;—the thawed snow found its way through the roof, and fell upon the middle of the floor; while the only furniture consisted of a long dirty divan, upon which the Count and Countess, the governess, and General Leo Naryshkin (who happened also to stay here) reclined until morning."[10]

In 1846 the Davydov family, traveling from Tambov Province to their grandmother's estate near Moscow, covered less than twenty miles in eight hours and were forced to spend the night in a swamp. On another occasion depar-ture from their estate Kulevatovo for Moscow was delayed because of rain. Davydov's mother wrote his father: "I am in despair because of our delay, but on the other hand it is fortunate that I put off the departure; according to news from Tambov the road is terrible; in 24 hours you can only make it from one station to the next, and around Ryazhsk the carriages sit for days [in the mud] waiting to be pulled out."[11] Like many other travelers, the Davydov family car-

143. "Excepting the chaussée from the western to the inland capital [St. Petersburg to Moscow], and from the former to Warsaw, there are really no roads." (*The Englishwoman in Russia*)

Mariamna Davydova. A carriage traveling through the spring mud. Watercolor. 1920s.
(Courtesy of Alona Vassiloff)

ried all their own provisions and tried to stop at the estates of friends along the way. One memoirist describes setting out with a huge block of frozen stew made from a variety of meats and vegetables. For each dinner a hunk was chopped off and thawed.

The Rhythms of Provincial Life

For all its difficulties, travel was an unavoidable (and hence habitual) aspect of provincial life. Elizaveta Yankova's chronicle of the estates and town houses she inhabited as a child, young woman, and wife, and of the trips she made during these years, gives some idea of the pattern of life for the Moscow elite from the reign of Catherine to the emancipation of 1861 (the year Yankova died). During Yankova's ninety-three years, hardly one passed without a major trip to see a relative, and each involved one or more trips from estate to town and back, a pattern that seems to have been typical. Born in 1768, Yankova was brought up at Bobrovo, the family estate near Kaluga, and spent her winters in Moscow as a child (fig. 144). Later the family moved to Pokrovskoe, in Tula Province. From there they traveled to Syaskovo, her maternal grandmother's estate (in the same province), living in Tula intermittently and also in Moscow. In the 1790s, as a young married woman, Yankova and her husband, Dmitry, spent spring through fall at their estate Gorky, thirty miles outside Moscow,

144. Artist unknown. One of the Moscow city gates. Late eighteenth century.
(Courtesy of the State Historical Museum, Moscow)

moving to Moscow for the winter. But the young couple also made regular trips to visit Yankova's father at Bobrovo and the Yankov relatives in Tula Province. In 1801 they moved to their estate Annino, in Tambov Province, 30 miles from the district town of Lipetsk. During their first two years there Dmitry traveled to Moscow on business three times, and at the end of September 1802 the whole family traveled 145 miles to Pokrovskoe. Yankova visited Petersburg only once, as a married woman with children.

Russian accounts of such trips, though often recorded in an offhand fashion, nonetheless provide some notion of the actual conditions of roads, towns, and accommodations in the provinces. Russian memoirists took pride in towns that could boast masonry houses and churches (rather than wooden ones) and paved streets. But they admitted that most provincial capitals were generally muddy, dirty, or dusty (depending on the season). V. A. Shompulev described the streets of Saratov (the self-styled capital of the Volga region) in the 1840s as "dusty in summer, and in spring and autumn covered with 8 inches of mud."[12] The only ornaments on the main street were narrow wooden sidewalks and occasional lamps. Certain provincial capitals were an exception to the rule. Tver, a model city when rebuilt in the mid-1760s, had thirty churches and an imperial palace. Yaroslavl, according to Gerakov, was "very clean and good, with a carriage way" and forty-four masonry churches (and therefore, in his view, infinitely superior to "dirty" Kostroma).[13] N. V. Davydov described Kharkov of the 1840s as "handsome" and "wonderfully designed, with a great number of solid masonry houses" and declared that it was "not like any of our provincial towns" (meaning those in Great Russia).[14]

Most foreigners, on the other hand, were outspokenly critical. The Englishman Robert Bremner had hardly a decent word to say about Orel in 1839: "It . . . has the filthy stream of the Orlyk stagnating among the long dingy streets of its lower quarter. The town . . . now spreads a full half-mile beyond it, the population, by the official ac-

counts, having increased eleven thousand in ten years! . . . We do not deny that this may be a flourishing town, but its look certainly does not indicate great prosperity. In the low quarter many of the houses, which are all of wood, appear to be deserted. . . . There is not a single shop with the substantial look which one would expect in a place of 31,000 inhabitants. . . . Comfort is a word which none would ever employ in speaking of [Russian towns]."[15] Bremner criticized the "vast squares and vast streets, out of all proportion with the insignificance" of most provincial capitals, although he found Kursk quite charming and bustling.

Whatever the shortcomings of Russia's provincial capitals, they were incomparably more developed than district towns (figs. 145, 146), many of which were little more than villages at the turn of the century. In 1801 Yankova termed Epifan, with its wooden houses, shingled roofs, and only two masonry churches, "a very ugly little city."[16] Her husband found Venev "a very pathetic little town," deplored Efremov for its streets awash in mud, and termed Lebedyan, despite its masonry cathedral, very poor. By mid-century at least some of these towns were more developed. One noble touring Tver Province found the layout of Rzhev attractive and its 12 churches impressive. Kashin (boasting 3 monasteries and 15 churches) was home, he noted, to "many noble families"; he was impressed by Torzhok's "many rather handsome buildings" and 13,500 inhabitants.[17]

By the early nineteenth century, possibly inspired by the success of Karamzin's *Letters of a Russian Traveler*, some Russian nobles were traveling for pleasure, bad roads notwithstanding, and writing literary accounts of their journeys. Prince Ivan Dolgoruky, a poet, playwright, and man of rare sensibilities, justifies his trip (with his wife and four comrades) to Odessa and Kiev in 1810 with the witty observation, "To stay endlessly at home bores even a sage." A romantic, Dolgoruky gazes up, not down, ignoring the mud and admiring the gleam of spires and the

199

145. View of Volokolamsk, a district town of Moscow Province, ca. 1900.

146. The meat market and other shops in Volokolamsk.

golden grain of distant fields. In Serpukhov he is enchanted by the ruins of a fortress built by Ivan the Terrible and reflects (not without a certain pride) that of a thousand people who walk there, "only perhaps two or three have glanced at it." Lunching at an inn in a village belonging to D. L. Naryshkin, he is amused by the latest graffiti on its walls: "From everything written above one has to conclude that few intelligent people travel by this road."18

District and provincial capitals, however undeveloped, were focal points of provincial socializing at certain periods of the year, bringing together nobles who otherwise associated little with one another. The months of December and January were full of festivities—balls (fig. 147), theater, and receptions. At other times of year the nobility gathered in town for fairs, for the opening of a new school or charitable institution, or for the public examinations of young relatives graduating from local institutes. Every three years the elections of provincial and district marshals brought nobles together at Assemblies of the Nobility. While the men, resplendent in military uniforms or the less prestigious uniforms of their province, politicked

in the great hall of the assembly, their wives and daughters socialized and watched the proceedings from the galleries. In the evenings the nobility might gather for a display of fireworks to benefit the poor or for a ball and late supper.

One can see the Russian provinces of the early nineteenth century beginning to flower in descriptions of these festivities from different periods. In 1802 Martha Wilmot, writing of an "excessively amusing" ball given by the governor of Smolensk, observed that the provincial elite differed distinctly from Moscow society:

The Princess [Dashkova] open'd the ball with a polonaise, after which she resign'd her handsome Cavalier Gen. Apraksin to me. We had a great number of country dances. . . . I find there is less of the *fire and fume* of a good education amongst the damsels of Smolensk than amongst the Muscovites who bewilder you to *shew off* their 4 or 5 languages, their musical abilitys & their profound knowledge of the great science of dancing. The Smolenskovites are consequently less affected & I am tempted to add *better bred*, as a tincture of diffidence is at least mingled with the *fearless inquisitive* fatiguing manner of half the fair damsels of my acquaintance at Moscow. At supper the Ladies only sat down to table, the Cavaliers wander'd about.[19]

In his travels almost two decades later the cosmopolitan Gerakov also noted a number of differences between provincial habits and those of the capital: provincials spoke Russian more often and observed the Lenten fast more strictly; also, the status-conscious provincials practiced a kind of "strict etiquette in order to be with everyone similarly acquainted." Yet the gap was visibly narrowing. Attending a ball at the Assembly of the Nobility in Tula, given in honor of the emperor's birthday, Gerakov noted women "dressed in the latest fashion, no worse than in the capital." Like Moscow, Tula had an English Club for the social elite. At a ball there on December 26, 1820, Gerakov described the women as "dressed very magnificently, with taste and some luxury," though the men wore mostly boots rather than dancing shoes.[20] Not all provin-

147. Count V. P. de Balmen. Sketch of a provincial ball. 1830s.
(*Stolitsa i usadba*, no. 74)

cial balls were as impressive. Nikoleva describes a New Year's masquerade at the Assembly of the Nobility in Smolensk at which the dancers' shoes stuck to the floor. It had been hastily painted the day before, and when the paint did not dry, they decided to cover it with a layer of glue mixed with resin. "The result was a scandal."[21]

Although Russia's provincial towns lacked the long cultural traditions of European urban centers, by the early nineteenth century some were developing an aura of sophistication imparted by a fashionable coterie of aristocrats and small circles of the well-educated. In these towns the elite met for festive meals, rounds of visits, card playing, theater parties, and balls, which became more frequent during the holiday season. For a few years Tver was enlivened by the presence of the Grand Duchess Ekaterina Pavlovna, sister of Alexander I. A woman of high culture, she was visited by Karamzin, Derzhavin, and Nikolai Lvov. In the 1820s Gerakov found a sophisticated group in Orel: Sergei Uvarov and his sister-in-law, Countess Natalya I. Kurakina (wife of Alexei Kurakin), and Generals Norov and Korff. At a breakfast given by Korff ("or rather a fabulous dinner") at 1 P.M. for more than thirty individuals, Gerakov (clearly feeling outclassed by the military guests) noted disdainfully that the local officials tended to put on airs.[22]

The provincial elite also traveled to "take the cure" or simply for a vacation. Although the aristocracy frequented fashionable watering holes abroad, the lesser nobility gathered at Russian spas. Yankova and her family twice summered in Lipetsk, which she found a "very jolly place," with a nice hotel, dance hall, theater, and troupe of traveling actors. Lipetsk continued to flourish, but some privately owned resort or spa towns were short-lived. Belov, touring Tver in the 1850s, passed through a ghost town he described as once having had a tavern, coffeehouse, and vauxhall for music and dancing, all of which had disappeared after the owner of the town died.

Alexander P. Nashchokin operated Rai-Semenovskoe,

near Moscow, as a luxurious sanatorium for about a decade, but it too failed to prosper. Rai-Semenovskoe had four springs, three of which produced waters rich in iron. At the turn of the century Nashchokin's father noticed the springs and in 1803 obtained an imperial decree giving him permission to develop the mineral waters he had found. In 1811 F. F. Reis, professor of chemistry at Moscow University, published a description and chemical analysis of the mineral waters, describing their location as "one of the most exquisite and picturesque in Moscow Province; from the village, and particularly from the landowner's house, one sees lovely vales covered with rich meadows, through which the limpid waters of the Nara River flow. The hills that rise gently on both sides of the vale are varied in appearance because of the various groves that cover them, the numerous trees planted along them, and the many streams that flow out of them and sometimes create waterfalls cascading over marble boulders."[23]

The sanatorium was already in operation by the war of 1812, because Nashchokin received an official letter from Moscow's Governor Rostopchin, thanking him for opening it for state needs. Soon Nashchokin decided to build up this enterprise on a grand scale. A stone marker on the road to Serpukhov alerted the traveler to the turnoff for the "waters of the Savior"; similar posts guided guests to the estate entrance. The sanatorium was located a short distance from the manor house. A round temple with twelve columns and a cupola marked the spring, and several bathhouses were available to guests. Those arriving for the cure could choose lodgings from twenty-seven specially appointed peasant houses, ten large houses (each with ten or eleven rooms), or a sixteen-room hotel grandly named Restauration aux Armes du Seigneur. Three paths led among the dwelling units, the last to a regular garden over half a mile long.[24]

A promotional brochure of 1817 advised that visitors would be awakened at sunrise with a cannon shot and serenaded with music throughout the day and evening. To entertain patients, the spa had a club as well as an amphitheater set in the English garden constructed of towering lime trees so artfully united "that the spectator imagines himself in a stone building." One memoirist says Nashchokin spared nothing to amuse the ill; he provided "a very good orchestra of serf musicians with a German choirmaster who really understood music, a house chorus with satisfactory singers, and a whole troupe of his actors with two very pretty, talented actresses and prima donnas."[25]

Unfortunately, the fame of his springs did not spread as Nashchokin had expected; soon after the spa opened, the guest quarters, which proved very expensive to maintain, were filled with ordinary boarders. The laudatory brochure of 1817, probably written by Nashchokin himself, came too late. Moreover, the healing properties of Rai-Semenovskoe's waters seem dubious: at the end of one man's cure in 1814 his daughter noted ominously, "My father had visibly begun to weaken and tremble."[26] A. E. Labzina writes that a relative suffering from dropsy spent March through September of 1819 at the waters but does not mention whether he was helped.[27] By 1820 the whole enterprise had been shut down, possibly because it was unable to compete with the new spas of the northern Caucasus, such as Pyatigorsk.

Provincials unable to travel to Moscow for shopping were sometimes forced to patronize the poorly stocked shops and markets of provincial towns (fig. 148) to obtain

148. The neo-Gothic trading rows in the provincial capital of Kaluga. Late eighteenth century.

149. Weekly fair outside the gates to Glubokoe, the Heiden estate. (Courtesy of Nicholas Volkov-Muromtsov)

dry goods, hardware, or other necessary items not produced on the estate. Fairs were a preferred alternative for such purchases, whether it be the renowned annual bazaar of Nizhni Novgorod (which drew two hundred thousand) or lesser ones (fig. 149).[28] As at the elections for noble marshals, business was mixed with pleasure at these gatherings. In 1822 Nikoleva's family traveled from Po-

krovskoe to the trading town of Khislavichi (owned by a Count Saltykov) for its annual summer fair. Nikoleva noted, "Many of our friends went, including the Rimsky-Korsakovs and Engelharts." There she went to her first ball (given for the nobility but attended by merchants as well), where she successfully charmed a young man "by playing the role of a naive country fool." At the ball the following evening Nikoleva wore a "new white dress of gossamer on satin, with a red rose in my hair, another at my waist, and around my shoulders a red voile scarf that my mother had bought from a Turkish prisoner." Her cavalier of the previous day gazed at her "with arms folded like Napoleon, not moving." Suddenly the evening took a Gogolian twist. Startled by shouts, the Nikolevs ran out of the ballroom to discover their coachman nearly lifeless. He had been trampled by their horses, who had stampeded, frightened by the Polish policeman shouting at him to make way for the carriage of the marshal's wife! The policeman begged forgiveness of Nikoleva's mother on his knees and paid for the damage, but the ball ended.[29]

The following year Nikoleva and her sister traveled with the Rimsky-Korsakovs to the week-long fair at their district capital, Dorogobuzh. A festive atmosphere was ensured by the local marshal of the nobility, a lively, well-educated man, and by the presence of a regiment (with the usual supply of eligible officers) currently quartered in the town. Nikoleva, a wreath of fragrant fresh flowers on her head, danced with her friends until 4 A.M. in the noble assembly hall, specifically to annoy a Moscow family in the house across the street who had let it be known that they did not like provincial entertainments.[30]

Such occasions gave the lesser nobility the opportunity to observe the dress and habits of the wealthy or sophisticated set. Bakarev, architect to Alexei Kurakin, describes this process at work even at the Saturday bazaars at Kurakino, the village of the prince that was closest to the manor house. There, merchants and small-estate owners mingled with Prince Kurakin's retainers, who "came and went from Petersburg with him and brought new styles of clothing and new customs from there, all of which country dwellers greedily noted and gradually introduced among themselves."[31]

By the 1850s even in winter Tambov was "filled with landowners living in very jolly fashion." The daughter of Yury Golitsyn (then marshal of the Tambov nobility) re-

calls the weekly balls that marked her introduction to society: "I remember my ball costume: a white tarlatan dress and white satin slippers; [my sister] Sonya had the same, only rose-colored." Although she insists that her father was not proud, merely a "real noble and prince," his conduct reflected the customary social distinctions. Once when he received a group of merchants, a nouveau-riche tax farmer from Voronezh rudely put out his hand in greeting rather than waiting for the prince to extend his. Returning the insult, Prince Golitsyn pulled a paper ruble from his pocket and put it into the outstretched hand.[32]

When members of the imperial family were passing through local towns, provincial nobles journeyed there for the ceremonies, celebratory dinners, and balls these visits occasioned. As a child Nikoleva remembers almost swooning with delight when Alexander I stopped in Elnya on his way to the Crimea in 1825. Because of the large crowd Nikoleva was pressed up against the walls of the house in which the tsar was staying; suddenly the tsar himself opened a window directly in front of her, and she found herself two paces from the person "whom I loved inordinately by reputation, although I had never [before] seen him." In February 1826 the funeral cortege of Alexander I passed through Tula; the entire Miliutin family traveled to town and young Dmitry watched the procession from a second-story window that was open "even though it was winter." In the late 1830s Nikoleva's family traveled to Smolensk to see the tsarevich en route to Europe and to enjoy the ball and fireworks presented in his honor.[33]

Throughout the year there were excursions to the estates of relatives, friends, and neighbors for name-day celebrations, baptisms, weddings, church dedications, and funerals. The host always gave a banquet, and guests often spent the night, males in one part of the house, females in another. As Makarov commented, "Not to spend the night meant grievously insulting the host."[34] On small estates, says one memoirist, male guests would amuse themselves playing tag (usually with the maids!) around the courtyard while their wives gossiped and did needlework. Later they would listen to peasant singing or sing themselves. The arrival of new residents to a district provoked rounds of visits. Custom dictated that the newcomers call on neighbors to introduce themselves; these calls were then reciprocated.

Hunting to hounds was a major autumn pastime that, for men, often meant being away from one's estate for several weeks. Those taking part in the chase usually gathered from several districts at one wealthy person's estate. After a hearty breakfast of *solyanka* (made of salted meat, cabbage, and onions), curd cakes, chopped beef cutlets, and pickled pork washed down with homemade drink, the army of hunters, huntsmen, and dogs would set out for the remote fields containing the prey. Carriages of women and children sometimes accompanied sportsmen for the first day. At night the hunters bedded down at neighboring estates, in local villages, or in the open air.[35]

Culture in the Provinces

More than one memoirist insists that feasting and hunting were the main distractions in the cultural wasteland of provincial Russia in the late eighteenth and early nineteenth centuries. Literature tends to confirm this, portraying most provincial nobles as barely literate boors. If so, Russia was hardly unique: in other European countries the well-educated were also a small fraction of the rural population. Most landowners were far too preoccupied with practical concerns to have the time or inclination for extraneous reading. In the provinces, moreover, reading matter was in short supply, which perhaps explains why most Russian estates of this period lacked even the modest libraries characteristic of many an English country house. This inadequacy is hardly surprising when one considers that the first Russian printing presses began operating only in the reign of Peter. For the next half century they produced mainly technical manuals and official decrees, de-

votional works and schoolbooks, and press runs were small. Between 1763, the year the first Russian novel was published, and 1775, only 12 original novels appeared, whereas 123 novels were translated into Russian during the same period.[36] In England, by comparison, between 1740 and 1770 at least 20, and sometimes as many as 40, new novels appeared annually.

In the reign of Catherine, private presses and provincial publishing started competing with state-controlled, centralized printing and book distribution. Between 1776 and 1801, thirty-eight private or institutional presses in Moscow and St. Petersburg published over two-thirds of all Russian books. By the middle of Catherine's reign, the reading public had become large enough to create an audience for nearly every kind of book for which there was a market in the West. In the quarter century before the onset of censorship in 1795, nearly eight thousand titles were produced in Russia, over three times the total produced in the previous two centuries.[37]

Provincial literary life also took off in Catherine's reign. Five provincial journals appeared from the late 1780s to the early 1790s. In Tambov, Derzhavin's arrival sparked the creation of the *Tambov News*, which he founded and edited for a year, stimulating local literary life. His friend Evgeny Bolkhovitinov played a similar role in Yaroslavl. By 1801 twenty-six secular presses had appeared in twenty-three provinces, though most survived only a short time. In spite of this activity, the supply of reading material to the provinces was small: at the end of the eighteenth century even Ireland had more bookshops than Russia. Publishing activities picked up again in the reign of Alexander, who reopened presses and regularized censorship. Local publishing still lagged behind that of the capitals, however, and the provincial's access to books was limited. In the 1840s, Kohl claimed, Kharkov's three bookstores (two secular and one French) sold books "by the pound," which was nonetheless an improvement over the single store of 1830.[38]

150. N. I. Tikhobrazov. Watercolor of the veranda of an estate belonging to the Lopukhins, showing a young woman busy with her correspondence. 1844. (Courtesy of the Tretiakov Gallery, Moscow)

Provincial publishing and bookselling statistics tell only a small part of the tale, however, because provincials secured reading matter mainly by ordering books from the capitals or buying them on trips (fig. 150). Newspapers and journals were also sent by mail to subscribers in obscure corners of the empire; and books, newspapers, and journals were shared among friends. On trips to Moscow in the 1760s Bolotov scoured the shops for books on gardening and was delighted to discover that the Moscow Academy bookshop had "all the books I had seen in Königsberg and

Prussia, every kind of French and German book."[39] These treasures were added to his library at Dvoryaninovo. In the late 1760s as well, Nikolai Tishinin, another provincial, on his remote estate Tikhvinskoe (Yaroslavl Province), was receiving all the latest news on literature and art, as well as books, journals, magazines, paintings, and engravings (even a camera obscura) from his godfather in St. Petersburg, Mikhail Makhaev.[40] Thus, some estates were being transformed into substantial provincial outposts of culture, even in this early period.

But the wide-ranging literary and cultural interests of men like Bolotov and Tishinin were outside the scope of the average Russian. The ordinary eighteenth-century provincial might read some pietistic literature, but his staples were how-to manuals and agricultural works such as Bolotov's *Economic Magazine*, published in Moscow expressly for those living in the country. Many a provincial considered the adventures and romances popular in the capitals morally suspect, especially for women (Labzina recalls her mother warning her against them). Country dwellers may have absorbed some idea of the habits of a world beyond their ken from belles lettres, but they were far more influenced by observing outsiders visiting the provinces and, in the late eighteenth and early nineteenth centuries, by newspapers and journals.

At the turn of the century the most popular and widely read papers were the official *Moscow News* and *St. Petersburg News*, which broadcast political news and events. By the 1820s there were a number of specialized weekly or monthly journals that brought the ideas, fashions, and happenings of the capital to the provinces: *Magazine for Women* (1823–33), one of the most popular, was a cultural potpourri; *Northern Flowers* compiled romantic literature; the *Neva Observer* took a satirical swipe at doings in St. Petersburg; *Pages for Worldly People* (1839–44) and the *Magazine of Women's and Men's Fashions* kept provincials abreast of the latest styles. As a form of advertising, some magazines listed the names and locations of annual

subscribers, which gives an idea of the geographical range of these publications. In 1821 the *Neva Observer* had subscribers not only in provincial capitals of central provinces such as Tula, Kaluga, Tver, Pskov, Kursk, Chernigov, and Yaroslavl but in fifty-six smaller or more remote cities such as Zmiev, Orekhov, Berdychev, Glazov, and Slobodsk. By the 1830s *The Library for Reading*, with its serialized fiction, reviews, and original articles, was among the most popular of the new encyclopedic journals available in the provinces.

Too few inventories of estate libraries exist to give an accurate picture of provincial reading, but we can be sure that it increased considerably in quantity, if not necessarily in quality, in the first half of the nineteenth century. As literary portraits suggest, most young ladies in the provinces may have gone no further than French romances, the Gothic tales of Radcliffe or, later, the novels of George Sand, while their fathers read only practical literature. In the 1830s a literary Muscovite sketched a rather condescending portrait of a "landowner's family in the steppe, reading everything it comes across, from cover to cover." According to him, "The daughter reads [romantic Russian] tales. The son, member of a new generation, reads Timofeev's verses and the tales of Baron Brambeus; the father reads articles on the two- or three-field system, on different ways of fertilizing the soil, the mother about new ways of caring for consumption and dyeing yarn."[41]

Yet some memoirs aver that by the 1820s and 1830s other types of literature existed in the countryside for a minority of curious intellects. Karamzin's *History*, the novels of Sir Walter Scott, and Daniel Defoe's *Robinson Crusoe* were staples of a Russian provincial education, along with Russian romantic fiction. The works of French enlightenment philosophers also circulated in the provinces. Nikoleva tells us that at Pokrovskoe her father, occupied with estate management during the day, ruined his eyesight at night by reading his favorite authors: Voltaire, d'Alembert, and Diderot. In the 1820s the noted diarist and memoirist Nikitenko (a freed serf of Dmitry She-remetev who became an imperial censor) termed Ostro-gozhsk the Athens of Voronezh Province. Here, he said, merchants and other common folk owned translations of Montesquieu, Beccaria, and Voltaire, and he saw a young officer ordering Montesquieu's *L'Esprit des lois* at the an-nual fair.[42]

Journals and books were shared. Nikoleva's father reg-ularly read his copy of *Moscow News* to his acquaintances. In far-off Penza Province in the 1830s Natalya Tuchkova owed her education to her neighbor Grigory Rimsky-Korsakov: "Like the whole educated minority of that time, a follower of Voltaire and the Encyclopedists . . . [he] had a remarkable library of French books." Rimsky-Korsakov made a catalog of his books for the Tuchkovs' governess, who selected "everything needed for our education, and he sent us a whole crate of books; a year later we returned them very accurately."[43] Near Orel, the mother of Timofei Granovsky, a future professor of history at Moscow Uni-versity, borrowed reading matter from wealthier neighbors for her son. In such fashion the eyes of a generation of country-bred Russian intellectuals were opened to other worlds.

Provincial Life Disrupted

A survey of the rhythms of country life during the century preceding the emancipation of the serfs would not be com-plete without some attention to two events that disrupted the normal life of landowners, the Pugachev rebellion and the invasion of Russia by Napoleon. In each case, the re-sults were more economically devastating and psycho-logically threatening than the customary small-scale and random depredations by neighbors or outlaws. The mas-sive peasant insurrection of 1773–74, led by Emelyan Pugachev (fig. 151), quickly became the stuff of legend for both the landowners and peasants who lived through it. Pugachev, a Don Cossack, rallied his followers behind the banner of Catherine's deposed husband, Peter III, who, ac-

151. Gilliers. Emelyan Pugachev in the cage in which he was transported to Moscow for execution. 1775. Engraving. (Courtesy of the State Historical Museum, Moscow)

cording to Pugachev, had not died; claiming that Peter was Russia's rightful ruler and a friend of the peasant, Pugachev declared that his aim was to restore Peter to the throne. Traveling along the Volga with a royal impostor in tow, Pugachev recruited his first followers among the Cossacks of the eastern Volga. The movement spread like a forest fire as Pugachev incited the serfs of Kazan, Simbirsk,

Penza, and other provinces to rise up against their masters, kill them, and join the march on Moscow. News of Pugachev's early successes sent shock waves of fear through the serf-owning nobility, particularly those whose estates lay in his path.

As we have seen, in ordinary times patriarchal Russia appeared to be populated by benevolent landowners and deferential peasants. The Pugachev rebellion created a breach in what one scholar, describing peasant resistance to elites, terms the "public transcript," the normal terms of discourse between landowners and serfs. Periods of crisis, he says, bring the "hidden transcript"—the things both groups feel about each other but normally express only behind closed doors—to the surface. Investigators misinterpret these moments of crisis, imagining that the crisis has engendered unusual hostility and rebellious sentiment rather than having simply revealed its existence.[44] In both the Pugachev rebellion and the Napoleonic invasion, the hidden transcript of lord-peasant relations surfaced.

On the landowner's side, the hidden transcript read that serfs were not happy, obedient children but malevolent, potentially dangerous adversaries. Bolotov's reaction to the rebellion gives us a glimpse of the landowner's usually invisible distrust of the peasant. For his time Bolotov was an enlightened and humane landowner who, in his memoirs, registered strong disapproval of the scurrilous treatment of serfs, remarking that one incident "left a black mark on the whole nobility."[45] In the dreadful year of 1774, upon learning from his village elders that Pugachev was close, Bolotov became upset: "'What are you saying!' I shouted, and my heart shook, and I was so frightened that for a long time I was in no condition to utter a word." His womenfolk burst into tears, imagining what might befall them. But taking heart, Bolotov went about mustering the most trustworthy peasants from local villages and arming them for local defense. In one village he turned to the strongest-looking peasant and told him he

was sure he could kill ten men by himself. "'Well,' [the peasant] replied to this, smiling malevolently, 'would I kill my brothers! But if it were you boyars, I'd be prepared to run ten through with this lance.'" From the talk in Moscow, Bolotov says ominously, it was clear that "in their hearts everyone in general was rebelling."[46] The poet I. I. Dmitriev concurred, noting that at the first signs of rebellion "from town and estate [the nobles] dashed to safety, everyone racing to where he thought there was the least danger."[47]

Dmitry Mertvago's memoirs bring home the horrors Bolotov and Dmitriev anticipated but never experienced. Mertvago was fourteen when his family fled from their estate in Kazan Province in an attempt to reach Alatyr, a garrisoned district town where they thought they would be protected. En route they received word that its inhabitants had handed over the town, greeting Pugachev with the traditional bread and salt. For three days the Mertvago family and their servants hid in a forest but on the fourth were discovered. Dmitry's father was hauled off and killed; Dmitry, his little brothers, and their nanny fled farther into the forest, then wandered aimlessly through nearby fields. "Suddenly we heard the terrible cry, 'Catch them, beat them!'" Dmitry grabbed one brother, and the two hid in the tall grass of the riverbank, while their nanny ran along the road. "The evildoers, taking her for a noblewoman, fell upon her, and one of them hit her with a hatchet; in her fright she raised her arm, which, however, didn't defend her; the blade, having cut off part of her hand, came down on her shoulder; her terrible cry pierced my heart." Dmitry came out of hiding, but his life was spared, because Pugachev needed a literate scribe.

Taken by the band to Alatyr, he traveled by the ruins of estates on which he had played. As he passed these familiar places, he was filled with grief: "I could not only see but even recognized the bodies of friends and relatives; my heart was so shattered that I no longer wanted to stay alive." He found his mother in the Alatyr jail. For two days she had been speechless and was "already showing signs of dementia." "Where is your father?" were her first words to young Dmitry. At last the maid of a cousin who had been murdered arrived at the prison with news of Dmitry's father. 'Yesterday they hanged him at your village," she cold-bloodedly told mother and son.[48]

The Pugachev rebellion put into high relief the deep divide between Russia's landowners and their peasants. As during later rebellions and revolutions, loyal retainers protected some landowners from mob violence, but many peasants, as Bolotov suspected, secretly if not openly sympathized with the rebels. They looked on Pugachev, like Stenka Razin before him, as a folk hero who would deliver them from the evil boyars.[49] Peasant accounts of the mass slaughter in Saratov (where landowners were disemboweled, butchered, thrown into the Volga or, more mercifully, shot) reflect complete indifference to their overlords' painful end. But the nobility was hardly more humanitarian toward the rebels. In Moscow it gleefully flocked to watch Pugachev drawn and quartered, and Bolotov was "unbelievably happy" when he got a good position near the scaffold. After the execution (which Bolotov both described and drew) his only regret was that Pugachev's sufferings were lessened when his head, not his hands and feet, was chopped off first.

Napoleon's invasion of Russia in 1812 was the second event to unveil concealed hostilities between lord and peasant. Noble families fled the areas in Napoleon's path, finally deserting Moscow, while peasants were either conscripted into local militias or simply left to fend for themselves. The landowner was required to deliver one-tenth of his souls for the defense effort. Conscription into the army was considered so terrible a fate that peasants often maimed themselves to avoid it. In this instance, however, the serfs were being called on to protect their own lands, and some memoirists aver that they joined willingly. The Yankovs, with approximately one thousand male serfs, contributed thirty-two peasants from Gorky and twenty-

two each from their Tula, Tambov, and Novgorod estates. "At Gorky Dmitry Alekseevich called a meeting of all inhabitants after church; speaking to them from the porch, he told them that the French were coming and that the fatherland had to be defended, and asked for volunteers. More than 32 stepped forward," Yankova insists.[50]

Details from other memoirs paint a different picture. Ekaterina Bibikova, a wealthy Muscovite, fled "with many servants in several carriages and wagons" for Nizhni Novgorod with her seven daughters, one daughter-in-law, and her youngest son, Alexander, whom she had refused to let join the army. At one post-station a crowd of peasants surrounded their carriages, determined not to let them have fresh horses. One shouted, "These people are fleeing from the French and sending us to fight, to certain death!" A daughter saved the day by rolling down the glass to speak to the angry peasants: "Don't you see that we are only women? How are we to fight? I have five brothers; four are at the front, one already badly wounded. One is here, he's still a child and wants to go to war; Mama forced him to come with her."[51]

The Nikolev estate Pokrovskoe lay not far from the post road leading to Moscow from Smolensk, which Napoleon captured on August 5. When Nikoleva's brother, an officer in a guards regiment, burst in on them one day at dinner with the news that the French were only fifteen miles away, her family fled eastward to Butyrki, her Aunt Protopopova's estate in Tula Province.

> The carriages were readied, suitcases filled with whatever was at hand. . . . Father gathered the peasants from the field and ordered the rusks we had prepared for the [Russian] troops to be distributed to the peasants as a gift, and some sacks to be filled with rusks for the road. A cart was filled with provisions. My sisters regretted leaving the cherries behind . . . and they filled baskets with them, leaving mother and nanny to gather more

211

152. S. Tonci. Portrait of Fyodor Rostopchin. Early nineteenth century. (Wilmot and Wilmot, *The Russian Journals of Martha and Catherine Wilmot*)

The caravan set off, followed by thirty horses from their stud farm, which had to be abandoned after a short distance because they slowed the convoy.

From Smolensk Napoleon moved on Moscow. The governor-general of Moscow, Rostopchin (fig. 152), insisted that the city would not fall to the enemy. Until the very last minute he urged people not to leave the city. In the haste of the subsequent evacuation many family valuables were left behind to be stolen or needlessly burned. When it was clear that Napoleon's troops would seize Moscow, the volatile governor, on the same impulse that led him to put the torch to his beloved estate Voronovo, either ordered or encouraged the burning of the city (fig. 153). He further directed that fire-fighting equipment be removed, so that once fires started it was impossible to check or contain them.

Muscovites fled, mostly to estates in distant provinces. The Yankovs declined their steward's advice to take their best furniture to Gorky (only thirty miles away), based on the reasoning that if Napoleon took Moscow, Gorky would also go. (As it happened, the French halted ten miles short of Gorky.) Elizaveta Yankova left precipitously with her two daughters, the nurse, and "the most necessary silver," headed for Kashira and then for their estate Petrovo, in Venev district. From there they intended to continue on to their Tambov estate.

This period brought some Muscovites an unexpected exposure to provincial life, and some provincials their first glimpse of sophisticated fashion. In Nizhni Novgorod the usually well-chaperoned Bibikov daughters, their mother having taken to her bed at the news of her favorite son's death in battle, were free to stroll through the town. The family stayed in Nizhni for the duration of the war. The Nikolev family, on the other hand, after some months in Tula, moved to Bruslanovo (the estate of a relative in Tambov Province) at Christmastime. During an unforgettable trek across the snow-covered steppes, the convoy got lost in a snowstorm. After going around in circles for two days,

necessary things. Our journey began at sunrise—I was in a carriage with mother and a large doll, dressed in my favorite rose dress. . . . Father followed us in an open carriage with my sisters, then there was a cart with a servant, another with provisions, and a wagon with our baggage.[52]

they finally saw a light and found shelter at the Khrushchevs' estate thirty miles from their destination.

Nikoleva's description of the Khrushchev house gives us some idea of the remote provinces in midwinter. The house was large and unbearably cold. Although estate houses were customarily built with thick walls and double-paned windows, in this instance many of the outer panes were broken and stuffed with rags. Because of the expense of firewood, only the bedroom of the mistress (who had just delivered a child) was heated, landowners considering it humiliating to use straw for fuel, as their peasants did. The Nikolev children remained in their fur coats. Their host summoned his serf orchestra and invited his guests to dance to the music, which was how his four children had been keeping warm. At last the travelers were offered food. From the way the family's tutor fell upon it, Nikoleva concluded that their host was a miser.[53]

While the Nikolev family was fleeing eastward, the French were retreating to the west. After a month of indecision, in late October Napoleon began the withdrawal from Moscow. French morale rapidly disintegrated during the retreat; on December 12 the remnants of the Grande Armée, decimated by cold and starvation, crossed the Niemen River near Kovno and left Russia. Later that month

153. Schmidt. "The Fire in Moscow in September, 1812." Early nineteenth century. Tinted engraving from the original by Christian-Johann Olendorf. (Courtesy of the Pushkin Museum, Moscow)

Alexander I made the decision to pursue the French; on March 31, 1814, he and his troops entered Paris as the liberators of Europe.

Although the Pugachev rebellion had a huge psychological impact on the nation, the war of 1812 can be said to have transformed Russian national consciousness in a more profound way. In 1812, some around Alexander, mindful of the precedent of 1773–74, predicted a peasant uprising. Isolated incidents of peasant violence (of the sort described below) did occur, but there was no general rebellion: the victory was truly a national one, achieved by noble officers and conscripted serfs fighting as one. In Paris, the triumphant feelings of Alexander's young officers in Paris were tempered by shame and a sense of injustice at the serfdom of the brave fighting men they had come to see as fellow human beings.[54] Russia's greatest military triumph had highlighted its political and social inadequacies: the desire for reform engendered by this victory would culminate in the uprising of December 1825, led by some of these very officers.

For estate owners, the economic consequences of the Pugachev rebellion were mild in comparison to Napoleon's invasion. Few families, particularly in central Russia, were financially ruined by Pugachev's marauders. (In fact, a few fortunes were made when landowners whose estates had been occupied by the rebels subsequently found caches of loot buried on their lands.) The burning of Moscow and the devastation of the surrounding countryside during the war of 1812, in contrast, had substantial impact on the life of many gentry families. In Moscow, the devastation of the Prechistenka region (southwest of the Kremlin), where many old families had houses, was almost total. Yankova was not even able to look at the ruins of the house they had recently completed. For years thereafter Muscovites were deeply divided over Rostopchin's behavior. Many, despite their losses, considered his actions deeply patriotic; few believed the pamphlet he wrote a few years later, in which he defended himself from widespread rumors that he had ordered Moscow burned. Yankova, a supporter, insists that most owners set fire to their own houses. But others blamed him both for the fire and for not giving them sufficient time to save their belongings.[55]

The French destroyed or severely damaged many suburban Moscow estates. The French marshal Michel Ney, billeted at Ostankino with his cavalry, looted the house and used its priceless busts and portraits for target practice. Some estates, like Rostopchin's Voronovo, were torched by patriotic owners. Thus Moscow and its environs after the war were in shambles. Grandees and the wealthy sustained their losses relatively easily. The wealthy S. S. Apraksin, upon seeing the ruins of his house, declared to Margarita Volkova that he would not leave Moscow "for anything in the world," and by November 1813 his new mansion was ready for a housewarming ball. The Yankovs had lost their house and most of their possessions but were able to rebuild after reluctantly selling their Tambov estate, one of four they owned. Suburban Gorky had been spared. When the Yankovs returned to it, they held a service of thanksgiving in the church. "All the house servants gathered to meet us, and on Sunday the peasants also came from their villages to the service and then to the house and expressed their joy at seeing us again." From the nanny, who had remained, they learned that the only looting had been done by Cossacks, not by the French, who merely helped themselves to wine and provisions.[56]

The fighting along Napoleon's route to Moscow (from Smolensk, skirting Elnya, through Vyazma, then on to Borodino and Mozhaisk) had taken a heavy toll on the area. Nikoleva states that the devastation of this region ruined the lesser nobility completely and had serious consequences even for a wealthy family like her own. In spite of the obvious sympathy Alexander I felt for the nobility's losses, the government's limited subsidies for rebuilding could not restore life as it had been. Nikoleva says wistfully, "Before 1812 we lived practically luxuriously." The following summer, when the family returned to Smolensk, they discovered the damage to Pokrovskoe: "The house was ruined, as were the church and the service buildings. Everything that could be taken was gone; the windows were broken, floors ripped up, furniture smashed, the piano torn apart, even the iron from the stoves had been ripped out." The French had burned the Nikolev house in Smolensk, and the houses and suburban estates of their relatives in Moscow had been destroyed. "After 1812 we were no longer in a position to go to Moscow frequently."[57]

Most, but not all, of the destruction could be blamed on the French. On numerous estates the invasion had unleashed peasant hostility against owners. Says Nikoleva, "We found that we'd barely left when the peasants began to gather at the house, while the house serfs fled." The Nikolevs' own peasants, not the French, inflicted most of the damage. In fact, Nikoleva relates the report of a house serf that one French officer who came upon Pokrovskoe was struck by a portrait of Nikoleva's oldest sister and drove a group of looters off the property, threatening to shoot them. A more serious incident took place on the Smolensk estates of Andrei Lykoshin, who owned two thousand souls. Like the Nikolevs, Lykoshin and his wife had fled at Napoleon's approach, leaving their son Pavel in charge. Young Pavel, upon hearing that the peasants at one of their estates near Dorogobuzh were beginning to divide up his father's goods among themselves, set off with his steward and a poor noble named Berdyaev to talk to the rebels. Lykoshin may not have had time to say anything, for the official report of the incident reads, "No sooner had he arrived at the village square when he was surrounded on all sides, murdered together with Berdyaev, and both bodies thrown into the lake." A company of Cossacks quelled the rebellion and punished the ringleaders.[58]

Arkhangelskoe, Princess Dashkova's Troitskoe, and L. K. Razumovsky's Petrovskoe were damaged or torn apart by enraged or needy peasants. "Of the huge [Petrovskoe] library collected lovingly over fifteen years and valued by the librarian who catalogued it at 400 thousand rubles, not one book was saved. After the French had left, the incredible orangery with up to 50 rare specimens of lemon and orange trees was burned down by the peasants, angered by the gardener who upbraided them for their indifference and lack of desire to help him eradicate the disorder the French had brought."[59] It is hardly surprising that in 1812—and again in 1905 and 1917—the village serf would regard the fairy-tale world his masters had vacated as fair game. Provisions were carried off; gazebos and columned galleries were taken apart for firewood; flocks were pastured in the estate park. Landowners moved to restore the normal order, insofar as possible, as swiftly as they could. After the Nikolevs returned to Pokrovskoe, Nikoleva's father managed to persuade the peasants to return to work, but that year the fields were unsown and their income was down.

In spite of the widespread destruction, the burning of Moscow and the looting and gutting of estates like Ostankino, Arkhangelskoe, and Shklov, some members of the Russian elite (admittedly writing decades after the fact) displayed sneaking admiration for the invaders, representatives of a culture they had long admired. Memoirs recount tales of French gallantry alongside descriptions of peasant heroism. Yankova, for instance, describes the courteousness of the French officers who arrived while their neighbors the Golovins were dining at their estate, Dednevo-Novospasskoe. They merely requested that the Golovins not ring the church bells. The French prisoners and wounded aroused compassion in some Russian nobles, who for decades had been tutored by French emigrants and had spoken the French language in preference to their own. Natalya Tuchkova's grandmother baked fresh bread for prisoners who passed by her estate. One of the Bibikova daughters, observing a prisoner eating dreadful-looking kasha, remarked, "You're having a very meager repast." The prisoner, eloquent as well as gallant, replied, "Yes, mademoiselle, but to season it I am growing a plant called patience."[60] In Orel, where fifty thousand French lay wounded in September 1812, nobles took the officers into their houses. The wealthy V. I. Kireevsky (father of the Moscow intellectuals Ivan and Peter) reportedly spent forty thousand rubles on the prisoners and contracted typhus ministering to them. He died from the disease and was buried at Dolbino, the family estate.

Yet for Russia perhaps the most profound consequence of the Napoleonic wars, which culminated in a struggle of all Russians against the French invaders, was a distinct shift in the hitherto cosmopolitan cultural identity of the elite. By 1805, reports D. I. Sverbeev, there was considerable dislike for the French, "even for their language." French émigrés were becoming less frequent and therefore too expensive as tutors, and French governesses were considered atheists and possibly spies. Hence "true patriots" had given up on having their children taught French.[61] The experiences of 1812 redoubled these sentiments: Russian patriotism was aroused by the invasion, and Russian pride ran at an all-time high after the victory over Napoleon. In a telling incident from 1812, peasant soldiers detained young Nikita Muraviev, the future Decembrist, who was trying to join the army defending Moscow. Because he spoke Russian so badly, they suspected he was a spy.[62] After the war, a poor command of Russian—the elite's classic linguistic marker of being a "resident foreigner"— was no longer fashionable, leaving cosmopolitans such as Prince Dmitry Golitsyn in difficulties. Golitsyn, reared in Paris, spoke Russian badly; upon being appointed governor of Moscow, he initially had to have his speeches translated from French. Yankova and others relate that speaking French went completely out of fashion for a time and that for the elite fluency in reading and writing Russian became the norm.

Like an earlier generation that had been raised on tales of the Pugachev rebellion, another now grew up on eyewitness accounts of the war of 1812. Two of Russia's gallant officers, both related to Ekaterina Samoilova, became par-

154. Silver snuffbox depicting General N. N. Raevsky and his two young sons bearing arms against the French. Made by I. Kalmykov, a Moscow master craftsman. Early 1820s.
(Courtesy of the Hermitage Museum, St. Petersburg)

ticularly legendary. General Nikolai Raevsky, her heroic son, was acclaimed for taking his two young sons into battle against the French (fig. 154). And in Denisov, of *War and Peace*, Tolstoy immortalized the fabled poet and partisan leader Denis Davydov, who was the cousin of Ekaterina's second husband. After the war, armed with these legends as well as their own experiences, Russia's landowners and peasants, and the life of town and country, slowly reverted to previously established patterns of existence (fig. 155), patterns sustained up to and even beyond the emancipation.

155. Artist unknown. Family life at Nikolskoe, an estate in Moscow Province. 1820s–30s.
(Courtesy of the Literary Museum, Moscow)

8

The Kingdom Divided

LORD AND SERF

Serfdom itself, despite its being contrary to human sentiment, produced differing results. In some it developed noble laziness, in others animal evil; in yet another a consciousness of worth, a feeling of obligation and responsibility, an enlightened independence which arose from the habit of command. —**Boris Chicherin**

156. G. V. Soroka. View of the dam on the estate Spasskoe (detail). In this painting of a manor house and agricultural fields separated by water, the strong line of the dam symbolizes the divide between the world of the peasant mowers and their landowner. 1840s. (Courtesy of the Russian Museum, St. Petersburg)

THE COMPLICATED, DEPLORABLE, AND PECULIARLY Russian institution of serfdom was the precondition for the world of the estate described in this book.[1] As early as 1767, in her instructions to her Legislative Commission, the enlightened Catherine II dealt gingerly with serfdom, noting that in some instances "slavery" served the interests of the state and that a general emancipation was not advisable. The law, she wrote, should guard equally against abuses of slavery and the danger of rebellion. The tension between these two goals marked the history of serfdom for the next century. Catherine's descendants took much the same tack, lamenting the institution more vociferously but continually raising the specter of social chaos to explain the inadvisability of emancipation. Then in 1858, the young tsar Alexander II declared to the assembled Moscow nobility that it would be far better to abolish serfdom from above than to await the day when it began abolishing itself from below. His words were a strong signal of his commitment to emancipation.[2]

Serfdom was indubitably a moral evil, as most Russians by 1858 recognized. Numerous historians have also argued that the institution was not only a brake on economic development generally but also largely responsible for the high percentage of landowners hopelessly in debt at the time of the emancipation. At the same time, the fact that serfdom survived as long as it did indicates that at least on some level it was a functional way of life, meeting the perceived needs of the Russian state, landowner, and even enserfed peasant. What was the underlying rationale of this socioeconomic system, how did it operate, and what were its economic and psychological effects on the landowning elite?

Manor House and Village

One memoirist describes her grandmother's estate as divided into "two kingdoms" that faced each other across the banks of the river running through the estate: "On 'this side' was grandmother's kingdom: 'her' people lived there:

the nanny, maids, lackeys, coachman, cook, scullery, gardener, and water carrier, who was also the night guard. On the 'other side' was the kingdom of [the steward], with the working horses, poultry, and dogs on chains, laborers, stable hands, cattle keepers, and two cooks" (fig. 156).[3] If a landowner's own kingdom consisted of dependents and domestics, he or she also ruled the other side: the conglomeration of illiterate farmers, craftsmen, and artisans living in the village or villages on the estate. The landowner's decrees on dues or work, issued from the estate office, usually passed through intermediaries—from the steward to craftsmen and village elders and officials. In his own kingdom the landowner was sole ruler, but in certain dealings with the other kingdom (for example, in collecting the state tax on all adult males, sending recruits to the army, making his serfs work on road maintenance, and maintaining order) he was also acting as the tsar's agent.

Tensions between the two kingdoms ran particularly high during the spring sowing and fall harvesting (figs. 157,

157. A. G. Venetsianov. *Spring Sowing.* Ca. 1827. (Courtesy of the Tretiakov Gallery, Moscow)

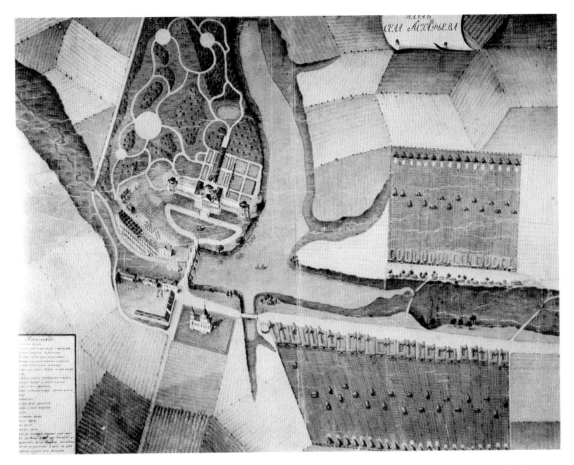

158. I. Vakhromeyev. Plan of the estate of Ostafievo, showing its two kingdoms. On the left, the park, house, church, and quarters for house serfs and artisans; on the right, across the pond, peasant villages and fields. 1805. (Courtesy of the Ostankino Museum, Moscow)

158). Arable land was customarily divided into long, narrow strips of property, as this meant fewer turns of the plow per strip. Approximately half the strips were the serf villagers', half the landowner's—though the serfs, of course, cultivated them all. The discrete areas were intermingled, and in critical periods the peasant's concern for his harvest competed with that of his owner. One owner of a small estate only narrowly averted a peasant rebellion during harvesting. Seeing that the family's grain was lying unharvested while the peasants worked on their own strips, she suggested that they switch their days of work in order to finish harvesting her grain. After apparently agreeing, the next day the whole village gathered in the courtyard instead of going to work.

Mama went out to them . . . [and] spoke in a strict tone; some did not answer in friendly fashion. Then she raised her voice and demanded that they hand over the initiators of the disorder or she would send for the policeman. The steward standing near Mama seemed feverish and muttered, "Your Highness! Leave, these are robbers, they will murder us." But Mama continued to speak; the peasants one after another took off their caps, finally went on their knees, asked for forgiveness, turned over the guilty ones and went straight to work. As a punishment Mama asked for two extra days [of peasant labor] and sent the guilty peasants to the gaol.[4]

If the steward brought offenses from his kingdom to the landowner's attention, justice was dispensed from the porch of the manor house. By law the noble was empowered to decide the fate of the offender, as warranted by the particular misdeed; the owner might choose to send the serf to Siberia, to the army for life, or to one of his distant estates; or he might merely have him beaten in the stables or at the local police station.

A supreme irony of the evolution of serfdom in Russia was the gradual perversion of its somewhat cloudy but quasi-rational original justification into a de facto system of personal slavery. According to the original principle, never written into law but widely accepted, serfs were obligated to serve the owner of an estate because he served the tsar. They were bound to the land they worked, not to an individual, for their work produced the income necessary for the state servitor to carry out his official responsibilities. The most common Russian word for nobleman, *dvoryanin,* or attendant at the court, reflected his duties, precisely as the word for house serf, *dvorovoi* (from the same root, *dvor,* meaning either "the court of a prince" or "a nobleman's seat"), mirrored the latter's obligations. The peasant, however, commonly believed that although the lord owned him, the land he worked was his.

The beginning of serfdom is usually dated to the reign of Ivan the Terrible (1533–84) or to the Law Code of 1649,

which permanently bound the peasant to the estate where he lived; this law abolished the right of the serf to migrate from estate to estate, a practice that had gradually been restricted in the previous century. In the eighteenth century serfdom was reinforced by the decree of Peter I concerning compulsory noble service to the state. The enserfed population swelled as the crown generously granted populated estates to individuals and extended serfdom into newly acquired territories. Until 1762, serfdom was a state business, the ownership of serfs and land being officially connected to the noble's service. After the noble was released from his part of the agreement (the obligation to serve), his right to continue to own serfs became the key element of an unwritten compact between crown and noble: "Support us and we will let you keep your 'living wealth.'" The laws on serf ownership during this period were unclear and contradictory, however. Numerous merchants, other non-nobles, and even foreigners could, or did, in effect, own serfs. The Demidov family, for instance, whose fortune was made in mining, controlled thousands of serfs assigned to the mines and factories the Demidovs established and operated. The process of restricting estate ownership to the nobility began with a decree of 1758, which ordered all those not entitled to own populated estates to sell them within six months.[5] Significantly, the decree did not apply to house serfs. As late as 1777 in the town of Smolensk burghers were allowed to own serfs, as were landowners in the Polish lands Catherine annexed, where the constitution decreed that anyone could own serfs.

By the end of the eighteenth century the privilege of owning populated estates had been restricted to the hereditary nobility (which now included self-made men like the three Demidov heirs, who had been ennobled and granted ownership of thousands of serfs). Although this was a fluid class to begin with, questions arose when a noble married out of it. In 1788 the Senate ruled that a noblewoman who married a non-noble be allowed to keep her estates, but

Nicholas I, embarking on a serious effort to restrict estate ownership, rescinded the decree in 1841. In subsequent years he ruled that nobles with no populated property could not buy serfs; that serfs who had become ennobled could not buy the settled lands they, their fathers, or their grandfathers had inhabited; that nobles who married serfs could not own their spouse's estate of origin (unless it had been inherited); and that non-Christian nobles could not own Christian peasants (except in the western provinces).

Just as the serf, in theory, provided the material foundations for the lord's service, so too the lord, in theory, acted as guardian of his peasants. The majority of landowners, aware that their own prosperity depended on the peasants' prosperity, conformed to the normal demands on the peasant. The peasant owed the landowner either work on his land (*barshchina*), which was customarily (and by law) limited to three days a week, or annual monetary dues (*obrok*, a form of quitrent), the average amount of which rose slowly as Russia's currency inflated during the last century of serfdom. On some estates the landowner exacted a mixture of the two forms of dues from his peasants. As noted, on barshchina estates the land was divided more or less evenly between master and serfs, with variations in the quality of the arable soil meticulously factored into the division. The Reverend William Coxe, wondering why Bolotov did not take the best land for himself, questioned him about this system. Bolotov gave the standard reply: it would not be fair. If his peasants did not prosper, neither would he.

Peasants on obrok were given passports to ply their trade off the estate and gave their owner part of the proceeds from their salaried work or sales of agricultural produce, honey, or handicrafts. Skilled serf craftsmen on quitrent were often more valuable to their owners and more prosperous than serf farmers. A few of Nikolai Sheremetev's serfs became wealthy entrepreneurs whose net worths were reckoned in millions of rubles and who owned both real property and serfs (registered in their master's name).[6] Some privately owned villages specialized (as do some Russian villages to this day) in the highly profitable production of lace, ceramics, and leather goods. To determine the extent of this entrepreneurship on his vast domains, in December 1798 Sheremetev ordered his steward to compile a list of "what kinds of industries the peasants of each estate have, where their factories and enterprises are, what such entrepreneurs make for their wares, and if possible, the annual amount for each" (fig. 159).[7]

159. L. K. Plakhov. *In the Blacksmith's Shop.* 1845. (Courtesy of the Russian Museum, St. Petersburg)

Landowners could drive hard bargains with wealthy serfs: one entrepreneur had to pay Sheremetev the princely sum of three hundred thousand rubles for his freedom.

In Gogol's *Dead Souls* the roguish Chichikov, pondering the list of dead craftsmen he has bought, lingers on two names and ponders their probable fortunes as entrepreneurs. He imagines that "Stepan the Cork," a carpenter, was on his way to becoming wealthy. "Like as not, he'd lug home a hundred solid silver rubles every time, and maybe he'd even sew a government note in his linen breeches." But "Maxim Teliatnikov," a talented shoemaker, might have made a fatal miscalculation: "'Why, how I'll start a little place of my own,' you said . . . and so, having paid a considerable quitrent to your master, you set up a little shop. . . . You'd gotten yourself some rotten leather somewhere, at one-third the regular price, and sure enough, you make a double profit . . . but within a fortnight the boots you'd made were all cracked and split . . . that little shop of yours became deserted, and you started taking a drop now and then."[8] The obrok system was more prevalent in northern Russia, where poor soil made agriculture less profitable. One Kostroma memoirist says that here the prosperous peasants were almost all on obrok (figs. 160, 161).

> Their huts . . . were very clean and spacious, two stories, with glass windows. . . . Practically all were artisans and craftsmen. . . . Some built boats, for which they got a lot of money. In other districts they mostly went . . . to Moscow, but preferably to Petersburg, where as boys they were apprenticed to some master craftsman: a blacksmith, locksmith, woodcarver, mahogany furniture maker, all possible industries. At the end of their studies, already hired by master craftsmen, they paid their masters a good obrok, returned home for a while and married. Then, having spent Lent and Easter at home, they returned to Petersburg, leaving the farming to their fathers, mothers, sisters and wives, sending them various sums of money from time to time.[9]

The peasant proverb "God is in His Heaven, and the Tsar is far away" reflected the serf's consciousness of being at the mercy of the estate owner or steward. The lord set the amount and type of work or dues the serf owed and meted out punishments as he or she saw fit. Although the law forbade it, peasants were sold without their families or the land they worked, unfairly punished, and sometimes beaten to death. Yankova fastidiously refused to trade a shiftless serf girl to a fisherman for his catch but happily sold her to the same man for a paltry twenty-five rubles.[10] Sporadic attempts were made to regulate the behavior of serf owners, but the de facto powers of the owner were always greater, and the position of the serfs more vulnerable, than the law allowed.

The estate, as a nineteenth-century official described it, was thus "a small state within a big one. . . . It is impossible not to notice how much trouble and expense it costs

160. A prosperous peasant's house in central Russia. Nineteenth century. (Museum of Wooden Architecture, New Jerusalem Monastery, Istra, Moscow Province)

161. Restored interior of a peasant's house at Petrovskoe, the estate of
Pushkin's grandfather.

the central government to penetrate this little state, to enforce its power and have its statutes upheld."[11] Only in the most notorious cases did local officials, many of whom were in awe of local grandees, try to interfere with a landowner's behavior. If they did so, they might be met by an armed band of retainers at the gates of the estate and threatened; those who persisted might be beaten or killed. One Voronezh landowner habitually greeted local officials by shooting at them, pistols in both hands.

Some eighteenth-century landowners were notorious for beating serfs in front of guests. As this suggests, only flagrant abuse was prosecuted. Court records tend to confirm the old nobility's assertion that parvenus—those recently enriched and ennobled—were more likely to abuse

serfs.[12] Yury Grinshtein, whom Empress Elizabeth rewarded with 927 serfs for his part in her seizure of power in 1741, was exiled from St. Petersburg for beating his serfs. Kannabikh, a Gatchina veteran to whom Paul I awarded 1,000 serfs for a chance remark, was also legendary for cruelty. Yet the most infamous tyrant of the mid-eighteenth century was Saltykova, a member of the old nobility.

Authorities were required by law to investigate reports of torture. On the estate of Major Orlov, in Orel Province, they found forty wounded serfs shut inside cattle barns without food and evidence that other serfs had been chained to a wall or put in irons or stocks for small crimes. At Major General Pobedinsky's estate in Yaroslav Province

225

they discovered instruments of torture covered with coagulated blood. In 1851 officials in Kherson Province investigating the suicide of an eleven-year-old serf learned that his mother had spent the previous five years chained to a post in the kitchen for trying to bathe in the river after a brutal beating.

Against this background of actual court cases Sergei Aksakov's account of Mikhail Kurolesov's behavior seems entirely probable. After marrying the orphan heiress Praskovya Ivanovna, he bought land in the eastern steppes and resettled his wife's serfs there on three estates. Kurolesovo, built for the family, was located in Simbirsk Province; Parashino and Ivanovka (named for his young wife) were in Orenburg Province. At Kurolesovo a magnificent manor house and church arose for the family, while Parashino, safely removed from its young mistress's gaze, became the setting for orgies of bloodthirstiness and debauchery. On prolonged "inspection" trips there Kurolesov's lawlessness gradually increased: he turned to stealing things he admired from his neighbors (including a married serf girl whom he bigamously married to his own servant). From the Parashino house serfs he assembled fifteen cutthroats who took part in their master's drinking bouts and shared his conviction that he was above the law. Whether serf, official, or noble, anyone who crossed Kurolesov was seized and locked up in a cellar or mercilessly flogged, sometimes on his own estate in front of his family. A good flogging made the sadistic Kurolesov quite amiable and gay, and during the height of his orgiastic behavior he spent most of his time piously supervising the construction of a church for Parashino. Memoirs provide similar accounts of tyrants, but few of them are as outrageous as Kurolesov.[13]

Karamzin's *Poor Liza* sentimentally tells of a peasant girl, seduced and then betrayed by a young noble, who throws herself into a lake and drowns. The story reduced a generation of readers to tears but did not alter the fact that landowners considered it their right to seduce or rape their female serfs, maiden or married, for which they were rarely prosecuted. In a curious case that took place in 1827, a house serf belonging to Captain Baturin of the Ryazan cavalry complained to officials that his master was going to send him to Siberia in order to enjoy his wife, from whom he begged not to be parted. This case went all the way to the Committee of Ministers in St. Petersburg (at that time the court of final appeal), which ruled that Baturin could legally send the serf to Siberia but that his wife must go with him![14] Landowners kept harems with impunity, and memoirs and literature abound in instances of peasant women being exiled from their families or forcibly married off to someone loathsome as punishment for resisting their masters. As late as 1855 a provincial privy councillor in Orenburg Province enforced *ius primae noctis* on his estate (for which he was, however, prosecuted).

With little chance of legal recourse against a tyrannical master, the peasant resorted to flight, revolt, murder, or suicide. Thousands of serfs ran away annually, their escape sometimes fueled by rumors of land and freedom on distant soil. In the eighteenth century many fled to Poland, and in the early nineteenth century, to Bessarabia and New Russia (made up of Ekaterinoslav, Kherson, and the Tauride Provinces). Hence many landowners had special employees who tracked down runaways and demanded their return. Harboring or employing runaways was illegal but common in a country with a chronic labor shortage. In 1827, when landowners of New Russia argued that the return of runaways they had taken in would ruin them, their sympathetic governor limited discovery of runaways to two years and decreed that former owners could be compensated by money: 250 rubles for a male, 150 for a female.[15]

The landowner, responsible for the tranquility of the Russian countryside, could summon troops against serf rebels. In 1750 three thousand rebel serfs fought off a regiment of dragoons sent in to pacify them and took its commander captive. Six regiments were then dispatched with orders to burn the rebels' houses. Such uprisings often provoked others on nearby estates. Peasant villages might rebel when faced with the threat of being sold to a harsh landowner or in reaction to other news that affected their lot. In 1760, when Count Vorontsov sold his Arzamas serfs to the court councillor Bezsonov, the peasants armed themselves against local officials, and troops had to be sent in to quell the uprising. In 1762, the year that Peter III issued his manifesto freeing the nobility from compulsory state service, 314 revolts were recorded, possibly because the logical corollary to freedom for nobles would have been freedom for serfs.

Fear of agrarian revolts intensified after the Pugachev rebellion. Monarch and landowner alike used the specter of Pugachev as an excuse for not tampering with the system. When three thousand peasants owned by Pozdeev, of Vologda Province, complained to the authorities that they had no clothes or shoes and were dying from cold and hunger, Pozdeev tried to dismiss their complaints, warning local officials that he foresaw "a revolt clearly developing similar to that of Pugachev, for all the peasants are inspired by the idea left from the time of Pugachev, that there be no nobles."[16]

Usually, however, the customary myths ruled: the authorities preferred to see rebellions as the work of a few rabble-rousers inciting normally docile serfs, and the serfs mistakenly envisioned the tsar as their protector against evil authorities.[17] Such was the case in the summer of 1821, following a rebellion among the peasants of Count K. G. Razumovsky. When the bailiff ordered the serfs flogged and their pleas to the count went unanswered, the serfs resorted to passive opposition—a work slowdown. Alarmed by reports of village meetings, the count called in local troops to arrest the agitators. Meanwhile the revolt spread to nearby estates. Some rebels set off for St. Petersburg to see the tsar; two hundred others stormed the jail to free the arrested. Early in 1822 the St. Petersburg criminal court sentenced five ringleaders to flogging with

the knout and to forced labor in Siberia.[18] Personal reprisals against bad owners also occurred: one Tambov landowner had his nose cut off; other owners (including Struisky's son and heir) were murdered.

Village revolts continued up to the emancipation and increased in the years immediately following the decree, reflecting the peasants' bitter disappointment in the terms. Yet the reported accounts of peasant revolts and vengeful acts against tyrannical owners are few in number (rarely over one hundred a year), which lends credence to the argument that most landowners were not tyrants. Some memoirists have undoubtedly exaggerated the bucolic harmony between lord and serf. But the great prerevolutionary historian Romanovich-Slavatinsky, after presenting a painstaking catalog of tyrannical behavior, also defends the Russian landowner. "The miseries of the position of enserfed peasants cannot be attributed to an entire class. Who does not know of landowners who cared for their serfs as if for their own family, for whom providing support for the serfs was a holy obligation they fulfilled in the most honorable fashion? The people, in any event, knew such landowners and created a proverb about them: 'If the grain does not suffice, the lord will give it.' The people loved such landowners and were not even happy about the end of serfdom, which ended their age-old link with their *barin-batyushka* [master-little father]."[19]

The *krestyanin* (the usual word for "peasant") was considered not only his master's "living wealth" but his "baptized property" (as the root *krest*, meaning "cross," indicates), which Russian Orthodoxy enjoined the noble to support and protect. Even grandees could adopt the role of patriarch. Nikolai Sheremetev, for instance, appears to have kept a close and kindly eye on his Kuskovo peasants. On May 13, 1797, he ordered his "home chancellery" to see that the peasants Nastasya and Varvara Matveeva be given five hewn trees each to repair their cottages. In February 1798 he ordered his steward to send him a list of the "superfluous workers who are just a burden to the peasants, for they live at Kuskovo unoccupied and are of no benefit." On June 4, 1799, he decreed that the situation of the poor in his villages be improved and that the sick and old be completely exempted from paying dues.[20]

By the early nineteenth century the peasant's helpless, childlike, and improvident nature (which allowed him to be easily misled and therefore to require paternalistic guidance) had become a major justification for the system. Gerakov, accompanying a rich young friend on a tour of his numerous estates in 1820, makes a remark typical of this attitude when he notes that at Nikolskoe the peasants crowded around the young master "like children around their father."[21] During the reign of Alexander I (1801–25),

Russia witnessed the establishment of the first public philanthropic organizations, the freeing of the serfs in Prussia, the end of slavery in England, and Alexander's experimental decree (1803) allowing nobles in some areas to free entire villages of serfs (though not individual peasants belonging to a peasant commune). Events such as these promoted a spirit of noblesse oblige among most educated, relatively well-off landowners, who felt obliged to provide decent cottages and clothing for their peasants and to keep grain reserves for their villages for periods of famine, as the law required, even when its sale would have been profitable (fig. 162). Estate owners began to build hospitals and schools for peasants on their estates (as does Andrei Bol-

162. Peasant cottages at Bolshaya Aleshnya, the estate of A. S. Ermolov, during spring flooding.
(*Stolitsa i usadba*, no. 30)

228

konsky at Bogucharovo in *War and Peace*) and generally to provide, at their own expense, the type of social welfare support that the zemstvos would assume after the emancipation.[22] In 1825, a famine year, for example, Countess Musina-Pushkina made sure her peasants at Valuevo had enough grain and even had bread baked for them.[23]

Yet the most benevolent master could not purge the system of some perennial sources of misery. One was the requirement that the village supply able-bodied recruits for the army, few of whom would return after their twenty-five years of service. Village elders tried to offer up the most shiftless peasants, but this was not always possible. Hence the heart-rending scenes, first recorded in Radishchev's *Journey from St. Petersburg to Moscow*, of women weeping and fainting when sons, fiancés, or husbands were selected, chained and placed under guard (lest they run away), and finally led off. Natalya Tuchkova's father, a liberal landowner elected marshal of the nobility four times in a row, hated recruitment so much that he often developed a fever from "trying to seem indifferent when inside he was deeply affected." Tuchkov became somewhat of a hero to the peasants in his district: he tried to ensure that only lazy, less healthy, or orphaned peasants were selected, and he investigated all rumors of cruelty to peasants. In the dark years that closed the reign of Nicholas, Tuchkov was arrested for his liberalism. Conservative neighbors told his house serfs, "He should have been sent away a long time ago, your master—a noble, but always on the side of the peasants!"[24]

Serfdom was the lowest rung on imperial Russia's hierarchy of servitude. Peasants suffered from the severe command styles many landowners acquired in military service. One retired naval officer was determined to run his estate in ship-shape fashion. At 6 A.M. on winter mornings he would set out for "the Admiralty," as he called the office, workshops, and school on his small estate. He kept the accounts himself and was considered a strict manager who liked to be obeyed, demanding shipboard perfor-

163. A. Malynin. *Girl with a Sickle*. Lithograph from a painting by A. G. Venetsianov. 1820s. (Courtesy of the Russian Museum, St. Petersburg)

mance from his peasants and his children. His son terms him harsh ("In the present day he would be considered cruel") and blames this alteration in a man who "by nature was tender and impressionable" on the two types of serfdom he had experienced: service in his youth and peasant enserfment.[25]

Although it is impossible to generalize from individual instances, both foreigners on the spot and modern scholars have been favorably impressed with the Russian peasant's standard of living. Martha Wilmot called the picturesque mowers (fig. 163) she saw from her window at Troitskoe in the summer of 1805 "better clothed and fed than our Paddys."[26] A recent study of the serfs of Petrovskoe, a Gagarin estate in Tambov Province, concludes that with the exception of famine years, the peasantry was as well nourished as any in Western Europe. The author concludes that as a system serfdom was probably more socially oppressive than economically exploitative. Over a two-year period, for instance, 79 percent of the prosperous Petrovskoe serfs were flogged, 24 percent more than once (roughly the same rate of punishment as slaves received on an American plantation).[27]

It would be anachronistic to evaluate the estate's system of justice by modern standards of oppression. In an age when the ideal master was stern but fair, village elders supported a master's decision to have the local police flog a thief or a drunken, unproductive peasant. Many punishments, however severe in modern terms, were considered justifiable at the time. Dmitry Miliutin never forgot seeing his father flog the serf steward of Titovo "mercilessly. . . . But thus were the mores in those times: a good landowner considered [flogging] unavoidable to keep his serfs in line. . . . The punished individual would come to thank the master afterwards for the 'lesson' he had received."[28]

The serf might have a favorable view of a stern yet just lord, but quite different feelings about the steward or bai-

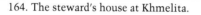

164. The steward's house at Khmelita.

165. The steward's house at Karabikha, the estate of Prince A. P. Golitsyn, governor of Yaroslavl Province. The poet N. A. Nekrasov bought the estate from the prince's descendants in the 1860s; after 1917 Nekrasov's former coachman ran the Karabikha collective farm.

liff who directly controlled his life (figs. 164, 165). As many, if not more, peasant complaints were directed toward estate stewards as toward owners. In line with their paternalistic thinking landowners also tended to blame stewards more than peasants, mostly for thievery or mismanagement. The well-intentioned Dashkova was shocked when, on a visit to her Belorussian estate, she found that "innumerable depredations had been committed by my Polish steward on the mistaken belief that I should be dispatched to Siberia. I took a number of measures on behalf of my peasants and appointed a Russian to administer the property."[29] On his first visit to Bolshye

Vyazemy, in 1803, young Boris Golitsyn wrote his mother that he had found "appalling disorder. . . . Nothing is organized sensibly, and all this is the fault of the steward. The income comes barely to 3,000 rubles, and the orangeries and house serfs eat that all up, so there is nothing left."[30]

Stewards, the mediators between the demands of the lord and the peasants' ability to produce, rarely escaped charges of cruelty or venality. Many must have been tempted to enrich themselves at the landowner's expense. Very wealthy landowners, who lived as a rule either in Moscow or St. Petersburg, relied entirely on a hierarchy of functionaries to manage their estates: the Gagarins, for

166. G. V. Soroka. The office of the house at Ostrovki, where Miliukov conducted his business. 1844.
(Courtesy of the Russian Museum, St. Petersburg)

example, had a central office in Moscow that kept the accounts, as did other families such as the Sheremetevs, Vorontsovs, Yusupovs, and Naryshkins. Some aristocrats left everything to their underlings, with disastrous results. In the 1830s, when the Decembrist V. L. Davydov was in exile in Siberia, Kamenka's unsupervised stewards spent their time in drunken revelry; soon the main house was in disrepair and the family fortune jeopardized.[31] Alexander Dumas was appalled that his wealthy friend Naryshkin did not even know how many serfs or acres he owned; Dumas was convinced that Naryshkin's steward was stealing from him. Financial shenanigans by two of Sergei Poltoratsky's stewards (along with his own profligacy) completely ruined the family fortune.[32]

It was all too easy for stewards to line their own pockets with profits extorted from the peasant, who sometimes took his revenge. Serfs murdered Nikolai Yusupov's head steward, a cruel Frenchman, for which they were sent to Siberia, in addition to receiving fifteen lashes with the knout and having their nostrils torn off and the word "murderer" branded on their faces.[33] Landowners also punished wayward officials: Nikolai Sheremetev sentenced some offenders (accused of squeezing the peasants, accepting bribes, and "other abuses") to a sound beating and transferred them to agricultural work at Ostankino, "until I give further instructions."[34]

The Estate Economy

The theoretically benevolent dictatorship of lord over serf held the noble legally responsible for feeding his peasants in time of famine, providing timber for their housing, and seeing that they were clothed. The law also forbade demanding "ruinous" exactions from peasants, such as exorbitant cash dues or working the lord's lands more than three days a week. In practice, some landowners abandoned their patriarchal role out of desperation, greed, or profligacy. Some used state funds provided for peasant famine relief for themselves. Others freed elderly or sick serfs so as not to have to care for them or pay their poll taxes. Some moved their serfs from estate to estate in order to avoid taxes. In the 1850s one landowner moved his serfs from Penza to Orenburg, sold their Penza houses for his own profit, and made them pay for the new ones in Orenburg.

Other nobles took advantage of the low-interest loans provided by state banks for the nobility (first established in 1754). Intended to stimulate capital investment in estates and agricultural improvements, these loans became an easy way of living beyond one's means. As one deputy to Catherine's legislative commission testified in 1767, most nobles who took advantage of these loans were not the poor and deserving; they were individuals with luxury-loving habits.[35]

Extending credit, it would appear, undermined rather than improved Russian agriculture. Statistics on the Russian landowning nobility during the first half of the nineteenth century paint a grim picture: the gap between rich and poor was enormous, and the majority of landowners were in increasingly dire economic straits. Just before the emancipation, roughly 75 percent of Russia's 103,194 landowners owned fewer than one hundred serfs each, and as a group less than one-fifth of the souls, while the richest 3.7 percent owned over 1,000 souls each, amounting to almost half the total. In the preceding 22 years the number of landowners had decreased by 18¼ percent.[36] Between 1820 and 1859 the percentage of privately owned serfs mortaged to a state credit institution rose from 20 to 66

167. E. M. Cheptsov. *They Are Listening*. Villagers getting the news from a literate peasant. Kursk Province, mid-nineteenth century. (*Stolitsa i usadba*, no. 29)

percent; this number reached 71.3 percent in the central agricultural region.[37]

Landowners sometimes tried to raise cash by selling an estate to the crown for an inflated sum. In the early 1850s Princess Tatyana Potemkina decided to do just this with Mikhailovka, a large estate in Kursk Province that Peter the Great had granted her great-grandfather M. M. Golitsyn for victory at Poltava. At the current price of 25 rubles per desyatina (2.7 acres), its 14,587 desyatinas (or 39,385 acres) were worth 364,675 rubles. When the princess discovered that the Ministry of State Domains was willing to pay 1.2 million rubles for the estate, she concluded the deal without informing the Mikhailovka peasants, a group of 5,000 artisans who made a handsome living selling handmade boots. Up to that time they had paid the princess only 9,000 rubles in annual dues; under the new arrangement their dues would be fixed at 18 rubles per soul, or 90,000 rubles. The Mikhailovka peasants understandably resisted the transfer. When a ministry official came to inspect the property, they rudely informed him that they were private serfs, not state peasants, and therefore not subject to his orders. A "revolt" was reported, and troops were about to be called in when Reshetov, a local noble, was sent to intervene. Just as he was addressing the peasant representatives, a total eclipse of the sun occurred. He told them this was a sign of God's displeasure with peasants who did not obey authority, and the frightened peasants agreed to the transfer.[38]

Russian literature confirms the pattern of spending beyond one's means and the mortgaging of souls and land as the time-honored solution to a poor cash flow. Beginning with Pushkin, literary portraits of noble profligacy and estate mismanagement are the rule, setting the stage for Chekhov's portraits of the decline and death of noble estate culture. When Tolstoy introduces Count Rostov, he points out that the count has plenty of cash that year because all his estates have been mortgaged to the hilt. Mortgaging serfs was so widespread a practice by the 1840s that

a character in Turgenev's *A Month in the Country*, wishing to present himself as an eligible suitor, pointedly notes that his 320 serfs are unmortgaged. In 1841 Emperor Nicholas I found it necessary to repeat the hope he had expressed in 1830, that nobles would use loans not to buy luxuries or repay other debts but to improve estates.

Some landowners did, in fact, manage their estates carefully, even attempting to increase their income by introducing new agricultural methods. Traveling through Russia in the 1840s, Kohl found some estate owners attempting to "keep progress with the march of improvement."[39] August von Haxthausen admiringly describes the estate of Goropyatnitskaya, which functioned according to principles of scientific farming its owner had picked up on travels in England, France, and Germany. In spite of the "obstinacy and ignorance of the people, their blind attachment to tradition, and their hatred of innovation" the owner had managed, says Haxthausen, to make gradual improvements, to blend the new with the old, and to bring the estate up to a level that Haxthausen had not seen elsewhere in Russia.[40] Increasing income through improved agricultural methods was attempted on a very limited scale, however, and viewed as eccentric. Alexander I visited D. M. Poltoratsky's model farm at Avchurino, which followed the English pattern and employed the English plow rather than the traditional wooden one, known as a *sokha*. But the volatile Rostopchin, after hiring an English agronomist to help him set up a similar farm, abandoned his experiment and published a pamphlet in 1806 entitled "The Plow or the *Sokha*," a xenophobic attack against foreign implements. The Russian peasant, as Haxthausen noted, was equally resistant to innovation (fig. 168). The Marquis de Custine recounts that the peasants of one village in Nizhni Novgorod assassinated their owner because they did not like the agricultural innovations he was proposing.[41] This resistance to innovation, along with the three-field strip system of cultivation, a dearth of fertilizer, and poor accounting, made the average yield of Russian fields extremely low by European standards.

To increase income nobles often set up some form of income-producing enterprise. The nobility shared with the state a monopoly on the distilling of alcoholic beverages: virtually all estates produced spirits, liqueurs, and some form of beer, which were sold to taverns in their villages. Stud farms were also profitable. In the late eighteenth century, as the luxury market expanded, a number of nobles started porcelain or glass factories on their estates. Most were very small (employing under twenty workers) and evidently not profitable in that they lasted less than a decade. In 1799, at Perovo, Alexei Razumovsky's Moscow estate, for example, a Prussian founded a factory for the manufacture of porcelain teacups, vases, and statuettes, with only eighteen workers. Sold to a German shortly before the Napoleonic invasion, it ceased operations, probably because of the war. Maria V. Maltseva,

168. A. G. Venetsianov. *The Threshing Barn.* 1822–23. A variety of traditional agricultural tools are pictured.
(Courtesy of the Russian Museum, St. Petersburg)

who owned a number of glass factories, set one up on her Kaluga estate in 1797. For two years it was run by a Swiss engraver and sculptor, Francis Gattenberg, but then closed for lack of capital.[42] The fate of I. L. Lazarev's silk factory, opened in the late eighteenth century on Fryanovo, his estate near Moscow, is unknown. One must conclude that in some instances these "factories" were playthings for the wealthy, producing prestige rather than income. Enterprises involving sugar and sunflower oil, on the other hand, proved more durable. When the price of refined sugar rose after the war of 1812 (from 1⅔ to 3 rubles per pound), profitable sugar-beet enterprises sprang up on estates such as the Davydovs' Kamenka, in Kiev Province, and Anton Gerard's Golubino, only fifteen miles from Moscow.[43]

The memoirs of V. A. Bakarev, Prince Alexei Kurakin's architect, give a detailed account of the economy of one large estate over an eight-year period (1820–28). Kurakino's more than sixty thousand acres were home to four thousand souls. Kurakino was run by a chief administrator and a chief controller (who submitted weekly, monthly, semiannual, and annual accounts to the prince), assisted by numerous accountants in the estate office. Kurakin also had an official in Orel who handled transactions there. The prince himself kept an eye on the smallest details, saying, "If I pay attention to the trifling, it is only a matter of time until I get to the important." Says Bakarev, "The property was like a web with the prince at its center. . . . [He] knew everything, whether it behooved him or not." For a new wooden spoon or broom to be issued, the old item had to be presented, and the latter was kept in one of many "closets filled with old and broken things of no use to anyone."[44]

The prince, interested in innovation, replaced the sokha with the plow and introduced new crops and machinery, new enterprises such as a linen-bleaching shop, and new breeds of livestock. The estate derived income from various products and activities: grain; fruit from its orchards, which generated up to 2,000 rubles a year; spirits (including vinegar, which sold for as much as 2 rubles per bucket); weekly village bazaars; and an annual fair in Alexandrovka (the largest village), which attracted nobles and merchants from surrounding areas and neighboring cities. But Kurakin's losses and expenditures on other enterprises exceeded this income. The linen factory cost him 150,000 rubles before he shut it down. He hired a Swiss cheesemaker whose products spoiled, costing him 5,000 rubles. He planned but never completed a potentially profitable inn at the post-station village on his property. Many workshops, manufacturing items such as carpets, lace, embroidery, and bricks (fig. 169), produced only for the estate.

Noblesse oblige was costly. Kurakin kept a handsome table, "always replete with tasty food and delicacies," at which his provincial neighbors were welcome. Fine wines and champagne (the prince's preferred drink) were served, always accompanied by light music from the winter garden. He loved to entertain, and his guests, each of whom was assigned a beautiful apartment, a servant, and sometimes a carriage, stayed for a few days "or on a few occasions, for a whole summer." Kurakin, says Bakarev, "personified every day the nobility in all its glory, that is, he lived not so much for himself as for the nobility of his district, who saw in him a state official, good natured master, and benefactor."[45]

Even Kurakin's main income, half a million rubles from a fish-catching lease in Astrakhan (granted to him and his brother by Paul), could not offset his enormous annual expenditures, which included 38,600 rubles in salaries to the most important officials of his domain; 43,300 rubles for the upkeep of his enterprises and house serfs; and 110,000 rubles for such personal expenses as wine, carriages, his servants' elegant livery, and the rental of a house in St. Petersburg. Kurakin spent at least 350,000 rubles annually to placate creditors and to cover unforeseen expenses (grain for his peasants during famine years; gifts to his daughter, Countess Zotova, whose husband's gambling debts were immense, and to his other daughter's illegitimate children). He died 7,000,000 rubles in debt.

169. Artist unknown. *A Brickyard on the Estate.* Late eighteenth century.
(Courtesy of the State Historical Museum, Moscow)

Karpinskaya's memories of her grandfather Pavel Mikhailovich Yablochkov offer a rare glimpse of the hardworking, successful estate owner who managed to accumulate wealth during this period of decline. In the early nineteenth century Yablochkov inherited the family votchina in Tula Province, consisting of 1,400 acres with 120 peasants and a 36-room house with 100 house serfs. With his wife's dowry (7,000 assignat rubles) he set up a profitable small distillery and bought oxen that he fattened up and sold for a profit. Then, during a prime time for buying land and peasants, his aunt left him a small inheritance.[46] Through a series of clever real estate transactions, Yablochkov acquired sufficient capital to buy 3,000 fertile acres on the border between Kharkov, Poltava, and Ekaterinoslav Provinces. The peasants he settled on it were soon so wealthy as to be the envy of many local landowners.

In 1820 Yablochkov bought the disreputable estate of

Zheleznovka, in Ryazan, which had been confiscated from a landowner whose band of serf robbers had terrorized everyone within a hundred miles. Although the peasants were not used to working, the territory was rich in iron ore and timber. Within four or five years he had constructed a water mill, profitable potash and soap factories, and a distillery that employed five hundred peasants and brought in eighty thousand rubles the first year. Yablochkov, says his granddaughter, "didn't spend a kopeck on luxuries." He never wore fancy clothes, nor did he purchase champagne or foreign wine. His sole indulgence was the large sum he gave his wife for home entertainments, which included serf performances of plays she had written.[47]

Estate Management in Fiction

Prudent landowners, save for Tolstoy's Constantine Levin, are virtually absent from Russian literature. Negrov, a retired major general in Herzen's *Who Is to Blame?* is a typical figure. Says Herzen, "His theory of management was very simple: he upbraided his bailiff and the village elder every day, he rode to shoot hares and walked to shoot snipe. Unused to attending to any business at all, he could not imagine what was to be done, so he devoted his efforts to trifles and was content. The bailiff and elder were content too" (fig. 170).[48] In *War and Peace* Rostov's steward, faced with the count's exorbitant demands for cash, siphons money from the countess's estates to support those of his master.

In literature, only individuals who have been exposed to other management models through travel abroad or in service attempt to change routines in a substantive manner. In Pushkin's *Tales of Ivan Belkin* we meet Ivan Petrovich Berestov, a retired guards officer in a remote province. "He had his house built according to plans drawn up by himself, set up a cloth-factory on the estate, increased his income, and regarded himself as the wisest man in the whole district. . . . He kept all the accounts himself, and read nothing but the Proceedings of the Senate."[49] But

sensible economic management more often takes second place to changes intended to assert or maintain status through the imitation of European (particularly English) patterns. In *A Nest of Gentlefolk* Turgenev tells us that Lavretsky's father, having become a confirmed Anglophile abroad, decides to change everything at home. "New furniture arrived from Moscow: spittoons, bells, and washing stands were introduced, breakfast was served in a new way; foreign wines replaced vodka and homemade liqueurs; new liveries were made for the servants; a new motto was added to the family arms: 'in recto virtus.'"[50] One will recall that Muromsky, Berestov's nearly bankrupt neighbor, similarly "wasted his substance" on an English garden, English jockeys, English governess, and foreign agricultural methods that did not work.[51] Landowners concerned with substantive as opposed to cosmetic changes are few, and on the defensive. Islayev, a main character in *A Month in the Country*, personally supervises the remodeling of barns and building of dams. He feels obliged to justify his unusual attitude, telling another noble, "I'm a practical man, born to look after my land—and nothing else."[52]

In *Oblomov* Goncharov tackles the psychological roots of the landowner's improvidence head-on. In the famous dream chapter that is key to Goncharov's theme, young Ilya Oblomov, unable to deal with his responsibilities as a minor official in St. Petersburg, dreams of his idyllic childhood on Oblomovka, the family manor.[53] At first glance the apposition of the small wooden house of Oblomovka, with its fussy old-fashioned interior, to Verkhlyovo, the grand estate of a neighboring prince, seems a typical commentary on the provincial social mosaic. But Verkhlyovo, we learn, formerly belonged to the Oblomovs. Goncharov employs telling details—broken steps on the porch, stains on the sofa upholstery—to transform the Oblomovs' cozy gentry nest into a symbol of sloth and torpor. Life at Oblomovka, says the author, is permeated by "primeval laziness, simplicity, peace, and inertia." The house becomes both a personification and indictment of the ignorant country patriarch's psychology, which rejects both productive work and change. Ilya's dream is a bright, almost festive celebration of the joys, rites, and rituals of country existence in pre-emancipation Russia, a world in which only serfs and foreigners work. Even in the city the adult Ilya's style of management, learned from his father, is a parody of the landowner's: he shouts at his lackey and does nothing.

Like *Oblomov*, *War and Peace* provides a literary portrait of generational decline, as sons inherit their fathers' inability to make a connection between work and income. Like Ilya Oblomov, young Nikolai Rostov dreams of the good life on his future estate, imagining his "charming wife, children, a good pack of hounds, ten to twelve leashes of swift harriers, the estate to look after, the neighbors, election to offices, perhaps, by the provincial nobility"—in other words, a life very much like his father's. When

170. Artist unknown. *Report of the Steward.* 1810. A dwarf holds the landowner's pipe.
(Courtesy of the State Historical Museum, Moscow)

Nikolai realizes that the family fortunes are in trouble, he throws the steward out, accusing him of robbing the Rostovs blind. "After this," says Tolstoy, "young Rostov took no further part in business of any sort but devoted himself with passionate interest to everything to do with the chase, which was kept up on a great scale on the old count's estate."[54]

Estate Management in Memoirs

A number of memoirists, for the most part individuals aware of having come down in the world, similarly celebrate country life even while criticizing the patriarchal landowner's impracticality. Miliutin makes clear that his father lived beyond his means and that as a result Titovo had to be sold. More striking is Khvoshchinskaya's picture of her father squandering a huge fortune in a few decades. On her mother's side Khvoshchinskaya's family included the wealthy Dunins and Bakhmetevs; on her father's, the Golitsyns, Saltykovs, and Potemkins. After Ekaterina Bakhmeteva and Yury Golitsyn married, most of the family money was spent on music, the main passion of her romantic, talented, superbly educated husband. When Golitsyn met his future wife in Kharkov he had a chorus of 30 men; when they settled at Saltyki, he created a women's chorus and later put together a large choir of 150 men and women whom he presented in concert not only in St. Petersburg and Moscow but abroad. "At Saltyki a large hall, two stories with choir lofts, was built especially for the singers. The accoustics were so good that when I ran through the hall to father's half [of the house] to say hello or good-bye, the echo of my little steps resonated throughout the hall. . . . Those who heard Golitsyn's choir would say that they sang like one soul."[55]

After two years of estate living, the young couple moved to Moscow for three months; the large entourage that accompanied them included a chamberlain, jockey, hairdresser, laundress, housekeeper, and two liveried lackeys; an upholsterer charged with selecting furniture for Saltyki; a choir director to choose voices for the choir; a French chef and assistant; and coachmen and stable hands to care for the sixteen horses, two carriages, two troikas, and sundry carts. Over the housekeeper's protests Golitsyn lodged and fed all these people at the Hotel Chevalier. Golitsyn surrounded himself with artists whom he wined and dined. When the renowned singer Albani came to town, he rented a concert hall for her recital and bought two hundred tickets for his friends. Golitsyn also went to all the fashionable masquerades. Before leaving Moscow Golitsyn had to sell "diamonds, silver and even the carriages" to meet his huge bills.[56]

The young prince, says his daughter, "was against the golden mean." For his coming-of-age party at Saltyki he offered his many guests various types of entertainment, imported wine, a dance orchestra, and a lavish dinner (which men and women ate in separate rooms, according to provincial fashion). Such hospitality gained Golitsyn a reputation among his neighbors, and at the beginning of the 1850s he became marshal of the Tambov nobility. Shortly thereafter the ruined state of his finances became clear. Having decided to part with his choir "with grief and an aching heart," he endeavored unsuccessfully to sell it intact to the Ministry of the Court. Golitsyn was tormented by the knowledge that he could not set things right and that he had squandered not only his own fortune but his children's. He tried to sell Saltyki, then begged his friend Rakhmaninov to accept his power of attorney and settle his debts. Desperate, Golitsyn wrote, "If [Rakhmaninov] has the cruelty to refuse my prayer my fortune is lost. . . . I cannot do it myself, I am going crazy."[57]

After the sale of Saltyki, Golitsyn's wife (now separated from her unfaithful husband), the children, and their governess departed for the much smaller estate of Ogarevo, in Penza Province. No manor house or gardens existed on this estate, and the family had to adjust to a modest house with thatched roof. The Ogarevo peasants, in contrast to the "industrious, prosperous" Saltyki inhabitants, were "more similar to wild people, dressed poorly in bast shoes and blue shirts. . . . Practically none of their huts had chimneys." Although the children were delighted by their new surroundings, their mother had to adapt to radically reduced circumstances. "At Saltyki everything had been ordered for us from the best Petersburg and Moscow stores; mother also dressed richly and elegantly. In Ogarevo she made the children's linens from father's old shirts, and even sewed new boots for us out of the old."[58]

Thus, at the same time that Boris Chicherin's father catapulted the family fortunes upward, using careful management and his income from tax farming to increase their acreage and serf holdings, the Golitsyns moved, in one generation, from the most prosperous stratum of the nobility into the most ordinary, that of the small-estate owner.[59] Their situation at Ogarevo was quite similar (if not quite as bleak) to the Dostoevskys' struggle for survival in the small village of Darovoe, purchased in the summer of 1831. Mikhail Dostoevsky, son of a priest, was a self-made man whose skill in medicine earned him in 1828 the Order of St. Anna, and with it, the right to inscribe himself and his heirs (among them the future writer Fyodor) in the rolls of the hereditary nobility. As Joseph Frank suggests, part of Mikhail's reason for purchasing an estate was—if only subconsciously—to affirm his new status.[60] Darovoe was a very small and poor property by the standards of the day: it had less than four hundred acres, no nearby water source, no forests, no manor house (the Dostoevskys occupied the largest peasant house), and only eleven peasant households with a total of seventy-six inhabitants. In the first two years Dostoevsky suffered several setbacks. A fire in the spring of 1832 completely destroyed the village. Then a boundary dispute with an heir of the original owner, whose land surrounded Darovoe on three sides, compelled Dostoevsky to buy another poverty-stricken hamlet, Cheremoshnya (comprising eight households and sixty-seven peasants), lest he be completely encircled. For this he was forced to go deeply in debt. Dostoevsky undoubtedly counted on making some sort of agricultural profit from his peasants, but the following two years brought drought and famine.

Letters between Dostoevsky, who stayed in Moscow because of his practice, and his wife, who went to Darovoe early in the spring to oversee the planting, reveal the constant problems of the smallholder whose livestock were few and poorly fed. The Darovoe and Cheremoshnya peasants got behind on the spring planting because they did not have enough reliable plow horses; a cow delivered her calf stillborn; at the end of May there were no chicklets in the entire village. In August Dostoevsky wrote his wife, "My dear, our horses are extraordinarily thin. . . . Order them fed, for now perhaps they might get you to Kolomna; if you begin to feed them well they will pull you all the way to Moscow." The Dostoevskys built a new shed but had no straw for thatch. Existence was little better than hand-to-mouth from the moment Dostoevsky bought Darovoe until his death eight years later. A month before his death, in responding to one of his son Fyodor's frequent requests for money while at boarding school, Dostoyevsky reveals a continually bad state of affairs:

Remember, that I wrote you both some months ago that the grain crop is bad, last year I wrote the same, that the winter wheat did not produce anything; now I write you that the present summer will bring decisive and complete ruin to our situation. Imagine to yourself a winter which lasted almost eight months, keep in mind that with our bad fields even in good years we have had to buy not just grain but straw, so that now I have had to spend from 500 to 600 rubles on grain and straw. Snow was on the ground until May, and consequently the livestock had to be fed somehow. All the [thatched] roofs have been taken down for fodder. . . . From the beginning of spring until now, not a drop of rain. . . . Terrible heat and winds have ruined everything, the winter wheat fields are as black as though they had not been sown. . . . This threatens [us] not only with ruin but with complete famine![61]

In 1836 A. Putyata, in his book *The Experienced Landowner, or a Most Trustworthy Guide for Landowners on Increasing Incomes from Their Real Property to Three or Four Times That of the Present, and on How to Preserve Mortgaged Estates from Public Sale,* addressed landowners like the Dostoevskys. Putyata emphasized sternness in dealing with one's peasants, whom he painted as generally unreliable. Dostoevsky's attitude was much the same. In contrast to his wife's sympathy for their peasants, he was a strict, demanding, and suspicious landowner, writing his wife, "Kharlashka, I hear, is a do-nothing, lazy, he must be watched more carefully and beaten if necessary." When a cow failed to calf, Dostoevsky told his wife, "If it was the fault of the [female] cattle-keeper, you have behaved very badly if you only chastised her lightly and did not punish her as an example to others."[62] According to descendants of some of his serfs, Dostoevsky once had a peasant beaten for not bowing to him, even though he was plowing a field and had not seen him. Another was punished for not removing his cap as he should in the presence of the master.

From the time of Dostoevsky's death until recently it was widely believed that his peasants had murdered him, though the official investigation failed to produce evidence of this.[63] The rumor, it turns out, was spread by a neighboring landowner who hoped to snap up the property cheaply. If Dostoevsky's peasants did have murderous feelings toward their master, they were undoubtedly more the result of his harsh punishments for petty infractions of etiquette than of the inescapable poverty of their existence, about which he could do little.

Steven Hoch points out that as a system of social control, serfdom functioned well; in this respect both landowners and the state had a vested interest in maintaining it.[64] As an economic system, serfdom was less profitable than it might have been, owing to noble profligacy and inertia and to peasant conservatism, all of which conspired against progressive change. From the moral point of view, the absolute power that serfdom gave the landowner over fellow human beings was not merely unjustifiable; that power also corrupted the landowner, as Andrei Bolkonsky insists in *War and Peace,* speaking to Pierre Bezukhov, presumably in 1812: "I know men who are ruined morally, who are devoured by remorse, who stifle [it] and grow callous from being able to inflict punishment. . . . I have seen good men, brought up in the traditions of unlimited power, with the years, as they grew more irritable, become cruel and brutal, conscious of it yet unable to control themselves, and growing more and more miserable."[65]

This remark was true but anachronistic for 1812. As Alexander Bakunin's protest against those who called serfs "slaves" indicates, most of Russia's patriarchs did not see serfdom as a moral evil at this time. Eventually, moral imperatives would become the driving force that produced the emancipation. After 1861 male peasants could no longer be beaten for failing to tip their caps, or women sexually violated. In other respects, however, the emancipation changed estate life less than might be thought. By leaving the communal structure of the village and the system of strip farming unaltered, the emancipation preserved many age-old social and economic habits. Moreover, many common values and patterns of interaction between noble and peasant on the estate were carried into the new era.

171. Count F. P. Tolstoy. *Pastorale.* Silhouette. Ca. 1818. (*Stolitsa i usadba,* no. 50)

III
The Cultural Arcadia

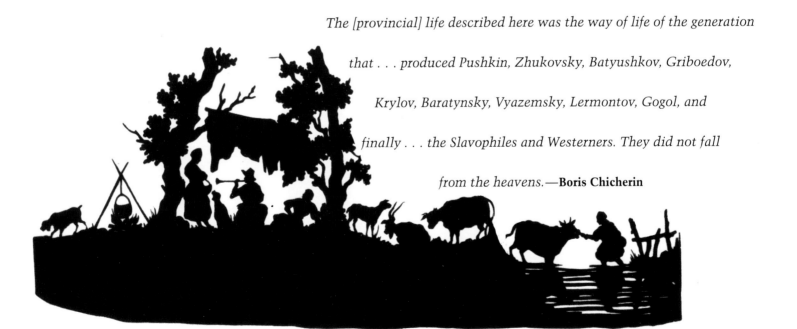

The [provincial] life described here was the way of life of the generation

that . . . produced Pushkin, Zhukovsky, Batyushkov, Griboedov,

Krylov, Baratynsky, Vyazemsky, Lermontov, Gogol, and

finally . . . the Slavophiles and Westerners. They did not fall

from the heavens.—**Boris Chicherin**

9
Regiments of Artificers

SERF ARTISANS AND ARTISTS

Perhaps there will come a time when people will love the products of these serf joiners, furniture makers, carvers, jewelers, and painters as they have fallen in love with cottage industries or anonymous popular songs.—**Baron N. N. Vrangel**

THE COUNTRY ESTATE NOT ONLY reflected the cultural ideals of Russia's elite; it also had a determining role in shaping these ideals. From the reign of Catherine II to the revolution of 1917, the estate served, in effect, as a laboratory for exploring the nature of Russian culture. Not surprisingly, the focus of the cultural exploration and experimentation changed over time. Initially, as Russia's elite looked westward, the estate became an oasis of European culture reinterpreted in Russian terms. This focus transformed some estates into Russia's first training grounds for the fine, decorative, and performing arts.

Estate life also gave the creative elite access to national folk culture. Although the majority of nobles confined themselves to the sentimental pleasures of observing this culture from afar, in the romantic age a critical minority sought out folk music, folklore, and folk art, spanning Russia's cultural divide in the process. Somewhat later, Russian intellectuals, from the rural arcadias they cherished, began to call attention to the anomalies and paradoxes of Russian estate life, thereby ensuring its end. In the following chapters I explore the multiple cultural roles of the estate to determine what each contributed to the development of elite culture.

Estate Artisans

The country estate of pre-emancipation Russia was a unique cultural phenomenon largely because of its population of enserfed master craftsmen and artists. From Pharaonic Egypt to the present, the design, building, furnishing, and maintenance of elaborate country residences have depended on access to skilled designers and craftsmen with a wide range of talents. What set the Russian landowning elite apart was that its members personally owned this talent. Considerable time and money were spent discovering and developing the skills of estate serfs, for not only the landowner's standard of living but frequently his cash income depended on their abilities. Hence the role of country estates as schools of the arts was immense. Estate

master craftsmen, who produced virtually everything owners required, including cash revenues, were one of the major reasons large Russian estates were autarchic fiefdoms that were self-sufficient economically as well as culturally. Sometimes skilled serfs were rewarded and treated as their talents merited. Yet the fact that lordly caprice ruled human life meant that the potential for tragedy always existed.

The Russian noble's appetite for fine furniture, carpets, and other luxuries, which was the driving force behind the training of these legions of serf artisans, was evident by the mid-eighteenth century. The wealthy Cherkassky family, for instance (whose assets Peter Borisovich Sheremetev acquired by marriage), had 243 domestic serfs in Moscow, almost one-third of whom were skilled in various crafts. A few decades later the Sheremetevs, now enormously wealthy, were retaining triple this number for their major building projects at Kuskovo and Ostankino, having trained masters in some twenty specialized arts.[1]

Such specialists cost little for the value received. In 1786 the staff of Kuskovo comprised 171 individuals who were paid a total of 1,877 rubles. As 700 of these rubles went to the English head gardener, Kuskovo's serf artisans received on average a yearly token of seven rubles, in addition to housing, food, and clothing.[2] The master craftsmen included two engravers, a gilder, a sculptor, a marble worker, a spoon maker, two master stove makers, five cabinetmakers, three wood-carvers, an upholsterer, a solderer, two wood turners, and two window makers, all of whom had from one to three apprentices working with them. There were also two highly specialized metalworkers: one who made rims for carriage wheels, and another who produced bas-relief work on thin sheets of silver, bronze, or gold for icon *rizas* or decorative elements on furniture.[3]

Children were selected for training at about age ten from the vast pool of peasant families on the estate. These apprentices might begin their training under a master craftsman at home or at a neighboring estate. The most talented then were sent on to Moscow, St. Petersburg, or occasionally abroad for further training.[4] The apprenticing of serf children was often done in haphazard fashion, leading one to conclude that many of them learned arts or crafts they would never have known if left to their own devices. In 1777, for example, Prince Kurakin wrote his Moscow office that he was sending three boys from one of his estates to the city: "See if they are apt for domestic service," he instructed his agent, "or if they should be sent out for training in a craft, as woodworkers, blacksmiths, or something of the sort."[5] Nikolai Sheremetev, on the other hand, seems to have designated certain talented youngsters for specific crafts. In February 1798 he ordered Dmitry Spukhovachov assigned to the clavichord master, and Ivan Melnikov to a painter; in September he ordered his accountant to award Praskovya Yanpolskaya, an apprentice learning how to make lace cuffs in St. Petersburg, her food, six rubles in salary, and ten rubles for clothes.[6]

Remarkable talents were uncovered through this process of training. There emerged whole families of serf experts like the Argunovs (who produced two architects and three painters), owned by the Sheremetevs; or Anna Borunova (an actress) and her father and brother (both architects), owned by Nikolai Yusupov. The Sheremetevs also owned two other skilled architects, three other outstanding painters, and a number of unusually talented cabinetmakers. One historian suggested in 1910 that such serfs, who usually enjoyed a close relationship with their masters and had received serious artistic schooling, were "more 'wards' of their owners than involuntary servants."[7] But although serfs like the Argunovs were comparatively well treated, and sometimes received in polite society, the fact remains that they were poorly recompensed for their high level of skill and the important responsibilities they fulfilled. As Hilton points out, the Sheremetev artists had wide-ranging responsibilities. Grigory Mukhin created sets for the Sheremetev theaters; Alexei Mironov, Grigory Dikushin, and Pavel Argunov (on whose

knowledge and taste Sheremetev relied heavily) supervised building and decorating projects at Ostankino, including the theater and the Egyptian and Italian pavilions, even directing the work of the non-serf artisans Sheremetev hired. Two Argunovs advised the count on art acquisitions from abroad.[8] But in 1798 Nikolai Sheremetev allotted Pavel Argunov a mere forty rubles for clothes, and another forty as a bonus, while Nikolai Argunov was paid only eighty rubles for one of his superb portraits.[9] In comparison to the English gardener's annual salary, the payments to the Argunovs were trifling.

Their support of skilled artisans made Peter and Nikolai Sheremetev Russia's first grand patrons of the arts. Some Sheremetev projects were so grandiose as to necessitate hiring workers or commissioning certain things from outside the estate. To complete one project, for instance, 640 wooden lilies were commissioned from additional carvers, at 1.3 rubles apiece. (It should be noted that this one decorative element cost more than Bolotov's new manor house.) In May 1795 the Ostankino steward reported that Sheremetev's craftsmen had carved 500 flowers for another project and might be able to produce the same amount again, but that outsiders would have to be hired to produce the sphinxes required.[10] Nikolai Sheremetev apparently knew his best craftsmen by name. In December 1798, from St. Petersburg, he ordered his Moscow estate office to send "from Ostankino the cabinetmaker Fyodor Pryatchenko and another cabinetmaker with him, choosing the best one, and from Kuskovo the carver Egor Chetverikov and tailor Alexander Vostrotin, on rented horses with money for food, to me in Petersburg without delay."[11]

The scale of the Sheremetev establishment, the high quality of the training, and the abilities of the serf artists were exceptional. The Sheremetevs' only rival in the development of artistic talent was Nikolai Yusupov, who from 1814 to 1831 sponsored a school for artists at Arkhangelskoe. Yusupov's lavish life required not only ele-

172. Platter from the Yusupov porcelain factory depicting the palace of Arkhangelskoe. 1820s.
(Courtesy of the State Ceramics Museum, Moscow)

gant surroundings but numerous ornamental objects for official presentations, all of which were produced in his own workshops (figs. 172, 173). In the Arkhangelskoe studio, workers decorated porcelain imported from France with flowers, arcadian scenes, and even portraits; later the porcelain was commissioned locally, from the Popov factory. They also made copies of Yusupov's collection of paintings by European artists and produced illustrated catalogues of Yusupov's art collections, which included sculpture and bronzes. Yusupov, an entrepreneur as well as patron, obtained imperial permission to develop other

workshops of artisans. Some of his serf masters elsewhere also produced and painted porcelain; others wove upholstery for furniture made by Arkhangelskoe woodworkers. At the village of Kupavna, near Moscow, some seven hundred Yusupov workers created "shawls and Silks" that Catherine Wilmot termed "highly perfectionized . . . quite on a par with what I recollect at Lyons." She also mentions a paper factory and one producing watches as being among the many enterprises Yusupov owned.[12]

A staff naturally reflected the interests and means of the owner. Razumovsky's staff of 261 at Baturin included

40 stable hands and 45 serfs who took care of hunting or traveling, but only 28 craftsmen, which was far fewer than most grandees employed during this period.[13] An inventory of the Griboedovs' estate Khmelita during the 1770s lists serfs skilled in 43 arts and crafts, among them lace making (fig. 174) and carpet weaving (fig. 175).[14] If one adds to this list the numerous household serfs providing ser-

173. Presentation cup bearing a portrait of Nikolai Yusupov, copied from a portrait by J-B. Lampi. Manufactured by the Yusupov porcelain factory. Late 1820s. (Courtesy of the State Ceramics Museum, Moscow)

vices to the family, the proportion of peasants at Khmelita directly engaged in maintaining the household, as compared to the proportion engaged in agriculture, must have been high. At Khmelita, as at other such estates, all the necessities could be made to order for the master and his family. Davydov describes a similar abundance of artisans and craftsmen on his family estate Kulevatovo: "joiners, saddlers, ironmongers, coopers, dressmakers, bricklayers, coachmen, horse trainers, gardeners, truck gardeners, cooks, bakers, and so on; in one wing girls and women spun linen and made all sorts of handicrafts."[15] Even on his family's small estate, Dmitry Moroz recalls Demyan, the blacksmith, who told great fairy tales; Levko, the tailor, who produced clothes for the whole family; a cobbler who made all their shoes; and two violinists, the remnants of his father's orchestra.[16]

Artisans lived in special quarters near the main house, with workshops nearby. Many had apprentices, even from off the estate, since a landowner whose resources did not permit his sending serfs to St. Petersburg or Moscow for training often paid a certain sum to a wealthy neighbor to secure apprenticeships with his master craftsmen for a stipulated period. Serfs sometimes contributed to the payments, knowing that after their training they could expect an annual bonus from their master and an outside income higher than if they remained unskilled.[17]

Not all apprenticeships were successful, however. Prince Kropotkin speaks scathingly of the boys his father apprenticed to various Moscow tradesmen; after five years of thrashings, they still had learned nothing. Another memoirist recalls the return of the serf Kirill from four years of apprenticeship to a St. Petersburg tailor. The tailor had written his owner that Kirill was hopeless: lazy and disobedient, he had run away for weeks on end. Kirill was dressed "in the latest French fashion" and claimed to have learned to speak German but could not demonstrate any skill as a tailor. His owner, angry at having wasted his money, demoted Kirill to swineherd.[18] On other occasions

175. Carpet woven at the Khomiakov estate. Late eighteenth century. An estate house, wings, and garden, located downstream from a walled town, are depicted at lower right. (Courtesy of the State Historical Museum, Moscow)

174. V. A. Tropinin. *The Lace Maker.* 1823. (Courtesy of the Tretiakov Gallery, Moscow)

verbal arrangements broke down. When Countess E. A. Golovkina asked the architect Nikolai Lvov to return a young serf whom she had "lent" him several years before, Lvov demurred. He said that he had personally raised the boy and had arranged for him to study with the renowned composer Sarti. Evidently the boy had shown talent, for Lvov planned to free him. In response to the countess's suggestion that he return the boy and that she repay him for Sarti's lessons, Lvov replied that no payment would recompense him for the time and effort he had expended on this boy. He eventually prevailed.[19]

By the end of the eighteenth century a number of estates had serfs skilled in the decorative arts, and some provided training, facilities, and materials for these arts comparable to the resources of major cities. As Hilton points out, the cabinetmaking workshops on these estates must have contained not only tools but sophisticated materials, including imported woods, varnishes, glues, paints, and gold leaf. The estate cabinetmaker might be ordered to create furniture and furnishings ranging from elaborately inlaid card tables to parquet floors, elaborately carved paneling, candelabras and picture frames.[20] The widespread use of pattern books for furniture enabled the serf master to copy any style chosen by the owner. This habit persisted among the wealthy until the end of serfdom. One memoirist, writing of the 1850s, recalls that Princess Meshcherskaya, of Kursk Province, had a passion for fine furniture. Her rather plain estate house was filled with all sorts of "well-made necessary and unnecessary furniture . . . which her own cabinetmakers made according to her instructions from foreign drawings."[21]

Numerous foreign memoirists testify to the remarkable skills of the Russian artisan, particularly in woodworking and carving, perhaps the most native of Russian arts. In the 1830s Robert Bremner noted that "in place of the ten or twelve different instruments, which a carpenter in other countries must have constantly about him, a Russian has only three or four; indeed, his principal and often

sole companion is the axe. . . . We have often watched him at work, laying a floor or making a chair. . . . The ease and the grace even, with which he wields it—always with one hand—would be a lesson to the most skillful of our artisans."[22] Most furniture produced was in the Empire style, though frequently with an original Russian flair. Karelian birch veneer, uniquely Russian, often set these pieces apart from the European models. For owners with pretensions, serf masters turned their skills to the decorative vocabulary of neoclassicism, producing swans, lions, sphinxes, Egyptian figures, and lyres. (Swans, with which they were familiar, were their forte, but some provincial lions came out looking more like dogs or monkeys, which adds to their charm today.) They also introduced motifs traditional to Russian decorative wood carving, such as vases, baskets, and columns.[23] Ornamentation executed in brass or fabric for European furniture in Russia was often copied in carved wood, giving it an exuberant high relief (fig. 176). Foreigners remarked on the ability of serf artisans to copy anything placed before them. The celebrated painter Madame Vigée-Lebrun, visiting Bezborodko's suburban Moscow estate, recalls his showing her "salons filled with furniture by the celebrated cabinet-maker [Henri] Daguère; most of this furniture had been imitated by his slaves and it was impossible to distinguish the copy when it was next to the original."[24]

Grandees prided themselves on serf master craftsmen such as Fyodor Nikiforov, owned by Princess Shcherbatova, Matvei Veretennikov, owned by Alexander Saltykov, or Ivan Mochalin, owned by Nikolai Sheremetev, all of whom produced pieces of unquestionably high quality. Only a few pieces of furniture, such as Nikifor Vasiliev's famous marquetry scene of Kuskovo (fig. 177), or the two round marquetry tables P. T. Olimpiev made in 1839 at the Goncharovs' Polotnyany Zavod, bear the serf artist's signature. And little is known about the training of experts like Vasiliev or Veretennikov. As Hilton points out, skillful marquetry requires a sophisticated sense of perspective

176. Chair of provincial workmanship, with griffons on arms and back.
The skirt, executed in wood, imitates draped fabric.
(Courtesy of the Hillwood Museum, Washington, D.C.)

and familiarity with trompe l'oeil techniques. Clearly some designs were, with greater or lesser skill, copied directly from etchings (fig. 178). But to create an original scene the artist must have studied perspective, understood how to draw to scale, and picked up artistic conventions such as framing a scene by placing a tree or an anonymous figure in the foreground.[25] Anything beyond the capabilities of one's personal artisans could be ordered from a firm such as Spol, a furniture studio in Moscow that also employed and trained serf artisans. Some decorative items such as the popular Wedgwood medallions used as inlays for Russian furniture were ordered from abroad to be incorporated into these serf-produced pieces.

Serfs also produced high-quality porcelain, glass, and metal products. In addition to maintaining large staffs of artisans for their personal needs, entrepreneurial landowners catered to the taste of the nobility for opulence; many built factories that specialized in the production of a particular luxury item, most often porcelain and glass but also high-quality lace and leather goods. The two leading porcelain factories were those of F. Ya. Gardner, founded in 1766 at Verbliki, near Moscow, and A. G. Popov's factory, at nearby Gorbunovo, founded in the early nineteenth century. Yankova mentions buying cups and saucers from the Popov factory, which was near her estate (fig. 179). But many smaller factories were established as well. In 1815, for example, N. C. Khrapunov founded a third porcelain factory near Moscow, which was so successful that in 1828 he built another one at Gubinskoe, in Vladimir Province. Meanwhile Poskochin opened a faience factory near St. Petersburg that produced mainly tea services and decorative items; and A. M. Miklashevsky started a porcelain factory at Volokitino (in Chernigov Province), where excellent clay could be found. Although most of these factories owned by nobles shut down after the emancipation, during the preceding century they and other similar factories were responsible for turning numerous peasants into trained artisans.[26]

Serf Artists

Some art historians have claimed that the serf origins of many of Russia's early artists became the stimulus that transformed imported cultural models into genuinely Russian art. This may be overstating the case. And such a claim certainly oversimplifies the varied artistic schooling of serf artists (which ranged from self-instruction to study

177. Fragment of a tabletop by the master craftsman Nikifor Vasiliev, depicting the kitchen wing, grotto, and Italian House of Kuskovo. 1780s. Marquetry of oak, mahogany, Karelian birch, plane, walnut, ebony, and pear. (Courtesy of the Kuskovo Museum, Moscow)

at elite institutions) and hence the possible influences upon them. It also projects the values of a later age back in time. Although eventually some landowners came to appreciate the idiosyncrasies serfs introduced into their artistic work, in the late nineteenth century the cultural elite was searching for pure Russian art, and its passion was for folk art, not the cultural hybrids estate artisans had produced.

Two rather poor still lifes of 1737, executed, signed, and dated by Ostankino serfs, indicate an early demand for serf artists, about whom we know little more than we do of artisans. By the late eighteenth century skilled serf

178. Marquetry tabletop depicting the Kremlin. Late eighteenth century.
The anonymous provincial craftsman, working from an engraving,
has reversed the scene. (Courtesy of the Hillwood Museum, Washington, D.C)

179. Cup and saucer with pastoral scenes undoubtedly copied from a European etching. Manufactured by the Popov factory. Early nineteenth century. (Courtesy of the Hillwood Museum, Washington, D.C.)

portraitists like Prince Potemkin's Mikhail Shibanov or Count Benckendorff's Fyodor Tulov were prized possessions. If especially promising, the serf artist of an aristocrat might be enrolled as an auditor at the Academy of Fine Arts, in St. Petersburg, which by the late eighteenth century was not only training architects, painters, and sculptors but offering classes in ornamental sculpture, wood carving, bronze and gold work, miniature painting, and cabinetmaking.[27] The lives of several well-known serf art-

ists and the initial assistance, and subsequent retreat, of the academy in their training illustrate the complexity and pathos of the serf artist's position.

The career of Vasily Tropinin (1776–1857), son of A. S. Minikh's serf steward, is a striking example (fig. 180).[28]

180. V. A. Tropinin. Self-portrait at a window overlooking the Kremlin (detail). 1844. (Courtesy of the Museum of V. A. Tropinin, Moscow)

When Minikh's daughter married Count Irakly Morkov, the talented boy was part of her dowry. To Tropinin's father's request that he be trained as a painter, Morkov responded, "There won't be any talk of that," and shipped young Vasily off to St. Petersburg as apprentice to Count Zavadovsky's pastry cook. While there he took free drawing classes at the academy and in 1799 was admitted as an auditor to more advanced classes, including portraiture. When his contribution to the student exhibition of 1804 was widely praised, his professor suggested that Morkov either free the young artist or end his ambivalent status at the academy by removing him. Morkov chose the latter, sending Tropinin to his estate in Ukraine to work as a lackey and pastry cook. Tropinin also acted as steward, did painting for the house, and taught Morkov's children to draw (for a salary of thirty-six rubles a year). These varied duties, however, did not discourage Tropinin, whose equable temperament is evident in his self-portrait. In his spare time, he painted landscapes and copied European paintings.

In 1815 an incident occurred on the estate that must have had some effect on Tropinin's obdurate owner. Morkov took a visiting Frenchman to view Tropinin's studio on the second floor of the house; the Frenchman lavishly praised Tropinin's work and shook his hand. Later, at dinner, he tried to persuade Tropinin (who was a uniformed servitor for the evening) to sit down at table. That evening Morkov is reputed to have told Tropinin that he should not wait on table any more. Some seven years later Morkov and his household moved to Moscow, and finally in 1823 the count's friends persuaded him to free Tropinin. In his first year of freedom Tropinin produced *The Lace Maker* (fig. 174) in the "unpretentious and lively" style for which he would become famous.[29] As a free artist Tropinin went on to success as a portraitist in Moscow but continued to paint anonymous peasants for pleasure.

Andrei Voronikhin (1759–1814) likewise occupies an exceptional place in the annals of serf artists. Born in Perm

Province on an estate belonging to Alexander S. Stroganov, he may have been the latter's illegitimate son; in any event he enjoyed an exceptionally close relationship with the Stroganov family. Stroganov summoned Voronikhin to Moscow at the age of eighteen for training in art and architecture, during which period the young student worked with the architects Matvei Kazakov and Vasily Bazhenov. Then in 1785 Voronikhin was selected to accompany Stroganov's son Pavel and Pavel's tutor, Gilbert Romme, on an extended grand tour, which began with a trip south through Russia to the Crimea and along the Black Sea coast.[30] Upon their return Stroganov freed Voronikhin, at Romme's request. The following year the trio traveled to Switzerland and France. Voronikhin went on to renovate the Stroganov palace and dacha near St. Petersburg and designed buildings at Gorodnya, the Kaluga estate of Princess Golitsyna. In later years, as a professor at the Academy of Arts, he submitted the winning design for the Kazan Cathedral and also designed many items of furniture for imperial palaces. At his death in 1814 (possibly by suicide) he was one of the foremost architects of his day.

Successful serf artists must have been envied by other house serfs whose talents were not always commensurate with their ambitions. Madame Vigée-Lebrun relates the following tale of the "slave" Count Stroganov gave her to assist her in cleaning her brushes and palette:

[He] had persuaded himself that he was also a painter and gave me no rest until I had gotten his freedom from the count, so that he could go to work with students of the Academy. . . . The count, giving in to my plea, said, "be assured that in a short time he will want to come back to me." I gave 20 rubles to the young man, the count the same, and he ran off at once to buy the uniform of the painting students, with which he returned to thank me with a triumphant air. But two months later he returned, bringing me a large picture of a family that was so bad that I could not look at it, for which he had been paid so little that the poor young man had lost 8 rubles on it. As the count had foreseen, a similar disappointment made him renounce his liberty.[31]

Other serfs with real talent suffered at the hands of capricious or tyrannical masters. The life of Soroka (Grigory Vasiliev), a gifted painter, presents an unhappy contrast to the stories of Tropinin and Voronikhin.[32] Soroka

181. G. V. Soroka. Portrait of P. I. Miliukov. 1840s.
(Courtesy of the Hermitage Museum, St. Petersburg)

was born in 1823 in Pokrovskaya, a small village in Tver Province belonging to the wealthy N. P. Miliukov (fig. 181), and began to draw as a child. Then the Miliukovs summoned him to Ostrovki, their manor house on Lake Moldino, as a house serf, and Soroka entered a wider world of culture. "This position gave him the chance to see books and paintings, and to overhear Miliukov and his friends conversing about literature, culture and current events."[33] At some point in the course of his duties Soroka met the Miliukovs' neighbor, the painter Alexei Venetsianov (1780–1847), who took an immediate interest in the young artist.

Venetsianov (fig. 182), though self-taught, was a renowned portraitist. After making a sufficient amount of money he had retired to his small estate Safonkovo, where he ran an art school. Venetsianov's contribution to Russian portraiture and landscape painting was immense. The concept of painting from nature rather than copying other paintings was revolutionary in Russia of the 1820s and 1830s. According to Hilton, Venetsianov's many studies of peasants express "a sense of the harmony and continuity of landscape, peasant and seasonable labor comparable to that felt in folklore and art."[34] In this respect his peasant portraits anticipate Turgenev's empathetic descriptions of peasant life in his *Sportsman's Notebook*. This unusual feeling for the dignity (as well as the poverty) of peasant life partially explains the success of Venetsianov's school for poor would-be artists and his efforts to achieve freedom for his serf pupils. Venetsianov generally had little difficulty recruiting promising serf students (such as A. A. Zlatov and A. A. Alekseev, who produced the renowned painting *Venetsianov's Studio*), for an accomplished serf artist was a distinct asset for any noble.[35]

In anticipation of acquiring such a skilled serf, Miliukov agreed to let Soroka study at the Safonkovo school. But at the same time he insisted that Soroka's studies not interfere with his duties at Ostrovki (among them gardening and acting in Ostrovki theatrical productions), and

259

182. G. V. Soroka. Portrait of A. G. Venetsianov. 1840s.
(Courtesy of the Tretiakov Gallery, Moscow)

When Venetsianov died in 1847 Soroka lost his only champion and had to continue working as Miliukov's gardener and lackey. In view of his inner pain, it is striking that his portraits of Miliukov's daughters and son (though not of his master) are so clearly sympathetic. His landscapes of Ostrovki and of Spasskoe, the estate of Milivkov's uncle in Tambov Province (see fig. 156), are equally luminous, but in them serfs often appear in the foreground, separated from their master's world by a body of water. Perhaps this reflected Soroka's view of his unhappy position. In the 1850s Soroka married and moved back to his native village where he became the icon master. According to estate records, during this period he paid an annual quitrent of twenty rubles, earned by local painting jobs and from taking on a few pupils.

In 1861 Soroka, free at last by imperial decree, joined a group of peasants who wished to buy some farmland from Miliukov. But Miliukov's terms were exorbitant, and so Soroka agreed to compose a petition from the group to the tsar, complaining about Miliukov. An enraged Miliukov filed a counter-complaint, and Soroka was soon charged with "having committed crudeness and spread false rumors in the district." He was sentenced to three days in prison and a severe lashing. This humiliation dashed Soroka's last hopes and broke his spirit. He became melancholy, appeared disoriented to his fellow villagers, and on April 10, 1864, committed suicide, hanging himself from a beam in Ostrovki's ceramics workshop.[36]

By the early nineteenth century the incongruities between the abilities and circumstances of such gifted serfs, already illuminated in Radishchev's *Journey from St. Petersburg to Moscow,* led to soul-searching and finally action by the august Academy of Fine Arts. The case of Alexander Polyakov, a house serf owned by the landowner Kornilov, prompted a rule that no members of the academy could take serfs as students. Polyakov had been trained by the academician Yakov A. Vasiliev, who believed that he

hence Soroka frequently had to leave Safonkovo. Venetsianov often took his pupils to St. Petersburg for extended periods of study, sent their work to academy exhibitions, and tried to help his pupils get further training and professional positions, none of which Miliukov would allow for Soroka. For years Venetsianov tried in vain to persuade Miliukov to free the talented young man. Meanwhile he made his prize pupil his teaching assistant, helped him get a few outside commissions, and tried not to alienate Miliukov.

had Kornilov's agreement to free the boy should he prove successful. Young Alexander won academy medals, was received by educated society, and was well paid for his portraits of the St. Petersburg beau monde. In 1822 Vasiliev apprenticed Polyakov to the renowned artist Gau, who was at that time creating a gallery of portraits of the heroes of 1812. Polyakov was so able that Gau is rumored to have simply signed some portraits actually executed by his student. But then Kornilov abruptly demanded that Polyakov be sent home. Vasiliev submitted a formal complaint to the Academy Council to no avail. Polyakov became Kornilov's postilion and "sometimes . . . ended up cleaning the steps of the carriage in front of those very houses where his paintings, in rich, gilded frames . . . constituted the family's delight and joy, and where he himself had formerly been received as a gifted artist."[37] The decision of the academy (endorsed by its president, A. Olenin, who declared, "Not one serf [student] has remained an upright person") was not without consequences. In 1829 the serf Myasinikov, a talented artist, committed suicide because he was not permitted to attend the school. This prompted another official decision: the provincial icon-painting school of A. P. Stupin, in Arzamas, which had earned the right to award official medals to outstanding students, could no longer do so, "because there have been cases in which serfs, having been granted medals but not having received their freedom from their owners, have fallen into despair and died."[38]

Most serf artists were more fortunate than Soroka or Myasinikov, in that their masters supported their formal studies. The majority of artists appear to have earned their freedom when they became recognized; one of Stupin's pupils even went on to found his own school. At least seven of Venetsianov's serf pupils were given freedom and the opportunity to study at the academy or even abroad. One became professor of portraiture at the Moscow School of Painting, Sculpture, and Architecture, where he taught founding members of the notable post-emancipation artistic movement, the Itinerants. Another became a member of the Academy of Fine Arts.

Below these serf artists whose names have survived was a much larger anonymous pool of painters who executed endless copies, landscapes, mediocre portraits of their owners' families, and the numerous wall and ceiling paintings to be found on estates throughout Russia. Sergei Aksakov's semifictional young Bagrov vividly describes the living room of Churasovo, its walls covered with "forests, flowers, fruit, strange birds, beast and trees . . . Chinamen, wild Americans, and palm trees, painted in the brightest possible colors."[39] Baron Vrangel remembers his father's study filled with engravings and etchings done by his "exceptionally gifted" serf Black Peter, who not only drew without having been taught but spoke French and German and was an excellent actor and a crack shot.[40] When Natalya Grot entered art school, Misha, her uncle's former serf artist, bought paints and brushes for her and supervised her efforts to copy still lifes.[41] Yankova recalls that all the walls and ceilings of her parents' Bobrovo were "covered with stretched linen painted in oil. In the great hall the hunt was depicted on the walls; in the living room were landscapes, as in the study; in the bedroom the walls were decorated with bouquets, which also adorned the draperies. Of course, all this was painted by home-grown daubers, but, I must say, not badly at all, even quite nicely, by the standards of the day."[42] Or consider the fantastic mythological frescoes executed by a similar house artist at Mednoe, in St. Petersburg Province, probably using house serfs for his models: "Malashka and Dunka, Fedka and Vanka were presented as mythological gods: the coachman as Paris, the milkmaid as Helen, the barefoot maids as goddesses" (fig. 183). By the end of the century connoisseurs were calling these frescoes artistic curiosities and appraising them as "wild but not devoid of charm."[43]

183. Wall frescoes by serf artists at Mednoe, the estate of Savva Yakovlev. (*Starye gody,* 1910)

Performing Artists

In serf-owning Russia, the worlds of art and theater were closely connected. Count V. G. Orlov's joiners at Otrada doubled as his actors and musicians, playing regularly at dinner and presenting instrumental and vocal concerts on Saturday evenings.[44] Serf artists produced the spectacular sets and costumes demanded for private productions. But serf musicians, singers, and actors were generally less trained and less valuable than serf artists. The famous forty-man horn orchestra fetched large sums, but the private market for musical virtuosos was smaller than that for artists. The same was true for performers, whose sad fate at the hands of profligate owners forms one of Chatsky's diatribes in *Wit Works Woe.*

The famous squire who, just to fill his leisure,
Bought up a serf ballet at every country fair,
Tore children from the arms of parents in despair;
His Zephyrs all his thought, his Cupids all his
    pleasure!
The town was all agape, to gaze on charms so great,
But as his creditors refused to wait,
Poor Cupids, they were sold in detail,
The Zephyrs, too, disposed of, retail.[45]

Painters and craftsmen were a necessity for estate life, whereas highly skilled performing artists were not, save for people with unlimited means and dedication to the arts. Foremost among these were the Sheremetevs, who in theater as in art set the standard for their peers. Future performers at Kuskovo and Ostankino, selected for schooling at the age of ten, underwent rigorous training (fig. 184). Along with vocal or instrumental instruction, these youngsters received a broad education unusual for its time at the estate school, in effect Russia's first school for the performing arts. To staff it Nikolai Sheremetev hired a number of instructors from abroad specializing in voice, dance, musical instruments, and foreign languages. All pupils became literate, and operatic performers were able to sing fluently in several languages. Like serf companions in wealthy families, who were raised with the sons and daughters of the house, the top Sheremetev performers acquired a worldly polish and education to complement their skills. After operatic performances at Ostankino, Nikolai Petrovich invited the audience to mingle, converse, and dance with his stars in one of the elegantly appointed pavilions. Among the serf performers, as we know, was his future wife, Praskovya.

At the turn of the nineteenth century virtually all members of the elite had troupes of entertainers. Even the architect Nikolai Lvov, who was not a grandee but who enjoyed composing operas, owned a twenty-eight-man orchestra.[46] Zorich, a favorite of Catherine II, maintained troupes of actors and dancers, a choir of singers, and two orchestras at Shklov.[47] Like the Hermitage Theater, the theater at Shklov featured light comedies, pantomimes, and ballets. On occasion aristocratic performers appeared on the stage: E. A. Dolgorukaya played roles in French opera, the talented amateur Prince P. V. Meshchersky and his wife performed in plays, and some grandees (notably I. O. Khorvat) even participated in ballets.

When the fantasy world of Shklov collapsed, the fate of Zorich's serf artists was typical for many singers, dancers, and musicians, whose best hope was to be purchased by the crown. In an age of lavishness, Zorich had been one of the biggest spenders (and a bad gambler). At his death in 1800 his estate was left with debts of over a million rubles. Sale of his artists was an obvious move, and Zorich's stepbrother, Davyd G. Naranchich, approached Alexander L. Naryshkin, director of the imperial theaters, with the suggestion that he take the Shklov dancers. Sensing an opportunity to acquire some seasoned performers, Naryshkin sent the ballet master Valberg to Shklov. There he selected eight males and six females from the troupe, all of whom were offered a salary of two hundred rubles a year in addition to housing, firewood, and between ten and twenty rubles for clothes. This was not the end of the matter, however, for in 1812 Zorich's nephew and heir, a Hungarian noble, sued the imperial theaters, claiming that the estate had not been recompensed for these artists. The slow procedures of Russian courts ended up working in favor of the imperial theater administration. By the time the suit was settled in 1820, the only five artists still living had been pensioned off; hence the crown claimed no restitution was in order.

For a serf musician, acquisition by the crown was a first step on the road to the coveted title of "free artist," conferred after ten years of service. This was the road traveled by several members of Naryshkin's own twenty-two-man choir. Like Zorich, Naryshkin was renowned for his lavish, old-fashioned hospitality and lived far beyond his means. As his financial position deteriorated, he hit on the expedient of renting out his choir to the imperial theater. In 1825 the choir members petitioned the crown to buy their freedom from Naryshkin; after long negotiations, 15 were freed for the sum of 8,000 rubles. Other owners also looked into such sales. In March 1820 the landowner Yakov Evgrafovich Arseniev offered Matvei Rumyantsev, the serf director of his choir, to Prince Tufyakin, an official of the imperial theaters, for 3,300 rubles. When Tufyakin seemed interested, Arseniev raised the price to 3,500, then refused to give Rumyantsev up because the choirmaster had insulted him by his complaints. The negotiations were

at last concluded in April and proved advantageous for the state, as official reports cite Rumyantsev as a "very industrious worker of praiseworthy conduct."

Sometimes serfs were purchased on the installment plan. In 1811, for instance, A. A. Maikov, the director of Moscow imperial theaters, arranged to pay 500 rubles a year for four years rather than 2,000 outright for Dmitry I. Kiselev's serf musician Ivan Pereletsky. Lastly, some serf musicians who had accumulated funds from outside salaries contributed their own money to be bought by the imperial theater. In 1822 the violinist Afanasy Amatov (who played first violin in the Italian theater for 960 rubles a year) negotiated on his own behalf. His owner, Vera I. Khlyustina, wanted 4,000 rubles for him; he suggested that he and the imperial theater split the amount, and the deal was concluded.[48]

As the fate of Zorich's and Naryshkin's singers suggests, in the course of the first half of the nineteenth century many privately owned, provincially trained performers made their way, often in tortuous fashion, into the public forum, most frequently state-supported theaters. A serf whom Yury Golitsyn trained in singing in Tambov in the 1850s later became an artist of the imperial opera. Provincial theaters also trafficked in serfs. The English traveler S. Edwards notes that "Madame Zeitto," the soprano prima donna of the Nizhni Novgorod operatic troupe, had been "formed" at the serf estate theater of her former owner, to whom she had paid only a small amount of her large salary. When the estate changed hands, however, the merchants of Nizhni had to pay "a considerable sum" to her new owner to gain permission to retain the "greatest adornment of the theatre."[49]

Of the serf actors whose careers were launched and prospered during this time, none was more remarkable

184. Nikolai Argunov. Portrait of I. Yakimov,
one of Sheremetev's young performers, costumed as Cupid. 1790.
(Courtesy of the Russian Museum, St. Petersburg)

than Mikhail Shchepkin, whose life story illustrates the barbarities of serf ownership but reverberates with a Horatio Alger quality.[50] By the 1830s Shchepkin was the toast of Moscow, and within one generation his family had attained status and security. His sons became professors and lawyers and his elder daughters actresses, securing through their civil service ranks the title of "honorary hereditary citizen." When Shchepkin died in 1863, he was eulogized by numerous members of the intelligentsia who had been his friends, among them Sergei Aksakov and Timofei Granovsky.

Shchepkin was born in 1788, son of the serf overseer of Krasnoe, the estate of Count G. S. Wolkenstein, in Kursk Province. As a child Shchepkin saw his first theatrical performance, an opera entitled *The New Family*, performed on a makeshift stage in Krasnoe's great hall. Shchepkin later acted on this stage, as well as in the local Kursk theater (run by two serf impresarios), while performing the normal duties of a house serf. Shchepkin's owners, noting his intelligence and diligence, sent him to the local school, where he was an outstanding student in the selective education offered serfs (he was bitterly disappointed at being forced to study German and Latin rather than French, the language of polite society).

In the summer of 1810, at the age of twenty-one, Shchepkin traveled to Prince Golitsyn's estate Yunokovka. There he saw the "savant and dilettante" Prince P. V. Meshchersky perform in *The Inveigled Dowry*, a Russian comedy. Shchepkin ranks this as the most significant event of his youth. Some years before, Meshchersky had asked Wolkenstein to lend him Shchepkin to copy a design from an alabaster vase in reduced scale, so that it could be used on a chest of drawers. Shchepkin had failed and was beaten. Now this episode was forgotten as Meshchersky's acting reduced Shchepkin to tears. "How many speeches and lines remained in my memory. . . . And how annoyed I was with myself: why hadn't I guessed from the start that that was the good thing about it, the fact that it was natural and simple! . . . Excellent acting, as it was then understood . . . involved incredibly ugly declamation . . . [delivered] as loudly as possible . . . [with] almost every word accompanied by gestures."[51]

Naturalness and simplicity were to become hallmarks of Shchepkin's style, and this performance, according to his biographer, "triggered Shchepkin's aspirations." These included not only fame as an actor but freedom for himself and his family. Shchepkin soon became the star of a large theater troupe in Kharkov, attracting the attention of Prince N. G. Repnin, then governor of Kharkov and Poltava Provinces. Aspiring to create a similar theater in Poltava, Repnin first asked Shchepkin's owner (now Wolkenstein's widow) for his transfer to Poltava. She assented, with the proviso that "this man with his skills and knowledge of land surveying . . . be sent back to me when I need him." When Repnin asked to purchase the Shchepkins, the countess took it as an insult and had her brother write the actor a letter: "Misha Shchepkin! Because you apparently don't want to be a servant and apparently are not disposed to be grateful for all that your father got when with the count, for the education given you, the countess wishes to give your whole family your freedom . . . for 8,000 [rubles], for it is quite a remarkable family. If you wish your freedom, come as soon as you receive this; don't waste time."[52]

Shchepkin had nothing like that sum, and his fate hung on a bidding war between Repnin and the notorious Count Kamensky, who wanted Shchepkin for his theater in Orel. Repnin managed to raise half the sum and asked to buy Mikhail alone; but the estate trustees for the recently deceased countess stuck to the original price. When an offer of ten thousand rubles arrived from Count Kamensky, Repnin promised the other four thousand, just in time to conclude the purchase before Kamensky doubled his offer. Shchepkin, who thought he had a promise of freedom from Repnin, was unhappy to learn that he would be the prince's serf until he could repay him three thou-

sand rubles. The legal transfer of ownership took three years. Meanwhile the Poltava theater slipped slowly into bankruptcy, and Shchepkin was hired at Tula. There he was discovered by V. L. Golovin, who was scouting provincial talent for the Moscow imperial theater and made Shchepkin an offer.

In accepting, Shchepkin became a serf employee of the government and eventually earned his freedom. His comic roles at the Maly made him famous: his impersonations of types he had known from his childhood, such as provincial eccentrics and the nouveau riche, gained favorable reviews from the young theatrical critic Sergei Aksakov (who nonetheless criticized his failures in less Russian roles). During the 1830s Shchepkin became acquainted with Pushkin, Belinsky, Herzen, and countless lesser luminaries, and his large Moscow household took on the patriarchal overtones of Shchepkin's childhood: the house was frequented by students and guests and filled with the noise of debate and music, and there were never fewer than twenty for dinner.

Success stories such as those of Voronikhin or Shchepkin, both possessed of extraordinary talent, must be weighed against numerous sad instances of lesser serf artists and performers being abused by their owners or denied permission to buy their freedom. Landowners derived no little sense of power from controlling the futures of talented serfs. As mentioned earlier, the Orel impresario Kamensky beat his actors for mistakes and treated his actresses as a harem. When one talented actress he had acquired from Kazan refused his amorous advances, Kamensky punished her by denying her roles and costumes. She retaliated by becoming pregnant. Shchepkin once heard her play the part of a falsely accused maidservant. "I barely heard her words, but I did hear her voice. 'Good lord!' thought I, 'how can such sounds issue from such a young breast. They are . . . the result of some dreadful experience.'"[53]

Many serf artists were psychologically scarred by their

treatment. Finogen, a "rather talented" and well-educated musician, the serf of the Nikolevs' neighbor Khlyustin, taught piano to the Nikoleva daughters (for two rubles a lesson). Nikoleva says that Finogen spoke French, Italian, and German "very well" and that he had a "velvet touch" on the piano. His "indeterminate position," she observes, oppressed him. Too well educated for the society of the other house serfs yet not accepted in polite society, he led a solitary life. His main pleasure was reading books from the Khlyustins' library. His having to ask his mistress for the key to the library embarrassed him, so he began taking it without her permission. When this was discovered, he was denied access to the library. Meanwhile, Khlyustin drew up a paper granting Finogen his freedom but entrusted it to the family doctor, who "from respect for the mistress" (evidently no friend of Finogen) refused to give it to Finogen. Finogen determined to steal the document but did not succeed; he ended up having to pay all his earnings (which amounted to five thousand rubles) for his freedom, turned to drink, and died "practically destitute" in Moscow.[54]

There is no way to assess how many Finogens and Sorokas were undone by the serf system that exploited their talent, or how many serf artists outlived or successfully negotiated their way out of serfdom. What is clear is that the cultural appetites of a large number of landowners had led to the discovery and development of artistic talent that otherwise would have been untapped;

and that for some of these artists, the training they received led to fame and freedom. Not only did the large pool of artisans and artists in the era of serfdom make estate culture possible, it also enriched Russian cultural life on many levels. One scholar has even asserted that "the average level of the arts under serfdom was incomparably higher than after the emancipation," owing to three factors: first, the Russian peasant's innate abilities; second, the landowners' ability to choose among their many serfs when they wanted to recruit promising artists; and third, the hiring of foreigners to train the serfs.[55]

Ironically, the very success of Russia's estate artisans and artists contributed to the demise of serfdom and the great age of estate culture along with it. From the start of the golden age of the estate some serf artisans and artists had been appreciated as outstanding talents, while others became casualties of the system. By the reign of Nicholas I, talented serfs had already joined the ranks of Russia's free artists, and others were to follow prior to 1861. But the anomalous position of those who remained enserfed undermined the system that had produced them, as their plight elicited increasing concern and protest. This last generation of serf artists thus rendered a double service to Russian culture: their achievements set a high standard for the future, and their tragedies hastened the day when Russia's artists would all be free.

10
The Kingdom United

ORTHODOXY, FOLKLORE, AND TRADITION

Where, how, when had this young countess, educated by a French émigrée, sucked in with the Russian air she breathed the spirit of that dance? . . . Anisya Fyodorovna, who handed her the kerchief she needed in the dance, had tears in her eyes, though she laughed as she watched that slender, graceful little countess, reared in silk and velvet, belonging to another world than hers, who was yet able to understand all that was in Anisya and her father and her mother and her aunt and every Russian soul.—**Leo Tolstoy**

THE THOUGHTS AND EMOTIONS TOLSTOY conjures up in the serf mistress Anisya as she watches Natasha Rostova perform a traditional folk dance were a projection of his own deepest longings, yet they also contained a measure of truth. On the country estate nobles and peasants not only coexisted but interacted in a proximity that seemed to breed mutual respect. Any observer of nineteenth-century Russia was aware of two distinct cultural worlds, one inhabited by the westernized noble, the other by the tradition-oriented peasant. Their differing values were expressed in sharply contrasting modes of education and upbringing, in dress, behavior, and cultural allegiance, in material possessions and circumstances, and even in language. In the countryside the contrast was physically illustrated by the vast difference between the Palladian manor houses of the wealthy and the small cottages of the peasant villages that supported them. The effort to find a bridge—indeed, a common language of discourse—between two worlds that often mistrusted each other's intentions is a major motif of the story of the Russian intelligentsia, a story with few moments of triumph to balance its most spectacular tragedy, the failure of the "to the people" movement in the summer of 1874.

The summer began with a mass migration of radical young nobles into rural villages. Dressed like peasants, they hoped to live and work with the villagers, learn from them, and convert them to revolution. Several thousand of the activists ended the summer in jail. They had been turned over to the police, because the peasants found their soft hands, glasses, and speech suspicious.[1]

The summer of 1874 echoed other moments of crisis in which many peasants, whether joining forces with a Pugachev or rebelling on a local level, made it clear that they wanted no part of their masters' foreign culture. Whenever the master was not clearly in control—as was the case in 1773, 1812, 1905, and 1917—some peasants took revenge on cultural symbols of oppression. On some hastily vacated estates a vengeful mob carted off needed tools, food, and building materials but not the useless artifacts of elite culture: the pianos, bric-a-brac, brocade curtains, mirrors, or works of art. These they ignored or angrily destroyed.[2]

On other estates, however, peasants helped their master and his family escape during these crises or hid them, as well as the family treasures, from rioters. The insistence of many post-emancipation memoirists that between numerous estate owners and peasants there existed mutual support, understanding of each other's ways, and shared traditions has too often been dismissed as upper-class apologetics, when in fact it merits investigation. The most prominent area of cultural interaction (which Natasha's dancing illustrates) was the sphere of Christian and pagan ceremony. On a more everyday level, peasants transmitted their folklore, music, and patterns of speech to nobles. Even the wide gulf in the decorative and fine arts gradually narrowed as some estate owners came to appreciate the uniqueness of the hybrid art their serfs had produced and Russian connoisseurs began to seek out folk art in the countryside—albeit well after the era of serfdom.

Orthodox beliefs, religious holidays, and traditional observances provided the broadest common ground for the population of provincial Russia (fig. 185). The estate calendar of work and rest revolved around religious holidays. Noble and serf worshiped at the same altar and were instructed by the same priest. Icon corners were found in peasant cottage and manorial living room, and both peasant and lord believed in visions and miracles. The Russian peasant has traditionally been portrayed as superstitious rather than religious, as having not a single but a double faith combining Christian and pagan beliefs. Although educated estate owners overtly condemned superstition, their world of faith had its strongly mystical elements.

Throughout the eighteenth and nineteenth centuries rural Russia teemed with Orthodox pilgrims, both wealthy and poor, traveling to holy places. Until the late imperial period, when inns near monasteries and convents

185. Mariamna Davydova. Service in the church at Matussov. The Lopukhin daughters and their mother are on the left; behind them are local peasants. Watercolor. 1920s. (Courtesy of Alona Vassiloff)

were established, pilgrims made their way from estate to estate, receiving food, shelter, clothing, and alms and often eating at the noble family's table. Like the local priest, pilgrims were welcome guests because, for one thing, they brought news to remote areas. More important, in the mind of noble or peasant there was always the possibility that one was entertaining a saint, particularly when the pilgrim was a *yurodivy*, or holy fool.

The religious behavior and beliefs of estate owners as recorded by memoirists tend not to fit the impression given by numerous historians—namely, that the elite's adherence to Orthodoxy derived more from habit than from true devotion. Estate owners celebrated Russia's religion in a number of ways: in the attention they paid to the building and decorating of estate churches, chapels, and bell towers; in their reverence for family icons; in the hospitality they offered religious pilgrims; and in the close links of many families to Russia's numerous monastic communities. If the belvederes and columns of provincial manor houses were material symbols of the nobility's external allegiance to western culture, the spires and bell towers of estate churches, rising above the belvederes, reflected the precedence given to Russian Orthodoxy. A small number of the educated elite were indeed private skeptics or atheists, yet among the nobility as a whole religion played a prominent role, and nowhere more so than on the estate. Here the nobleman's role (imitative of the autocrat's) was that of public defender of the faith; he saw to it that churches were built for the peasants in his villages and that they received religious instruction and practiced their faith.

For these reasons, to wealthy landowners the estate church was an important part of the architectural ensemble. As we have seen, the church sometimes antedated the manor house (fig. 186). In other instances a new house and church were built at the same time, or an existing church was remodeled. When Prince Kurakin finished the manor house at Nadezhdino, he replaced the dilapidated parish church with a magnificent cathedral modeled on the Palladian church at his family estate Kurakino, also adding a house chapel to Nadezhdino's upper story. In many instances, the pains taken by an aristocrat over his church were clearly a kind of showmanship. The church at Rai-Semenovskoe, designed by Kazakov and twenty years in the building, had an interior of expensive Italian marble and precious metals rather than the traditional gilded wood. The 1817 brochure advertising the glories of Rai-Semenovskoe boasted, "Nowhere in Europe, not even in Italy, is there a private individual who might have such a church." A contemporary described it as "Italian in style, with a light cupola and a high, handsome bell tower, which does not disrupt, as bell towers often do, but rather adorns the whole building; in addition it is distinguished by a faultless elegance inside. . . . The upper church, high, luminous, whose lofty cupola is supported by handsome little Corinthian columns of local marble, is particularly striking because of the outstanding iconostasis."[3] The white marble of the iconostasis, also designed by Kazakov, contrasted with interior columns made from a unique local marble with red and green veining, giving the church an unusual and magnificent appearance.

The Yankovs, though not nearly as wealthy as Nashchokin, spent considerable time and effort designing and building their church at Gorky; the iconostasis, of wood in this case, was painted by their serf artist. The war of 1812 destroyed the new house they had just built in Moscow, but in 1813 they interrupted its reconstruction to add a new chapel to the Gorky church. Yankova explains, "We thought that God had punished us because we had built the [new] house and not finished decorating the church, so now we decided to finish at least one of the chapels, and then worry about the house."[4]

Many wealthy noblemen seem to have been truly pious. The Marquis de Custine was astounded by a prince's behavior at the Convent of the Transfiguration in Yaroslavl. The prince kissed all the icons, as well as the relics of

a saint whose tomb was opened for them by a monk, and made the sign of the cross no fewer than fifty times. Custine comments disbelievingly, "This prince had gone to Paris with Alexander I."[5] The equally sophisticated Yury Golitsyn confessed daily during Holy Week and knelt before his peasants to ask their forgiveness before taking communion, an act his daughter says moved him to tears.

Male reverence, however, was expressed mainly in building churches and supervising peasant religious practice. Female piety was a more pervasive, private, and personal matter. Women were the icon keepers: their bedrooms usually contained the most elaborate icon corner of the house or were situated next to the oratory, and like their peasants, noblewomen shared a faith in the power of these images to produce miracles. While men built churches on their estates, women protected holy men and beggars, donated their handicrafts to churches, and created religious communities. Many even took religious vows.

The estate was connected to Russian Orthodoxy not only through churches and religious practices but by blood, in that most noble families had one or more relatives who had joined the Orthodox hierarchy or one of Russia's many monasteries or nunneries (fig. 187). Elizaveta Yankova lists only ten male relatives who became prelates or monks but insists that there were others. Two of her sisters went into women's monasteries after several years of preparation for a life of denial. Even though these communities to some extent served as genteel retirement homes for noblewomen, a serious commitment, sometimes accompanied by severe deprivation, was required of the noblewoman-turned-nun. One of Yankova's sisters, for instance, entered a strict order and asked Yankova not to visit until she became used to her new surroundings. The abbess sometimes ordered her to go without speaking for days; at other times she had no food or water.[6]

186. Interior of Marfino's Church of the Nativity of the Virgin (1701–06), designed by A. Golitsyn's serf architect V. I. Belozerov in French baroque style.

Perhaps because so many noble widows took monastic vows, throughout the imperial period numerous female landowners endowed or founded religious communities. In the 1820s Gavrila Derzhavin's wife directed that upon her death their estate Zvanka be turned into a female monastery. If this proved impossible, Zvanka was to be sold to the state and the serfs given their freedom; only if all else failed was the estate to go to a private individual, with the proviso that the serfs work no more than two days a week. (Zvanka did become a female monastery but lasted only a few decades, as the nuns were unable to support it.) Princess Avdotya Meshcherskaya, who had built a brick church and then an almshouse on her estate of Anosino, dreamed of founding a religious community there before her death and becoming part of it. She took her vows in 1823, received the permission of Metropolitan Filaret to establish a convent, and at his insistence became its abbess. Some fifty years later this community was still thriving, supporting the almshouse and a hospital for the nuns on the proceeds from its inn for pilgrims. In the 1840s Tatyana Potemkina, another devout princess, fulfilled a decades-old dream by endowing a male monastery at Svyatye Gory (Holy Hills), a site that, according to a local monk, contained the ruins of a former monastic community. With this knowledge, Potemkina persuaded her mother-in-law to buy the estate; when the princess eventually inherited Holy Hills, she restored the monastery at great expense and hosted an elaborate dedication ceremony for the new community. There is no reason to doubt her memoirs, in which she states, "I thank God for having let me be the witness to His great mercy to men."[7]

Like Potemkina, Varvara Golovina was a wealthy, deeply religious aristocrat who fulfilled her destiny by turning her estate into a religious community. By nature pious to the point of mysticism, Golovina became a strict observer of Orthodox fasting days after her first husband died and increased her visits to monasteries and pilgrimages. In the 1850s she married M. I. Golovin and be-

273

187. Aerial view of the monastery of Joseph of Volokolamsk. (Author's collection)

came the mistress of Golovino, a handsome estate with a spacious old park near Moscow. Gradually Golovino became home to a large number of religious types.

The steward of Golovino was charged with converting the basement of the estate house into a refuge for holy wanderers. In 1869 Varvara Golovina built a cell in a grove of the estate park as a hermitage for a monk who had arrived on her doorstep; somewhat later, she built a chapel in the woods, which became her favorite retreat. Golovina's daughter appeared to have inherited her religious zeal, and a special building was erected near the estate church in the

expectation of the daughter's becoming a nun. Its upper story was a chapel; the lower contained cells for a future religious community, whose first members were two peasant women who had arrived with the monk. By the 1870s Golovino was populated with "holy fathers, holy fools, wanderers, and sectarians, all traveling with their knapsacks from one end to the other of broad Mother Russia." Serafim, a deacon of the Danilov monastery in Moscow, settled at Golovino. A typical *starets* (holy father), he was "severe, gloomy . . . [and] spoke in allegories, his head bent low, not looking at the person he addressed." Varvara

Golovina seems to have moved easily between caring for her religious community and life in the great house, with its mahogany furniture, tall mirrors, and "patterned parquet floor [which] shone like a mirror."[8] At her death the estate was turned over to the commune; in 1914 her grand-niece visited Golovino and found the nuns offering daily prayers for the repose of their benefactors, "Boyar Mikhail and Boyarina Varvara, slaves of God."

Rasputin's nefarious influence among the Petersburg elite is foreshadowed in earlier tales of noblewomen falling under the influence of a particular holy man. In the 1820s the countess Orlova, pious daughter of the dashing Orlov-Chesmensky, resolved to devote her life to good deeds after being told by her confessor and religious instructor, Father Photius, that her wealth was ill-gotten. She followed Photius (her main adviser and the supervisor of her property) to the Yuriev Monastery, outside Novgorod; there she built a little retreat for herself, possibly took secret religious vows, and spent her fortune renovating the monastery, which subsequently became "one of the richest in Russia." Yet even for the 1820s, a period of religious obscurantism, Photius was considered too fanatical and was finally accused of having frightened the countess "with tales of the devil."[9]

Noblewomen were more likely than their male counterparts to practice personal charity, to make pilgrimages to monasteries, and to shelter pilgrims. Memoirists echo Tolstoy's portrayal in *War and Peace* of Princess Maria's devotion to her "holy folk," simple religious types she kept in her room, out of sight of her stern father. At Bobrovo Yankova's grandmother always took in begging monks, whom she sheltered, fed, and provided with money. Her son disapproved, as did the husband of another noblewoman, who sold household silver without his knowledge to support her mendicants. A third turned over an entire wing of her Moscow urban estate house to pilgrims and sold stockings she had knitted to raise money for them. On trips to and from Annino, the Yankovs frequently went out of their way to spend a day with cloistered relatives or a revered holy father. From Gorky there were annual pilgrimages to the St. Sergius-Trinity Monastery (at Sergiev Posad).[10]

In some cases noble piety bore a strong resemblance to peasant superstition. One noblewoman, raised by her aunt on her grandmother's estate, was protected by wearing clothing only of blue and white, the colors of the Virgin, until she was sixteen. Her parents had entrusted her to her aunt "because all the children before me had died, so they acted like peasants do in the country: when baby livestock die, they give the rest to another to bring up."[11] One woman never ate doves because the Holy Spirit had descended in their form.[12] Female memoirists often mention miracles worked by a particular family icon, or icons or amulets that when worn around the neck in wartime had miraculously deflected a bullet from their loved ones.

From the reign of Catherine to the revolution of 1917 provincial nobles lived and died in tune with their visions. After the death of her husband in the 1760s one distraught mother ignored her children and remained shut in her room, claiming to have had a vision in which her husband appeared and "told her he would never come back if she let anyone else in the room." After three years she suddenly began to pray and ask for her infants. Her sudden change was explained by a second vision, in which her deceased father had appeared; he told her that the first apparition had been the devil disguised as her husband.[13] Even sophisticated Muscovites believed their visions. In the 1820s Sergei Apraksin made a compact with his friend Yury Dolgoruky. "They agreed that if it is possible for the dead to communicate with the living, he who died first would appear to the other three times to warn him he was about to die. This happened: Prince Yury died in the year of the cholera, and Apraksin appeared to him three times, the last time three days before he died."[14]

Robert Bremner termed the "instances of credulity" among the Russians "most melancholy." Writing in the

275

1830s, he noted that "the belief in lucky and unlucky days, for setting out on a journey or commencing any undertaking—the evil consequences of meeting certain kinds of people such as a monk—the danger of having 13 at dinner, or of upsetting the salt; in fact, all the absurdities which were so prevalent in Scotland . . . reign here with undiminished authority."[15] In the 1840s Nikoleva and her sisters enjoyed teasing a "poor, little developed" neighbor prone to visions of evil spirits on the eve of holy days. "We would leave her alone in a room, and as dusk fell, we would dress up one of the maids and send her in; the old lady would run screaming into our mother's room, convinced she had seen a *kikimora* [a malevolent sprite]."[16] The typical memoirist evinces obligatory disdain for country superstition, even while telling the reader about it. Yankova lists the superstitions of her old grandmother: she never stepped on a thread on the floor or on a circle in the grass left by a watering can. "On the first day of the month she eavesdropped at the door of the maids' room: from what she heard she would decide whether the month was going

188. Mariamna Davydova. The Lopukhins entertaining Father Agathon at Matussov. Watercolor. 1920s. (Courtesy of Alona Vassiloff)

to be lucky or not. The maids knew her weakness, and when they heard her coming they'd make conversation that would be lucky."[17]

Shared superstitions and rituals were a leveling device between noblewomen and their female serfs (similar to the hunting rituals of males). On the estate almost all females participated in *gadanie,* or fortune-telling. The tradition clearly had pagan origins, even though the main period for it was demarcated by Christian feast days (beginning with St. Catherine's Day, November 24, and concluding on Twelfth Night, January 6). Pushkin, who spent his early years in the country, was one of the first Russian writers to identify such rituals and superstitions with native sensibilities. In chapter 5 of *Eugene Onegin* Pushkin describes Tatyana's belief, as a "true Russian," in popular superstitions: the purring of a cat while washing its face signified the arrival of guests; wishes on a shooting star were fulfilled; a hare or monk crossing one's path was an evil omen. The Larin housemaids and daughters drop melted wax into dishes, divining their fortunes from the shapes it takes. Tatyana's nurse instructs her how to use mirrors in the bathhouse to foretell the future. Too fearful to stay in the bathhouse, Tatyana goes to bed with a mirror under her pillow (and proceeds to dream of the duel between Lensky and Onegin).[18]

Sometimes the symbols of elite culture were appropriated for an old tradition, as Nikoleva describes fortune-telling during a Christmas spent with her cousins at Bruslanovo. "Cousin Maria Protopopova, who liked poetry, made up couplets of various content, each of which would define the fate of the person who got it. One of the sisters dressed up as Pandora, in a thin white dress with a veil over half her face, and on her head a green wreath that held the veil. Across her shoulders on a green ribbon hung a container with the couplets she handed out. Another, dressed as Hebe, bore the nectar of Olympus to everyone. . . . The third was a Vestal Virgin who carried the holy flame in a chafing-dish, and so on."[19]

These traditions of fortune-telling and superstitious acts were so ingrained in the national psyche that they lasted into the twentieth century (along with a general inclination on the part of the Russian elite, from at least the reign of Alexander I to the present, to consult ouija boards, fortune-tellers, or miracle workers). Mariamna Davydova (née Lopukhina) writes that during gadanie at Matussov, the family estate, she, her sisters, and their female servants practiced "all sorts of witchcraft to guess the future and especially anything that had to do with love and marriage." On St. Catherine's Day they would "arise before dawn, go out in the garden and pick cherry branches, put them into a bottle filled with water, and make a wish, hoping they would blossom before the 1st of January. If they did, the wish would be granted."[20] As for Tatyana a century earlier, for these girls the shapes of tea leaves and molten wax, like the visions in the bathhouse mirrors, assumed special significance.

The Russian bathhouse was, of course, in use throughout the year (fig. 189). Noble and villager used different buildings, but the Saturday night ritual was much the same in both. Catherine Wilmot described it as a "religious observance, as not one of the lower order would or could profane the Church without having been in the Hot Bath the night before." At Troitskoe the bathhouse for Dashkova and her friends had three chambers. One was similar to a steam bath, with "a gradation of stairs to increase the heat of a vapour bath." In the others were large tubs, one filled with "a composition of wormwood, nettles, Grass-seed, mint, and horsereddish!" After soaking in this, one proceeded to another "Great Tub" where, in water up to the chin, "the Ceremony is to scour oneself with Horsereddish until you smart, and then with soap." Wilmot confessed to having undergone this process frequently in the countryside.[21]

Young noblemen who grew up in the countryside played mostly with house serfs but also with villagers. One remembers the villagers coming to the manor house to

Hamam tout les Samedis.

189. Mariamna Davydova. The Saturday ritual in the bathhouse at Matussov. Watercolor. 1920s.
(Courtesy of Alona Vassiloff)

pick him up for sledding excursions and boating on the Oka. Through such contacts he acquired the peasant belief in pagan goblins such as the *domovoi* or the more threatening *leshi*. Nicholas Volkov-Muromtsov, who grew up at Khmelita in the early twentieth century, describes the domovoi as something like a polecat.[22] The peasants told him it lived in the stable rafters and enjoyed running up and down the backs of the horses, working them into a frenzy. For this reason, he recalls, billy goats were kept in the stable, as the domovoi was thought to dislike their smell. Leshi, wood goblins who preyed on people, were more frightening. If a person were passing through a forest at night and heard them cackle, he could be sure that the creatures were trying to lead him astray. Country dwellers believed the mythical leshi to be far more dangerous than wolves or bears.

Nobles raised in the country were immersed in peasant folklore and superstition. Peasant servants—housekeepers, nannies, maids, coachmen, footmen, and valets—introduced their masters to a wide range of folk tradition (fig. 190). This immersion in peasant culture had substantial impact on high culture. Pushkin's debt to his nurse, Arina Rodionovna, is well known: her "enchanting tales" (as a captivated Yazykov called them) provided the folkloric motifs of many of his poems and stories. Like Pushkin, many other scions of noble families heard these stories in the nursery or servants' hall. Appollon Grigoriev brilliantly describes the impact of country lore even on a Moscow childhood of the 1830s:

> Superstitions and legends surrounded my childhood. . . . The servants . . . all came from the country, and I experienced with them that whole world Goncharov conveyed with real mastery in Oblomov's dream. When relatives arrived from the country, [their] servants . . . added fire to my superstitious, or rather, fantastic, inclinations, with new stories about mysterious goats butting each other at midnight on the little bridge to the village of Malakhov, about the treasure in the Kirikov Forest, about the magician-peasant buried at the crossroads. . . . I played all the folk games with the servants in our broad courtyard. . . . I heard all the fables of the folk epics . . . in the autumn dusk from the village girl Marina, brought from the village especially for my entertainment. . . . Occasionally peasants arrived from Grandmother's estate. This is where I heard even more wonderful stories.[23]

Even after mid-century and emancipation, by which time early ethnographers had recorded many Russian folk songs and tales, the oral tradition continued to play an important role. Volkov-Muromtsov recalls his grandmother's housekeeper, Olga Semenovna, born a serf (the illegitimate daughter of Prince Mikhail Dondukov-Korsakov) but highly educated and sophisticated, regaling him with folklore and oral epics, most of which he thinks were not recorded. "Her knowledge of fairy tales seemed unlimited. I used to sit for hours while she was knitting, listening to these marvelous stories. In all of them the good always triumphed, in spite of terrific difficulties. Most of them had animals: the hero and the cleverest was always the hare, the nastiest the fox."[24] Volkov-Muromtsov also recalls a *bayan*, or wandering troubadour, arriving at Khmelita to delight a large audience. An aged blind man, he was led by a little boy of twelve who accompanied his high-pitched voice on the dulcimer. In ballads sung by the bayans (only some of which were recorded) Ivan the Terrible and Stenka Razin were popular heroes.

For all the contrasts between the life of the manor house and the village, religious ceremonies and traditional practices regularly united the two halves of the kingdom. Easter, the foremost religious holiday, brought collaborative, ritualized labor and common celebration. It was preceded by solemn confession and seven weeks of fasting during Lent, when all Orthodox Russians abstained from meat, eggs, butter, and sometimes sugar. Orthodox religious practices ignored class distinctions. Miss Wilmot, visiting Princess Dashkova's estate of Troitskoe, was amazed by the fact that prior to confession all Orthodox believers, from tsar to peasant, had to beg forgiveness for their sins from everyone around them. At Pokrovskoe, the Nikolev estate, the "day of mutual forgiveness" that preceded Lent was celebrated in the "old, patriarchal fashion." Nikoleva remembered that

> Mother sat down on the sofa in front of a table on which there was placed a tray with a round loaf of rye bread and a saltcellar. We all gathered on both sides. All our house servants, and the peasants, if any of them were in the courtyard at that time, were allowed in. Nanny Fedora cut the bread into

190. A. G. Venetsianov. *A Landowner's Morning.* 1823.
This painting suggests the close relationships on the estate.
The housekeeper, planning the day with her mistress, seems to
consider the viewer an intruder on a family conference.
(Courtesy of the Russian Museum, St. Petersburg)

The week before Easter was consumed with the baking of the traditional *kulichi* and *paskhi*—the tall cakes and the rich concoction of sweetened curds, butter, and raisins with which the Orthodox end their fast—and the dyeing of eggs, to be blessed by the priest and presented as gifts (fig. 191). Dmitry Moroz vividly describes Holy Week preparations on a modest estate in the early nineteenth century. Domina, a house serf married to one of the author's childhood companions (the son of his mother's cook), was in charge. On the first day of Holy Week, Domina, famed for her beautiful knot-shaped rolls, pies, and buns, commandeered his grandmother's kitchen and began preparing the pastry for the traditional Easter cakes. Dmitry's mother and older sisters joined her, spending "days on end" preparing pastry. The spinning and weaving that usually took place in this kitchen was transferred to the servants' quarters, and throughout Holy Week no man could enter this area as the cooking proceeded.[26]

Nobles and peasants attended services together on Easter eve. The congregation emerged after midnight to greet one another with a joyous "Christ is risen," accompanied by an exchange of three kisses (fig. 192). The noble family then distributed Easter cakes and decorated eggs to their peasants. At the Golitsyns' Saltyki a feast was set out for Easter Sunday on tables in the courtyard. "Father put me, a little three-year-old girl, on the table, and I greeted all the bearded peasants who looked at me lovingly and put colored eggs in my basket. Father himself sat at the table where the men sat, and mother at the women's. All the clergy were there with their families. There were no place settings so that [we] would not be any different from the peasants; we ate hot things from cups with wooden spoons and the rest with our fingers."[27]

No other religious holiday matched Easter week in duration or elaborateness of preparation, but other holy days or ceremonial occasions throughout the year followed much the same format. Lord and peasant prayed together in the estate church, and the service was followed

little pieces and salted them, or sometimes mother herself did this; then the mutual forgiveness began. Those taking part came up in turn to my mother, bowed to the ground, saying "Forgive me, mistress, if I have sinned in any way against you." Mother stood up, gave a half bow to the person, and said, "And thou also forgive my sins," and offered a piece of salted bread, expressing the hope that they would break the Lenten fast together.[25]

by some form of largesse to the peasants. Unkovskaya says, "On large holidays the peasants came to our estate and sang in chorus in the courtyard; the coachman Fyodor gave them little cups of vodka, which the peasants drank in a gulp after crossing themselves. . . . Our men chatted with the peasants, and our maids danced with the peasant women."[28]

Because of Russia's short growing season, the agricultural calendar, from sowing to harvesting, was a com-pressed period of hard work. Much of the remainder of the year was marked for celebration. Religious holidays throughout the year, particularly the Feast of the Virgin (October 1), Trinity Day, All Saints' Day, and Nikolin Day, were celebrated with song, dance, and a feast for the peasants. For the feast of the Intercession of the Virgin Mary, Nikoleva's father and mother used the large servants' hall opposite the house to set out tables laden with bowls of *shchi*, jellies, and cakes, and the family raised a glass of

191. Mariamna Davydova. The storehouse at Kamenka. The housekeeper is showing Mariamna Davydova the Easter *kulichi* and dyed eggs that will be distributed to the villagers. Watercolor. 1920s. (Courtesy of Alona Vassiloff)

vodka with their three hundred peasants. In good weather the feast would continue until dusk. Fiddlers provided music for dancing and singing, and Nikoleva and her sister sang along with the peasant girls and children.

Christmastime brought prolonged revelry. The mother of the composer Mikhail Glinka celebrated Christmas eve in the traditional fashion at Novospasskoe, her Smolensk estate, creating a manger in the largest room of her house. This symbol of the nativity consisted of a small pile of hay, covered with a cloth, upon which a bowl of *kutya* (a pudding of sweet barley or rice with raisins) was placed between two candles. The parish priest held a service in front of this mock manger; he then blessed the kutya, which was shared by everyone present. Often the hay beneath the kutya was also blessed and taken to the stables for the horses to eat. Holiday congratulations were exchanged, and the evening ended with dancing.[29]

Constant partying marked the holiday period known as Svyatki, the twelve days between Christmas and January 6. "According to country custom," says Nikoleva, "neighbors visited one another . . . initially visiting landowners, then officials, and gradually going lower and lower [on the social ladder]; each house could be confident that its time to entertain would arrive. The third day of the holiday was my parents' turn."[30] The amusements during Svyatki reflect the mixed culture of the estate: masters appropriated the peasant traditions of fortune-telling, mumming, and folk dancing, while house servants were

192. Mariamna Davydova. The priest blessing the celebrants and their Easter food after the midnight service. Watercolor. 1920s. (Courtesy of Alona Vassiloff)

193. Mariamna Davydova. Father Agathon blessing the Easter feast at Kamenka. Watercolor. 1920s. (Courtesy of Alona Vassiloff)

introduced to elite, western-style dancing. To the tunes of the house musicians (four violinists), the entire Nikolev household—masters and servants—and their guests enjoyed waltzes, *écossaises*, and other dances. Nikoleva and her sisters, dressed as gypsies and shepherdesses, taught their maids the steps and figures of the "Grossvater" and "matradur." At Troitskoe and other estates Martha Wilmot visited, house servants likewise joined the dancing. "Tis by no means uncommon to see Masters and Slaves mingle in the same dance, and in visiting at a strange house, I have been more than once puzzled to find out which was the Mistress and which the femme de chambre," she wrote her mother.[31] Nikoleva recalls one of the male servants, "a handsome lad," dancing folk dances with the best dancer among the maids, ending with a rousing *trepak*, the Ukrainian dance in which the legs are kicked out from a squatting position.

Clearly traditional Russian dances had great reso-nance for the nobility. Consider the performance of Dmitry Gedeonov, dressed as a coachman, and his cousin Maria Engelhardt, in peasant *sarafan* (Russian national dress for women) and *kokoshnik* (a national headdress, varying, like the sarafan, from province to province), dancing for their grandmother on her name day in the early nineteenth century: "They both danced very well; when she, as if fleeing from the young man pursuing her, jumped onto a low pedestal and shook her finger at him, it was so delightfully artistic that the stern grandmother herself jumped up from her chair, began to shake her shoulders and gesture, then fell back into her seat and burst into tears. All her children and grandchildren rushed up to her, surrounded her, and kissed her hands."[32]

Khvoshchinskaya describes her sensations while dancing in similar fashion at a New Year's ball some forty years later at Obrochnoe, her uncle's estate in Novgorod Province. Although her memoir might well have been influenced by Tolstoy's description of Natasha Rostova's instinctive dancing to her uncle's accordion, her emotional connection to native culture appears genuine. "Since childhood I have passionately loved Russian dancing. . . . The orchestra played the trepak! When I heard the familiar native sounds we had played at Ogarevo on the accordion or piano, and here there was an orchestra, my blood stirred and my feet moved of their own accord! I took off my ball attire, threw the flowers from my head, wound my hair in a braid, put on my sarafan and kokoshnik with a veil, and flew into the ballroom!" In the 1890s, when Khvo-shchinskaya was writing her memoirs, heightened nationalism had bred a newfound respect for folk-art traditions in the Russian elite, expressed in everything from architecture and furnishings to themes for masquerade balls. This trend undoubtedly colors her sentimental reminiscence of herself as a child: "In each unstudied movement [of national dance] the character of a nation is visible. . . . No one taught me to dance, but I was a real 'Russian girl,' who grew up in the Russian countryside; when I heard the song

'The maiden went for water, for cold spring water,' my arms involuntarily rose above my head and I felt like moving as swans glide across the water, practically without touching the floor."[33] Nikoleva, also writing in the 1890s, similarly stresses her Russianness: "I was dressed in a Cossack jacket with braid—I was so pleased that even now, a half century later, I remember standing on a chair and trying to act like a Cossack girl, imitating our maids who were taking part in the masquerade."[34]

The country estate was often the site of entertainments for the local nobility in which the peasantry played an important role. As we have seen, on grand estates those peasants chosen and trained for elaborate theatrical productions were introduced to the elite culture of opera, plays, and music. More often, however, peasants entertained the manor house with traditional song and music. Martha Wilmot mentions Princess Dashkova's maid Nastasya gathering her friends to perform "all the old Russian amusements such as national songs, and as they are sung by all most [sic] all the Company who move in a large circle, two are placed in the Centre and act the little Story that is told."[35] Throughout the age of the country estate, nobles at all levels enjoyed listening to and learning folk songs from their peasants. Kuskovo had renowned peasant choristers who delighted strollers with their native costumes and songs on festival days. At Ostankino they appeared on stage. On one visit Alexander I and his entourage were moved when the Ostankino theater curtain rose to reveal these choristers (and several outstanding soloists) in a romantic Russian birch grove, serenading them with evocative folk songs.

Mikhail Glinka (1804–54), Russia's first renowned composer, was originally inspired by the peasant folk songs he heard at home and the performances of his uncle's serf orchestra, which often appeared at his mother's Novospasskoe. As a young composer Glinka learned much from two serf musicians, the Netoev brothers, one a violinist, the other a bass player. In exchange for information about songs, phrasing, and musical styles, he took them to St. Petersburg and paid for their music lessons. For almost twenty years during his visits home, Glinka invited village singers to the manor so that he could transcribe their songs.[36] Later he used these familiar melodies in his own compositions, which may explain the enormous popularity of "A Life for the Tsar" and "Ruslan and Ludmila" (an orchestration of Pushkin's famous version of an old Russian fairy tale) for elite audiences right to the end of the old regime.

Glinka was merely the most famous aficionado of folk songs of his day, for this art form aroused widespread interest in the romantic age. Khvoshchinskaya's claim that her father, Yury Golitsyn, was "the first to interest the Russian public in popular songs that his choir rendered so magnificently under his direction" is hence probably exaggerated, but that she makes it at all is significant.[37] From other memoirs it appears that nobles learned folk songs as a natural part of estate life. Dmitry Moroz's mother, sisters, and their maids spent long winter evenings doing needlework, entertained by the folk singing of Gapka and Nadya, his sister's young chambermaids. Their repertory was huge, with a new offering almost every night, and the two girls frequently quarreled over what to sing. Moroz's mother often sang with them, and he too joined in as a child.

Although noblewomen were not supposed to weave or sew, young ladies often learned from house serfs the fashionable accomplishments of embroidery, petit point, beadwork, and painting on velvet. Many types of needlework were ancient Russian folk arts that serf women produced in copious amounts for clothing and furnishings, as well as for sale. Moroz's account makes his mother the head of her needlework circle, but other observers cite instances in which expert serf needleworkers taught techniques to their mistresses.[38]

A number of important transitions on the agricultural calendar were solemnized by ceremonies of Orthodox, pagan, or mixed origins; often these occasions brought villagers and estate owners together. All estates, for example, had beehives, which produced much-needed honey and wax. One memoirist relates that a religious procession complete with priest and icons (of the bees' patron saint) accompanied the beekeeper when he transferred the hives from their winter home in the garden to the woods for the summer. A summer drought at Krasnoe, in Tula Province, produced a similar procession that involved the noble family walking with their villagers and priest to the fields to pray for rain, aided by icons and holy water.[39]

Numerous other events in the life of the estate called for solemn celebrations that drew lord and peasant together. Whenever a church or chapel was dedicated or a new house completed, the priest was summoned to offer a service of thanksgiving and to anoint the new structure with holy water. Guests were invited, the peasants gathered, and festive celebration followed. Name-day celebrations frequently began with a service and ended with a feast. Estate owners often became godparents of their serfs' children. Most landowners were interred in their estate church, with their serf servants among the mourners.

Arrivals and departures called for traditional ceremonies. Witness the opening scenes of Turgenev's play "A Poor Gentleman," in which an estate steward bustles about, freshening up the servants' livery and summoning the estate musicians to welcome the absentee owner with a celebratory fanfare. A safe arrival called for a service of thanksgiving and a greeting from the peasants; before the owner departed, a service was said for the journey, and the villagers bid farewell to the traveler. In his memoirs Gerakov recounts the elaborate rituals of arrival and departure he and a young friend encounter as they travel from St. Petersburg to Tbilisi to inspect the friend's many holdings. Not far from Rostov they came to his sizable estate of Bogoroditsk, where they spent the night. This is what he writes: "No words can describe the joy of the peasants, seeing their lord for the first time." They laughed and cried with delight as they presented the traditional *khleb-sol* (a word meaning, literally, "bread and salt" and, figuratively, "hospitality"). The manor house, in which no one had slept for thirty years, was in perfect condition, as were the park and the church. When the travelers left two days later, the peasants ran alongside their carriage for eight miles, singing and dancing "as if it were a festival."[40] Twentieth-century cynicism prompts the suspicion that the young master's departure, possibly for another thirty years, might well have been cause for serfs to celebrate. But the incident highlights the fact that in such rituals the serf and the master were playing familiar parts.

Hospitality was, according to one nineteenth-century Russian, "the general character of the whole nation."[41] It was perceived as a welcome obligation not unconnected with religion, an opportunity to make a small gift to God in gratitude for having a roof over one's head. Russian readiness to take in unknown travelers for the night was legendary. This explains the warm welcome peasants extend to the narrator of Turgenev's *Sportsman's Notebook*. There was no such thing as an unwanted guest; indeed, some descriptions of name-days mention totally unexpected or unknown people arriving for the party.

The custom of offering some form of gift (always called khleb-sol) to a visitor or new arrival was universal, whether it be the rich ornaments presented to royal guests on lavishly decorated silver platters or simply bread offered on a wooden trencher. When Yury Golitsyn brought his young bride to Saltyki, a crowd of peasants gathered to meet them several miles from the estate. The entire group went immediately to the church for a thanksgiving service. At its conclusion Golitsyn turned to the crowd, dressed in holiday clothes, and said, "Here is my wife, and your princess. Serve her as you do me, well and faithfully— she will always be good to you, will be your defender and helper in need." The village elders then carried forward a large white cake decorated with flowers, and the elder's wife offered a towel filled with fresh rolls. The peasant

285

women approached their new mistress and kissed her three times, calling her "our darling, you beauty!"[42] Princess Dashkova's arrival at Troitskoe after a few weeks' absence followed the same routine. First she went to the chapel, where "the Priests gave her the crucifix to kiss and sang Psalms." Then two of her house serfs, meeting her at the entrance gates with "a great loaf of black bread and a handful of salt on top . . . greeted the Princess as though she'd been away much longer."[43]

Holidays likewise began with a church service, followed by a procession and feasting (fig. 194). Yankova first met the peasants of Gorky as a new bride soon after the feast of the Virgin of Kazan. After the church service her husband presented her to the peasants on the front porch; "if they asked, I let them kiss my hand." All the men were given beer, wine, and cakes, the women earrings and necklaces; treacle and nuts were thrown to the children out of the windows. Says Yankova, "This was how all large

194. A religious procession passing before the gates of the church at Khmelita. Early twentieth century.
(Courtesy of Nicholas Volkov-Muromtsov)

195. P. E. Zablotsky. *After Harvesting.* 1822. Villagers dancing in the courtyard of an estate for their master, mistress, and the house serfs. (Courtesy of the Russian Museum, St. Petersburg)

church holidays were formerly celebrated on all estates."[44]

One is hard-pressed to accept at face value some memoirists' accounts of happy peasants seemingly engaged in continual merrymaking. Slavutinsky writes that his peasants, whom he describes as "very jolly," took at least three days to celebrate each of the important holy days. Every Sunday, he claims, from the end of the harvest until the spring sowing, the peasants sang and danced late into the evening (fig. 195). "I remember with pleasure that this practically always took place in view of the manor house, sometimes even in the courtyard, and not on command, not by a summons, but of their voluntary will." On this estate, even the harvesting was "frequently done as if it were a holiday: the young men, women, and girls dressed in their best, and there were usually jolly songs."[45] One wonders if the peasant, usually pushed to the limit at this season, really felt on holiday; but numerous noble families treated harvesting as an event to celebrate, taking picnics to a nearby glade whence they could observe the peasants mowing and listen to their singing.

Cultural values are deeply embedded in patterns of speech. In imperial Russia language was a striking cultural divide, immediately distinguishing town from country, noble from peasant. Peasant speech, with its wealth of proverbs, imagery, and colloquialisms drawn from folklore, was richer than upper-class Russian and practically unintelligible to those bred in the city; conversely, the peasant had a hard time understanding the bureaucratic or militaristic language of recently retired or absentee landowners, or the barely passable Russian of an aristocrat raised abroad. Peasants inevitably presumed that the appearance of such a foreigner in their midst meant trouble. An unfinished sketch from Turgenev's *A Sportsman's Notebook* graphically portrays miscommunication and peasant distrust when a well-meaning absentee landowner tries to take inventory of the villagers' equipment as a first step toward benevolent agricultural reform. Yet throughout the nineteenth century noble children who had been raised on the estate and had played with serfs learned to understand the pattern of peasant speech, including the significance of the proverbs and "riddles" that distinguished it. Volkov-Muromtsov insists that in the maelstrom of revolution peasants distinguished not between rich and poor but between city and country: a person from the country was identified by verbal clues and subsequently protected as kin.

Russian folk art drew on the same sources of inspiration that informed peasant language, namely, popular legends and fairy tales. An uninformed appreciation of folk art seems to have begun to penetrate elite consciousness early in the nineteenth century, as a curious by-product of its interest in replicating the European material culture of the city. As we know, the furnishings and decor of the country house depended on the development of serf talent. The ambition of every landowner, says the anarchist Prince Kropotkin, was to have all household items made on the estate, by his own serfs—regardless of the quality.[46] Remarking on the typically mediocre hunting scenes and landscapes on most estate walls, Yankova echoes Kropotkin: "The most important thing was that the host could praise them and say, 'True, it's not very well drawn, but my serf masters did it.'"[47]

These paintings and pieces of furniture were the serf artist's compromise between his native impulses and the western artistic norms to which he had been introduced. Estate owners can be accused of having contributed to the decline of some traditional Russian arts by employing some of their most skilled artists to practice nontraditional art forms. Yet the estate must also be given credit for being the vehicle that kept an apparently culturally estranged elite in contact with traditional folkways. The extent of that estrangement is extremely hard to measure. Historians accustomed to seeing a wide gulf between elite and folk culture might argue that Russian nobles enjoyed folk songs and dances but undoubtedly considered them unrelated to their own lives. Throughout the nineteenth century, the nobility's participation in traditional folk culture was limited and in many instances took the form of conscious masquerade. But it is possible that the identification with native Russian tradition through song and dance, to which our memoirists testify, was as emotionally genuine as it was widespread.

If one looks at the phenomenon from the peasant's point of view, one could likewise argue that in dancing or parading before the manor house, jointly celebrating holidays with the master, or performing other ceremonies of ritual communion, the peasant was simply deploying the traditional conciliatory weapons of the weak. Yet many of these estate rituals continued after the emancipation (fig. 196). That, and the fact that nobles took pride in their familiarity with native tradition, may signify that on some level these traditions were deeply imbedded in the national psyche at all levels, thanks largely to estate life.

After 1861 the desire of the elite to reclaim native elements of its culture was most actively expressed in the efforts to revive folk art of connoisseurs like Savva Mamontov or Princess Tenisheva, who established studios on their estates, and in Tolstoy's adamant rejection of elite culture for peasant life at Yasnaya Polyana. On a wider, more private, and perhaps more profound scale it was also expressed in the relatively unchanged life of the country estate, which in its ritualized celebrations for over a century had provided the starting point for an abiding, evanescent dream: an eventual reconciliation of Russia's two cultures.

196. Mariamna Davydova. The Lopukhins going to the Holy Thursday service at the Matussov church in a *lineika*. Watercolor. 1920s. (Courtesy of Alona Vassiloff)

11
Ideal Worlds

THE IDYLL OF THE RUSSIAN INTELLIGENTSIA

I am staying in the country at the Davydovs, those charming and

intelligent hermits. I spend my time between aristocratic dinners and democratic debates.

Our group, now dispersed, was . . . a varied and gay mixture of original minds. . . .

Few women, lots of champagne, many bons mots, lots of

books and a little poetry.—**A. S. Pushkin**

THE WORD *INTELLIGENTSIA*, ONE OF the few to have passed from the Russian language into our own vocabulary, refers to a group of Russians first distinguishable in the upper-class literary circles of the late eighteenth century. In the broad sense, to be a member of the intelligentsia was to lead a life centered around ideas. In the narrow sense, *intelligentsia* later came to describe a discrete group of individuals who stood outside the system, the better to observe and describe it critically. As Mikhail Bakunin put it, "We lived, so to speak, outside Russian reality, in a world filled with feeling and imagination."[1] To be a member of this latter group was almost by definition to have an aversion for—as the intelligentsia saw it—the aristocratic frivolity of official Russia and the unthinking, ignorant patriarchalism of most Russian landowners.

The outlooks of virtually all the significant cultural figures of the first half of the nineteenth century were shaped in some way by extended periods spent on a country estate. There the writer or composer discovered Russian folklore from peasant storytellers and singers, and the abolitionist played with serf children. There painters and Slavophiles reveled in the Russian landscape, and statesmen hunted, fished, and swam. The estate worlds of their childhoods became talismans, to be re-created later for their own families or in their writing.

In Europe the end of the eighteenth century marked the beginning of an intellectual migration toward the utopian countryside of antiquity. The late-Enlightenment, early-romantic idealization of the countryside might be characterized as a poetic, intuitive response to the first stirrings of industrialization. In Russia this particular impetus would not arrive for almost a century, but its absence was more than compensated for by indigenous features of Russian life from which sensitive souls sought refuge. Most prominent among them were the Russian's sense of being harnessed to the mighty needs of the state and the confinement of intellectual life by a system of censorship and surveillance. As Boris Chicherin put it much later,

"Whereas in the capital one felt that heavy despotism stifling every living thought, where power was felt at every step and gave rise to oppositional feelings . . . in the provinces the endless distances weakened the operation of the system. . . . Even in the darkest days . . . everyone coming to the country felt he breathed more freely, could think and say what he wished."[2]

In their country retreats Russia's nobly-born intellectuals and artists united these more mundane impetuses with the philosophical pursuit common to their age: a search for the Arcadia of classical poetry, for a life of pastoral simplicity. Withdrawal to the countryside, even when the exile was involuntary, became a cleansing experience that put one in touch with the classical world and that was, as a result, widely celebrated in verse. Gavrila Derzhavin, the poetic giant of Catherine's age, invoked Pindar's example when he sang of his life of simple pleasures at Zvanka, his estate on the Volkhov River, north of Novgorod. Constantine Batyushkov, no less steeped in antiquity, lyrically enumerated the objects protected by his Penates, the deities guarding his country refuge: the creaky three-legged table, the half-rusted ancestral sword hanging in a corner, old notebooks, and a hard bed. These he declared more precious than the riches he could obtain from court life: "I won't beg and bow in Petersburg as long as I have a crust of bread." The reader looks on as Lileta (his sultry muse, or imaginary mistress?) enters his refuge, symbolically drops her soldier's uniform at her feet, looses her curly hair from under her man's cap, and whispers to him, "I am yours, yours!"[3]

By the early nineteenth century, as Russian provincial life developed, the country estate rivaled the urban salon as a gathering place for writers, intellectuals, and artists. This setting provided an environment for work and relaxation, a peaceful context for artistic experimentation, and a safe haven where ideas opposed to the ideology of official Russia could be fearlessly thrashed out among close friends and nativist roots reclaimed. Intellectual currents

197. V. A. Tropinin. Portrait of Alexander Pushkin. 1827.
(Courtesy of the Pushkin Museum, Moscow)

witty friends. Meanwhile in more private fashion the future Decembrists assembled at estates like the Bakunins' Pryamukhino and the Davydovs' Kamenka to concoct remedies for the social and political evils of their day.

The intelligentsia of pre-emancipation Russia were the first to call for a better life and full individuality for the oppressed peasant, whose humanity they vividly portrayed in their writing. They were also the first to decry the educated elite's apostasy from native culture and to identify the peasant as the bearer of this culture. Yet—and this was the tragic conflict—the cultivated Russian, no matter how liberal, was almost assuredly from a landowning family, and hence a co-conspirator in the system. Few men of letters prior to the 1860s derived their primary income from writing; many, despising military or government service, subsisted, for better or worse, on the labor of enserfed peasants. Given this fact, the attitudes of Russian intellectuals toward the countryside in the era of serfdom, their behavior on the estate, and the philosophies they developed take on a particular poignancy. Some expressed the conflict between ideals and reality in creative works that undermined serfdom—and with it the estate life they loved. Others denied the existence of this conflict; still others were destroyed by it. The lack of occupations commensurate with many a noble's education and ideals accounts for Russia's "superfluous men," its fictional Pechorins and real-life Katenins, talented but eccentric or cynical, whose lives revolved around vain gesture and who died forgotten.

Ideal Worlds

For roughly fifty years, from the 1780s to the 1830s, Russia's intellectuals spoke mostly in poetry. The estates they inhabited, now physically vanished, have lived on as the ideal, poeticized worlds their owners described. Derzhavin's Zvanka stood in close proximity to Gruzino (fig. 198), the country seat of General Alexei Arakcheev; but intellectually and spiritually Zvanka was worlds removed,

contributed to this development, particularly the romantic cult of nature, which was at its peak in the first third of the century. By the end of Alexander's reign these idyllic country retreats formed a network of nerve cells through which the energy of Russian intellectuals pulsed. A painting of that period shows A. N. Olenin, president of the Academy of Fine Arts, in a red fez, entertaining at his country retreat, aptly named Priyutino (or Refuge).[4] Pushkin (fig. 197) was a welcome guest there, as well as at Ostafievo, where Prince Peter Vyazemsky welcomed his

its spirit and routine directly opposed to that of Gruzino. There Arakcheev devised and practiced a military model of life that was copied not only by retired officers but by Paul I, at his favorite estate, Gatchina. The military colonies of soldier-farmers Arakcheev set up in the last ten years of Alexander's reign enshrined the model. In the colonies an abiding dream of Russian monarchs was realized: the perfectly ordered, clockwork empire where everything was regulated, where uniformed peasants arose, were mustered out, worked, ate, and slept in military precision according to a "minute, rigid, and relentless schedule."[5]

The poetic Zvanka, designed by Nikolai Lvov (fig. 199), was a living reproach to this model. Derzhavin's relative and closest friend and possibly the most creative architect of his day, Lvov designed numerous estates, including the elegant Raek (figs. 200, 201) for General Glebov. A writer, artist, and inventor as well, Lvov translated and published the first volume of Palladio's magisterial *I*

198. M. N. Vorobiev. View of Gruzino from the Volkhov River. 1811–15.
(Courtesy of the State Historical Museum, Moscow)

199. Artist unknown. Portrait of Nikolai Lvov. Late eighteenth century. (*Starye gody*, 1911)

quatri libri dell' architettura and his own book on perspective; he collected Russian folk songs; he wrote poetry and operatic librettos that he illustrated himself; and he pioneered in the production and use of a new building material of compressed earth and clay. After Lvov's death Derzhavin praised him as "one of those excellent and rare beings who are endowed with a marked receptiveness to that refined feeling which, delightfully filling the heart with lightning speed, often expresses itself in a tear. . . .

He was accomplished in mind and knowledge, loved the sciences and the arts and was distinguished by a subtle and elevated taste."[6]

Zvanka, a Palladian cube situated majestically on a hill overlooking the Volkhov River (fig. 202), was designed for comfort, privacy, and family life. The exterior, with its porticoes, pillars, and belvedere, resembled Lvov's own Nikolskoe-Cherenchitsy, and the interior Derzhavin's Petersburg residence (also designed by Lvov). Of generous proportions, the two-story house had almost six thousand square feet of living space. But unlike Raek, designed for a general's entertaining, it had no central hall or enfilade. Lvov was a devotee of Palladio but felt his designs must be modified for a different climate and age to provide the "diverse comforts contributing to the pleasure of life and health," among them less drafty rooms and better ventilated stoves.[7]

On either side of the entrance hall were the personal offices of the master and mistress. Behind Derzhavin's study was a spacious dining room, the largest room in the house. One end of it was semicircular, with a row of pillars, beyond which were the pantry and room for male servants. The main staircase and master bedroom occupied the middle of the house opposite the dining room, and a game room and divan room (a favorite retreat for Derzhavin) spanned the rear facade. On the second floor were his wife's dressing room, a billiard room, and accommodations for guests, family, and Derzhavin's secretary. Servants reached the second floor via two spiral staircases concealed inside the thick walls, their ground-floor entrances disguised as stove fronts.[8]

Lvov and other friends—Derzhavin's brother-in-law V. V. Kapnist (a fellow poet), P. L. Veliaminov, and the publisher and future metropolitan Evgeny Bolkhovitinov—frequently traveled to Zvanka. In pastoral surroundings the members of this close-knit circle read drafts of their works, discussed the political and cultural news of the day, hunted and fished, and staged amateur theatricals, estab-

200. Drawing of a cross-section of the main house at Znamenskoe-Raek, the estate of General Glebov, designed by N. Lvov. (Budylina, Braitseva, and Kharlamova, *Arkhitektor N. A. Lvov*)

lishing a pattern of country life for the intelligentsia. Spouses and dependents became part of one extended spiritual family: when Lvov and then his wife died, Derzhavin and his wife took on the upbringing of Lvov's younger daughter, Praskovya.

Although every member of this circle had official positions and spent time in St. Petersburg, they all at one time or another expressed the strong emotional attachment to country living characteristic of their age. As has been seen, Derzhavin (1743–1816) was no stranger to court life. After his ode "Felitsa" won him Catherine's favor in 1783, he became her poet laureate, served for a while as a provincial governor, and—to judge from his memoirs—enjoyed the pomp of court spectacles. In 1807, when he wrote his lengthy poem "Zvanka" (dedicated to Evgeny Bolkhovitinov), Derzhavin was serving as minister of justice. Yet in the first two stanzas of "Zvanka" Derzhavin rejects the life of a grandee, "office worries," and the "gold and honors of the court" in favor of Zvanka's "golden freedom," solitude, and quiet.[9] Kapnist had similar feelings about Obukhovka, his "cherished cloister" (also designed by Lvov): "I am searching for my real happiness . . . in the contemplation of beautiful, virgin nature. . . . I am using my hands in decorating and clearing my garden (more beautiful than most kings have), in supervising the farming, in all kinds

of rural, peasant, and, one might say, peaceful labors. . . . We are living happily."[10]

Although Derzhavin referred jokingly to Zvanka as his "little estate," it consisted of nearly two thousand acres, most of which were forest, and the small village of Zvanka. In his poem Derzhavin describes himself rising, sometimes feeding his doves before breakfast, and enjoying the sounds of shepherds tending his cattle. When the family and guests assemble at the round table, their talk is "of dreams, of urban or rustic rumors," of the deeds of the ancestors whose portraits gaze down on them, or of Russian heroes such as the immortal Suvorov. In the course of the morning, peasant women present the mistress with their handiwork—linens, embroidered napkins, tablecloths, rugs, lace, and knitting—while farm produce such as honey, butter, purple grapes, and silvery mushrooms is paraded before the master. The doctor, having visited the infirmary, reports on his patients; the "whiskered elder" of the village gives an accounting; young craftsmen come to show their carving or painting and are rewarded with a gift. Before lunch Derzhavin might play a heated game of cards, then slip into his "sanctuary" to "commune with Pindar" or dictate to his secretary.

At noon, writes Derzhavin, his "slaves" hasten to lay the table, which is quickly transformed into a "flower bed" of dishes that include green *shchi*, rosy-yellow apple tarts, white cheese, red crayfish—not a feast, he insists, but "fresh, healthy" fare washed down with wine from the Don and Crimea and homemade cordials and beer. The meal is accompanied by lively, amusing conversation and concludes with a diplomatic standing toast to the tsar and family. Chess or other games, or bathing in the "crystal waters," follow. Derzhavin liked to sit on his balcony and survey his "kingdom—seas, forests, a whole world of beauty before one's eyes." He was pleased when the children of his house serfs ran up to him "not for lessons" but for biscuits and rolls ("they don't see me as a bogeyman"). A young relative enlarges the picture of life at Zvanka

201. View from the main house of the colonnade encircling the courtyard of Znamenskoe-Raek. (Courtesy of *Nashe Nasledie*)

depicted in the poem. He tells us that Derzhavin had serf musicians who played for the family on holidays. During the dinner celebrating Derzhavin's name day two cast-iron cannons on the balcony were fired, and his nieces and nephews set off fireworks. At a mooring in the river stood Derzhavin's skiff *Gavrila*, in which he paid visits to his neighbors. His secretary and his wife's housekeeper fished from the dock; occasionally Derzhavin hunted hares along the riverbank.

"Life at Zvanka" abounds with visual images and lyrical pastoral romance. The windows of Derzhavin's "cathedral-like" house gleam as the sun sets on the Volkhov, the happy peasants dance and sing, shepherds bring garlands of flowers to their sweethearts. Yet the poem pays homage to the rulers of Derzhavin's day: Catherine, Paul, and Alexander. At the end, sentimentally imagining a time when house and garden will have vanished, when "nowhere will the name of Zvanka be remembered," Derzhavin calls on his friend Evgeny ("a witness to my songs here") to ascend the "awesome hill" where his tomb is located, to bear witness that "here lived the minstrel of the goddess—Felitsa."

In 1816 Derzhavin died at Zvanka, the symbol of the simple life and idyllic relationship to nature his generation had sought. Although in reality life at Zvanka had many aristocratic touches, Derzhavin's poetic insistence on his pastoral, patriarchal routine in the country typified the intelligentsia's rejection of aristocratic luxury. Life at Prya-

202. Artist unknown. View of Zvanka from the Volkhov River (detail). Engraving. Early nineteenth century. (Courtesy of the State Historical Museum, Moscow)

mukhino, Alexander Bakunin's estate, and at Lvov's Nikolskoe, both near Torzhok, epitomized a similar rejection of fashionable aristocratic "openness" for an idealized, private family life. Lvov planned the renovation of his friend Bakunin's old wooden estate house, adding three Doric porticoes to dress up the main entrance and the facades of the two wings. Lvov also designed the elegant neoclassical church at Pryamukhino (see fig. 209) and planned the park, with ponds and cascades similar to those at Nikolskoe, a grotto, and a summerhouse on an artificial hill. In a poetic letter to Bakunin, Lvov described his life at Nikolskoe, in terms no one could better appreciate than Bakunin: "I am convinced, my friend, that if fortune's favorite (were his heart not altogether hardened) were to look in on us at Nikolskoe and see us finishing our daily round with a song, gathering to rest in the summer evening under the lime tree in the meadow, surrounded by family life, a healthy clutch of children and a merry throng of people who love us, he would say: 'How blessed they are.'"[11]

After Bakunin's retirement from service in 1797, at the age of twenty-nine, Pryamukhino, like Zvanka and Nikolskoe, became a magnet for artists and intellectuals (the eminent painters Borovikovsky and Levitsky, in addition to Derzhavin, Lvov, and Kapnist). In 1810 Bakunin, then forty-three, married eighteen-year-old Varvara Muravieva, and thereafter the couple devoted most of their attention to raising their eleven children. Their eldest son, Mikhail, was to become Russia's first revolutionary anarchist.

Much of what we know of life at Pryamukhino is contained in Bakunin's long poem "Osuga" (named for the river on whose banks Pryamukhino was situated), which was begun around 1817 and written over a number of years. From it we learn that Pryamukhino was a large but modestly furnished family house "without parquet floors, expensive rugs, or solemn furniture, not even card tables." In the corner of the dining room, says Bakunin, stands a

clock "about the same age as I am," and opposite it a "sacred ivy" and a lark and two nightingales in cages. "There are no valuable dishes; my furnishings are three or four simple platters and the shining faces of my children." A large mirror hung in the divan room, and a portrait of Catherine II graced the living room (where the dustcovers over the tapestried furniture were removed only on holidays).

The Bakunins gave their children an exemplary home education. Alexander taught them natural history, geography, physics, elementary astronomy, and history. Varvara Aleskeevna, a worldly young girl at the time of her marriage, became a model housekeeper and mother, giving orders to her staff, keeping the accounts, and teaching her children voice and piano. Governesses taught French, German, and at one point Italian: one line of "Osuga" mentions five languages being used in the children's rooms. All studied music (the girls the piano, their brothers the violin) and art. Not surprisingly, "Osuga" celebrates, above all, domestic life, simple pleasures such as family evenings in the country. "In the evening when the whole family gathers together like a swarm of bees, then I am happier than a tsar."[12] Some read, some talked while doing needlework; the family played games and music. The Bakunins spent some winters in town. For one departure Bakunin composed a farewell song to Pryamukhino—to the church, the village, the garden, the spring, the "shining waters of the Osuga," and "village freedom"; so affecting were his words that his family burst into tears singing it.

A third idyllic retreat was Ostafievo (figs. 203, 204), south of Moscow, the estate Pushkin dubbed the "Russian Parnassus" for its role in Russian intellectual life during the first two decades of the nineteenth century. Its owner, the talented poet Prince Peter A. Vyazemsky (fig. 205), was

203. "Washington" oaks frame the portico of Ostafievo. Imported as seedlings from George Washington's grave at Mount Vernon, they were planted in the 1860s by Karamzin's daughter.
(Courtesy of *Nashe Nasledie*)

an attentive host; Ostafievo's visitors during his long life included all the major literary figures of several generations, among them the poets Baratynsky, K. N. Batyushkov, V. K. Kuchelbecker, Denis Davydov, V. L. Pushkin (Alexander's uncle), and Vasily Zhukovsky. Other visitors were Alexander Griboedov, the bard of Poland Adam Mitskevich, the novelist Nikolai Gogol, the historian Mikhail Pogodin, and Alexander Pushkin, twelve years Vyazemsky's junior. Here Nikolai Karamzin, Vyazemsky's brother-in-law and guardian, wrote his *History of the Russian State*, while Griboedov used Ostafievo's visitors and host as models for some of the characters in his play *Wit Works Woe*.

Ostafievo was the votchina of Prokopy Lyapunov in the early seventeenth century. In the mid-eighteenth cen-tury it belonged to K. M. Matveev and in 1792 passed into the hands of Peter Vyazemsky's father, Andrei, a Catherinian aristocrat of ancient lineage. The spacious neoclassical manor house he built has weathered the past two centuries well. A grand six-columned Corinthian portico before the two-story central house, crowned by a belvedere, greets visitors; colonnades extend laterally to two symmetrical wings, one of which housed the kitchen. Some details suggest that I. E. Starov drew up the plans, but according to family lore Vyazemsky (who fancied himself an architect) personally designed the house.[13] In typical fashion a large oval great hall in the center of the house opens into the garden.

Ostafievo was atypical in having a major library. In Prince Andrei's time it contained five thousand volumes,

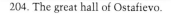

204. The great hall of Ostafievo.

205. Joseph Sontag. Portrait of Prince Peter Vyazemsky. 1821. (Courtesy of the Pushkin Museum, Moscow)

able qualities for a successful career in Russian service at that time. Disgusted with provincial corruption, Prince Andrei resigned his position as governor-general of Penza Province in the reign of Paul, explaining in no uncertain terms to the emperor, "nature has filled my soul with a limitless loathing for crooked paths."[15]

Prince Andrei's iron will had its uses, however. When he fell in love with a married Irish woman (Eugenia O'Reilly) on a trip abroad, he helped her obtain a divorce and then married her. This was the future poet's mother. Eugenia and Andrei brought up their son in Spartan fashion, teaching him to swim by throwing him in the pond one evening. When Prince Andrei died in 1808, Prince Peter, then sixteen, became the ward of Nikolai Karamzin, his older sister's husband.

Nikolai Karamzin, one of the most important literary and intellectual figures of his age, wrote poetry, travel literature, sentimental fiction, literary criticism, and history, influencing his own and subsequent generations in all fields. His elegant language became a model of literary style. The stunning impact of his history, the first truly readable, coherent account of Russia's past, was eloquently summarized by one contemporary: "Now at last I know I have a fatherland." In 1808, the year he became guardian of Prince Peter, Karamzin had been living at Ostafievo for seven years. He remained there until 1816 and later recalled, "Ostafievo is memorable to my heart: there we reveled in the whole delight of life. . . . There the middle if not the best years of my life were passed, devoted to family, work, and feelings of general wellbeing, an oasis amid stormy passions."[16]

Prince Peter described Karamzin's day:

Karamzin arose usually at 9 in the morning, and immediately thereafter walked or rode, no matter what time of year or weather. This lasted an hour. Upon his return from the excursion, he breakfasted with the family, smoked a pipe of Turkish

to which his son added seven thousand and his grandson ten thousand more. Peter Andreevich recalled his bibliophile father spending "the major part of the day sitting at the fireplace. . . . Every day [the library] was enriched by new French literary works. . . . Historical and philosophical works were his favorite reading."[14] Prince Andrei was an eccentric, described by his son as a man of "firm" character who inspired fear rather than love. Others did not scruple to call him rude, haughty, and unbending, undesir-

tobacco and then immediately went into his study and worked until dinner time, that is until 3 or 4 o'clock. . . . While working he took no rest, and his morning belonged exclusively to his *History [of the Russian State]* and was inviolable and untouchable. . . . His wife frequently sat at work or reading in his study, while the children played, and sometimes made noise. Then he would look at them, smiling, say a word and again set to writing. This entire order was strictly observed and inviolable, primarily for hygienic purposes: he took care of his health and looked out for it not just from fear of illness and suffering, but as a tool necessary for uninterrupted and free work.[17]

Karamzin's study on the second floor looked onto the park through a Palladian window. Mikhail Pogodin, later professor of Russian history at Moscow University, recalls its simplicity: bare stuccoed walls painted white, a high pine table standing in front of the window, a simple wooden chair, several boxes with lids, in which were manuscripts, books, notebooks, papers. "There wasn't a single cupboard, armchair, couch, étagère, carpet, or pillow. A few decrepit chairs stood in disarray along the walls."[18]

Only Karamzin's dearest friends dared visit him at Ostafievo. Interruptions from his work, he felt, deprived him of "spiritual food," and guests might find him tiresome, since he thought, spoke, and dreamed only about the topic he was working on. Not only did Ostafievo provide Karamzin with an ideal setting in which to work, but by a stroke of good fortune the manuscript of his *History of the Russian State* at Ostafievo escaped the flames that accompanied Napoleon's march across Russia. (The other copy, in the Kremlin archives, burned in 1812.) The *History* was an instant success and universally acclaimed. Pushkin called it "not only the creation of a great writer but the triumph of an honest man." But as a liberal, Pushkin disapproved of Karamzin's conservatism and may have written

this oft-quoted, biting political epigram: "In his 'History' elegance and simplicity show us, without any bias, the necessity of autocracy and the glories of the knout." Nonetheless, Pushkin and an entire generation of writers and historians read the *History* repeatedly, as much for its literary merits as for its content. Pushkin fittingly dedicated his historical tragedy *Boris Godunov* to the "memory, invaluable for a Russian, of Nikolai Mikhailovich Karamzin."

Peter Andreevich frequently entertained members of his literary group, The Society of Obscure Arzamas Men of Letters, at Ostafievo. "To tell the truth, here I know of nothing cleverer than the Arzamasians," wrote Karamzin; "one could truly live and die among them."[19] The group became famous for its witty verbal sallies against literary enemies. Vyazemsky, nicknamed "Asmodei" (Demon), found this his natural element, and Ostafievo a natural base of operations. More often than not he would write a friend, "In a few days I am off to Ostafievo, and all of Moscow's Arzamas with me."[20] They included Pushkin (fig. 197), a welcome visitor at Ostafievo. In 1827 he composed a short, mock hortatory verse for Peter Andreevich's son Pavel, then ten, who remembered Pushkin's amusing visits in the winter of 1830–31, just after the lifting of the quarantine for the cholera epidemic. Pushkin pranced around the room during evening tea exclaiming, "I'm a burgher, I'm a burgher, just simply a Russian burgher!" and later recited his new poem "My Genealogy" to the family.[21] Theater, poetry, and politics filled the Ostafievo atmosphere. On a visit to Ostafievo in the 1820s, possibly from Khmelita, his uncle's estate where he spent a number of summers, A. S. Griboedov played the female role of Eremeevna in Fonvizin's comedy "The Minor." He also reputedly read Vyazemsky his new play, *Wit Works Woe*, and received a few small suggestions for it.

The Idyll Interrupted

Prior to the war of 1812 few members of Russia's intelligentsia were bothered by the contrast between the country idylls they celebrated in verse and the serfdom of their villagers—as Derzhavin's casual use of the word *slave* in his poem would indicate. Consider, for instance, the actions of the elegiac poet Zhukovsky (1783–1852), both a translator and imitator of Thomas Gray. Zhukovsky (fig. 206) was the illegitimate son of the wealthy landowner Afanasy Bunin. His mother was reputedly a Turkish woman from a harem given to Bunin by a friend; like many illegitimate children of nobles, Zhukovsky received his name from a poor noble who lived nearby. In a later age this background might well have evoked a feeling of kinship with the powerless. Yet Zhukovsky, upon inheriting his father's estate, took on the attitudes of a landowner. A letter Zhukovsky wrote in 1809 to P. I. Golubkov, a school friend who had become chief of police in Tula, is revealing. Zhukovsky asked Golubkov to help him out of a troublesome business by preventing three of his master craftsmen from filing a petition for their freedom. The three men claimed that their serfdom was illegitimate since they were sons of a Polish émigré who had voluntarily become a serf, but Zhukovsky insisted that their petition had no merit and carried the day.[22]

After the war of 1812, in the course of which sensitive participants had come to view the serf soldier as a human being, a younger generation began to view such actions—and indeed the institution of serfdom itself—as unjustifiable and to talk privately about its abolition. One can detect the early phases of the debate over serfdom in "Osuga," where Alexander Bakunin defended serfdom in a manner that his friend Derzhavin a mere decade earlier had found unnecessary. Looking at his "peaceful settlements of industrious villagers" Bakunin exclaimed, "I do not know why our learned men call them slaves!" Bakunin went on to argue that serf benefited as much as master from this equitable system and that it represented the "unchange-

206. Otto Oesterreich. Portrait of V. A. Zhukovsky. 1820.
(Courtesy of the Pushkin Museum, Moscow)

able foundation" of "holy Rus'." Bakunin also talked about the insecurity of hired hands, who had no landowner to protect them.

Among the challengers of Bakunin's patriarchal views were radical young relatives who some six years later would participate in the abortive uprising known as the Decembrist Rebellion. The rebellion on December 14, 1825, was precipitated by two weeks of interregnum, for upon the sudden death of Alexander I, his brother Nicholas had refused to accept the throne until his older brother

303

Constantine (then viceroy of the Kingdom of Poland) publicly renounced his claim. This involved communication between St. Petersburg and Warsaw, a lengthy process in 1825. The climate of indecision prompted the rebel officers of the Northern Society, one branch of the conspiracy, to call out their troops to Senate Square in St. Petersburg to demonstrate in favor of Constantine and a constitutional regime (Constantine being mistakenly viewed as more liberal than Nicholas). The rebellion was quickly put down by loyal troops. After a lengthy inquiry, on July 14 five Decembrists were hanged, and thirty-one were sent into exile for life. This event reverberated throughout Russia, as virtually every noble family discovered a Decembrist in its ranks.

Most of the Decembrists had been members of one of the secret societies devoted to social welfare that had sprung up after the war. Modeled on Masonic lodges and the German patriotic society Tugenbund, these societies were devoted to Russia's moral and spiritual regeneration rather than political change. During the decade that preceded the rebellion, the disaffected, idealistic young had also been congregating at country estates, expounding their ideas (which increased in radicalism as the conservatism of Alexander I became more apparent) in these relatively safe havens. In Smolensk Province Ivan Yakushkin (who married a Sheremetev) invited his friends every summer to Zhukovo. Among them were a number of liberal-minded youths with whom he and his brother (along with his country neighbors the Lykoshin brothers) had studied at Moscow University: Alexander Griboedov, M. A. Fonvizin, N. I. Turgenev, Artamon and Nikita Muraviev, and Peter Chaadaev. Griboedov's letters chronicle the progressive estrangement of this group from their elders. In 1818, returning to Moscow, he wrote a friend, "In Moscow nothing is to my liking. Idleness, luxury, unconnected with the slightest notion of good." By 1825, however, shortly before the debacle of December 14, he was asking A. A. Bestuzhev, "What are you writing? Tell me. All I know is that

you have described Yusupov's orgies with a master's brush; . . . What an old infamous wretch of a courtier!" He told Bestuzhev that he had read the Yusupov tale to "other outstanding men in confidence" and asked that Bestuzhev give Kondraty Ryleev (a poet and leader of the Decembrist Northern Society) a warm embrace for him "in republican style."[23]

Among Varvara Bakunina's cousins were four Muravievs and two Muraviev-Apostols, all of whom became Decembrists. Alexander Muraviev, founder of the secret society, The Union of Welfare (1818–21), was particularly close to the Bakunins. His conversations with Alexander Bakunin at Pryamukhino in the early 1820s were heated. Bakunin, a moderate by nature, defended autocracy, telling Muraviev that his insistence on the necessity of changing Russia's form of government was the product of the imagination of a small circle of youths who had not troubled to weigh the inevitably tragic consequences of even the smallest weakening of the country's ruling power.

Meanwhile at Kamenka, far to the south, Vasily Davydov headed one branch of the Decembrists' Southern Society. In contrast to the constitutionalist Northern Society, the Southern favored a republic for Russia. The meetings of the faithful at Kamenka included Prince S. G. Volkonsky, General Mikhail Orlov, and Alexander and Nicholas Raevsky, sons of Davydov's famous half-brother, General N. N. Raevsky, and good friends of Pushkin. (Their sister Maria, with whom Pushkin was half in love, later married Volkonsky and followed him to Siberia.) General Raevsky and Pushkin, not privy to the conspiracy, enjoyed the "democratic debates" of the early 1820s at Kamenka, which sometimes included Ivan Yakushkin, a charter member of the Northern Society. In December 1825, shortly before the uprising in the south, triggered by the abortive revolt in St. Petersburg, the police, acting on a tip from an English employee of the Kamenka sugar refinery (who had eavesdropped on Davydov and his friends as they swam in the Tyasmin River), arrested Davydov. Of the hundreds of conspirators arrested, he was among the thirty-one condemned to hard labor and exiled for life in Siberia.

This far-flung conspiracy, by scions of the most distinguished families in Russia, stunned, scared, and divided the elite. Many felt their names had been dishonored. When the terrible news of the arrests reached Pryamukhino, Bakunin hastened to burn the incriminating letters, diaries, and drafts of constitutions the Muravievs had left. In Moscow Nadezhda Sheremeteva summoned her steward from Pokrovskoe, told him that her son-in-law, Yakushkin, had hidden secret correspondence under a floorboard and ordered him to burn it immediately.[24]

But for the intelligentsia, the Decembrists were martyrs to the noble cause of freedom and justice. A year after the debacle on Senate Square, his friend Ryleev among the five hanged, Griboedov disconsolately wrote a friend: "Who will respect us bards of true inspiration, in a land where worth is measured in the number of one's decorations and serfs? In our country, in any event, Sheremetev overshadows Homer; he is a pig, but an aristocrat and rich as Croesus. It is painful to be an ardent dreamer in the land of eternal frost."[25] Inevitably, such private views emerged in literature. Chatsky, hero of *Wit Works Woe*, has the liberated views, penetrating gaze, and cynical tongue of this generation. Chatsky's sallies were so true to the Decembrist mentality that the play was suppressed for over a decade. As for Famusov, father of the heroine and a conservative pillar of society, to judge from an essay by Griboedov entitled "The Character of My Uncle," he had a good deal in common with the owner of Khmelita, Alexei Griboedov.

> Here is a character which . . . twenty years ago was dominant . . . a kind of mixture of vices and kindness, external chivalry in mores, while the heart lacked any sort of feeling. . . . Let us explain the whole thing: every one had dishonesty in his soul and lies on his tongue. . . . My uncle belonged to that epoch. He fought like a lion against the Turks under Suvorov, then fawned in the antechambers of all sorts of people in Petersburg, and in retirement lived on scandal. His example is morally instructive.[26]

The Arzamas group at Ostafievo also had Decembrist sympathizers. In contrast to the revered but conservative Karamzin, Peter Vyazemsky and Pushkin were outspoken social liberals, at least in verse. Vyazemsky's politically direct "Indignation" (1820) and "The Russian God" (1828) scathingly portrayed the Russia of mistreated, barefoot serfs and their loutish masters, implicitly attacking serfdom, while similar suspect verse by Pushkin earned him brief periods of exile.

The incongruities of such daring attacks on serfdom from men subsisting on serf labor are highlighted in an episode involving Pushkin and Vyazemsky in the spring of 1826. Pushkin was then living in exile at Mikhailovskoe, his small family estate (figs. 207, 208), his solitude broken only by conversations with his nanny, Arina Rodionovna, and visits to Trigorskoe, the Wulfs' nearby estate (where the poet Yazykov would spend that summer). In early May, Vyazemsky, then in Moscow, was surprised by the arrival of young Olga Kalashnikova, the daughter of the serf steward of Mikhailovskoe, obviously in a pregnant state. She bore the following letter from Pushkin:

> A very sweet and good girl, whom one of your friends carelessly knocked up,[27] bears this letter to you. I am counting on your humanity and friendship. Shelter her in Moscow and give her as much money as she needs—and then send her to Boldino (to my votchina, where they raise cocks, hens, and bears). . . . With fatherly tenderness I also beg you to concern yourself with the future offspring, if it is a boy. I do not want to send him to the Foundlings' Home—wouldn't it be possible for the time

being to place him in some village—perhaps at Ostafievo. My dear, before God I am ashamed about her . . . but it is no longer a question of conscience.[28]

Pushkin's letter, for all the slang and typical humorous asides, reflects a sensitive awareness of having taken advantage of the system and his regret about the consequences. Curiously, however, he did not take the usual steps to ensure his son's status. Pavel was born July 1 at Boldino and registered as the son of a peasant sexton there; his later fate is unknown. Nor did Pushkin apparently respond to Olga's laments at being married off to an elderly drunkard.

Pushkin's great novel in verse, *Eugene Onegin*, tells us much about his generation's attitude toward the countryside, an outlook later generations inherited. Like Karamzin's *History of the Russian State*, *Eugene Onegin* had enormous impact on contemporaries, and its characters and themes continued to influence later writers. Tatyana's honesty and morality, Pushkin implies, derive from her provincial upbringing, just as Eugene's boredom and amorality are engendered by the superficial life of St. Petersburg. Natasha Rostova, of aristocratic lineage yet Moscow-bred and Russian to the core, was the lineal descendant of Tatyana Larina, Pushkin's heroine. Onegin similarly inspired scores of later fictional superfluous men, characters

207. The restored main house at Pushkin's Mikhailovskoe.

208. The restored steward's house at Mikhailovskoe.

without a firm moral core or a purpose to their lives, such as Lermontov's Pechorin, a questionable hero of his time, or Turgenev's Rudin (in the novel of the same title), an eloquent talker unable to commit himself to action.

By the time of Pushkin's untimely death in a duel in 1837, it was becoming increasingly difficult to have a foot in the two worlds of official and intellectual Russia, as had Derzhavin, government official and court poet, or Zhukovsky, poet and tutor of a future tsar. The tragic example of the idealistic Decembrists cast a long shadow. Like the Pugachev revolt and the war of 1812, the Decembrist rebellion became part of the nobility's folklore, reinforcing conservatism in some but also inspiring the next generation of radical nobles. The rebellion, the hanging of the ringleaders, and the exile of others to Siberia made St. Petersburg increasingly synonymous with official Russia, home to a pomp and sycophancy that personified the dead hand of autocracy. Moscow, the city of intellect and culture, defiantly raised its standard ever higher. In Moscow salons and on suburban estates the Russian intelligentsia battled first over poetry and philosophy, then over the "accursed questions" of the day: the nature of Russia's present condition, its proper direction, and its ultimate destiny.

Slavophiles, Westerners, and the World of Love at Pryamukhino

With the exceptions of Sergei Aksakov and Peter Vyazemsky (who outlived everyone else of his generation), the main figures of the 1830s and 1840s were a new generation of intellectuals and writers. Because of their sharply contrasting views they became known as Slavophiles and Westerners in the mighty debate that raged over the future of Russia during the remarkable decade of the 1840s. Aside from Belinsky (of plebeian origins), sons of landowners dominated the intellectual circles of this period. All had intimate ties to country life; yet their reactions to this life varied enormously. Nikolai Stankevich, whose humane idealism attracted everyone with whom he had contact, was raised at Uderevka, the son of a wealthy, liberal Voronezh landowner. Stankevich's father sent serfs to school along with his son, who inherited his liberalism. Bakunin's upbringing in the deliberately isolated, smotheringly patriarchal idyll of Pryamukhino, by contrast, very likely inspired rebellion. Alexander Herzen, the illegitimate son of a wealthy aristocrat, derived his happiest childhood memories from summers spent on the family estate Vasilievskoe. Yet like the anarchist Prince Kropotkin, Herzen traced his first radical notions to the empathy he felt with his father's tyrannized serfs. His closest friend, Nikolai Ogarev (who at the age of fifteen stood with Herzen on Sparrow Hills, outside Moscow, and swore to remain faithful to the memory of the Decembrists), was likewise the son of a wealthy landowner. Ogarev's lonely, sickly youth was passed in the isolated atmosphere of his father's house. He resented his father's insistence on formality and subservience to power, whereas he remembered with gratitude the devoted attention of his nanny and male nurse. Ogarev would be the only member of the intelligentsia to liberate the serfs on one of his three estates.[29]

In some respects the writer Fyodor Dostoevsky, though the son of a smallholder, had had country experiences similar to those of his wealthier peers. At Darovoe his father played the role of stern master, while Fyodor was entrusted to a devoted serf nanny. He played with the village children, roamed the countryside, and forty years later wrote, "That small and inconspicuous spot . . . left a deep and strong impression upon me for my whole life. . . .

There everything to me was full of dearest memories."[30] Dostoevsky never forgot the kindness of his father's oppressed peasants toward him. Easily recognizable figures from Darovoe such as the female village idiot (re-created as Lizaveta Smerdyakova) filled his later novels, as did nearby locales (the village of Cheremoshnya in *The Brothers Karamazov*). Dostoevsky's empathy with the peasants because of his father's harsh treatment of them, and his admiration of their humane, moral qualities, may have sown the seeds of both his early liberalism and his later devotion to Orthodoxy and pan-Slavism.[31]

Turgenev's liberal conscience was undoubtedly awakened as a boy by his tyrannical mother's behavior at Spasskoe-Lutovinovo. Another liberal from Orel, Timofei Granovsky, later professor of world history at Moscow University, grew up playing with serf children on Pogorelets, his father's small estate not far from Orel. Yet rural Russia bred Slavophiles as well. Ivan and Peter Kireevsky were also Orel natives, raised on the far more substantial estate of Dolbino. After they lost their father to disease and their mother remarried, the family wintered in Moscow but returned to Dolbino annually. Alexei Khomyakov's father was a substantial Smolensk landowner with about three thousand serfs. The sons of the less affluent Sergei Aksakov were both born on remote family estates, Constantine at Aksakovo, in Orenburg Province, Ivan at Nadezhino-Kuroedovo, in Ufa Province.

In the 1830s this varied group began to coalesce in student circles headed by Stankevich in Moscow and Herzen in St. Petersburg. Stankevich's luminous personality united individuals who would later find themselves on opposite sides in the great debates of the 1840s, among them Bakunin, the Kireevskys and Aksakovs, Vissarion Belinsky and Vasily Botkin (the only non-nobles of the group), Turgenev, and Granovsky. The enchanted world of Pryamukhino took on new life when Bakunin and his friends discovered the German philosopher Johann Fichte; the object of their existence became the search for harmony, the Absolute, and love so remote and idealized as to be unattainable.

One by one Bakunin's friends traveled to Pryamukhino (fig. 209) and fell in love with his four sisters. Stankevich, the first, wrote a friend, "You will gradually be enthralled by these women, who are like beautiful creations of the gods, you will see, you will listen, you will want to hold them and forever behold these angelic faces. . . . The Bakunin family is an ideal family. We must go to Pryamukhino to be reformed."[32] Stankevich exchanged love letters with Lyubinka, the oldest of the sisters; then he formally proposed. Shortly thereafter, however, overcome by his inability to sustain the lofty beginnings of this relationship, he began to question whether this was, indeed, the ideal, absolute love. The situation was further complicated when his doctor urged him to go abroad for his health (already threatened by consumption). Lyubinka, feeling betrayed, languished and died shortly thereafter.

The next to be charmed was Vissarion Belinsky. At Pryamukhino, he wrote, "My surroundings breathed harmony and blessedness [which] penetrated my soul. I saw my images of woman brought to life." The three months he stayed at Pryamukhino were filled with debates in Bakunin's smoke-filled rooms, arguments about poetry, philosophy, God, and eternity that continued on walks along the banks of the Osuga or in the dining room ("What? We haven't even resolved the question of the existence of God, and you're calling us to dinner!"). Belinsky fell in love with Alexandra, though it was Tatyana who hung on his impassioned words. Morbidly absorbed with his own feelings and overcome by self-doubt, he slipped away from Pryamukhino without resolving his feelings for Alexandra. He later confessed that "even as a boy, without having yet felt the need for love, I had already created for myself an ideal of love and loved according to the instructions of this ideal. . . . Idealism is my chronic disease, more deeply rooted in my organism than hemorrhoids."[33]

Bakunin hovered over these relationships between his male soul mates and his sisters, jealously probing, examining, and talking them out of existence. When Varvara married a neighboring landowner, Bakunin declared him intellectually unworthy and demanded that she leave her husband. At first Varvara refused to comply. Later, however, she went abroad, ran into the consumptive Stankevich in Rome, realized that she had always loved him,

209. The estate church at the Bakunins' Pryamukhino, designed by Nikolai Lvov, pictured on the cover of *Nashe Nasledie*. (Courtesy of *Nashe Nasledie*)

and held him in her arms as he died. Meanwhile, Alexandra fell in love with Vasily Botkin and managed to overcome her father's strenuous objections to her marrying a merchant. This was the only Pryamukhino romance to have a happy ending.

The last romance was that of Tatyana and Ivan Turgenev. "Welcome him as a friend and brother," Mikhail wrote his sisters from Berlin (where he was studying). Arriving at Pryamuhkino, the young writer felt the brotherly love he was supposed to for this young woman three years his senior; she adored and idolized him. "You are holy, you are miraculous, you are chosen by God. On your forehead I see the imprint of His greatness, His glory," she wrote Turgenev. Tatyana might have been speaking for all of her sisters when she later wrote her brother Pavel: "His words, his glances, that seeming love aroused my soul, and I, without thinking, without reasoning, gave in to that feeling. Only when it had passed did I understand that there was no true love in it, that all this was nothing more than the fantasy of an overheated imagination . . . for which I, of course, paid with tears and my health."[34]

In Berlin, Bakunin, like others of this generation, abandoned Fichte and love for Hegel and politics. With his conversion the second Pryamukhino idyll, a world of overheated debate and undermined romance, drew to a close. By the late 1830s Russia's intellectuals were integrating their childhood experiences of rural Russia with the western philosophies they had studied; they were becoming immersed in what they termed the "accursed questions": the nature of Russia's present condition, its proper direction, and its ultimate destiny.

In 1836 Peter Chaadaev had thrown down the gauntlet by publicly proclaiming that Russia, cut off from the dynamic culture of the Catholic West, had no past, therefore no present, and possibly no future. (For this lèse-majesté Nicholas I branded Chaadaev a madman and sentenced him to house arrest under the care of a doctor.) Peter the Great, Russia's heroic Tsar Transformer, stood at the center of the controversy. The debaters had violently opposed views of Peter, each of which, in retrospect, we can see contained a measure of truth. The Slavophiles blamed Peter's forcible westernization of the elite and his bureaucratization of the state for introducing a cultural rift into the Orthodox Russian polity. They called for a return to an idyllic world of cooperation between tsar and people, lord and serf, a world of consensus rather than law. Slavophiles like Constantine and Ivan Aksakov came to believe in the patriarchal world of their youth re-created in their father's autobiographical fiction. The Westerners, by contrast, hailed Peter's determined effort to force Russia out of isolation but saw the status-quo policies of Nicholas I as the degenerate offspring of Petrine dynamism. They called for the completion of his program through emancipation of the serfs and political modernization. Herzen and Ogarev, having moved from Hegel to the utopian socialists, began to view the peasant village structure, with its communal landholding and primitive self-government by village council, as proof of the Russian peasant's innate socialistic tendencies.

Herzen summed up the consensus of Westerners and Slavophiles in the early 1840s that they were friendly enemies. The Slavophiles' religiously based romantic nationalism, which insisted on the uniqueness of Holy Russia and on the peasant's innate communalism (as opposed to western individualism) derived from European philosophical sources. So did the Westerners' equally ardent conviction that Russia must travel the path taken by Europe. Initially the two camps were more united by joint antipathy for Russia's current state than divided by their opposed solutions. "We had the same love, but not the same way of loving—and like Janus or the two-headed eagle we looked in different directions, though the heart within us was but one," Herzen wrote upon the death of his close friend but intellectual adversary Constantine Aksakov.[35] The Moscow intelligentsia, whatever their differences, formed a select knighthood sworn to a moral, principled fight with a system they branded hypocritical, corrupt, and dehumanizing.

The Idyll and Idols Shattered

Life at the Aksakovs' Abramtsevo (fig. 210), an estate west of Moscow near the St. Sergius-Trinity Monastery, exemplified this consensus, though it was also party to its unavoidable breakdown. Abramtsevo, the last ideal world of the pre-emancipation period, belonged, appropriately, to a Slavophile. When Sergei Aksakov bought it in 1843, he described it to his son Ivan as "a beautiful, peaceful, unified little corner, where everything we need is gathered together." The brilliant descriptions of the Russian countryside in *A Family Chronicle*, written at Abramtsevo, reflect Aksakov's abiding passion for nature, acquired during his childhood in Ufa Province and rekindled in the picturesque rural surroundings of Abramtsevo. Aksakov wandered through the woods in search of mushrooms, carefully captured birds for the cage that stood on the dining room table, and fished in the nearby Vora River. A passionate angler, Aksakov wrote a paean (disguised as a treatise on fishing) to the exalted state the Russian coun-

210. The park facade of Abramtsevo.

tryside inspired in him. Autumn was his favorite season. "Everything has turned yellow, the leaves are gently falling, the water has changed its color, the autumn bird has flown to its home and roosted. . . . I'll run this minute to the river, set up my fishing rods, smoke a cigar and sit—where I sit and what I'll begin to think about or feel, I don't know, but I feel a thirst for this moral state," he wrote a friend.[36]

Aksakov's two sons, noted Slavophiles, inherited both their father's patriarchal attitudes and his love of nature and the countryside, though they expressed it in different ways. Constantine, the closest to his father, took to dressing in what he fancied was Russian costume, an eccentricity both his opponents and friends deplored. Ivan, collector of Russian folklore, dressed conventionally but shared his brother's conviction that country life brought one close to the people.

> In a Russian field it is difficult to sing anything except a Russian song: the same simplicity, the same endlessness and expanse, the same peacefulness and the same quietly variegated uniformity. . . . And amidst all of this, perched on a sawhorse, in only a shirt, tsar and lord of all of this, sits the Russian peasant; his soul freely admits this nature into itself.[37]

At Abramtsevo the rhythm of life was simple and patriarchal, in some respects replicating Aksakov's childhood at Novoe Aksakovo, in Ufa Province. It also bore marked resemblance to Derzhavin's life at Zvanka. Both writers had re-created the idyll of childhoods on estates in remote Ufa Province (Derzhavino, Derzhavin's family estate, was only about sixty-five miles from Aksakovo). In the morning the Abramtsevo inhabitants pursued their own occupations; dinner was served to all in the dining room; in the evening everyone gathered in the living room for literary readings, chess, or a family play. From this splendid isolation Aksakov kept abreast with the latest

literature and political currents, reading "Notes of the Fatherland," "Messenger of Europe," and other journals. In the evening Aksakov's daughters took turns reading parts of Aksakov's *Family Chronicle* or *Notes of an Angler* or from works by Pushkin, Gogol (an intimate family friend), and Lermontov.

Yet at Abramtsevo, as at Pryamukhino, idyllic contemplation of nature sometimes gave way to highly charged discussions. The historian Pogodin recalls Aksakov's study being filled with clouds of blue smoke and the air reverberating with ongoing literary debates. Abramtsevo attracted a ceaseless flow of guests, among them the poet F. I. Tyutchev (who later married Sergei's daughter), Evgeny Baratynsky (from nearby Muranovo), Zhukovsky, Turgenev, Gogol, and the actor Shchepkin.

The misinterpretation of the work of Nikolai Gogol (fig. 211), a brilliant writer but tormented man, by Slavophiles and Westerners alike highlights the relations between the friendly enemies of the 1840s. By 1842, when *Dead Souls* was published, Gogol was already plagued by spiritual torments. He intended *Dead Souls*, subtitled *A Poem*, to be the first of a three-part epic of sin and resurrection modeled on Dante's *The Divine Comedy*. In the only part Gogol completed, his hero Chichikov races around the Russian provinces buying up dead souls from delighted landowners. A landowner was obliged to pay a tax for every soul registered as his on the tax rolls during the decade from one census to the next, whether or not the peasant was still alive. Thus he would save money by selling dead souls still on the books. Normally, of course, no one would buy them, but Chichikov plans to use the deeds of sale to establish fraudulent credentials as a landowner of substance. He can then take out a large mortgage on his supposed "living wealth." Inevitably the scheme is uncovered and Chichikov must flee. Gogol completed a second part of his epic but burned it shortly before his death; the third, in which Chichikov's own soul presumably is saved, was never written.

211. E. A. Dmitriev-Mamonov. Portrait of Nikolai Gogol. Lithograph. 1852. (Courtesy of the Pushkin Museum, Moscow)

Upon reading *Dead Souls* the Westerners mistakenly hailed it as a realistic, masterfully biting, satirical attack on landowning Russia. Gogol, to be sure, presents readers with a gallery of rogues, and the factual details he supplies about their attire, houses, habits, and food give it an aura of realism. But Gogol intended his portrait of the world into which Chichikov plunges to be an intentionally exaggerated, comic inferno, the beginning of a moral epic, not realistic social commentary. The work abounds with philosophical digressions, while the lyrical descriptions of the countryside through which Chichikov's troika flies might have been written by Aksakov himself. Small wonder, then, that the Slavophiles also hailed Gogol as a natural ally.

The battle to define Gogol's work as a triumph for one side or the other filled the press and the salons. Constantine Aksakov and Belinsky were the chief rivals, each proclaiming *Dead Souls* a masterpiece validating his point of view. But in 1847, when Gogol published his *Selected Passages from Correspondence with Friends,* the "friendly enemies" were forced to unite in condemnation. Gogol had come to believe that both the Russian state and patriarchal Russia were immutable and foreordained by God, part of the unity and communality of Holy Russia. And—much as the Orthodox icon painter is considered a medium whose work is a channel for God's wishes—Gogol now insisted that the artist is called and directed by God, not an independent creative individual. In *Passages,* a religious treatise more than anything else, Gogol insisted on the sanctity of the present Russian state and the religiously ordained power of lord over serf. Awed by the perfection of the status quo, he expressed doubt that education for serfs was advisable, though he urged landowners to be kind to their "living wealth." His former arch-defender Aksakov, now bitterly offended, accused him of perverting the Gospel and bowing to the establishment. An equally disappointed Belinsky publicly castigated Gogol for abandoning his artistic calling for that of "apostle of the knout."

The Slavophiles' appealing view of the Russian peasant as the embodiment of a particular and uniquely Russian virtue outlived the Westerners' protests, linking the men of the 1840s to subsequent generations. This view of the peasant reemerged first in the Populists' theories of the 1860s and 1870s and later in Tolstoy's utopian vision of a peace-loving, egalitarian agricultural polity. By the end of the 1840s, however, whatever one thought of the peasants' inner world, most considered their outward bondage Russia's moral disgrace. In 1847 the first of a series of stories of Russian country life by Turgenev appeared (which were later published together as *A Sportsman's Notebook*). The sketches, as autobiographical as Aksakov's *Family Chronicle*, portray the people and landscape near Turgenev's Spasskoe-Lutovinovo (fig. 212). Often called the Russian *Uncle Tom's Cabin*, the *Notebook* galvanized Russian popular opinion in favor of emancipation. The stories purport to be the reflections of the hunter-narrator as he roams the countryside with his huntsman, Yermolai, and their dogs. But hunting takes second place to stories of local peasants and nobles and to lyrical celebrations of the Russian countryside that rival Aksakov's (and were the

basis for their friendship). Few Russians either at the time or subsequently thought these stories fictional, a fact confirmed by the comment of a Spasskoe native in the 1880s:

My grandmother and mother told me that practically all the people mentioned in *A Sportsman's Notebook* were not imaginary, but modeled on real people. . . . Yermolai and even his [hound] Valetka existed, and, of course, Dianka, Turgenev's dog; so did Biryuk, whom his peasants murdered in the woods, and Yashka Turchenok, the son of a captive Turkish woman. I even personally knew one of the Turgenev heroes, namely, Anton Suchok, whose name was changed from Kuzma by Mistress Varvara Petrovna [Turgenev's mother].

212. The estate church at the entrance to Spasskoe-Lutovinovo, Orel Province.

Bezhin meadow, the Parakhinsk grove, Varnavitsy, the Kobyky heights and so forth—all these places had the same names.[38]

Turgenev's dispassionate tone (in contrast to Harriet Beecher Stowe's) if anything increases the harrowing effect of the world he describes, a world of misery, thwarted dreams, tyranny, and degradation. He presents "model" landowners who punish serfs "for their own good," declaring, "They must be treated like children." One tyrannical noble prevents his wife's personal maid from marrying the footman she loves, then shaves her head, dresses her in sackcloth, and sends her to the countryside for her "ingratitude" toward his wife, an "angel incarnate." In "Lgov" we meet the sixty-year-old serf Suchok, who was page, postilion, gardener, whipper-in, and cobbler for his first master, then for his second owner (Turgenev's mother, who called him Anton rather than Kuzma, his real name) cook, coffee server, and actor in the estate theater. "They would take me and dress me up; then I would walk, all dressed up, or stand, or sit, as the case might be. They'd tell me what to say—and I'd say it. Once I played the part of a blind man. . . . They put a pea under each of my eyelids. . . . Yes, that's how it was." Subsequently he became a coachman and finally a fisherman. Suchok accepts this bewildering series of roles with resignation and humility.

Turgenev's countryside also abounds with nobles fallen on hard times. Some play the fool for wealthier patrons. Another, known as a "dangerous, crazy, proud fellow" throughout his district, "came of an old family that had once been wealthy. His ancestors had lived sumptuously, after the manner of the steppes; that is to say, they received all and sundry, fed them to surfeit, allowed visiting coachmen a quarter of oats for each troika, kept musicians, singers, buffoons and hounds, treated their people to wine and home-brewed beer on feast days, drove away in the winter to Moscow in heavy traveling coaches drawn by their own horses, and now and then sat for months on end

without a farthing and lived on home-grown poultry." This man's father lost the family fortune indulging himself in crazy schemes: "He had the idea of building a church, on his own of course, and without the help of an architect. He burned up a whole forest in baking the bricks, he laid the foundations . . . fit for a cathedral in a provincial capital! He built the walls, and started putting on the dome: the dome collapsed. He started again. . . . A third time the dome collapsed. . . . He pondered [that] . . . there must be an evil spell on it . . . so suddenly he ordered that all the old women in the village were to be whipped . . . but all the same the dome never went up."[39] This same master "in the interests of orderliness and Cost Accounting" had numbers sewn on his serfs' collars, which they had to cry out upon meeting him. In other stories Turgenev mocks the social pretensions of provincial nobles and introduces us to rural superfluous men.

The stories that had greatest impact, however, stressed the peasant's humanity, individuality, and long-suffering nature. Turgenev's character sketches of Khor, a "positive, practical fellow," Kalinich, the "idealist, romantic, enthusiast, dreamer," the superstitious lads of "Bezhin Meadow," and the heartrendingly stoical cripple in "A Living Relic" made his contemporaries see serfs as people. The last story, probably autobiographical, concerns Lukerya, formerly "the greatest beauty of all our household —tall, plump, pink and white—full of laugher and dancing and song . . . courted by all our young swains, for whom I too had sighed in secret." Now a petrified, shriveled, crippled mummy, Lukerya has been relegated to spending the winter in the shed for Spasskoe's beehives, and Lukerya herself insists that "it isn't possible to keep a cripple in the manor house."

Turgenev's panoramic approach to the countryside combined Aksakov's acute sensitivity to nature with a Gogolian appreciation of nuance, human identity, and the ridiculous. In so doing, the *Notebook* bridged the gap between the Slavophiles' myopic devotion to rural Russia and peasant virtue and the radical Westerners' harsh critique of Russia's social structure. His unique and memorable characters, peasant and noble, combined to convey the message that serfdom as a system was equally harmful to oppressor and oppressed. During the reign of Nicholas I another important group of intellectuals, liberal-minded like Turgenev but less visible than he or other writers, had come to the same conclusion. The "enlightened bureaucrats" and their friends—progressives in civil service positions, such as Dmitry Miliutin and his brothers, or Boris Chicherin, professor of law—would emerge as statesmen and reformers in the next reign. Like Russia's liberal artists, their views of Russia's needs had been shaped by the estate worlds they had known in childhood.

The Crimean War, which broke out two years after Turgenev's last sketch appeared, aroused widespread patriotism, anger, and despair. Nicholas's troops were magnificent on parade but unprepared for battle. The recruits were serfs; for want of railroads they had to march thousands of miles on scant provisions, to confront an enemy far better equipped and trained than they. Russian defeats in this war, which mercilessly revealed the nakedness of the old system, made the end of serfdom inevitable. Now even Vera Aksakova, who like her brothers had been under the spell of her father's vision of Russia's immutable order, called for change. In the middle of the war Vera confided to her diary: "Our position is totally desperate: not external but internal enemies threaten us—our government, acting hostile toward the people. . . . It is now clear that until the people receive eyes and ears to understand what is being done to it and around it, Russia cannot expect any resurrection; ears and eyes will open only when it is liberated from the slavery that paralyzes its ability, its blood, and its fortune."[40] The old order that had made possible the ideal worlds of Zvanka, Pryamukhino, Ostafievo, and Abramtsevo was on the eve of transformation. All that would remain were memories of the charm, the idealism of these worlds, perhaps best expressed almost fifty years later by Pavel Bakunin, Mikhail's brother. Writing a cousin from Pryamukhino, where he was going through old family letters, he mused:

> It's strange to hear the past in these distant voices, and to reconcile it with the great changes that have since occurred. . . . It is as though I hear the echo of distant music, a kind of sweet hallucination, a kind of elevated and naive folly, a ferment beneath serfdom's soil. You read, and you literally hear the chorus "Freischutz" being played by the hands of diffident girls; Michel, with the zeal of a propagandizer, declaiming about harmony, about the Absolute, God, . . . with the ardor of a barbarian in front of whom all the mysteries of European life had appeared. . . .
>
> Altogether this is the type of hallucination the spring thaw brings on like a confusing fog. . . . At night on all sides the brooks gurgle, deep and noisy, and the cries of cranes trouble the soul.[41]

Epilogue

A WREATH FOR THE ESTATE

I passionately love anything that is called an estate in Russia.

This word has still not lost its poetic sound.—**Anton Chekhov**

Since 1861 the country estate has survived almost as much because of its hold on the Russian imagination as for any other reason. The story I have presented in this volume is of a phenomenon that, though short-lived, was the crucible of Russian high culture. The estate was the physical and social setting for a cultural life of extraordinary scope and resonance. Russian culture is indebted to estate life not only for the luxurious appointments of its Palladian mansions fashioned by serf artists and for the beginnings of a rich theatrical tradition. In addition, throughout the imperial period, the visions of estate life and its real rhythms, sights, and sounds both provoked and provided material for such diverse cultural phenomena as romantic poetry, Decembrist plans for reform, the debates of Slavophiles and Westerners, and much of Russia's great art, literature, and music.

My present story ends with the emancipation of Russia's serfs, a momentous event that, inevitably, transformed reality. A full account of its aftermath deserves another volume. Yet my narrative would be incomplete without a brief sketch of the impact of the emancipation on estate life and the subsequent fate of the estate—a tale mostly of decline and destruction, but also of reinvention and resurrection (fig. 213).

213. The listing gates of Staro-Nikolskoe. Beyond them lie the crumbling remains of the estate that once delighted generations of Musin-Pushkins and Bibikovs. (Author)

The Emancipation Proclamation of February 19, 1861, fundamentally altered the age-old compact between noble and tsar, and the relationship between lord and peasant, thereby dooming estate culture as it had existed for over a century. As in the American South, Russia's landed elite was divided between "planters" and "abolitionists." Most landowners understood both the moral necessity of emancipation and the social chaos that might ensue if their villagers were merely emancipated and not also given land to support their families. But many, already in dire economic straits, resisted giving up more land than they had to, resorting to ploys such as the hasty transfer of village serfs to their household staff to lower the number of serfs entitled to land. The emancipation ruined struggling landowners, though historians still debate the scope of its devastating effect on the nobility as a whole.[1]

Most memoirists assure us that their families welcomed the changes, one even claiming that the emancipation "brought us closer to the peasants."[2] A pious noblewoman writing in her diary on February 19 called it a "great day, which will be remembered from generation to generation. . . . A centuries-old sin weighing on the nobility's conscience has been absolved, and our terrible responsibility before God lifted from us."[3] But some never adjusted to the new world. D. N. Filosofov, for example, owner of Bogdanovskoe, had maintained a serf harem that had traveled with him everywhere he went. In the 1860s, when his steward reported that some of his former girls planned to marry, Filosofov apoplectically shouted, "I forbid it!" Another prominent aristocrat never allowed the word *emancipation* to be spoken in his presence and eccentrically affected no knowledge of it.

In the decades that followed, landowners continued to react in a multitude of ways. Some ignored reality, others denied it. Some accommodated gracefully, others entirely reinvented estate life in idealized form. To the very end of the old regime Russia's courtiers migrated in the summers to their opulent estates. It would be easy, in retrospect,

214. V. M. Maximov. *It's All in the Past.* 1889.
(Courtesy of the Tretiakov Gallery, Moscow)

boldly to label this an era of aristocratic decline and delusion, but that would be an oversimplification. Forces of renewal and regeneration were also active, and only the superbly prescient could have anticipated in full the terrible finale of 1917.

By 1861 the era of photography had arrived, providing a new form of documentation. The evidence is contradictory. Some photographs show a surprising vitality to a way of life that by the turn of the century seemed an illusion, a "hallucination," as Pavel Bakunin put it, an already mythopoetic construction destined, as it turned out, to be swept entirely away by war and revolution. Other photographs reveal a life more clearly in disarray and decay. In the final half-century of imperial Russia, painters and writers were especially sensitive to the illusory quality of the estate and captured it even better than the camera (fig. 214). Yet these prophets of doom, among them Anton

Chekhov, son of a serf, were equally captivated by the idea of being estate owners. When Chekhov bought the run-down property Melikhovo (fig. 215), he celebrated by signing an ecstatic letter to his brother "Pomeshchik [Landowner] Chekhov."[4]

The Long Good-bye

It could, and perhaps should, be argued that estate culture retained its resonance (and appealed to self-made men like Chekhov) largely because it had for so long been the symbol of aristocratic power and privilege. Around Moscow the moneyed merchant class snapped up virtually all estates of one hundred or fewer former souls from noble owners who, as a marginal group even before the emancipation, were destroyed by the loss of their free labor. Old aristocrats coexisted with new owners, albeit in visibly decaying circumstances. When S. D. Sheremetev called on the aged owner of Rai-Semenovskoe in the late 1880s, he found the park unrecognizable and the famous springs invisible. Yet inside the manor house life was lived as it had been fifty years earlier. Sheremetev was treated to an "endless dinner" of family recipes served on platters with the Nashchokin crest, accompanied by fine old wines from the cellar served in equally splendid crystal. At the end his hostess served him the famous homemade cordial that her father, Peter Nashchokin, had always offered his guests. She then disclosed that his habit of entertaining hundreds had wiped out their fortune; the estate was worth one hundred thousand rubles but encumbered by an equal amount of debt.[5]

Numerous historic estates were in shambles by the end of the century, but a few were being rescued and restored. In the 1890s Count Peter Heiden, driving from Moscow to Glubokoe, his estate in Pskov Province, had spotted the crumbling mansion at Khmelita and bought it as a dowry for his daughter Varvara, who was soon to marry Vladimir Volkov-Muromtsov. The new owners found grain drying in the ballroom and sprouting in the cracks of the

parquet floor. One wing and both pavilions had disappeared, the other wing was badly damaged, and the park was in disarray. Within a decade the young couple had restored the fifty-eight-room mansion and wing, the twelve-room pavilion, and Khmelita's elegant grounds, and Vladimir had been elected marshal of the nobility for Vyazma district, an office he would hold in 1917.

Life at Khmelita in the prewar decades mirrored estate life for the still-prosperous members of Russia's aristocratic elite (fig. 216). It was an existence that would end both in Russia and throughout Europe with the Great War. Six children grew up at Khmelita (fig. 217) surrounded by family retainers (many of them former serfs) and tended by the usual nannies, governesses, and tutors. In summer they played in the haystacks that Russia's legendary mowers created; in winter the servants built an icy toboggan run for them from Khmelita's upper story down to the pond. There were long summer interludes at their grand-

215. The small estate house at Melikhovo, the estate near the town of Serphukhov, which Chekhov purchased in 1892.

216. Vladimir and Varvara Volkov-Muromtsov at Khmelita. 1912. (Courtesy of Nicholas Volkov-Muromtsov)

parents' Glubokoe, not far from Pushkin's Mikhailovskoe. Sunny afternoons there meant excursions in ancient carriages to the fanciful, ruined Grecian temples some ancestor had erected on the shores of Lake Glubokoe, and once a summer a traveling puppet show delighted young and old, parading lifelike figures of Salome, Herod, and Pontius Pilate across a miniature stage. Sergei Obolensky, a young man in the prewar period, recalls a similarly idyllic life on their estate Krasnaya Gorka, in Nizhni Novgorod Province, where he and his father divided their time between local affairs, agriculture, and hunting.[6] Far to the south, Lev Davydov's skillful management of the sugar factory and grain production at Kamenka allowed him to enlarge the estate from fifty-four hundred to about thirty-two thousand acres, thereby reassembling a portion of Potemkin's once-vast holdings.

If these estates were a late-imperial variant of aristocratic patriarchy, others contributed to the ongoing evolution of Russian high culture. Krechetnikov's Mikhailovskoe (fig. 218), restored and enlarged, had become the family seat of Sergei Dmitrievich Sheremetev (fig. 219), grandson of Nikolai and Praskovya (and one of the wealthiest landowners in Russia). Sheremetev, a born historian, was deeply committed to the goal of gathering and publishing the records of the past tucked away on his family's estates. Married to a Vyazemsky, he acquired historic Ostafievo and began publishing its archives as well as excerpts from his family's records.[7] A photograph from 1911

321

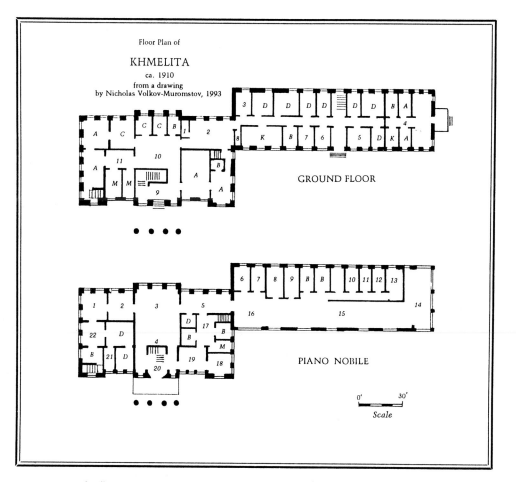

217. The floor plan of Khmelita in the early twentieth century. (Author's collection)

Ground Floor

1. Larder
2. Servants' hall
3. Pump room
4. Separate flat for long-term
   visitors
   (2 bedrooms, drawing room,
   kitchen, bath and WC)
5. Housekeeper's room
6. Laundry
7. Cook's room
8. Lamp room
9. Entrance hall

10. Vaulted hall
11. Cupboard room
    A. Guest room
    B. Bath and WC
    C. Teacher's room
    D. Servant's room
    K. Kitchen
    M. Room for lady's maid

Piano Nobile

1. Drawing room
2. Father's study
3. Ballroom

4. Minstrel gallery
5. Formal dining room
6. Tutor's room
7. Patrick's room
8. Classroom
9. Playroom
10. Alexandra's room
11. Nicholas's room
12. Room of Marina and
    nursemaid
13. Room of Mrs. Tidswell
    (governess)

14. Billiard room
15. Picture gallery
16. Library
17. Scullery
18. Nursery
19. Blue (family) dining room
20. Upper hallway
21. Cupboard room
22. Parents' bedroom
    B. Bath and WC
    D. Dressing room

218. The manor house at Mikhailovskoe, bought by S. D. Sheremetev in 1870. The estate is now a sanatorium.

shows a group assembled there for the unveiling of the granite monument Sheremetev erected on the centennial of Karamzin's *History of the Russian State.* One sees generations of Sheremetevs, local officials, servants, and—in the back rows—the local peasantry, agape at the goings-on of the swells on this historic day.

Two other cultural figures of this epoch assigned the estate a different yet related historical mission. Savva Mamontov, at Abramtsevo, and Tolstoy, at Yasnaya Polyana, committed their energies to the age-old purpose of bridging the gulf between elite and peasant culture, but in radically differing fashions. Mamontov, who was thrilled by his purchase of historic Abramtsevo from Sergei Aksakov's heirs in 1871, epitomizes the dichotomies of the era. A man who had made his fortune in railroads, the symbol of Russia's impending industrialization, he used his money largely to prevent the disappearance of old Russian culture, a heritage that, one artist claimed, was being swept away by "the currents of modern life. . . . Only in a few places, deep in the most remote areas, are its last feeble sparks still smoldering."[8] Mamontov's remedy—one of the antiurban populist currents historians often overlook —was to create a school for folk art at Abramtsevo that would teach peasants how to produce salable products, thus luring them away from the factory. He enlisted an assortment of friends, among them Russia's leading contemporary artists: I. E. Repin, V. D. Polenov (themselves landowners), V. M. Vasnetsov, and M. A. Vrubel. They de-

219. Count S. D. Sheremetev with his eldest grandson and namesake in Georgian costume. (Courtesy of Kyra Cheremeteff)

"to raise [peasant] children up out of the commonplace tenor of daily life into the realm of heroism and beauty."[9] These same children were studying at Abramtsevo's school and learning folk-art techniques in its workshops, while their parents were seasonally employed to carve items sold in Moscow. Ironically, some of these Russian folk-art items, like those being simultaneously produced at Princess M. K. Tenisheva's Talashkino, near Smolensk, were in fact of foreign origin. The most familiar Russian item in the western world today, the *matryoshka,* or nest of dolls, dates from this period and was adapted from a Japanese model.

Meanwhile, at Yasnaya Polyana Leo Tolstoy (fig. 224) had embarked on a different type of crusade: to save the soul rather than the body of national culture. Few figures of this period are as contradictory as Tolstoy, the aristocrat turned peasant, the renowned writer of fiction turned religious prophet. From an early age Tolstoy was morbidly obsessed by the vices of his own class. Like his peers he served in the military, kept a serf mistress, and was a passionate hunter. But as a young man in the 1850s Tolstoy had already set himself apart by learning to plow and harvest and by founding and teaching in a peasant school at Yasnaya Polyana. One day, a former student recalled, Tolstoy told his students that his ambition was to live like a peasant, to marry one, and to become a farmer. "We were all silent. Each of us tried to discover whether [he] was serious or joking. As if one could turn a nobleman into a *muzhik* [peasant]!"[10]

In his fiction Tolstoy drew heavily on his aristocratic antecedents. For *War and Peace* he relied as much on family history as on painstaking research. His mother's ancestors, a Volkonsky field marshal and his son, a hero of 1812, were models for old Prince Bolkonsky and Andrei. Sukhanovo (see fig. 35), the Volkonsky estate where Tolstoy

signed charmingly archaic new buildings for the estate—an "old Russian" church (fig. 220), where Mamontov would be buried, a bathhouse (fig. 221), and a fairy-tale playhouse on chicken legs that evokes the hut of Baba Yaga, the mythical figure used to frighten generations of Russian children (fig. 222). In Mamontov's studio they tried their hand at ceramics and sculpture; roaming the countryside, they covered countless canvases with evocative landscapes, some of which were hung in the Abramtsevo dining room (fig. 223).

Mamontov also sponsored operatic theatricals at Abramtsevo for a local audience, presenting scaled-down versions of his extravagant Moscow productions. By offering peasants the chance to see scenes from *Boris Godunov, Prince Igor,* and *Sadko,* Mamontov hoped, says Polenov,

220. The church at Abramtsevo. The chapel at left sits over the tombs of Savva Mamontov and his son.

221. The bathhouse at Abramtsevo, the first of the new outbuildings that Savva Mamontov erected in old Russian style after buying the estate.

Estate Life Besieged

While these cultural experiments were being launched in the Russian countryside, court aristocrats continued to travel to their lavish, well-staffed estates for the summer. Unlike Russia's patriarchs, the courtiers seem to have been remarkably out of touch with the harsh realities of the countryside. Paul Grabbe recalls the "sullen faces" of the village children (with whom he was not allowed to play) at his family's estate Vasilievskoe and his parents' indifference to the efforts of Vanya, the steward's son and his childhood friend, to gain admission to a technical school.[11]

Russians had their first taste of revolution in 1905. The upheaval began in St. Petersburg, when, on January 9, imperial troops fired at a procession of unarmed workers and their families bearing icons and petitions to the tsar at the Winter Palace, a response whose brutality shocked the nation. Unrest and violence spread to Moscow and into the countryside. By October a reluctant Nicholas II saw no

222. The children's playhouse at Abramtsevo.

lived while he did some of the writing, was a suggestive prototype for Bleak Hills and its setting. But Platon Karataev, the long-suffering, sooth-saying muzhik, was Tolstoy's personal model. In the 1880s Tolstoy entered the final phase of his quest to renounce his past for the simple life and truths of the peasant. Leaving his wife to worry about managing Yasnaya Polyana (a traditional income-producing estate) and supporting their many children, Tolstoy adopted simple peasant dress, worked with his peasants, ate their food, and slept in a small, cell-like room. In the terrible famine of 1890–91 he organized hundreds of soup kitchens for the starving peasants, then returned to writing moralistic tales for peasants and philosophical tracts advocating passive resistance to violence. These activities attracted swarms of disciples from around the world and evoked government surveillance and eventually excommunication by the Orthodox church.

223. The Abramtsevo dining room. On the easel is V. A. Serov's portrait of Mamontov's daughter, Vera.

other course than to grant Russia its first central elective governing body, the Duma (whose powers, however, paled in comparison to those the autocrat and his appointees retained). The flames that engulfed manor houses across Russia during the long summer of its first revolution in 1905 were the signal for the beginning of an exodus of nobles from the countryside. Count Grabbe hastened to Vasilievskoe expressly to avert its destruction and the next year sold it. Yet aristocratic life went on. The Nabokovs, abroad in 1905, returned to Russia, and in the summer of 1906, while exploring the attic of his mother's estate Vyra, young Vladimir found the dusty book that inspired his life-long passion for lepidoptera. No chronicle is as full of vivid images of country life in this period as Nabokov's bittersweet autobiography *Speak, Memory.* Soon after the revolution a new journal, aptly titled *Bygone Years,* appeared, its aim being to record and stimulate preservation of a cultural world now clearly under siege. Its photographs of estate exteriors and interiors, furniture and furnishings, offer a unique glimpse of prerevolutionary Russian splen-

dor. But almost every issue of *Bygone Years* sounded the tocsin with a black-bordered chronicle of estates that had recently been burned or vandalized or were simply falling into ruin from neglect. The once-grand Khoten, a prime example, was rotting because of discord among the heirs of P. S. Stroganov. Profiting from the situation, the steward had sold the furniture; as at Khmelita local peasants were storing grain in Khoten's reception rooms (fig. 225). The second floor had been converted into a tuberculosis sanatorium for children (a portent of things to come under the Bolsheviks). By 1914 huge chunks of the elaborately painted ceilings had fallen down, the parquet had been ruined, and the bronze mounts on the fireplaces torn away. Only inscriptions on empty, broken picture frames catalogued the once-priceless art collection that had hung there.

Another chronicle of this period, *The Capital and the Estate,* an elite social commentary published between 1914 and 1917 (subtitled *Journal of the Beautiful Life*), leaves quite the opposite impression of the Russian aristocracy on the eve of its demise. On its large, glossy pages, articles on individual estates are interspersed with betrothal portraits of prominent nobles, along with photos of court balls, maidens at the Smolny Institute, the occasional princess with her devoted pug, and the wartime volunteer nursing activities of the empress, her daughters, and various noblewomen. Here we see the final echoes of estate theatricality and of the general fascination with folk culture. At Gremyach, in Chernigov Province, colorfully clad peasant women are photographed sweeping a long allée in formation. Two others pose decoratively with a guitar on the steps of a quaint wooden cottage in the park. Most telling for the life of this "Russian Versailles," as contemporaries called it, is a snapshot of Princess Maria V. Golitsyna in peasant dress, milking a cow (fig. 226). This image, an eloquent statement about aristocratic visions of estate culture, seems in retrospect as incongruous for 1916 as do the portraits of courtiers dressed in magnificent pre-

Petrine court costumes for the famous ball of 1903, another famine year.

As the war progressed, a note of urgency can be discerned among other groups. In 1916 the Archaeological Commission of Novgorod Province sent out a questionnaire to 130 estate owners, asking specifically about items of historical importance they possessed. In the introduc-

tion to its report on the findings, the commission referred to a triple threat to the artifacts of estate culture: their destruction by fire, their sale to new owners unconcerned with preservation, or their removal to the city; as a result of these circumstances, went the report, "every year it becomes more difficult to find and gather elements of the past." The "disturbances of 1905–06," the commission

224. L. N. Tolstoy (left) playing chess with P. F. Samarin on the terrace of Samarin's estate house at Molodenki. 1887. (*Stolitsa i usadba*, no. 53)

225. Grain drying in the reception rooms of Khoten, the Stroganov estate. (Lukomsky, *Usadby Kharkovskoi gubernii*)

noted, had greatly increased the Novgorod nobility's "desertion" of their estates. "There were few cases of murder, but houses were burned down rather frequently with everything in them . . . [and] many estates were sold, passing into the hands of other classes, or more rarely other nobles, but not ones who loved antiquity."[12] Of the 68 responses the commission received to its questionnaire, more than 50 mentioned holdings of old papers: land grants from various tsars, family letters, eighteenth-century books and manuscripts (including Andrei T. Bolotov's, at Gorka, his great-great-grandson's estate), and numerous old family portraits. This was the heritage of Russia's "nests of gentlefolk"—not just a way of life but the record of a past doomed, as the commission feared, to be demolished in the whirlwind of 1917–21.

The Storm

Had there been no revolution, one could imagine Russian estate life gradually and gracefully receding as it did elsewhere in Europe after the war. At present there would certainly be fewer grand estate houses than in 1916, their maintenance perhaps financed by paying guests or reproductions of Ostankino treasures and Yusupov porcelain. Wealthy landowners like the Volkov-Muromtsovs and Davydovs might still be found in the countryside, surrounded by historic relics but, in all likelihood, living a radically different life. Many of Russia's manor houses, as elsewhere, would undoubtedly have disintegrated, been sold and converted to other uses, or been razed to make way for housing developments. Predicting what direction the lurching troika bearing Russia's history might have taken, given other circumstances, has always been a vain (if popular) pursuit. And so one is left with the actual tragedy: not the abrupt end to a particular way of life, for it was slated inevitably to perish, but the deliberate, irrevocable attempt to destroy a brilliant chapter of Russia's cultural

226. Princess Maria Golitsyna, in local costume, milking a cow at Gremyach. (*Stolitsa i usadba*, no. 50)

history—houses, artifacts, the record, and even the memory of the Russian country estate.

Throughout Europe the Great War dealt a mortal blow to the upper-class pastoral idyll celebrated by Pushkin and Wordsworth, Tolstoy and Rupert Brooke. But nowhere was it so savagely put to death as in Russia, where both the reality of this life was done away with and its memory forsworn. In the 1840s Prince Peter Vyazemsky, doing battle with radical literary critics who seemed intent on writing off the past as outmoded and unnecessary, issued a prophetic warning: "Is one to think that [time] commenced only when you arose? . . . Break the chain of sequence and tradition, and time and its achievements, that is, time in its spiritual sense, will turn to stone and come to a complete standstill. In tearing down, destroying and removing all the past as outlived and unnecessary, you are transforming yourselves, without guessing it, into primitive savages. . . . Grief will befall the people which does not respect its past!"[13]

The Bolshevik revolution was a cultural tragedy of colossal proportions, bearing out Vyazemsky's words. During it, estate culture was deliberately destroyed in two stages. In the first few years revolutionaries severed the cultural arteries that estate life had provided for provincial Russia. In 1917 and 1918, in a riot of vandalistic, spiteful destruction of luxury, young peasants swarmed through the gates and then the doors of countless manors, slashing paintings, decapitating statues, gleefully destroying orangeries, barns, and estate offices and their records, and finally either vandalizing or burning the house so that the owner could never return.[14] By 1919 the Volkov-Muromtsovs, Davydovs, Obolenskys, Nabokovs, and countless other estate owners whose activities had been the blood coursing through these arteries had left Russia. The "aunts' house" at Kamenka was burned. Khmelita was not destroyed, but its books and paintings were shipped to Moscow and Smolensk; other furnishings simply vanished. For a few years it was used as a "People's House," then abandoned to decay.

Estate churches were plundered, sometimes bulldozed by members of the League of the Militant Godless, or turned into warehouses or workshops. Those manor houses not destroyed or left to rot were transformed into sanatoriums, museums, or agricultural institutes. Near Moscow and in the Crimea, grand estates were reserved for the new elite. Lenin appropriated the Morozovs' Gorky, south of Moscow; A. V. Lunacharsky, his cultural commissar, moved into the main house at Ostafievo, allowing Pavel Sheremetev, Sergei's son, to live in a wing and act as director of the Ostafievo Museum. Some still remember his courteous tours of the house he had once owned; a photograph of his niece's wedding in 1921 (fig. 227) shows that life at that time, even if reduced in quality, was still bearable.

Until the mid-1920s the new regime, largely thanks to Lunacharsky, was relatively benevolent toward the small group of connoisseurs of estate culture left in Russia, among them former owners, preservationists, and museum directors. In 1922, eighty-seven of these individuals, including A. N. Grech, Pavel Sheremetev, and the sons of Polenov and the poet N. A. Nekrasov, founded the Society for the Study of the Russian Estate. Its members did historical research, wrote articles for the new periodical *Among Collectors*, and published guidebooks to suburban Moscow's estates.

After Lunacharsky's death and Stalin's consolidation of power in 1928 the second phase of destruction began. This was an assault not just on objects and people but on memory. Pavel Sheremetev was fortunate in merely being evicted from Ostafievo. Many of his collaborators were sent to the gulag, where they perished without a trace. Among the most remarkable artifacts of this repression is Grech's "A Wreath for the Estates," the 260-page manuscript he wrote in Solovki Prison. Dated 1932, it chron-

227. The wedding dinner of Pavel Sheremetev's niece, held in the Ostafievo colonnade. 1921.
(Courtesy of Kyra Cheremeteff)

icled what Grech could recall from memory of his years of research. A moving introduction summarized the significance and fate of the estate: "In 1917 the agony began, the doom of the Russian estate and everything connected with it. . . . Only the epilogue remained to be written, an epilogue to that which poets and writers had glorified, which musicians had heard in the noises and rustlings of the night, which artists had seen in the tender pastel tones of spring, in the flaming crimson of autumn sunsets. In ten years a grandiose necropolis has been created. In it lie two centuries of culture. The monuments of art and daily life, the thoughts and forms of Russian poetry, literature, and music lie buried here."[15]

It was precisely this necropolis—the fact that the estate lived on in Russian literature, music, and art—which kept its memory alive in Russian imagination. Up to and even after Stalin's death the conventions of Soviet historiography dictated that archives of estate owners be mined only for evidence of mistreatment and exploitation of serfs. Nabokov's command that memory speak could have been uttered only by an exile, because in Soviet Russia no positive reference to former estate owners was possible. It

331

is bizarre indeed to read scholarly works on estate architecture from this period. When possible, serf architects are given prominent attention; some authors artfully omit even the names of the nobles who commissioned Russia's estates and their parks, not to mention their sources of inspiration or their thoughts and emotions about the world they had created.

World War II brought a new round of physical destruction to central Russia. During it, all of Russia's imperial palaces were totally destroyed or severely damaged, and more estate houses lost. Khrushchev's massive onslaught on churches in the late 1950s targeted many estate churches that still served local parishes, and they too began to decay. But this period also provided the first intimations that officials were having second thoughts about letting the destruction continue. National pride (and, very likely, the hope of tourist revenues) inspired the Soviet government to embark on the most paradoxical phase of estate history. In the 1930s, as is well known, the Soviet state had re-enserfed Russia's peasants, herding them into collective farms. Now the state, in effect, re-enserfed Russia's skilled artisans. They were paid nominal salaries, almost comparable to those Sheremetev paid to his talented staff in 1786, to rebuild, recarve, restucco, regild, reweave, and repaint—in short, to re-create from scratch, by hand, what Soviet power had either destroyed or allowed to perish. Thus virtually all the Russian palaces and estates on view to tourists today have been twice built, both times by skilled, unfree artisans.[16] The results are extremely impressive, but only when compared to the losses—not to what life might have been like had the sacrifice never been made.

228. The ruins of the manor house at Petrovskoe-Alabino. (Author)

In the 1990s, provincial Russia seems in some respects farther away from Moscow than it was in the 1890s. When Russia's landowners fled, they took with them the vitality that their presence, support, and commerce had lent provincial cities and towns. In comparison to the prerevolutionary local elite's endowments for orphanages, schools, charitable societies, churches, and monasteries and their patronage of theaters, shops, and restaurants, the contribution of the impoverished Soviet state, and its new elite, to town life was inevitably pallid. And so the life of these towns withered, grayed, and has never recovered.

A different type of life has been invading the countryside in the past few years. Russia's new millionaires are building the latest generation of country houses in the greatest flurry of private construction since the revolution. In April 1992 the Society for the Study of the Russian Estate was reborn in Moscow. Its members are dedicated to recovering what has been lost, but its resources are limited, and the forces against which Russia's restorers and curators must compete for talent and material are both formidable and well funded. Perhaps one, or some, of these

229. The park facade of the mansion at Khmelita in 1992, during the restoration of its original appearance. In January 1995 Khmelita was reopened as a museum honoring Alexander Griboedov. (Author)

new self-made Russian aristocrats will, in time-honored fashion, decide to endow the restoration movement—but will the offer come in time to save mansions like Marfino (see fig. 45), now on the brink of ruin, or Petrovksoe-Alabino (fig. 228)? One day might an estate complex—Khmelita (fig. 229), for instance—be resurrected not only as a museum but as a model working estate, so that generations acquainted with estate culture only through literature can see what that life was really like?

Although such restorations have taken place in other countries, given Russia's chaotic financial situation it may prove easier at present to resurrect the estate on paper. That too will be difficult. Because the last witnesses to estate life are now close to or in their nineties, the importance of recording their precious memories becomes more pressing. Somewhere in the archives perhaps there exist stewards' accounts for Titovo or Karaul and sketches of estates we know only by name—Lyubichi, Dolbino, Veryakushki, or Zlobino. Buried in personal archives there are surely thousands of letters of ordinary estate owners that could amplify our understanding of their daily life. Perhaps they mention neighbors, thus providing additional fragments of the as-yet uncharted map of Russia's former estates. The task of painstakingly reassembling this precious data, and of fitting the pieces into the geographic, social, and cultural puzzles, is daunting. Yet it is a vital undertaking if we are ever to see the entire picture behind the wall, and if Russians are to reclaim fully their purloined heritage.

230. The bell tower of the estate church at Bolshye Vyazemy. Nearby is the grave of Alexander Pushkin's brother, Nikolai.

Notes

Introduction

Epigraph: Eleanor Cavanaugh, letter to her father, written from Troitskoe, October 4, 1805 (Wilmot and Wilmot, 187).

Part I
The Aristocratic Playground

Epigraph: Prince A. A. Bezborodko, letter to Count Semen Vorontsov, Russian ambassador to England, 1798 (*Arkhiv Knyazya Vorontsova*, 13: 379).

1
The Russian Noble

Epigraph: Catherine Wilmot, letter to Anna Chetwood, March 23, 1806 (Wilmot and Wilmot, 217)

1. Olearius, 126, 131, 147.
2. Ibid., 155.
3. Even S. L. Streshnev, an uncle of the tsar, and I. D. Miloslavsky, father of the tsar's first wife, were accused of sorcery because of their Western ways. Nikita Romanov, a cousin, had a suit of offensive foreign hunting clothes confiscated. For three years, between 1672 and 1675, foreign dress was permitted for a select group of high officials (and their servants) who had to deal with foreigners.
4. Lahana, 8, 9. Matveev was later stoned to death by an angry mob.
5. At the top of the service hierarchy was the *boyarin*; at the bottom, the *dumnyi dyak*.
6. The two play regiments into which Peter, as a boy, had inducted his friends—the Preobrazhenskii and Semenovskii—became the most prestigious real-life regiments after he assumed full power in 1698 and remained so down to 1917.
7. Zabelin, 332–33.
8. Peter Tolstoy, 35–36.
9. *Polnoe sobranie zakonov*, 3: 681–82.
10. Ibid., 5: 91–94.
11. Karnovich, 12. Nobles used the word *village* (*selo*) interchangeably with *estate* (*usadba*), as in this instance.
12. Ibid., 152.
13. Ibid., 22.
14. See Dolgorukaya.
15. Karnovich, 259.
16. Buturlin, *Russkii arkhiv*, 1897, 2: 215.
17. If legend is to be believed, Kirill kept a shepherd's crook and simple Ukrainian costume on display in a luxurious mahogany cabinet to remind his children of their humble origins.
18. Cited in Cracraft, *Petrine Revolution*, 229.
19. Cited in Ford, vii.
20. Cracraft, "James Brogden," 241.
21. Bluche, 178.
22. Wilmot and Wilmot, 45.
23. See Girouard, chap. 1.
24. Karamzin, 325.
25. Haxthausen noted in 1843 that "the [Russian] nobleman does not regard his estate as his homestead. . . . He will dispose of his inheritance immediately if he sees an advantage in doing so" (250). Some Russian scholars now believe that ancestral *votchinas* were more likely to stay within a family than were more recently acquired lands.

2
The Golden Age of the Pleasure Palace

Epigraph: Catherine II, letter to Baron Friedrich Melchior Grimm, 1779, cited in Chenevière, 22.

1. Shvidkovskii, *Gorod*, 14–72.
2. In the mid-1780s, upon viewing the almost completed palace on which Bazhenov had labored for a decade, Catherine ordered it torn down and redesigned by Matvei Kazakov, an order that luckily was only partially carried out. Her displeasure has often been attributed to the Masonic symbols Bazhenov included in the ornamentation, but Dmitry Shvidkovskii has recently suggested a second reason: the palaces Bazhenov had created for Catherine and for her son, Paul, were of equal size and therefore unacceptable to her.
3. The ideological component to Catherine's experiments has been explored by Dmitry Shvidkovskii; see his articles "Idealnyi gorod" and "K voprosu."
4. See Cross, *By the Banks*, chap. 9.
5. Stowe, possibly at Catherine's request, was allotted forty-four views, and Kew twenty-five. There were fourteen views of the less renowned West Wycombe; and Stourhead, Wilton, and Wrest Park were each depicted four or more times. See Hayden, "British Seats," 21; Cross, "Russian Gardens," 12.
6. See Petrova. Reception rooms in a baroque mansion tended to be indistinguishable in size, save for the two largest (the ballroom and the main living room). In the neoclassical house the enfilade was more likely to be punctuated with small rooms that emphasized the size of the larger chambers that preceded and followed them.
7. Like numerous other renowned Italian architects and designers who came to Russia, such as the Rastrellis, Gonzago, and Quarenghi, Camporesi spent the rest of his life there and hence might be considered a naturalized Russian.
8. The same is true of General G. I. Bibikov's Grebnevo, to the northeast, Count F. A. Tolstoy's Ivanovskoe, now within the city limits of Podolsk, and a few other country estate houses near Moscow.

9. Wilmot and Wilmot, 237.
10. B-va., "Iz istorii," 3.
11. Cited in Makarenko, 132.
12. Golombevskii, 14.
13. Cited in Morozov, 38.
14. Ibid., 3.
15. According to D. O. Shvidkovskii, pseudo-Gothic elements in Moscow estate architecture of the late eighteenth century almost invariably signaled that the estate owner was a member of a Masonic lodge—making him politically suspect in the eyes of Catherine toward the end of her reign.
16. The Marquis de Custine, visiting a log house near Moscow in 1839, immediately connected its appearance to native Russian culture. "I was received in a wooden house. . . . The interior of these huge cabins recalls the most beautiful palaces of Europe. . . . This is the sole dwelling which might be termed national in style" (3: 150). The narrator of Gogol's *Dead Souls* (1842) likewise describes these grandiose log cabins as "the only sign of patriotism" among Russia's French-, English-, and German-speaking aristocracy (190).
17. Golombevskii, 15.
18. In *Kuskovo*, G. S. Sheremetev describes both refuges, destroyed in 1812. Boris's hideaway was more elegantly furnished than his son's. The living room had a multitude of ornamental statuettes and French wallpaper. In the bedroom, filled with Chinese porcelain figurines, the alcove and bedspread were done in green taffeta. The boudoir had thirty-four mirrors, and the dressing room a parquet floor and corner cabinet filled with marble objects. In the 1820s Nikolai Yusupov's wife moved to the Caprice, a similarly elegant refuge on the grounds of Arkhangelskoe, when Yusupov's debauchery became the talk of Moscow.
19. Sverbeev, 2: 131–36. Kuskovo, the archetypal eighteenth-century pleasure palace, bears out Sverbeev's observation. Occupied sporadically in the summers down to 1917, the house had only decorative stoves, no plumbing, and no lighting other than candles.
20. Beard, 23.
21. Cross, "'The Great Patroness,'" 69.
22. Cox, "An English Gardener," 105.
23. Maikova, "Arkhiv," 11.
24. See Zinoviev, "Zhurnal puteshestviya."
25. Karamzin, 325.
26. Raevskaya, "Vospominaniya," 530.
27. Morton, 77.
28. Cited in Elizarova, 174, 62, 176. Sievers was the chief administrator of Novgorod Province (which until 1775 comprised most of the northwestern heartland, including the later provinces of Pskov, Tver, and Olonets). See Jones for Sievers's career.
29. Youssoupoff, 25.
30. The wealthy Yusupov was notoriously stingy. Moscow was scandalized when Arkhangelskoe burned down, reputedly because the count had economized by burning sawdust rather than firewood.
31. In less lavishly furnished estate houses, poplar veneer, which resembles Karelian birch in hue and grain and is less expensive, was often used for furniture.
32. *Arkhiv Knyazya Vorontsova*, 12: 310 (letter of February 22, 1805).
33. Makarenko, 146–47.
34. Glumov, 119.
35. O. I. Nosova, Tsaritsyno Museum; personal communication.
36. Blagovo, 25, 230, 295.
37. See Anisimov.
38. This expenditure was enormous even in comparison to extravagant purchases by other grandees. Countess E. A. Musina-Pushkina, for example, spent 6,200 rubles on a fancy carriage for her daughter; her son ordered one from Joachim, the best Moscow carriage maker, for 3,400 rubles. High-quality fabric for the liveries of the Musin-Pushkin Moscow servants cost between 12 and 17 rubles a yard. Military uniforms (made in England) cost the young Musin-Pushkins 1,800 rubles apiece, and a three-room campaign tent 1,000 rubles. A different standard of comparison is offered by the fact that by the mid-nineteenth century, a landowner's average income from a serf on *obrok* was 11.4 rubles (see Kolchin, 151). Thus the table was roughly equivalent to
an owner's revenues from 3,000 dues-paying serfs.
39. Vrangel, "Pomeshchichya," 19–20. In the 1860s one woman inherited an estate filled to the brim with old furniture and decided to order more fashionable things from a nearby town. The nearest rail station being forty miles away, she decided simply to burn the old.
40. This explains why, in *Anna Karenina*, Tolstoy shows Dolly Oblonskaya's instinctive aversion to Anna's lavish redecoration of the old estate house she and Vronsky are occupying. "All [Dolly] saw gave her the impression of abundance and elegance, of that novel European luxury which she had read about in English novels, but had never yet seen in Russia in the country. Everything was . . . costly and new" (559).

3
Tatyana's Garden

Epigraph: A. T. Bolotov, *Zhizn*, 2: 558.
1. Karamzin, 325.
2. Wilmot, 209; Bakarev, 255.
3. Cox, 108–09.
4. Ibid., 111–12.
5. Hayden, "Imperial Culture," 118–19.
6. Hadfield, 289.
7. Svinin, pt. 12: 32.
8. Lyall, 2: 359–60.
9. Custine, 3: 28–29.
10. *Sbornik imperatorskogo*, 13: 256, 259.
11. *Arkhiv Knyazya Vorontsova*, 6: 304.
12. *Arkhiv Knyazya F. A. Kurakina*, 5: 395–96.
13. Golombevskii, 17.
14. Sverbeev, 1: 283.
15. Cox, 107, 109.
16. Sivkov, 4.
17. S. D. Sheremetev, "Vremya Pavla," 91–92.
18. Anikst and Turchin, 174.
19. Golombevskii, 17.
20. Ibid., 19.
21. Denike, 38.
22. Bolotov, *Zhizn*, 2: 344, 3: 1137.
23. See Shchukina, 109–17.
24. Bolotov, *Zhizn*, 3: 1163.

25. Wilmot and Wilmot, 209.
26. Ibid.
27. Bolotov, *Zhizn*, 2: 1148, 1163.
28. Sedov, 19, 33, 23.
29. Hayden, "Pavlovsk," 223; translation by Hayden.
30. Likhachev, 227–42.
31. Bolotov, *Zhizn*, 4: 38.
32. Ibid., 2: 1148.
33. Baranova, 54. Kuskovo was open to the public for weekly summer festivals in the late eighteenth century. In the 1770s the landscape park was added to the formal park, one of the most magnificent in Russia.
34. Bolotov, *Zhizn*, 2: 1156–57.
35. See Cross, "The English Garden," on the relationship between translated and original works on gardening theory.
36. Kosarevskii, 30.
37. Pushkin, *Sochineniya*, 3: 222.
38. Grot, 96.
39. Pushkin, *Sochineniya*, 3: 254–55.
40. See Fleming and Gore, 131.
41. Pushkin, *Sochineniya*, 3: 30, 28, 128.
42. Ibid., 31, 123.
43. Bolotov, "Nekotorye zamechaniya," 59.
44. From Mikhailovskoe, Pushkin wrote D. M. Schwartz, "It's been four months since I find myself in the depths of the country—it's boring, but there's nothing to be done. . . . I spend the whole day riding, the evening listening to my nanny's tales; I think you saw her once, she is my only friend, and only with her am I not bored" ("Pisma," 120, letter of December 1824).

4
A Private Princedom

Epigraph: Martha Wilmot, letter to her mother, written from Troitskoe, October 19, 1803 (Wilmot and Wilmot, 56).
1. Cited in Tristram, 35.
2. Wilmot and Wilmot, 189.
3. Almedingen, 93; Blagovo, 55; Turgenev, "Sportsman," 157.
4. Golombevskii, 16.
5. Bakarev, 258.
6. Karnovich, 289.

7. Wilmot and Wilmot, 53.
8. Blagovo, 307–08; Nikoleva, 136; N. P. Makarov, 1: 15; see also Basova, 44.
9. Wilmot and Wilmot, 131–33.
10. Turgenev, *A Nest of the Gentry*, 172.
11. S. D. Sheremetev, "Vremya Pavla," 115, 226, 264, 270.
12. S. D. Sheremetev, "Ulyanka," 24.
13. Ibid., 11.
14. Raevskaya, "Prizhivalshchiki," 75–78.
15. Nikoleva, 144.
16. S. D. Sheremetev, *Vospominaniya*, 37, 7.
17. Wilmot and Wilmot, 204, 208–09.
18. Ibid., 206, 202, 200.
19. Bolotov, *Zhizn*, 3: 1185.
20. Wilmot and Wilmot, 273, 45.
21. Ibid., 60, 191, 210.
22. Ibid., 191, 205, 201, 145–46.
23. Bolotov, *Zhizn*, 3: 1186–87. Contemporaneous etchings show tent pavilions.
24. Wilmot and Wilmot, 207.
25. Ibid., 108.
26. Ibid., 63, 220.
27. Raevskaya, "Prizhivalshchiki," 74.
28. Herzen, *My Past*, 53.
29. Kropotkin, 41.
30. Ibid., 42–44.
31. Ibid., 44.
32. Herzen, *My Past*, 54.
33. Raevskaya, "Babushka," 355.
34. Raevskaya, "V pamyat," 204.
35. Herzen, *My Past*, 55–56.
36. S. B., 252.
37. G. S. Sheremetev, *Zapisnaya*, 21.
38. Raevskii, 395–96.
39. Tolstoy, *Childhood*, 33–35.
40. Kropotkin, 45–46.
41. Lavrov, 445–56.
42. Cited in P. Sheremetev, "Vyazemy," 87.
43. Ibid., 88.
44. Tolstoy, *Childhood*, 30–31, 35.
45. Neverov, 445–46.
46. Morton, 150–52.
47. Tolstoy, *War and Peace*, 470.
48. Bakarev, 257.
49. Ibid., 255.
50. Davydov, "Iz pomeshchichei," 198.
51. See my "The Country House as Setting and Symbol" for a comparative treatment of ar-

tistic and literary portraits in the nineteenth century.
52. The portrait is reproduced in *Starye gody*, January 13, 1911.

5
Emerald Thrones and Living Statues

Epigraph: From Dolgorukii's poem "My Theater" (1797), cited in V. G. Sakhnovskii, 42.
1. See Goodwin and Spring for comparative evaluations. Bush describes the "noble ideal of expenditure" as a "massive programme of consumption involving the maintenance of impressive households, stables, and entourages, the purchase of expensive and distinctive clothing, and the generous dispensation of hospitality and charity" (107).
2. See Lotman's "Poetics," "Decembrist," and "Khlestakov," in both *Semiotics* (Ithaca, 1985) and *Semiotics* (Ann Arbor, 1984), and his "Theater and Theatricality," in *Semiotics* (Ann Arbor, 1984).
3. Kurbatov, 620.
4. Anikst and Turchin, 174.
5. Cited in Cross, "British Sources," 24, 29; italics in the original.
6. Lepskaya, "Ostankinskii teatr," 62–78.
7. Cited by Lepskaya, 68.
8. Sakhnovskii, 48–49.
9. Drizen, "Shklovskii balet."
10. N. Ya. Afanasiev, Shepelev's choirmaster, describes the theater in his "Vospominaniya," 255–76.
11. Malinin, 15.
12. Derzhavin, "Zapiski," in Podolskaya, 157.
13. Senelick, *Serf Actor*, 48.
14. Senelick, "Erotic Bondage," 24–34.
15. Buturlin, *Russkii arkhiv*, 1897, 6: 190–92; see also his "Teatr grafa Kamenskago."
16. Troinitskii, 45; see Kolchin, 52, for a comparison with the 1795 census. Dynnik's list of 173 theaters overlooks many described in memoirs.
17. Vigel, 1: 237; Raevskaya, "Vospominaniya," 550.
18. Wilmot and Wilmot, 56–57, 186–87.

337

19. Pylyaev, 532. Bolotov's repertory included twenty-nine plays, some written by him.
20. Kolbe, 139; Lyall, 2: 505.
21. Anikst and Turchin, 93; Vrangel, *Venok*, 76.
22. Cited in Sakhnovskii, 23–26.
23. Troyat, 11–12. Gogol's father, related by marriage to Dmitry Troshchinskii, was major domo in this household, taking charge of theatricals and organizing revels. See Setchkarev, 6, 9.
24. Blagovo, 114–15.
25. Haxthausen, 110.
26. A. M. Turgenev, 175–77.
27. Kazarinov, 26–31.
28. De Madariaga, 534.
29. Lyubetskii, "Gulyane," 128–29.
30. Bibikov, one of Catherine's most trusted senior officials, was appointed marshal of her Legislative Commission in 1767; in 1773 he was given full authority to put down the Pugachev rebellion by any means possible and to conduct an inquiry as to its roots.
31. Raevskaya, "Vospominaniya," 541–42.
32. The Count de Segur, cited by Karnovich, 122.
33. Drizen, "Shklovskii balet."
34. Malinin, 13.
35. Lyubetskii, *Selo Ostankino*, 16.
36. Vrangel, *Venok*, 76.
37. Bovill, 81–82.
38. Youssoupoff, 14.
39. Lyall, 1: 28.
40. Coxe, 1: 313. Coxe may have been in error, because most likely this exotic melon was grown in Orlov's estate hothouse.
41. Wilmot and Wilmot, 68.
42. From de Staël's *Ten Years' Exile* (London, 1821); cited in Cross, *Russia under Western Eyes*, 305.
43. Lyall, 1: 24.
44. Karamzin, 310. Both English and Russian hospitality on the estate level involved extravagant expenditure, but they differed in terms of purpose, the frequency and duration of visits, and the character of entertaining.
45. Cited in Sakhnovskii, 45, 30.
46. Mengden, 326.
47. Blagovo, 249.

48. N. P. Makarov, 1: 28.
49. Lotman, "Poetics," *Semiotics* (Ithaca, 1985), 77–80.
50. Blagovo, 73.
51. More nativist but equally theatrical in terms of its deviation from traditional noble dress was the peasant costume affected by the occasional provincial eccentric.
52. Wilmot and Wilmot, 82. Noting that Russians brought "anything that can amuse" into the drawing room, she remarks, "*Mauvaise honte* is absolutely unknown, or if felt, 'tis banished as fast as possible as useless lumber."
53. Neverov, 445.
54. Raeff, "Home, School," 219–21.
55. Kropotkin, 39–42.
56. A. M. Turgenev, 482.
57. Wrangel, 42–43.
58. Lyall, 2: 363–64, and Kolbe, 120, comment on Russian extravagance.
59. Dashkova, 223. The village was about two miles from Troitskoe. Its new name appears on some nineteenth-century maps.
60. Vrangel, "Pomeshchichya," 52.
61. Raeff notes that "living nobly" was a legal concept in ancien-régime France (Banac and Bushkovich, 119 n. 1).
62. Lotman, "Poetics," *Semiotics* (Ithaca, 1985), 70.
63. Golovine, 2: 77.
64. Gerakov, 143–44.
65. Haxthausen, 110.
66. Sakhnovskii, 52–60.
67. Derzhavin, *Sochineniya*, 1: 383, 390–91.
68. Malinin, 21.
69. Cited in Sakhnovskii, 43.
70. Lotman, "Theater," *Semiotics* (Ann Arbor, 1984), 160.
71. See *The Diary of George Mifflin Dallas* for a personal account of court festivities, including a masquerade of 1842 designed as a medieval tournament. Lotman describes Alexander I as adept at theatrical posturing ("Theater," 156–59). The Marquis de Custine said of Nicholas I: "He poses incessantly; whence it results that he is never natural. . . . In Greece, the hypocrite was a man who masked himself to play comedy.

Thus I wish to say that the emperor is always in his role and fulfills it as a great actor" (*La Russie*, 1: 192–93).
72. Cited in Brown, 2: 109.

Part II
The Patriarchal Enclave

Epigraph: Excerpt from Alexander Bakunin's poem "Osuga" (1819), cited in Kornilov, 9–10. The fuller text of Bakunin's defense of serfdom as a mutually advantageous system for serf and owner reads as follows: "I see the peaceful settlement/Of hardworking villagers./I don't know why our learned men/Call them slaves!/They give us fixed dues/From work within their powers./And their share from that receiving—/Fields, granaries, cattle, and a house—/Just like the owner,/They are masters of their life./Dividing the day in half,/The half-free villager,/Giving three days to his master,/Is his own master for the other three./On this unchangeable foundation/Rests holy Rus./In the detestable slavery of words/A mutual alliance is concealed. . . ./With us, for better or worse,/The landowner is guardian of orphans,/Waters their family fields/And provides heat for the family stove!"

6
Nests of Gentlefolk

Epigraph: Mary Ann Pellen Smith, speaking of her visit to Krasnoe Selo (Beautiful Village), Ryazan Province, in the 1850s (*Six Years' Travels*, 2: 130–31).
1. Mironov, citing A. K. Korsak, 39.
2. S. N. Glinka, 8.
3. On noble insecurity, see Meehan-Waters, "Development and Limits," 300 and throughout, and Dukes, 145–50.
4. N. P. Makarov, 23–24.
5. Bolotov, *Zhizn*, 2: 887.
6. Blagovo, 11.
7. Bolotov, *Zhizn*, 2: 236.
8. Blagovo, 148.
9. Nikoleva, 154–55, 182.
10. Ibid., 120; Kohl, 522–23.

11. Raevskii, 216.
12. Blagovo, 103.
13. Ibid., 192–93, 147. The Table of Ranks (1722) established German titles for Russian court ranks.
14. Ostrozhskii-Lokhvitskii, 363.
15. Olga N. [S. V. Engelgardt], 164. Mosolov left Zhernovka only once, Engelhardt relates, traveling to Moscow to inspect a painting, allegedly by the Italian painter Domenico Zampierini, that Herzen's father had purchased abroad. Upon his return Mosolov scornfully proclaimed the painting an obvious fake (163).
16. Blagovo, 118.
17. Chicherin, 521.
18. See Hamburg, 21, 31.
19. Chicherin, 512–13.
20. Ibid., 508, 509–10.
21. Ibid., 502–04.
22. Ibid., 506–07.
23. Piksanov, 13, 22–23.
24. Ibid., 20, 22.
25. Tuchkova-Ogareva, 32, 29.
26. N. P. Makarov, 27. Chicherin echoes these sentiments when he speaks of Nikolai Krivtsov's being forced into retirement: "Thus, the government lost all these brilliant gifts, all this extraordinary training, this eagerness for the general good. A phenomenon which has subsequently and constantly been repeated: when the government does not value enlightened individuals, makes no effort to attract them and keep them . . . the government deprives itself of its best servants. They retire into private life and there leave traces of themselves, invisible, but sometimes no less fruitful" (504).
27. Herzen, *My Past*, 619 (excerpt from *The Bell*, 1859).
28. Nechaeva, 33–36.
29. Bolotov, *Zhizn*, 2: 307.
30. Chechulin, 29–30.
31. Bolotov, *Zhizn*, 2: 798.
32. Buturlin, *Russkii arkhiv*, 1898, 3: 403–04.
33. Vigel, 1: 144.
34. Shatilov, 168.
35. Buturlin, *Russkii arkhiv*, 1897, 2: 41.

36. Shestakov, 167.
37. A. Vereshchagin, 1.
38. Batyushkov, *Opyty*, 398–99.
39. Smith, 2: 124–30.
40. Ibid., 2: 125.
41. Buturlin, *Russkii arkhiv*, 1898, 3: 404; Vigel, 1: 144.
42. Shatilov, 248.
43. Shompulev, 324; Miliutin, *Vospominaniya*, 31.
44. Turgenev, *Nest*, 205; Nikoleva, 181.
45. Blagovo, 25–26.
46. Miliutin, *Vospominaniya*, 12, 27.
47. Khrapovitskii had "all the best French and German authors; he also bought all the Russian books Novikov published" (S. N. Glinka, 14–15).
48. Karpinskaya, 866.
49. Khvoshchinskaya, 1897, 4: 161.
50. Nikoleva, 115.
51. Miliutin, "Moi starcheskie," 3; Kropotkin, 28; Blagovo, 25; A. Vereshchagin, 12.
52. Nikoleva, 116, 155; Shestakov, 172.
53. Nikoleva, 169.
54. Blagovo, 27.
55. See Wachtel.
56. Nikolaeva [Tsebrikova], 27. Mosolov, the art connoisseur, had his son learn carpentry, on the example of Rousseau's Emile.
57. Labzina, 21.
58. "V chem sostoit raznitsa obrazovaniya," *Vospitanie* (1861), 172; cited in Tovrov, 188.
59. B-n., 4: 160, 5/6: 139.
60. Ibid., 4: 164.
61. Wilmot and Wilmot, 201.
62. Grot, 12, 88–89.
63. Khvoshchinskaya, 1897, 3: 518; Miliutin, *Vospominaniya*, 25.
64. Khvoshchinskaya, 1897, 3: 519.
65. Kovalevskaya, 36.
66. Cited in Tovrov, 190.
67. Karpov, 142–43.
68. A. Davydoff, 22.
69. Sabaneeva, 46–47.
70. Blagovo, 253–54.
71. See Durova's translated memoirs, *Cavalry Maiden*.

72. Nikolaeva [Tsebrikova], 43, 47, 49, 50, 52.
73. Gogol, 47.
74. Neverov, 437.
75. Ibid., 441.
76. Vigel, 1: 236.
77. Zaitsev, 662.
78. Cited in Longinov, 961–62.
79. Labzina, 26–57.
80. Freeze, 98–99.
81. Cited in Stites, *Women's Liberation*, 6–7.
82. This case is recounted in Adam, "Iz semeinoi khroniki."
83. Romanovich-Slavatinskii, 315.
84. Martynov, 1283.
85. Blagovo, 293–94.
86. See N. P., "Epizod iz vremen krepostnogo prava."
87. See Sokolova, A. L., "Dobrovolnaya zatvornitsa."
88. Nikoleva, 150–51.
89. Estates were often part of a girl's dowry, whereas men usually inherited estates upon their parents' death. Thus many males became fully independent relatively late in life, though frequently they managed their wife's property.

7
Town and Country

Epigraph: Nikoleva, *Russkii arkhiv*, 1893, 10: 176–77.
1. Cited in Dukes, 169–71.
2. Bolotov, *Zhizn*, 2: 963.
3. Carr, *Bakunin*, 4.
4. Lukomsky, *Kharkov*, 17.
5. See Selivanov, 146–47, and Shompulev, 322.
6. "M," 246.
7. Buryanov, *Progulka*, 102.
8. Coxe, 2: 67.
9. Gerakov, 110.
10. Morton, 165.
11. N. V. Davydov, "Iz pomeshchichei," 174, 191.
12. Shompulev, 321.
13. Gerakov, 9–10, 15.
14. N. V. Davydov, "Iz pomeshchichei," 178.

15. Bremner, 2: 331–33.
16. Blagovo, 96.
17. Belov, 18, 36–37, 79.
18. Dolgorukii, *Slavny*, 1, 4, 7.
19. Wilmot and Wilmot, 129–30.
20. Gerakov, 37, 163, 145, 157.
21. Nikoleva, 194.
22. Gerakov, 125.
23. S. D. Sheremetev, "Lopasnya," 72.
24. Denike, 33.
25. Sverbeev, 2: 131–36.
26. Ibid., 1:119.
27. Labzina, 158.
28. On Nizhni, see Yankova, 98–99;
    Gerakov, 17; Custine, 4: 54–60.
29. Nikoleva, 171.
30. Ibid., 187.
31. Bakarev, 255.
32. Khvoshchinskaya, 1897, 4: 170.
33. Nikoleva, 177; Miliutin, *Vospominaniya*,
    33; Nikoleva, 190–91.
34. N. P. Makarov, 12.
35. Ibid., 10–12.
36. V. V. Sipovskii, cited in Marker, 101.
37. Marker, 105.
38. Kohl, 506.
39. Bolotov, *Zhizn*, 2: 188–89.
40. B-va., 2.
41. Cited in Lotman, *Roman*, 56.
42. Nikitenko, 1: 66, 86.
43. Tuchkova-Ogareva, 30.
44. See Scott, *Domination and the Art of Re-
    sistance* and *Weapons of the Weak*.
45. See Bolotov, *Zhizn*, 4: 565, 1034–37,
    for other tales of landowners' cruelty to
    peasants.
46. Ibid., 3: 427–40.
47. Cited in Chaikovskaya, 198.
48. See Mertvago, "Pugachevshchina."
49. The uprising led by Stenka Razin, a Don
    Cossack, in 1670–71, was so similar in cer-
    tain respects to the Pugachev rebellion of
    1773–74 that a mythical link between
    them was forged in popular memory. Peas-
    ant songs called Pugachev the "son of
    Razin," and one old man declared in the
    1840s that Pugachev "had been the second
    coming of Razin after a hundred years"
    (cited in Avrich, 122).
50. Blagovo, 159.

51. Raevskaya, 357.
52. Nikoleva, 132.
53. Ibid., 137–38.
54. See Raeff, *Political Ideas*, 65–75.
55. Blagovo, 166. To this day the facts sur-
    rounding the burning of Moscow are un-
    clear. Kutuzov appears to have misled
    Rostopchin, who learned of the French ap-
    proach only the day before Moscow was
    taken. He belatedly ordered Moscow evacu-
    ated and—most likely—burned. See
    McConnell, 109–10.
56. Ibid., 235.
57. Nikoleva, 139, 141.
58. Piksanov, 65–66.
59. Nazimova, 845.
60. Raevskaya, 357.
61. Sverbeev, 1: 46.
62. A. P. Kern, cited in Chaikovskaya, 221.

8
A Kingdom Divided

Epigraph: Chicherin, 521.
1. On serfdom, see the two pioneering works
   of Semevskii, *Krestyane* and *Krestyanskii
   vopros*. More recent classic studies are
   Confino, *Domaines et seigneurs*, and
   Kolchin, *Unfree Labor* (a comparison
   of Russian serfdom and American
   slavery).
2. On landowner attitudes toward the emancipation, see Emmons, *The Russian
   Landed Gentry*, and Field, *The End of
   Serfdom*.
3. Unkovskaya, 23.
4. Khvoshchinskaya, 1898, 3: 570.
5. See Romanovich-Slavatinskii, 278–85.
6. See Shchepetov, 93–111, 182–201, 355.
7. S. D. Sheremetev, "Vremya Pavla," 201.
8. Gogol, 155–56.
9. N. P. Makarov, 1: 9–10.
10. Blagovo, 103.
11. Cited in Romanovich-Slavatinskii, 352.
12. Ibid., 306 and throughout.
13. Sabaneeva, for instance, merely says that
    the family always referred to her great-
    grandfather, a notorious tyrant, in whis-
    pers. In spite of his reputation, as a rich
    man retired from service he played an im-

portant role among the nobility of his dis-
    trict (31–33).
14. Romanovich-Slavatinskii, 289.
15. Ibid., 357.
16. Ibid., 363.
17. See Field, *Rebels*, which describes the
    myths on both sides and gives illustrations
    of their effect in practice.
18. O'Meara, 58. K. F. Ryleev, the principled lo-
    cal assessor of the court (and future De-
    cembrist), refused to endorse the sentence,
    declaring that "the case against the defen-
    dants is based solely on the testimony of
    Count Razumovskii's bailiff and the suppo-
    sitions of the chief of police" (ibid.).
19. Romanovich-Slavatinskii, 331.
20. S. D. Sheremetev, "Vremya Pavla," 125,
    249.
21. Gerakov, 31–32.
22. The zemstvo system, established in 1864,
    provided for elected representative bodies
    at the provincial and district levels to
    handle local concerns. The zemstvos, dom-
    inated by the local nobility, were seen by
    many as the first step toward a national
    parliamentary system.
23. See Sosnina-Putsillo for this and other in-
    stances of the Musin-Pushkins' patriarchal
    concern for their serfs.
24. Tuchkova-Ogareva, 45–49, 88.
25. Shestakov, 187.
26. Wilmot and Wilmot, 146–47.
27. Hoch, 87, 163.
28. Miliutin, "Moi starcheskie," 1. These addi-
    tional unpublished notes on his childhood,
    written some years after Miliutin published
    his memoirs, are much more frank about
    his father's occasional brutality toward
    serfs.
29. Dashkova, 282.
30. Cited in P. Sheremetev, "Vyazemy,"
    135–36.
31. See A. Davydoff, 30–31.
32. Dumas, 136; Almedingen, 145.
33. Youssoupoff, 12.
34. S. D. Sheremetev, "Vremya Pavla," 217.
35. *Sbornik Russkogo istoricheskogo
    obshchestva*, 4: 202.
36. Troinitskii, 85, 88.
37. Blum, 380.

38. Reshetov, 149–54.
39. Kohl, 523.
40. Haxthausen, 64–69.
41. Custine, 4: 96.
42. Popov, 266.
43. Blagovo, 424–25; also Tuchkova, 29–30. Another profitable enterprise of this period was the cloth factory at Ostafievo, which supplied the army.
44. Bakarev, 255.
45. Ibid., 259–60.
46. Count P. P. Sukhtelen's diary for May 1816 noted that more than six hundred estates and three hundred thousand serfs were then in receivership and for sale. "He who has excess money can make outstanding purchases" (348).
47. Karpinskaya, 189.
48. Herzen, *Who Is to Blame?* 37.
49. Pushkin, *Tales of Belkin*, 87.
50. Turgenev, *A Nest of the Gentry*, 179–80.
51. Pushkin, *Tales of Belkin*, 88.
52. Turgenev, *Three Plays*, 32.
53. Goncharov, chap. 11, "Oblomov's Dream."
54. Tolstoy, *War and Peace*, 602, 455–57.
55. Khvoshchinskaya, 1897, 4: 165.
56. Ibid., 169.
57. Ibid., 169, 175, 363.
58. Ibid., 364, 369.
59. See Hamburg, 18–22. Chicherin's father became an *otkupshchik*, an official appointed to conduct the alcohol trade for his own and the state's profit. The otkupshchik was required to buy a certain amount of liquor from state factories but could also buy from other sources (or sell his own spirits if he was a noble); he resold the liquor to taverns and collected the required taxes on it for the state.
60. Frank, 15.
61. Nechaeva, 46, 49.
62. Ibid., 45.
63. See Frank's discussion, 85–87.
64. Hoch, 187.
65. Tolstoy, *War and Peace*, 354.

Part III
The Cultural Arcadia

Epigraph: Chicherin, 522.

9
Regiments of Artificers

Epigraph: Vrangel, 34.
1. Dedyukhina, 85. This article includes archival information on the names, occupations, training, and products of Sheremetev serf artisans. I am indebted to Alison Hilton for letting me read in manuscript chapter 14 ("Serf Artists, Peasant Painters, and the Rise of Genre") of her *Russian Folk Art* (Bloomington, 1994), from which I gained vital information for this chapter.
2. An Englishman visiting St. Petersburg in 1790 estimated that the pound was worth approximately 7.5 rubles (Cross, "British Sources," 24). Thus the gardener's salary was a good one, to judge by Meader's figure of 100 pounds. The serf craftsmen, however, seem by any standard to have been underpaid.
3. Sivkov, "'Shtat' sela Kuskova," 6–7. A *riza* is an ornamental metal covering for an icon that usually leaves only the face and hands of the saint visible. Some rizas are ornamented with precious stones.
4. Count A. G. Tolstoy, for example, sent two painters and a clarinet player abroad to study in the late eighteenth century (Semevskii, *Krestyane*, 1: 151).
5. Popova, 157; cited in Hilton.
6. S. D. Sheremetev, "Vremya Pavla," 229, 179.
7. Vrangel, "Pomeshchichya," 33.
8. Hilton, "Serf Artists."
9. S. D. Sheremetev, "Vremya Pavla," 208.
10. Chenevière, 59, 61.
11. S. D. Sheremetev, "Vremya Pavla," 205.
12. Wilmot and Wilmot, 228.
13. Karnovich, 289.
14. TsGADA, fond 1355, delo 22, 306–07.
15. N. V. Davydov, "Iz pomeshchichei," 192–93.
16. Moroz, 6: 315–17.
17. Hilton, "Serf Artists."
18. Fon Ritter, 4.
19. Glumov, 95.
20. Hilton, "Serf Artists."
21. Reshetov, 428.
22. Bremner, 1: 162.

23. Hilton, "Serf Artists."
24. Vigée-Lebrun, 3: 71–72.
25. Hilton, "Serf Artists."
26. See the catalogue edited by N. A. Asharina for a listing of all known ceramics and glass factories by province and district; and Popov for a list of private factories.
27. Pronina, 82–83; cited in Hilton.
28. On Tropinin's career, see Kovalenskaya and Savinov, 514–40; Hilton, "Serf Artists"; and Vrangel, *Venok*, 64–65.
29. Hilton, "Serf Artists."
30. During this trip they visited Bogoroditsk and delighted Bolotov by praising his gardens. In Paris, Pavel joined the Jacobin Club and, along with his tutor, ended up on the barricades. His father hastily summoned him home.
31. Vigée-Lebrun, 2: 316–17.
32. On Soroka's career, see Alekseeva, 267–331, and Hilton.
33. Hilton, "Serf Artists."
34. Ibid.
35. Yankova admits that their serf artist Grigory Ozerov was good only at copying. He had studied art "somewhere" but produced "wry-mouthed faces, lanky and awkward bodies" when creating work of his own. Nonetheless the Yankovs sold him (with his wife and daughter) for the respectable sum of two thousand rubles (Blagovo, 255–56).
36. Alekseeva, 330.
37. Vrangel, "Pomeshchichya," 32–33.
38. Pospelov discusses the school and this case. Stupin's school was sponsored by Nikolai Sheremetev. One of Stupin's students founded a similar school in Kozlovo, Tambov Province. See also Vrangel, *Venok*, 64–65.
39. Aksakov, *Childhood Years*, 414, 417.
40. Wrangel [Vrangel], 37.
41. Grot, 106.
42. Blagovo, 25.
43. Vrangel, "Pomeshchichya," 34.
44. Orlov-Davydov, 2: 14.
45. Griboedov, 111.
46. Glumov, 131.
47. Drizen, "Shklovskii balet," 10.
48. See Drizen, "Pokupka artistov."

49. Edwards, 168.
50. For details of Shchepkin's early life, see chaps. 1–3 of the illuminating biography by Senelick.
51. Cited in Senelick, 27–28.
52. Ibid., 29, 39, 42.
53. Ibid., 49. Similar anecdotes Shchepkin told in Moscow in 1839 furnished the material for Herzen's "*Soroka-vorokha*" (The thieving magpie), a heart-rending tale of a serf actress that greatly stimulated abolitionist sentiment in the 1840s.
54. Nikoleva, 149.
55. Vrangel, "Pomeshchichya," 25.

10
The Kingdom United

Epigraph: Tolstoy, *War and Peace*, 477.
1. See Venturi, 469–506, for a summary of the movement, which provided the plot for Ivan Turgenev's novel *Virgin Soil*.
2. Stites, *Revolutionary Dreams*, 63.
3. Cited in Denike, 37.
4. Blagovo, 235.
5. Custine, 4: 19–20.
6. Blagovo, 319.
7. Cited in Khvoshchinskaya, 1898, 4: 147.
8. M. Marina, "Golovino," 46–47.
9. Blagovo, 369–70.
10. Ibid., 21, 303, 99–100.
11. Unkovskaya, 4.
12. Moroz, 309.
13. Labzina, 17.
14. Blagovo, 432.
15. Bremner, 1: 138.
16. Nikoleva, 172.
17. Blagovo, 40.
18. Mariamna Davydova recalls as particularly "thrilling . . . the seance in the [bathhouse]," using images straight out of *Eugene Onegin*. "One had to sit there with two lit candles between the two facing mirrors. They and the lights reflected from one to the other created a long corridor, at the end of which was supposed to appear the most significant event of the year. The apparition did not appear right away. Often one had to wait for hours alone at night. Our chambermaids told us that some young girls had seen coffins and that they had died during the year: others had seen wedding processions and had married" (M. Davydoff, 22).
19. Nikoleva, 138–39.
20. M. Davydoff, 22.
21. Wilmot and Wilmot, 202–03.
22. Letter to author, May 31, 1991.
23. Grigoriev, 17–18, 23–24.
24. Letter to author, April 17, 1992.
25. Nikoleva, 131.
26. Moroz, 6: 302–03.
27. Khvoshchinskaya, 1897, 4: 162–3.
28. Unkovskaya, 24.
29. Nikoleva, 188.
30. Ibid., 107.
31. Wilmot and Wilmot, 48.
32. Nikoleva, 152.
33. Khvoshchinskaya, 1898, 3: 581.
34. Nikoleva, 138–39.
35. Wilmot and Wilmot, 141.
36. Stites, "Old Smolensk," 15–16.
37. Khvoshchinskaya, 1897, 4: 165.
38. See Vrangel, *Venok*, 62.
39. Unkovskaya, 24–25.
40. Gerakov, 68–69.
41. Gurowski, 186.
42. Khvoshchinskaya, 1897, 3: 533–34.
43. Wilmot and Wilmot, 188.
44. Blagovo, 71.
45. Slavutinsky, 214–15.
46. Kropotkin, 28.
47. Blagovo, 25.

11
Ideal Worlds

Epigraph: A. S. Pushkin, letter to P. N. Gnedich, written from Kamenka, early 1820s, cited in A. Davydoff, 27.
1. Cited in Kelly, 22–23.
2. Chicherin, 514–15.
3. Batyushkov, 4: 168.
4. The artist Fyodor Solntsev provided a key to the individuals he depicted at Priyutino in his painting (Pushkin Museum collection).
5. McConnell, 143. The first small colony was set up between Smolensk and Minsk before the war of 1812. At their height the colonies comprised one-third of the Russian army; the experiment was profitable to the state but detested by the colonists and punctuated by rebellions.
6. Commentary to "In memory of a friend," cited in Hughes, 289–90.
7. Budylina, 46–47.
8. For floor plans of Zvanka, see Nikitina, "Ob usadbe," 516–17.
9. "Evgeniyu: Zhizn Zvanskaya," in Derzhavin, *Stikhotvoreniya*, 326–34.
10. Cited in Glumov, 64.
11. Cited in Hughes, 295.
12. For "Osuga," see Kornilov, vol. 1, chaps. 1–5.
13. Ilin, *Podmoskove*, 123.
14. P. A. Vyazemskii, *Polnoe sobranie*, 7: 91.
15. *Arkhiv Knyazya Vyazemskogo*, 48.
16. Cited in Verkhovskaya, *Karamzin*, 92.
17. Cited by P. S. Sheremetev, 36–37.
18. Cited in Veselovskii, 376.
19. See Karamzin, *Neizdannye sochineniya*, 1: 165.
20. *Ostavievskii arkhiv*, 1: 47. The name of the group—Arzamas—derived from a literary quarrel. Vyazemsky's friends admired the modern Russian literary language Karamzin used and abhorred what they termed the "biblical style" of A. A. Shakhovskoy, author of the popular play "Lipetsk Waters" (1815). One day N. D. Bludov, pausing in the district town of Arzamas (Nizhni Novgorod Province) on the way to his estate, overheard some obscure writers discussing literature and wrote a satirical "Vision in an Arzamas Tavern" in Shakhovskoy's style, casting him as one of the obscure writers. Upon reading it, Zhukovsky recognized the incident's possibilities: "In a glance he envisioned a long series of jolly evenings, an unending chain of clever and decorous pranks" (Vigel, 2: 64).
21. P. P. Vyazemskii, *Sobranie sochinenii*, 528.
22. The letter was first published in *Russkii arkhiv*, 1863, 926–27.
23. Piksanov, 73.
24. G. S. Sheremetev, *Zapisnaya knizhka*, 20.
25. Piksanov, 74. After the Decembrist revolt, Griboedov was arrested in the Caucasus

and brought to St. Petersburg, but in spite of his many close friends among the conspirators he was set free.

26. Ibid.
27. *Obryukhatil* in the original.
28. Pushkin, *Polnoe sobranie*, 13: 274–75.
29. See Tarakanov; also Carr, *Romantic Exiles*, 161. The grateful serfs of Beloomut, Ryazan Province, bought the estate from Ogarev by installments over a number of years.
30. Dostoevskii, 2: 752.
31. See Frank, chap. 3.
32. Cited in Nosik, 150.
33. Ibid., 152.
34. Ibid., 154.
35. Herzen, *My Past*, 287.
36. Cited in Arzumanova, 19, 20–21.
37. Ibid.
38. A. I. Zamyatin, cited in Bogdanov, 1.
39. Turgenev, *Notebook*, 307–09.
40. Cited in Arzumanova, 61.
41. Cited in Nosik, 154.

Epilogue

Epigraph: Anton Chekhov, letter to N. A. Leikin, owner and editor of the St. Petersburg weekly *Fragments*, congratulating him on the purchase of an estate, October 12, 1885 (Simmons, 82).

1. See particularly Becker, chap. 1; also Manning.
2. S. B., 160.
3. Cited in Piksanov, 59–60.
4. Simmons, 271.
5. S. D. Sheremetev, "V doroge," 4, 54–69.
6. See Obolensky, chaps. 1 and 2.
7. See especially Sheremetev's "Mikhailovskoe."
8. Cited in Hilton, "Serf Artists."
9. Ibid.
10. Cited in Chute, 37.
11. Grabbe, 39, 49–50.
12. Anichkov, 5–6.
13. Vyazemskii, *Polnoe sobranie*, 5: 192–4.
14. Stites, *Revolutionary Dreams*, 62–63.
15. Grech, *Venok*, 1–2.
16. For a detailed picture of destruction and heroic restoration, see Massie, pt. 2.

Works Cited

Primary Sources

Adam, M. "Iz semeinoi khroniki" (From a family chronicle). *Istoricheskii vestnik* (1903) 12: 816–27.

Afanasiev, N. Ya. "Vospominaniya" (Reminiscences). *Istoricheskii vestnik* (1899) 8: 255–76.

Aksakov, S. T. *A Family Chronicle* and *Childhood Years of Bagrov Grandson*. Translated by O. Shartze. Moscow, 1984.

———. "Vospominaniia" (Reminiscences). In *Sobranie sochinenii* (Collected works), vol. 2. Moscow, 1955.

Arkhiv Knyazya F. A. Kurakina (The archive of Prince F. A. Kurakin). 5 vols. Saratov, 1890–94.

Arkhiv Knyazya Vorontsova (The archive of Prince Vorontsov). 40 vols. Moscow, 1870–95.

Arkhiv Knyazya Vyazemskogo (The archive of Prince Vyazemsky). St. Petersburg, 1881.

B., S. "Iz nedavnyago proshlogo (bytovye ocherki)" (The recent past [notes on daily life]). *Russkaya starina* 143 (1910) 8: 246–66; 9: 441–59.

B-n., S. "Vospominaniya" (Reminiscences). *Russkaya shkola* (1911) 4: 155–76; 5/6: 127–59; 7/8: 163–92; 9: 79–95.

Bakarev, V. A. "Usadba nachala devyat-nadtsatogo veka" (An estate of the beginning of the nineteenth century). *Krasnyi arkhiv* (1936) 5: 254–62.

Bardakova, M. M. "Golovino." *Russkii arkhiv* 3 (1915) 9/10: 44–54.

Batiushkov, K. N. *Sochineniya* (Works). Moscow, 1955.

Belov, I. *Putevye zametki i vpechatleniya po Moskovskoi i Tverskoi guberniyam Yosifa Belova* (The travel observations and impressions of Joseph Belov on Moscow and Tver Provinces). Moscow, 1852.

Blagovo, D. *Razskazy babushki: Iz vospominanii pyati pokolenii* (Grand-mother's tales: The reminiscences of five generations). St. Petersburg, 1885.

Bolotov, A. T. *Zhizn i priklyucheniya Andreya Timofeevicha Bolotova* (The life and adventures of Andrei Timofeevich Bolotov). 4 vols. Moscow, 1873.

———. "Nekotorye zamechaniya o sadakh v Rossii" (Some observations about gardens in Russia). *Ekonomicheskii magazin* 20 (1784): 53–60.

Bremner, Robert. *Excursions in the Interior of Russia*. 2 vols. London, 1839.

Burianov, V. *Progulka s detmi po Rossii* (A stroll with the children around Russia). St. Petersburg, 1839.

Buturlin, Mikhail D., Count. "Teatr grafa Kamenskago v Orele v 1827 i 1828 godakh" (The theater of Count Kamenskii in Orel in 1827 and 1828). *Russkii arkhiv* (1869) 3: 1407–14.

———. "Zapiski" (Memoirs). *Russkii arkhiv* (1897) 2: 213–47; 3: 396–444; 4: 597–601; 5: 5–47; 6: 177–256; 7: 337–439; 8: 529–601; (1898) 1: 125–64; 2: 239–76; 3: 388–424; 10: 153–222.

Chicherin, B. N. "Iz moikh vospominanii" (From my reminiscences). *Russkii arkhiv* (1890) 4: 501–25.

Coxe, William. *Travels in Poland and Russia*. 2 vols. in 1. New York, 1970.

Custine, Marquis de. *La Russie en 1839*. 4 vols. Brussels, 1843.

Dallas, G. M. *The Diary of George Mifflin Dallas, United States Minister to Russia, 1837–1839*. New York, 1970.

Dashkova, Ekaterina D., Princess. *The Memoirs of Princess Dashkov*. Translated by Kyril Fitzlyon. London, 1958.

Davydoff, Alexander. *Russian Sketches: Memoirs*. Ann Arbor, 1984.

Davydoff, Mariamna. *Memoirs of a Russian Lady*. New York, 1986.

Davydov, N. V. "Iz pomeshchichei zhizni proshlogo stoletiya" (The life of a land-owner in the last century). *Golos minuvshego* (1916) 2: 164–200.

———. "V Spasskom" (At Spasskoe). In *Iz proshlogo* (From the past). Moscow, 1913.

Derzhavin, G. R. *Sochineniya* (Works). 9 vols. in 1. Cambridge, Eng., 1973.

———. *Stikhotvoreniya* (Poems). Leningrad, 1957.

Dolgorukaya, Natalya. *The Memoirs of Princess Natalja Borisovna Dolgorukaja*. Translated by Charles Townsend. Columbus, 1977.

Dolgoruky, Ivan M. *Slavny bubny za gorami, ili puteshestvie moe koe-kuda 1810 goda* (Travelers have the privilege of lying, or my trip to various parts in 1810). Moscow, 1870.

———. *Sochineniya* (Works). Moscow, 1919.

Dostoevskii, Fyodor M. *The Diary of a Writer*. 2 vols. Translated by Boris Brasol. London, 1949.

Dumas, Alexandre. *Voyage en Russie*. Paris: Hermann, 1960.

Durova, Nadezhda. *The Cavalry Maiden*. Translated by M. F. Zirin. Bloomington, 1989.

Edwards, Sutherland. *The Russians at Home*. London, 1861.

The Englishwoman in Russia. London, 1855. Reprint, New York, 1970.

Freeze, G. L. *From Supplication to Revolution: A Documentary Social History of Imperial Russia*. New York, 1988.

Gerakov, G. V. *Putevye zapiski po mnogim rossiiskim guberniyam 1820* (Memoirs of travel through many Russian provinces in 1820). 2 vols. St. Petersburg, 1828, 1830.

Glagolev, A. *Zapiski russkago puteshest-vennika A. Glagoleva* (The memoirs of the Russian traveler A. Glagolev). St. Petersburg, 1855.

Glinka, F. N. *Izbrannoe* (Selected works). Petrozavodsk, 1949.

Glinka, S. N. *Zapiski* (Memoirs). St. Petersburg, 1895.

Gogol, Nikolai. *Dead Souls*. Translated by B. G. Guerney. New York, 1960.

Golovine, Ivan. *Russia under the Autocrat Nicholas the First*. 2 vols. Reprint, New York, 1940.

Goncharov, Ivan. *Oblomov*. Translated by N. Duddington. New York, 1960.

Grabbe, Paul. *Windows on the Neva*. New York, 1977.

Griboedov, Alexander S. *Wit Works Woe*. Translated by B. Pares. In *Masterpieces of the Russian Drama*, edited by G. R. Noyes. New York, 1933.

Grigoriev, Apollon. *My Literary and Moral Wanderings and Other Autobiographical Material*. Translated by R. E. Matlaw. New York, 1962.

Grot, N. P. *Iz semeinoi khroniki: Vospominaniya dlya detei i vnukov* (A family chronicle: Reminiscences for [my] children and grandchildren). St. Petersburg, 1900.

Gurianov, I. "Progulka v Lyublino" (A stroll at Lyublino). *Otechestvennye zapiski* (1825) 66: 201–28.

Gurowski, A., Count. *Russia as It Is*. 2d ed. New York, 1854.

Haxthausen, August von. *Studies on the Interior of Russia*. Edited by S. F. Starr. Translated by E. Schmidt. Chicago, 1972.

Herzen, Alexander. *My Past and Thoughts*. Edited by D. Macdonald. Translated by C. Garnett. Berkeley, 1973.

———. *Who Is to Blame?* Translated by Margaret Wettlin. Moscow, 1978.

Karamzin, N. M. *Letters of a Russian Traveler*. Translated by F. Jonas. New York, 1957.

———. *Neizdannye sochineniya i pere-piska*. 2 vols. St. Petersburg, 1862.

Karpinskaya, Yu. N. "Iz semeinoi khroniki" (A family chronicle). *Istoricheskii vestnik* (1897) 12: 853–70.

Karpov, V. N. *Vospominaniya* (Reminiscences). Moscow-Leningrad, 1933.

Khvoshchinskaya, E. "Vospominaniya" (Reminiscences). *Russkaya starina* (1897) 3: 514–33; 4: 159–78; 5: 357–74; (1898) 3: 559–85; 4: 137–48; 5: 407–21, 6: 631–44; 7: 157–74.

Kohl, J. G. *Russia Observed*. London, 1844.

Kolbe, Edward. *Recollections of Russia during Thirty-Three Years' Residence, by a German Nobleman*. Edinburgh, 1855.

Kornilova, O. I. *Byl iz vremen krepost-nichestva* (A tale from the days of serf-dom). St. Petersburg, 1890.

Kovalevskaya, S. *Vospominaniya detstva* (Reminiscences of childhood). Moscow, 1960.

Kropotkin, Peter, Prince. *Memoirs of a Revolutionist*. New York, 1971.

Kurakin, F. A., ed. *Vosemnadtsatyi vek: Sbornik statei i materialov* (The eighteenth century: A collection of articles and materials). 2 vols. Moscow, 1904–05.

Labzina, A. E. *Vospominaniya* (Reminiscences). St. Petersburg, 1914.

Lavrov, P. S. "Dnevnik" (Diary). *Russkii arkhiv* (1878) 2: 444–59.

Lyall, Robert. *Travels in Russia, the Krimea, the Caucasus, and Georgia*. 2 vols. London, 1825.

"M." "Cherty iz zhizni russkikh dvoryan v kontse vosemnadtsatogo veka" (Aspects of the life of Russian nobles at the end of the eighteenth century). *Moskovskii nablyudatel* 2 (September 1936): 243–52.

Makarov, N. P. *Moi semidesiatiletnyia vospominaniya* (My seven decades of rec-ollections). 2 vols. St. Petersburg, 1881.

Marina, M. "Golovino." *Russkii arkhiv* (1915) 9–10: 44–54.

Marina, M. M. [M. M. Bardakova]. "Iz semeinoi khroniki minuvshago veka" (From a family chronicle of the preceding century). *Istoricheskii vestnik* (1910) 10: 184–206.

Martynov, A. M. "Selo Stepanovskoe" (The village of Stepanovksoe). *Russkii arkhiv* (1895) 4: 534–35.

Mengden, E. "Iz dnevnika vnuchka" (From the diary of a granddaughter). *Russkaya starina* (1913) 1: 103–31.

———. "Luchi proshlago" (Light of the past). *Russkaya starina* (1908) 4: 97–116; 5: 325–48.

Mertvago, D. B. "Pugachevshchina" (The time of Pugachev). *Russkoe bogatstvo* (1857) no. 7, book 1.

Miliutin, D. A. "Moi starcheskie vospominaniya za 1816–1873 gg." OR GBL, f. 169, k. 11.

———. *Vospominaniya* (Memoirs). Tomsk, 1914. Reprint, Newtonville, 1979.

Moroz, D. K. "Iz moego davnoproshed-shago" (From my distant past). *Kievskaya starina* 49 (1895) 5: 31–64; 6: 301–22.

Morton, Edward. *Travels in Russia, and a Residence at St. Petersburg and Odessa in the Years 1827–1829*. London, 1830.

"N." "Opisanie botanicheskago sada E. S. Grafa A. K. Razumovskago, v Gorenkakh bliz Moskvy" (Description of the botanical garden of [His Excellency] Count A. K. Razumovskii at Gorenki near Moscow). *Vestnik Evropy*, pt. 52 (1810) 13: 52–62.

N., Olga [S. V. Engelgardt]. "Iz vospominanii" (From my memories). *Russkii vestnik* 1887 (191), 10: 690–715; (193), 11: 159–80.

Nazimova, M. G. "Babushka Grafinya M. G. Razumovskaya" (My grandmother, Countess M. G. Razumovskaya). *Isto-richeskii vestnik* (1899) 3: 841–54.

Neverov, Ya. M. "Stranitsa iz istorii krepostnogo prava" (A page from the history of serfdom). *Russkaya starina* (1883). 11: 429–46.

Nikitenko, A. S. *Moya povest o samom sebe: Zapiski i dnevnik, 1804–77* (My story about myself: Memoirs and Diary, 1804–77). 2 vols. St. Petersburg, 1904.

Nikolaeva, M. [Tsebrikova, M. K.]. "Stranitsa k istorii nashego zhenskago domashnyago vospitaniya v nedavnyuyu starinu" (A page for the history of our home education for women in the recent past). *Russkaya shkola* (1893) 5/6: 30–63, 7/8: 29–56.

Nikoleva, M. S. "Cherty starinnago dvoryanskago byta" (Aspects of the old way of life of the nobility). *Russkii arkhiv* (1893) 9: 107–20; 10: 129–96.

Obolensky, Serge. *One Man in His Time*. New York, 1958.

Olearius, Adam. *The Travels of Olearius in Seventeenth-Century Russia*. Edited and translated by Samuel Baron. Stanford, 1967.

Orlov-Davydov, V. P. *Biograficheskii ocherk grafa V. G. Orlova* (A biographical sketch of Count V. G. Orlov). 2 vols. St. Petersburg, 1878.

Ostavievskii arkhiv kniazei Vyazemskikh (The archive of the princes Vyazemsky at Ostafievo). Edited by S. D. Sheremetev. 3 vols. St. Petersburg, 1899.

Ostrozhskii-Lokhvitskii, I. O. *Zapiski* (Memoirs). Kiev, 1896.

P., N. "Epizod iz vremen krepostnogo prava" (An episode from the time of serfdom). *Russkaya starina* 125 (1906) 1: 163–68.

Podolskaya, I. I., ed. *Russkie memuary: Izbrannye stranitsy XVIII vek* (Russian memoirs: Selected pages from the eighteenth century). Moscow, 1988.

Polnoe sobranie zakonov Rossiskoi imperii (Complete collection of laws of the Russian empire). 1st ser. 45 vols. St. Petersburg, 1830.

Pushkin, Alexander S. "Pisma, 1815–30" (Letters, 1815–30). In *Sochineniya*, vol. 9. Moscow, 1977.

———. *Polnoe sobranie sochinenii* (Complete collected works). 17 vols. Leningrad, 1937–39.

———. *Sochineniya* (Works). 3 vols. Moscow, 1962.

———. *The Tales of Ivan Belkin*. Translated by I. and T. Litvinov. Moscow, 1954.

Radishchev, A. *Puteshestvie iz Peterburga v Moskvu* (Journey from Petersburg to Moscow). Moscow, 1950.

Raevskaya, E. I. "Babushka Ekaterina Aleksandrovna Bibikova" (My grandmother Ekaterina Aleksandrovna Bibikova). *Russkii arkhiv* (1883) 4: 352–60.

———. "Prizhivalshchiki i prizhivalki" (Male and female hangers-on). *Russkii arkhiv* (1883) 3: 70–79.

———. "V pamyat V. A. Zolotova" (In memory of V. A. Zolotov). *Russkii arkhiv* (1883) 1: 200–06.

———. "Vospominaniya" (Reminiscences). *Istoricheskii vestnik* (1898) 11: 523–56; 12: 938–75.

Raevskii, I. A. "Iz vospominanii" (From my recollections). *Istoricheskii vestnik* (1905) 8: 391–409.

Reshetov, N. F. "Dela davno minuvshikh dnei" (Deeds of the distant past). *Russkii arkhiv* (1885) 5: 149–54; 6: 300–04; 7: 428–41; 11: 443; 12: 539–47; (1886) 2: 212–18; 3: 363–68; 4: 525–33; 10: 221–39; 12: 497–515; (1887) 3: 350–55.

Ritter, A. A. von. *Otzvuki minuvshago* (Echoes of the past). 3d ed. Moscow, 1899.

Rostopchina, L. A. *Semeinaya khronika* (A family chronicle). Moscow, 1912.

Rusov, N. N., ed. *Pomeshchichya Rossiya po zapiskam sovremennikov* (The Russia of landowners in contemporary memoirs). Moscow, 1911.

Sabaneeva, E. A. *Vospominaniya o bylom* (Reminiscences of the past). St. Petersburg, 1914.

Sbornik imperatorskogo russkogo istoricheskogo obshchestva (Anthology of the Imperial Russian Historical Society). 148 vols. St. Petersburg, 1867–1916.

Segur, Louis Philippe. *Zapiski grafa Segura o prebyvanii ego v Rossii* (Notes by Count Segur of his stay in Russia). St. Petersburg, 1865.

Selivanov, V. V. *Sochineniya* (Works). 2 vols. St. Petersburg, 1881.

Sh., A. "Podlinnyia vospominaniya byvshago krepostnago" (Actual recollections of the former epoch of serfdom). *Russkoe bogatstvo* (1885) 5/6: 342–70.

———. "Pomeste Saltychikhi" (The estate of Saltychikha). *Russkii arkhiv* (1871) 7/8: 1281–86.

Shatilov, N. "Iz nedavnago proshlago" (From the recent past). *Golos minuvshago* (1916) 1: 165–201; 4: 205–25; 10: 45–47.

Shch., A. "Semeinye vospominaniya" (Family recollections). *Atenei* (1858) 11/12: 462–69.

Sheremetev, S. D. *Domashnaya starina* (The old days at home). Moscow, 1900.

———. "Vremya Imperatora Pavla" (The times of Emperor Paul). In *Otgoloski vosemnadtsatogo veka* (Echoes of the eighteenth century), vol. 11. Moscow, 1905.

———. *Vospominaniya detstva* (Recollections of childhood). St. Petersburg, 1896.

Shestakov, I. A. "Zapiski" (Memoirs). *Russkii arkhiv* (1873) 2: 164–200.

Shompulev, V. A. "Iz proshlogo Saratovskoi gubernii" (From the past of Saratov Province). *Russkaya starina* (1897) (89), 3: 535–40; (92) 11: 323–30; (1898) (94) 4: 191–95; 5: 347–50; (95) 8: 321–35; (1901) (105) 3: 733–38.

———. "Piknik pod Nikolin den: Iz zapisok starago pomeshchika" (Picnic on St. Nikolas' Day: From the memoirs of an old landowner). *Russkaya starina* 134 (1908) 6: 611–12.

Slavutinskii, S. F. "Rodnye mesta" (Native places). *Russkii vestnik* (1880) 5: 198–240.

Smith, M. A. P. *Six Years' Travels in Russia*. 2 vols. London, 1859.

Sukhtelen, P. P., Count. "Iz zapisnoi knizhki grafa P. P. Sukhtelena" (From the notebook of Count P. P. Sukhtelen). *Russkii arkhiv* (1876) 3: 346–55.

Sverbeev, D. I. *Zapiski* (Memoirs). 2 vols. Moscow, 1899.

Svinin, P. P. "Stranstviya v okrestnostiakh Moskvy" (Peregrinations in the environs of Moscow). *Otechestvennye zapiski* (1822), pt. 9, no. 12: 3–34; pt. 12, no. 30: 3–32.

346

Tolstoy, Leo. *Anna Karenina.* Translated by Aylmer Maude. New York, 1970.

———. *Childhood, Boyhood and Youth.* Translated by Rosemary Edmunds. Baltimore, 1964.

———. *War and Peace.* Translated by Constance Garnett. New York, n.d.

Tolstoy, Peter. *The Travel Diary of Peter Tolstoi.* Edited and translated by Max J. Okenfuss. DeKalb, 1987.

Tolycheva, T. *Semeinye zapiski* (Family memoirs). Moscow, 1903.

Tuchkova-Ogareva, Natalia A. *Vospominaniya* (Reminiscences). Moscow, 1959.

Turgenev, A. M. "Zapiski" (Memoirs). *Russkaya starina* 47 (1885) 12: 473–86.

Turgenev, I. S. *Fathers and Sons.* Translated by B. Makanowitzky. New York, 1959.

———. *Rudin* and *A Nest of the Gentry.* Translated by Kathleen Cook and Bernard Isaacs. 2 vols. in 1. Moscow, 1985.

———. *Sochineniya* (Works). 28 vols. Moscow-Leningrad, 1961.

———. *A Sportsman's Notebook.* Translated by C. and A. Hepburn. New York, 1957.

———. *Three Plays.* Translated by Constance Garnett. London, 1934.

Turgenev, N. I. *Dnevniki i pisma Nik. Iv. Turgeneva* (The diaries and letters of Nikita Ivanovich Turgenev). 3 vols. Moscow, 1911–21.

Unkovskaya, A. *Vospominaniya* (Reminiscences). Petrograd, 1917.

Vereshchagin, Alexander. *Doma i na voine, 1853–81* (At home and at war, 1853–81). St. Petersburg, 1885.

Vereshchagin, V. V. *Detstvo i otrochestvo* (Childhood and adolescence). St. Petersburg, 1875.

Vigée-Lebrun, Marie-Louise-Elisabeth. *Mémoires.* 4 vols. Paris, 1835.

Vigel, Filipp F. *Zapiski* (Memoirs). 2 vols. Moscow, 1928.

Vinitskii, F. N. *Razskazy iz bylogo vremeni* (Tales of bygone days). Moscow, 1874.

Vinskii, G. S. "Moe vremya" (My times). *Russkii arkhiv* (1877) 1: 77–123.

Volkova, M. A. *Otgoloski 1812–13 godov v pismakh* (Echoes of 1812–13 in letters). Moscow, 1912.

Von Gun, O. *Poverkhnostnyia zamechaniya po doroge ot Moskvy v Malorossii k oseni 1805 g.* (Superficial observations while on the road from Moscow to Little Russia in the autumn of 1805). Moscow, 1806.

Vulf, A. N. *Dnevniki* (Diaries). Moscow, 1929.

Vyazemskii, P. A. "Ocherki i vospominaniya" (Sketches and reminiscences). *Russkii arkhiv* (1877) 3: 305–14.

———. "Zametki iz vospominaniya" (Notes from my reminiscences). In *Polnoe sobranie sochinenii* (Complete collected works), vol. 7. St. Petersburg, 1882.

Vyazemskii, P. P. *Sobranie sochineniya* (Collected works). St. Petersburg, 1893.

Wilmot, Martha, and Catherine Wilmot. *The Russian Journals of Martha and Catherine Wilmot.* London, 1934.

Wrangel, Peter N., Baron and General. *From Serfdom to Bolshevism.* Philadelphia, 1927.

Youssoupoff, Felix, Prince. *Lost Splendor.* New York, 1954.

Zagoskin, S. N. "Vospominaniya" (Reminiscences). *Istoricheskii vestnik* 79 (1900) 1: 41–48; 2: 489–530; 3: 921–46; 4: 51–72; 5: 403–29; 6: 790–815; 7: 36–61; 8: 416–34.

Zaitsev, I. K. "Vospominaniya starogo uchitelya" (Recollections of an old teacher). *Russkaya starina* 54 (1887) 6: 33–45.

Zhukovskii, V. A. "Pismo V. A. Zhukovskago k P. I. Golubkovu, 25 Maya 1809" (Letter of V. A. Zhukovskii to P. I. Golubkov, 25 May 1809). *Russkii arkhiv* (1863) 5: 925–27.

Zinoviev, V. A. "Otryvki iz dnevnika" (Diary excerpts). *Russkaya starina* 23 (1878) 12: 611–30.

———. "Zhurnal puteshestviya po Germanii, Italii, Frantsii, i Anglii, 1786–90" (Journal of a trip through Germany, Italy, France, and England). *Russkaya starina* 23 (1878) 12: 593–610.

Secondary Sources

Alekseeva, T. V. *Khudozhniki shkoly Venetsianova* (Artists of the Venetsyanov school). Moscow, 1982.

Almedingen, E. M. *Life of Many Colours.* London, 1958.

Anichkov, I. V. *Obzor pomeshchikh usadeb Novgorodskoi gubernii* (Survey of the estates of landowners of Novgorod Province). Novgorod, 1916.

Anikst, M. A., and V. S. Turchin. *V okrestnostyakh Moskvy* (In the environs of Moscow). Moscow, 1979.

Anisimov, Iu. "Olgovo." *Podmoskovnye muzei* no. 4. Moscow-Leningrad, 1925, 7–65.

Arzumanova, O. I., A. G. Kuznetsova, T. N. Makarova, and V. A. Nevskii. *Muzei-zapovednik Abramtsevo* (The Abramtsevo museum and estate). Moscow, 1983.

Asharina, N. A., ed. *Iz istorii Russkoi keramiki i stekla semnac̆tsatykh-devyatnadtsatykh vekov: Sbornik trudov* (The history of Russian ceramics and glass from the seventeenth to the nineteenth centuries: Collected essays). Moscow, 1986.

Avrich, Paul. *Russian Rebels, 1600–1800.* New York, 1972.

B-va., A. "Iz istorii odnogo ugolka na Volge" (The history of one nook on the Volga). *Rodnoi krai* 3 (June 8, 1922): 2–5.

Banac, I., and P. Bushkovich, eds. *The Nobility in Russia and Eastern Europe.* New Haven, 1983.

Baranova, O. *Kuskovo.* Leningrad, 1983.

Basova, E. "Byt vysshikh sloev obshchestva." (The life of high society). In *Iz epokhi krepostnogo khozyaistva vosemnadtsatykh i devyatnadtsatykh vv: Stati i putevoditel* (From the epoch of serfdom of the eighteenth and nineteenth centuries: Articles and a guide). Moscow, 1926.

Beard, Geoffrey. *The Work of Robert Adam.* London, 1978.

Becker, Seymour. *Nobility and Privilege in Late Imperial Russia.* DeKalb, 1985.

Bluche, François. *La vie quotidienne de la noblesse française au dix-huitième siècle.* Paris, 1973.

Blum, Jerome. *Lord and Peasant in Russia.* New York, 1965.

Bogdanov, B. "Na rodine I. S. Turgeneva" (In the homeland of I. S. Turgenev). Moscow, 1984.

Bovill, E. W. *English Country Life, 1780–1830.* London, 1962.

Brown, W. E. *A History of Russian Literature of the Romantic Period.* 4 vols. Ann Arbor, 1986.

Budylina, M. V., O. I. Brattseva, and A. M. Kharlamova. *Arkhitektor N. A. Lvov* (N. A. Lvov, architect). Moscow, 1961.

Bush, M. L. *Rich Noble, Poor Noble.* 2 vols. Manchester, 1988.

Carr, E. H. *Michael Bakunin.* New York, 1961.

———. *The Romantic Exiles.* Boston, 1961.

Chaikovskaya, Olga. "*Kak lyubopytnyi skif . . .*": *Russkii portret i memuaristika vtoroi poloviny vosemnadtsatogo v.* ("Like a curious Scythian . . .": The Russian portrait and memoir in the second half of the eighteenth century). Moscow, 1990.

Chechulin, N. D. *Russkoe provintsialnoe obshchestvo vo vtoroi polovine vosemnadtsatogo veka* (Russian provincial society in the second half of the eighteenth century). St. Petersburg, 1889.

Chenevière, Antoine. *Russian Furniture: The Golden Age, 1780–1840.* New York, 1988.

Chute, Patricia. *Tolstoy at Yasnaya Polyana.* New York, 1991.

Confino, Michael. *Domaines et seigneurs en Russie.* Paris, 1963.

Cox, E. H. M. "An English Gardener at the Russian Court, 1779–87." *New Flora and Silva* (1939) 1: 103–12.

Cracraft, James. "James Brogden in Russia, 1787–1788." *Slavonic and East European Review* 108 (1969): 241.

———. *The Petrine Revolution in Russian Architecture.* Chicago, 1988.

Cross, A. D. "British Sources for Catherine's Russia: (1) Lionel Colmore's Letters from St. Petersburg, 1790–91." *Study Group on Eighteenth-Century Russia Newsletter,* no. 17 (July 1989): 24–29.

———. "*By the Banks of the Thames*": *Russians in Eighteenth-Century Britain.* Newtonville, 1980.

———. "The English Garden and Russia: An Anonymous Identified." *Study Group on Eighteenth-Century Russia Newsletter,* no. 2 (September 1974): 25–29.

———. "'The Great Patroness of the North': Catherine II's Role in Fostering Anglo-Russian Cultural Contacts." *Study Group on Eighteenth-Century Russia Newsletter,* no. 6 (September 1978): 67–82.

———. "Russian Gardens, British Gardeners." *Garden History* (1991) 1: 12–20.

———. *Russia under Western Eyes, 1517–1825.* New York, 1971.

Dedyukhina, V. S. "K voprosu o roli krepostnykh masterov v istorii stroitelstva dvoryanskoi usadby XVIII v. (na primere Kuskovo i Ostankino)" (On the question of the role of serf masters in the history of the construction of the eighteenth-century noble estate [as exemplified by Kuskovo and Ostankino]). *Vestnik Moskovskogo Universiteta (Istoriya),* ser. 8, no. 4, 1981.

De Madariaga, Isabel. *Russia in the Age of Catherine the Great.* New Haven, 1981.

Denike, B. "Rai-Semenovskoe." *Sredi kollektsionerov* (1924) 9–12: 31–38.

Drizen, N. V., Baron. "Naryshkinskie pevchie" (Naryshkin's singers). *Stolitsa i usadba* (1914) 14/15: 13–15.

———. "Pokupka artistov" (The purchase of artists). *Stolitsa i usadba* (1915) 29: 6–9.

———. "Shklovskii balet" (The Shklov ballet). *Stolitsa i usadba* (1914) 12/13: 8–11.

Dukes, Paul. *Catherine the Great and the Russian Nobility.* Cambridge, 1967.

Dynnik, Tatyana. *Krepostnoi teatr* (Serf theater). Moscow, 1933.

Elizarova, N. A. *Teatry Sheremetevykh.* Moscow. 1944.

Emmons, Terrence. *The Russian Landed Gentry and the Peasant Emancipation of 1861.* Cambridge, Eng., 1968.

Field, Daniel. *The End of Serfdom: Nobility and Bureaucracy in Russia, 1855–1861.* Cambridge, Mass., 1976.

———. *Rebels in the Name of the Tsar.* Boston, 1989.

Fleming, L., and A. Gore. *The English Garden.* London, 1979.

Ford, Franklin. *Robe and Sword.* Cambridge, Mass., 1965.

Frank, Joseph. *Dostoevsky: The Seeds of Revolt, 1821–1849.* Princeton, 1976.

Girouard, Mark. *Life in the English Country House.* New Haven, 1978.

Glumov, A. *N. A. Lvov.* Moscow, 1980.

Golombevskii, A. "Pokinutaya usadba: Selo Nadezhdino, byvshee imenie knyazei Kurakinykh" (An abandoned estate: The village of Nadezhdino, the former estate of the princes Kurakin). *Starye gody* (1911) January: 3–25.

Goodwin, A., ed. *The European Nobility in the Eighteenth Century.* London, 1953.

Grech, A. "Sobiratelstvo v staroi Moskve" (Collecting in old Moscow). *Sredi kollektsionerov* (1923) 7–10: 61–63.

———. "Venok usadbam" (A wreath for the estates). Manuscript, 1938(?). Manuscript Division, Russian Historical Museum, Moscow.

Hadfield, Miles. *A History of British Gardening.* London, 1960.

Hamburg, G. M. *Boris Chicherin and Early Russian Liberalism.* Stanford, 1992.

Hayden, Peter. "British Seats on Imperial Russian Tables."*Garden History* 13 (1985) 1: 17–32.

———. "Imperial Culture at Pavlovsk." *Country Life,* June 1987, 118–19.

———. "A Note on Jacques Delille." *Garden History* (1990) 2: 195–97.

———. "Pavlovsk." *The Garden*, June 1982, 219–24.

———. "Russian Patrons of English Pottery." *Britain-USSR* 72 (December 1985): 6–9.

Hilton, Alison. "Serf Artists." In *Russian Folk Art and the Patterns of Life*. Bloomington, 1995.

Hoch, Steven L. *Serfdom and Social Control in Russia*. Chicago, 1984.

Hughes, Lindsey. "N. A. Lvov and the Russian Country House." In *Russia and the World of the Eighteenth Century*, edited by R. P. Bartlett, A. G. Cross, and Karen Rasmussen. Columbus, 1984.

Ilin, M. A. *Podmoskove* (The environs of Moscow). Moscow, 1966.

Ivask, Yu. *Selo Sukhanovo* (The village of Sukhanovo). Moscow, 1915.

Jackson-Stops, Gervase, and James Pipkin. *The English Country House: A Grand Tour*. New York, 1985.

Jones, Robert E. *Provincial Development in Russia*. New Brunswick, 1984.

Karnovich, E. P. *Zamechatelnyia bogatstva chastnykh lits v Rossii* (The remarkable wealth of private individuals in Russia). St. Petersburg, 1874. Reprint, The Hague, 1965.

Kazarinov, L. "Krepostnoi teatr pomeshchika Obreskova" (The serf theater of the landowner Obreskov). *Istoricheskii sbornik Chukhlomskogo otd. Kostrom. nauchn. O-va*, no. 3, Chukhloma, 1928.

Kelly, Aileen. *Mikhail Bakunin*. New Haven, 1987.

Kolchin, Peter. *Unfree Labor: American Slavery and Russian Serfdom*. Cambridge, 1987.

Kornilov, A. A. *Molodye gody Mikhaila Bakunina* (The youthful years of Mikhail Bakunin). 2 vols. Moscow, 1915.

Kosarevskii, I. A. *Iskusstvo parkogo peizazha* (The art of park landscape). Moscow, 1977.

Kovalenskaya, N. N., and A. A. Savinov. "V. A. Tropinin i portretisti nachala devyatnadtsatogo veka" (V. A. Tropinin and portraitists of the early nineteenth

century). *Istoriya Russkogo iskusstva*. Vol. 8, pt. 1. Moscow, 1963.

Krasnov, Vasily. "Usadba Goncharovykh" (The Goncharov estate). *Stolitsa i usadba* 5 (March 1, 1914): 3–6.

Kvyatkovskaya, N. K. *Marfino*. Moscow, 1985.

———. *Ostafievo*. Moscow, 1990.

Lahana, Martha. "Breaking the Rules in Muscovy: The Example of A. S. Matveev." Paper presented at the twenty-eighth annual meeting of the Southern Conference on Slavic Studies, Savannah, Ga., 1990.

Lansere, Nikolai. "Zabytaya prigorodnaya usadba vosemnadtsatogo veka" (A forgotten suburban estate of the eighteenth century). *Sredi kollektsionerov* (1924) July–August: 36–44.

Lazarevskii, Ivan I., and V. Egor, eds. "Ostafievo, Muranovo, Abramtsevo." *Podmoskovnye muzei* (1925): 9–36.

Lepskaya, L. A. "Novoe o krepostnykh shkolakh kontsa vosemnadtsatogo-nachala devyatnadtsatogo v. v votchinakh Sheremetevykh" (New findings about the serf schools of the late eighteenth and early nineteenth centuries on the Sheremetev ancestral lands). *Pamyatniki kultury* 13 (1987): 71–76.

———. "Ostankinskii teatr: Predystoriia. Zamysl. Voploshchenie" (The Ostankino theater: Prehistory. Design. Realization.). In *Novye materialy po istorii russkoi kultury: Ostankinskii dvorets-muzei, Sbornik trudov* (New materials on the history of Russian culture: Ostankino Palace-Museum, collection of essays). Moscow, 1987: 62–78.

Likhachev, Dmitry S. *Poeziya sadov* (The poetry of gardens). Leningrad, 1982.

Logvinskaya, E. Ya. *Interer v Russkoi zhivopisi pervoi poloviny XIX veka* (The interior in Russian painting in the first half of the nineteenth century). Moscow, 1978.

Longinov, Mikhail N. "Neskolko izvestii o Penzenskom pomeshchike Struiskom" (Some information about the Penza land-

owner Struiskii). *Russkii arkhiv* 31 (1865) 958–63.

Lotman, Yu. M. *Roman A. S. Pushkina "Evgenii Onegin": Kommentarii* (A. S. Pushkin's novel "Eugene Onegin": A commentary). Leningrad, 1983.

Lotman, Yu. M., L. Ia. Ginsburg, and B. A. Uspenskii. *The Semiotics of Russian Cultural History*. Edited by A. D. Nakhimovskii and A. S. Nakhimovskii. Ithaca, 1985.

Lotman, Yu. M., and B. A. Uspenskij. *The Semiotics of Russian Culture*. Edited by A. Shukman. Ann Arbor, 1984.

Lukomskii, Georgii. "Dva tainstvennykh dvortsa Razumovskikh" (Two secret palaces of the Razumovskiis). *Stolitsa i usadba* 16–17 (September 1, 1914): 3–8.

———. *Pamyatniki starinnoi arkhitektury Rossii* (Monuments of old Russian architecture). Petrograd, 1916.

———. *Starinnyia usadby Kharkovskoi gubernii* (Historic estates of Kharkov Province), vol. 1. Petrograd, 1917.

Lyubetskii, S. N. "Gulyane v Kuskove, pri Imperatritse Ekaterine II, vo vremya prazdnovaniya 25-letiya ee tsarstvovaniya" (A promenade at Kuskovo during the reign of Empress Catherine II, at the time of the celebration of the twenty-fifth anniversary of her reign). *Sovremennaya Letopis*, no. 27, 1866.

———. *Selo Ostankino s okrestnostyami svoimi* (The village of Ostankino and its surroundings). Moscow, 1868.

McConnell, Allen. *Tsar Alexander I*. Northbrook, 1970.

Maikova, K. A. "Arkhiv Orlovykh-Davydovykh" (The archive of the Orlov-Davydovs). *Zapiski Otdela Rukopisei* (Notes of the manuscript division), Lenin State Library, no. 32 (1971): 5–60.

Makarenko, N. "Lyalichi." *Starye gody* (1910) July–September: 131–51.

Makarov, Y. K. "A. Bolotov i sadovoe iskusstvo v Rossii" (A. Bolotov and landscape architecture in Russia). *Sredi kollektsionerov* (1924) May–June: 26–57.

Makovskii, S. "Dve podmoskovnyia

knyazya S. M. Golitsyna" (Two suburban estates of Prince S. M. Golitsyn). *Starye gody* (1910) January: 24–37.

Malinin, D. I. *Nachalo teatra v Kaluge* (The origins of theater in Kaluga). Kaluga, 1913.

Manning, Roberta. *The Crisis of the Old Order in Russia.* Princeton, 1982.

Marker, Gary. *Publishing, Printing, and the Origins of Intellectual Life in Russia, 1700–1809.* Princeton, 1985.

Massie, Suzanne. *Pavlovsk: The Life of a Russian Palace.* Boston, 1990.

Meehan-Waters, Brenda. "The Development and the Limits of Security of Noble Status, Person, and Property in Eighteenth-Century Russia." In *Russia and the West in the Eighteenth Century,* edited by A. G. Cross. Newtonville, 1983.

————. "Popular Piety: Local Initiative and the Founding of Women's Religious Communities in Russia, 1764–1907." *St. Vladimir's Theological Quarterly* 30 (1986) 2: 112–42.

Miller, G. P. "Sudba odnogo imeniya" (The fate of one estate). *Istoricheskii vestnik* (1901) 12: 1072–81.

Mironov, B. N. *Russkii gorod v 1740–1860 gody* (The Russian town from 1740 to 1860). Leningrad, 1990.

Morozov, V. F. "Dvorets Rumyantsevykh-Paskevichei v Gomele" (The Rumyantsev-Paskevich Palace at Gomel). *Arkhitekturnoe nasledstvo* 30 (1982): 37–45.

Nechaeva, V. S. *V seme i usadbe Dostoevskikh* (In the family and on the estate of the Dostoevskys). Moscow, 1939.

Nekrasov, A. I. *Zabytaya podmoskovnaya* (A forgotten suburban Moscow estate). Moscow, 1925.

Nikitina, A. B. "Ob usadbe G. R. Derzhavina Zvanka" (The estate of G. R. Derzhavin, Zvanka). *Pamyatniki kultury* 10 (1984): 508–22.

Nosik, B. "Ottsy i deti" (Fathers and sons). *Nashe nasledie* 3 (1990) 15: 149–56.

O'Meara, Patrick. *K. F. Ryleev.* Princeton, 1984.

Petrova, A. "Osobennosti anfiladnoi sistemy v russkoi arkhitekture serediny devyatnadtsatogo veka" (Particularities of the enfilade system in Russian architecture of the mid-nineteenth century). *Kultura i iskusstvo Rossii devyatnadtsatogo veka.* Leningrad, 1985.

Piksanov, N. K. *Griboedov i staroe barstvo* (Griboedov and the old nobility). Moscow, 1926.

Pirumova, Natalia. "Dvoryanskoe gnezdo" (A nest of gentlefolk). *Nashe nasledie* 3 (1990) 15: 144–48.

Podyapolskaya, E. N., ed. *Pamyatniki arkhitektury Moskovskoi oblasti.* 2 vols. Moscow, 1975.

Popov, V. A. *Russkii farfor: Chastnye zavody* (Russian porcelain: Private factories). Moscow, 1980.

Popova, Z. "Krepostnoi master Matvei Yakovlev, syn Veretennikova" (The serf master Matvei Yakovlev, son of Veretennikov). In *Pryanik, pryalka i ptitsa sirin* (Gingerbread, distaff, and the siren bird), edited by S. Zhigalova. Moscow, 1971.

Pospelov, G. G. "Provintsialnaya zhivopis pervoi poloviny devyatnadtsatogo veka" (Provincial paintings in the first half of the nineteenth century). In *Istoriya russkogo iskusstva,* vol. 8. Moscow, 1964.

Pronina, I. A. "O prepodavanii dekorativno-prikladnogo iskusstva v vosemnadtsatom v." (On teaching the decorative and applied arts in the eighteenth century). In *Russkoe iskusstvo vosemnadtsatogo veka* (Eighteenth-century Russian art), edited by T. V. Alekseeva. Moscow, 1973.

Pylyaev, M. I. "Polubarskie zatei" (Semi-noble caprices). *Istoricheskii vestnik* (1886) no. 9.

Raeff, Marc. "Home, School, and Service in the Life of the Eighteenth-Century Russian Nobleman." In *The Structure of Russian History,* edited by M. Cherniavsky. New York, 1970.

————. *Political Ideas and Institutions in Imperial Russia.* Boulder, 1994.

————. "The Russian Nobility in the Eighteenth and Nineteenth Centuries: Trends and Comparisons." In *The Russian and East European Nobility,* edited by I. Banac and P. Bushkovich. New Haven, 1984.

Romanovich-Slavatinskii, A. V. *Dvoryanstvo v Rossii ot nachala vosemnadtsatogo veka do otmeny krepostnogo prava* (The nobility in Russia from the beginning of the eighteenth century to the end of serfdom). St. Petersburg, 1870. Reprint, The Hague, 1968.

Roosevelt, P. R. "The Country House as Setting and Symbol in Nineteenth-Century Literature and Art." In *Russian Narrative and Visual Art: Varieties of Seeing,* edited by R. Anderson and P. Debreczeny. Coral Gables, 1994.

Rozantseva, S. A. "Fayansovyi zavod v Arkhangelskom" (The faience factory at Arkhangelskoe). *Pamyatniki kultury,* no. 9 (1983): 444–51.

S., E. "Vospominaniya o Lyalichakh" (Reminiscences of Lyalichi). *Istoricheskii vestnik* (1910) 4: 129–41.

Sakhnovskii, V. S. *Krepostnoi usadebnyi teatr: Kratkoe vvedenie k ego tipologicheskomu izucheniyu* (Serf theater on the estate: A brief introduction to its typological study). Leningrad, 1924.

Salias, E. A. *G. R. Derzhavin, pravitel tambovskago namestnichestva* (G. R. Derzhavin, administrator of the Tambov vicegerency). Tambov, 1871.

Scott, James C. *Domination and the Art of Resistance: Hidden Transcripts.* New Haven, 1990.

————. *Weapons of the Weak: Everyday Forms of Resistance.* New Haven, 1985.

Sedov, A. P. *Yaropolets.* Moscow, 1980.

Selinova, T. A. *Ivan Petrovich Argunov, 1729–1802.* Moscow, 1973.

Semevskii, V. I. *Krestyane v tsartsvovanie Imperatritsy Ekateriny II* (Peasants in the reign of Empress Catherine II). 2 vols. St. Petersburg, 1901–03.

————. *Krestyanskii vopros v Rossii v vosemnadtsatogo i pervoi polovine devyatnadtsatogo veka* (The peasant question in Russia in the eighteenth and first half of the nineteenth century). 2 vols. St. Petersburg, 1888.

Senelick, Laurence. "The Erotic Bondage of Serf Theatre." *Russian Review* 50 (1991) 1: 24–34.

———. *Serf Actor: The Life and Art of Mikhail Shchepkin*. Westport, 1984.

Setchkarev, Vsevolod. *Gogol: His Life and Works*. New York, 1965.

Shchepetov, K. N. *Krepostnoe pravo v votchinakh Sheremetevykh* (Serfdom on the ancestral lands of the Sheremetevs). Moscow, 1947.

Shchukina, E. P. "Naturalnyi sad russkoi usadby v kontse vosemnadtsatogo v." (The natural garden of the Russian estate at the end of the eighteenth century). In *Russkoe iskusstvo vosemnadtsatogo veka* (Eighteenth-century Russian art), edited by T. V. Alekseeva. Moscow, 1973.

Sheremetev, G. S. *Kuskovo do 1812 goda* (Kuskovo before 1812). Moscow, 1899.

———. *Zapisnaya knizhka* (Notebook). No. 1. Moscow, 1903.

Sheremetev, Pavel. *Karamzin v Ostafieve, 1811–1911* (Karamzin at Ostafievo, 1811–1911). Moscow, 1911.

———. *Vyazemy*. Petrograd, 1916.

Sheremetev, S. D. "Lopasnya i Semenovskii-Rai" (Lospasnya and Semenovskii-Rai). In *V doroge* (On the road), no. 4. Moscow, 1906.

———. *Mikhailovskoe*. Moscow, 1906.

———. *Ostafievo*. St. Petersburg, 1893.

———. *Ulyanka*. St. Petersburg, 1893.

Shvidkovskii, D. O. *Gorod russkogo prosveshcheniya* (The city of the Russian Enlightenment). Moscow, 1990.

———. "Idealnyi gorod russkogo prosveshcheniya" (The ideal city of the Russian Enlightenment). In *Deni Didro i kultura ego epokhi* (Denis Diderot and the culture of his age), edited by M. Libman. Moscow, 1988.

———. "K voprosu o prosvetitelskoi kontseptsii sredy v russkikh dvortsevo-parkovykh ansamblakh vtoroi polovini vosemnadtsatogo veka" (The question of the enlightenment concept of the envi-

ronment in Russian palace-park ensembles of the second half of the eighteenth century). In *Vek Prosveshcheniya* (The century of enlightenment), edited by Irina E. Danilova. Moscow, 1983.

Simmons, Ernest J. *Chekhov: A Biography*. Chicago, 1962.

Sivkov, K. V. *"Shtat" sela Kuskova, 1786 g.* (The "staff" of the village of Kuskovo, 1786). Moscow, 1927.

Sokolov, M. S. *Interer v zerkale zhivopisi* (The interior through the looking-glass of painting). Moscow, 1986.

Sokolova, A. I. "Dobrovolnaya zatvornitsa" (The voluntary recluse). *Istoricheskii vestnik* (1917) 1: 78–85.

Sokolova, T., and K. A. Orlova. *Glazami sovremennikov* (In the eyes of contemporaries). Leningrad, 1982.

———. "Russkaya mebel nachala devyatnadtsatogo veka" (Russian furniture of the early nineteenth century). *Dekorativnoe iskusstvo* (1974) 7: 39–43.

———. "Russkaya mebel serediny vosemnadtsatogo veka" (Russian furniture of the mid-eighteenth century). *Dekorativnoe iskusstvo* (1973) 12: 42–46.

Sosnina-Putsillo, E. V. "Ilovna i ego obyvateli" (Ilovna and its inhabitants). Typescript. Yaroslavl (private collection), ca. 1920.

Spring, David, ed. *European Landed Elites in the Nineteenth Century*. Baltimore, 1977.

Starikova, L. M. *Teatralnaya Moskva* (Theatrical Moscow). Moscow, 1989.

———. "Teatralno-zrelishchnaya zhizn Moskvy v seredine XVIII veka" (Theater and spectacle in the life of Moscow in the mid-eighteenth century). *Pamyatniki kultury* 12 (1986): 133–88.

Stites, Richard. "Old Smolensk." Paper presented at the Kennan Institute, September 1993.

———. *Revolutionary Dreams*. New York, 1989.

———. *The Women's Liberation Movement in Russia*, Princeton, 1978.

Tarakanov, N. G. *N. P. Ogarev*. Moscow, 1974.

Tarnovskii, M. V. "Kachanovka." *Stolitsa i usadba* 40/41 (1915): 4–12.

Tartakovskii, A. G. *Russkaya memuaristika vosemnadtsatogo–pervoi poloviny devyatnadtsatogo veka* (Russian memoir literature in the eighteenth and first half of the nineteenth century). Moscow, 1991.

Tikhomirov, N. *Arkhitektura podmoskovnykh usadeb* (The architecture of suburban Moscow estates). Moscow, 1955.

Toropov, Sergei. "Petrovskoe Demidovykh." *Sredi kollektsionerov* (1924) 7/8: 20–25.

———. "Yaropoltsy: Zametki" (Yaropolets: Observations). *Sredi kollektsionerov* (1924) 7/8: 45–55.

Tovrov, J. *The Russian Noble Family: Structure and Change*. New York, 1987.

Tristram, Philippa. *Living Space in Fact and Fiction*. London, 1989.

Troinitskii, A. *The Serf Population in Russia according to the Tenth National Census*. Translated by Elaine Herman. Newtonville, 1982.

Troyat, Henri. *Gogol: The Biography of a Divided Soul*. Translated by Nancy Amphoux. London, 1974.

Veiner, P. "Zhizn i iskusstvo v Ostankine" (Life and art at Ostankino). *Starye gody* (1910) May–June: 38–73.

Venturi, Franco. *Roots of Revolution*. Translated by Francis Haskell. New York, 1966.

Vereshchagin, V. "Razorennoe gnezdo" (A ruined nest). *Starye gody* (1908) March: 133–49.

Vergunov, A. P., and V. A. Gorokhov. *Russkie sady i parki* (Russian gardens and parks). Moscow, 1988.

Verkhovskaya, N. *Karamzin v Moskve i Podmoskove* (Karamzin in Moscow and its environs). Moscow, 1968.

Veselovskii, S. V. *Podmoskove* (Suburban Moscow). Moscow, 1962.

Vrangel, N. N., Baron. "Pomeshchichya Rossiya" (The Russia of landowners). *Starye gody* (1910) July–September: 5–79.

———. *Venok mertvym: Khudozhestvenno-istoricheskie stati*

(A wreath for the dead: Essays on art and history). St. Petersburg, 1913.

Wachtel, Andrew W. *The Battle for Childhood.* Stanford, 1990.

Yezhova, I. K. *Zubrilovka. Nadezhdino: Dvortsovo-parkovye ansambli v povolzhe kontsa vosemnadtsatogo-nachala devyatnadtsatogo veka*

(Zubrilovka. Nadezhdino: Palace and park ensembles along the Volga at the end of the eighteenth and beginning of the nineteenth centuries). Saratov, 1979.

Zabelin, I. E. *Opyty izucheniya russkikh drevnostei i istorii* (Essays on the study of Russian antiquities and history). Moscow, 1873.

———. "Oranzherei i sady podmoskovnykh votchin. kn. Dmitriya Mikh. Golitsyna 1737" (The orangery and gardens of Prince Dmitry Mikhailovich Golitsyn's ancestral estate in the environs of Moscow in 1737). *Zhurnal sadovodstva* (1857) 3: 52–58.

Index

Estates that do not appear on the two maps are identified by owner and province in this index. Map references appear in boldface; figure references in italics.

Durnov, Efim, 122
Durova, Nadezhda, 182–83
Dvoryaninovo, **2:69**, *123*, xiv, 85–87, 126, 167, 208

Education, home, 23, 125, 179–83, 298, 301. *See also* Schools
Edwards, S., 265
Egotov, I. V., 45
Egremont, Lord, 144
Eismond, Elizaveta, 112
Ekaterinburg, 187
Elagin Island, **2:3**, 83
Elizabeth, empress of Russia, 18, 225
Elnya, 192, 205, 214
Emancipation of *1861*, xii, xiv, 158, 220, 318–19
Engelhardt family, 159, 160, 204; Engelhardt, Maria, 283; Engelhardt, Sophia, 162
England, 12–13, 29, 31–33, 56–57, 70, 143–44; Russian travelers to, 12, 30–31, 37, 58, 78, 80–81, 162
Enlightenment, the, 45, 50, 291; philosophers of, 79, 96, 180, 208–09. *See also individual philosophers*
Epifan, town, 199
Ernovo (Ekaterina Shishkova), Ryazan Province, 190–91
Esipov, P. V., 139, 187
Estates, English, 30, 38–39, 58, 81, 83, 144
Estates, Russian, *22, 158*, 16–18, 22, 26, 31–32, 37, 47, 98, 112–13, 119, 162, 184, 188, 234, 335n25, 339n89; architecture and decor, 12, 22, 26, 36–79 passim, 114–16, 130, 167–73, 184–86, 188, 212, 288, 294, 335n6; churches, *9, 11–12, 19, 26, 29, 44, 73, 89, 185–86, 196, 209, 212, 220, 230*, 271, 332; comfort of, 52, 56, 115–16; dependencies and outbuildings, *30, 42, 72, 90–91, 101, 114, 164–65, 189, 191*, 18, 26–27, 36, 277; economy, *169*, 118, 126, 130, 175–76, 221, 223–24, 231–38, 240–42, 248; entertainment, xiii, 45, 72, 98, 117–18, 120, 125–26, 135–53, 160, 162, 174–75, 202–03, 213, 238, 240, 284–86, 296–97, 338n44, 338n52; household, *82–83*, 56, 90–91, 103–08, 110–12, 148, 178–80, 240; management, *120*, 187–88,

220–22, 230–33, 238–42, 247. *See also* Furniture and furnishings; Gardens; Landowners; Serfs; Theater
Esterhazy family, 32

Family life, *155*, 120–23, 125–26, 179–82, 298
Fichte, Johann, 308–10
Filaret, Metropolitan, 273
Fili, **1:53**, *12*, 10
Filimonki, **1:85**, *136*
Filosofov, D. N., 187, 319
Folk art. *See* Culture, folk
Fonvizin, D. I., 302; Fonvizin, M. A., 304
Food, 18, 116–18, 120–21, 144, 170, 179–80, 198, 206, 280, 282, 296
France, 17, 31, 58, 214, 216, 258; estate life in, 29
Fraser, John, 78
Frederick II, the Great, king of Prussia, 18
Freemasonry, 37, 304, 335n2, 336n17
Fryanovo, **1:28**, 236
Furniture and furnishings, *58, 176–78*, 52–53, 56–73, 173, 252–53, 258, 336n18, 336n39, 336n40. *See also* Serfs: artists, craftsmen

Gagarin family, 8, 71, 231; Gagarin, Prince Matvei, 16; Gagarin, Sergei, 39
Gamiltonovka, 150
Gardens, *27, 60–63, 67–69, 75–79*, xii, 12, 14, 21, 23, 26, 29, 37–38, 40, 46, 70–71, 74–98, 100–01, 118; *fermes ornées*, 37, 98, 146
Gatchina, **2:7**, 293
Gau, Vladimir (court portraitist), 261
Gedeonov, Dmitry, 283; Gedeonov, Ivan, 160
Gerakov, G. V., 151, 180, 195–96, 199, 201–02, 228
Gerasimov, P. A., 94
Germany, 12, 58
Girouard, Mark, 30
Glazov, town, 208
Glebov, General F. I., 70, 293
Glinka, Evgenia A., 282; Glinka, Mikhail, 282, 284; Glinka, S. N., 158–59, 176–77
Glinki, **1:48**, 20–21
Glinskaya, Princess, 161

Glubokoe, **2:37**, *149*, 320–21
Gnezdilovo (Osipov), Smolensk Province, 161
Gogol, Nikolai, xv, 33, 243, 312–13, 338n23; *Dead Souls*, 186, 224, 300, 312–13; *Inspector General*, 151; *Selected Passages from Correspondence with Friends*, 313–14
Golitsyn family, 8, 12, 33, 45, 50, 85, 104, 113, 122, 143, 240; Golitsyn, Prince A. B., 122–23, 144; Golitsyn, Prince A. M., 122; Golitsyn, Prince A. P., governor of Yaroslavl, *165*; Golitsyn, Prince B. A., 10, 122; Golitsyn, Boris V., 231; Golitsyn, Prince D. M., 12; Golitsyn, Prince D. V., governor of Moscow, 71, 216; Golitsyn, Field Marshal M. M., 234; Golitsyn, Prince N. A., 42; Golitsyn, Prince N. M., 122–23; Golitsyn, Field Marshal S. F., 85, 162; Golitsyn, Prince V. V., 12–13; Golitsyn, Prince Vladimir B., 58, 122; Golitsyn, Yury N., 177, 182, 205, 240–41, 265, 284–86
Golitsyna (née Bakhmeteva), Ekaterina, 240–41, 285–86; Golitsyna, Princess Maria V., *226*, 327; Golitsyna (née Chernysheva), Natalya Petrovna, 122
Golovchino (Khorvat), **2:129**, 146
Golovin family, 90; Golovin, Fyodor, Admiral, 20, 22; Golovin, Mikhail I., 273–75; Golovin, V. L., 266; Golovin, V. V., 146
Golovina (née Baratynskaya), V. I., 273–75
Golovino (Golovin), Moscow Province, 146
Golovkina, Countess E. A., 252
Golubino, **1:71**, 236
Golubkov, P. I., 303
Golubtsov family, 160
Gomel, **2:111**, 47, 50
Goncharov, Ivan: *Oblomov*, xv, 238–39, 279
Goncharov family, 50, 93; Goncharov, Afanasy, 16; Goncharov, Nikolai, 75
Gonzago, Pietro, 80, 83
Gorchakov, Prince, 159
Gorenki, **1:60**, *34*, 45, 78–79
Gorka (Bolotov), Novgorod Province, 329
Gorky, **1:92**, 330
Gorky, **1:10**, 198, 211–12, 214, 271, 275, 286

Turgeneva, Varvara P., 190, 314–15
Tver: province, 138, 202, 259; town, 199, 202, 208
Twickenham (England), 30, 81, 83–84
Tyurin, Evgraf, 67
Tyutchev, F. I., 312

Ubory, **1:68,** 10
Uderevka, **2:132,** 308
Ufa Province, 308, 312
Ukhtomsky, D. V., architect, 21
Ukraine, 18, 28, 257
Ulyanka, **2:2,** 108, 113
Umatovo, **2:26,** 139
Umet, **2:103,** 162
Universities. *See* Schools
Unkovskaya, A., 281
Ushakovo, **2:54,** 160, 179
Ustinov, A. M., 162
Uvarov family, 28; Uvarov, Count Fedor S., 163; Uvarov, Count Sergei S., 163, 202
Uvarova (née Golovina), Countess Darya I., 163

Valuevo, **1:84,** *72,* 44, 89, 229
Vanbrugh, John (architect), 38
Vasiliev, Nikifor, *177,* 59, 252; Vasiliev, Yakov A., 260–61
Vasilievskoe (Grabbe), **2:51,** 326–27
Vasilievskoe (Yakovlev), **1:79,** 119–20, 308
Vasnetsov, V. M., 323
Veliaminov, P. I., 294
Venetsianov, A. G., *157, 158, 182,* 259–61
Vereshchagin, Alexander, 169, 179; Vereshchagin, V. A., 150
Veretennikov, Matvei, 252
Veryakushki, **2:38,** 123, 147, 172, 183–87, 333
Veshnyakovo (Cherkassky), Moscow Province, 21
Vienna, 32
Vigée-Lebrun, Elisabeth, 252, 258–59
Vigel, F. F., 139, 148, 187
Vitruvius Britannicus, 37
Vodolagi, **2:138,** 112, 172, 181
Volga River, 142, 209, 211

Volkonsky family, 45, 71, 324; Volkonsky, Prince S. G., 304
Volkonskaya (née Raevskaya), Maria V., 304
Volkov family, 8; Volkov, Abram A., 8; Volkov, Alexei, 13
Volkov-Muromtsov family, 330; Volkov-Muromtsov, Nikolai V., 278, 279; Volkov-Muromtsov, Vladimir, *216,* 320–21
Volkova, Margarita A., 214
Volkova-Muromtsova (née Heiden), Varvara P., *216,* 320–21
Volokitino (A. M. Miklashevsky), Chernigov Province, 253
Volokolamsk, *145, 146*
Voltaire, 79, 208, 209
Voronezh: province, 18, 209, 308; town, 205
Voronikhin, Andrei, 80, 258–59
Voronovo, **1:110,** *41,* 50, 214
Vorontsov family, 8, 232; Vorontsov, A. R., 70; Vorontsov, Illarion G., 39, 50; Vorontsov, Count M. S., 196–97; Vorontsov, Count Mikhail I., 18, 27, 80; Vorontsov, Count Semen R., 47, 58
Vorontsova (née Branicka), Countess E. K., 196–97
Vrangel, Baron N. N., 148, 150, 153, 187
Vrubel, Mikhail A., 323
Vyazemskaya (née O'Reilly), Eugenia, 301
Vyazemsky family, 33; Vyazemsky, Prince A. A., 300–01; Vyazemsky, Prince Peter A., *197,* 75, 76, 100, 243, 292, 301, 305, 307, 330
Vyazma, 22, 214
Vyra, **2:6,** 327
Vyshenki (P. A. Rumyantsev), 143

Walpole, Horace, 81
War of *1812,* xiii, *153,* 50, 68, 120, 158, 202, 209, 211–17, 271, 302, 307, 324, 340n55
Water closets, 56, 62, 68, 186
Wedgwood, Josiah, 57
Westerners, xiv, 243, 307–10, 312–15
Wilmot family, 29, 113; Wilmot, Catherine, xv, 2, 45, 75, 113–19, 144, 277; Wilmot,

Martha, *87,* xv, 29–30, 102, 106–07, 113–19, 279, 284
Wilton House (England), 58
Wolkenstein, Count G. S., 265
Wotton, Sir Henry, 103
Wrack, Peter, 83

Yablochkov, P. M., 237–38
Yagotin, **2:135,** 39
Yakushkin, Ivan, 304–05
Yankov family, 33, 159, 161; Yankov, Dmitry, 24, 199
Yankova (née Rimskaya-Korsakova), E. P., 71–72, 103, 141, 161–62, 174–75, 179–80, 182, 198–99, 212, 224, 261, 273, 276–77, 286–88
Yaropolets, **1:18,** 92–93, 98, 143
Yaropolets, **1:19,** *30, 43,* 50, 75, 93, 101, 137
Yaroslavl: province, 42, 122; town, 142, 199, 206, 208, 271
Yasenevo, **1:73,** 20
Yasnaya Polyana, **2:77,** xii, xv, 289, 324–26
Yazykov, N. M., 279, 305
Yurasovky family, 140–41
Yusupov family, 28, 33, 232; Yusupov, Prince Nikolai, 144, 148, 233, 247–48, 304, 336n30

Zaitsev, Ivan, 187
Zaraisk, 165
Zavadovsky, Count Peter, 39, 47, 69–70, 257
Zemstvos, 229, 340n22
Zheleznovka, **2:80,** 177, 238
Zhernovka, **2:72,** 162
Zhukovo, **2:53,** 304
Zhukovsky, V. A., 186, 243, 300, 303, 312, 342n20
Zinoviev, V. N., 58
Zlatov, A. A., 259
Zlobino, **2:70,** 159
Znamenskoe-Gubailovo, **1:44,** 93
Znamenskoe-Raek, **2:27,** *200–01,* 293–94
Zorich, Semen, 137, 143
Zubrilovka, **2:109,** 162
Zvanka, **2:13,** *202,* 39, 273, 291–97, 316